The Knights Next Door

The Knights Next Door

Everyday People Living Middle Ages Dreams

By Patrick O'Donnell with contributions from Mael Patraic mac Domnaill

iUniverse, Inc.
New York Lincoln Shanghai

The Knights Next Door
Everyday People Living Middle Ages Dreams

iUniverse, Inc.

For information address:
iUniverse, Inc.
2021 Pine Lake Road, Suite 100
Lincoln, NE 68512
www.iuniverse.com

ISBN: 0-595-32530-0 (Pbk)
ISBN: 0-595-66633-7 (Cloth)

Printed in the United States of America

CREDITS

Front cover artwork by the Barony of the Cleftlands Scribes Guild, with work done by Elena Inghean Ronain/Laura Gilmour and Kiriena Kirova Doch' Rysenkova/Cat Kenney. Illumination is based on "The Annunciation to the Shepherds," a page from a French Book of Hours completed in Paris c.1410. The border was drawn out on a piece of calf's skin, also known as vellum, which was prepared with pumice so it would accept paint. Hide glue sizing was applied to the areas that would later be gilded, or covered with 24-karat gold leaf and polished with an agate burnisher. Gouache, an opaque watercolor, was used to paint the background colors of the bars and un-gilded leaves. White gouache details were applied with a fine sable brush to complete the design.

Front cover photo courtesy of Tracey Griffin and www.pennsic.net.

Back cover battle photo courtesy of Carla C. Emmons and www.winterstarlight.com

Other back cover photos by Patrick O'Donnell except for Darkyard marching, courtesy of Maistor Iustinos Tekton called Justin/Scott Courtney

Interior photos by Patrick O'Donnell with the exception of:

Duke Edmund and all photos of the Middle Kingdom coronation courtesy of EUSTACIO HUMPHREY © 2002 The Plain Dealer. All rights reserved. Reprinted with permission.

The Clan Tynker at Pennsic opening ceremonies and the Pennsic woods battle courtesy of Maistor Iustinos Tekton called Justin/Scott Courtney

The SFU group courtesy of Emer nic Dougal/Amanda Morlocke

Duchess Elina courtesy of Duchess Megan nic Alister/Margaret Silvestri and www.history.westkingdom.org.

Kildonon Hall courtesy of Master Erik of Telemark/Ed Kreyling and

Duke Baldar courtesy of www.houseasgard.com.

ACKNOWLEDGEMENTS

I would like to thank many people for their help with this book and for the aid and understanding they provided to help me overcome a fully modern setback connected to it.

Heartfelt thanks go out to:

Every SCA member who talked to me for this book, whether they spared an evening to talk by phone or suffered through an out-of-period interview at an event.

All of the members of SFU/Portus Aurelius for putting up with constant questions and note-taking, most of all Sean for opening his house, Rob for suffering through shield punches to the chest, and Craig for the hours of help with photos.

Darkyard and Legio Draconis for accepting a questionably-competent shieldman.

William of Fairhaven/Pat Savelli for videotapes of events I could not attend.

Valharic/Tom Noble for enduring questions more personal than he had to.

My employer, the Plain Dealer, for the use of some photos in this book, for giving me reasonable scheduling allowances to attend events, and for the understanding of both management and my co-workers of a seemingly endless recovery process. The help of Ron Rutti, Jesse Tinsley, John Kuehner, Julie Washington, Stuart Warner and Alana Baranick is especially appreciated.

I owe extra thanks to my girlfriend Cat Kenney for understanding me spending half my life at the keyboard, and to my parents and grandparents for not complaining that I all but ignored them for more than two years. Double thanks to Cat and my parents for being there when I needed them most.

None of it would have mattered without the help of Michigan state police, the Air Care helicopter rescue crew, Marshall Fire and Rescue, the staff at Bronson Methodist Hospital in Kalamazoo and everyone on 8A at MetroHealth Medical Center in Cleveland.

Dr. Usha Tandra, Jamie Merkle, Tracy Porter and Chloe Gasson helped make this book and the rest of my mental well-being possible. Please let your new TBI patients know there is a light at the end of the tunnel.

And if the good Samaritan with a cell phone on I-69 about midnight 10/19/2001 can reach me, I owe you a free copy of this book. It's the least I can do.

O for a Muse of fire, that would ascend
The brightest heaven of invention,
A kingdom for a stage, princes to act,
And monarchs to behold the swelling scene!
Then should the warlike Harry, like himself,
Assume the port of Mars; and at his heels,
Leash'd in like hounds, should famine, sword, and fire,
Crouch for employment. But pardon, gentles all,
The flat unraised spirits that hath dar'd
On this unworthy scaffold to bring forth
So great an object. Can this cockpit hold
The vasty fields of France? Or may we cram
Within this wooden O the very casques
That did affright the air at Agincourt?

O, pardon! since a crooked figure may
Attest in little place a million;
And let us, ciphers to this great accompt,
On your imaginary forces work.
Suppose within the girdle of these walls
Are now confin'd two mighty monarchies,
Whose high upreared and abutting fronts
The perilous narrow ocean parts asunder.

Piece out our imperfections with your thoughts:
Into a thousand parts divide one man,
And make imaginary puissance;
Think, when we talk of horses, that you see them
Printing their proud hoofs i' th' receiving earth;
For 'tis your thoughts that now must deck our kings,
Carry them here and there, jumping o'er times,
Turning th' accomplishment of many years
Into an hour-glass; for the which supply,
Admit me Chorus to this history;
Who prologue-like, your humble patience pray
Gently to hear, kindly to judge, our play.

Prologue to the tale of King Henry V, by William Shakespeare

No shit, there I was...
Usual prologue to Current Middle Ages tales

CONTENTS

Vouchsafe to those that have not read the story,
That I may prompt them: and of such as have,
I humbly pray them to admit the excuse
Of time, of numbers and due course of things,
Which cannot in their huge and proper life
Be here presented.

—Prologue, Act V, William Shakespeare's *Henry V*

THE TRAVELER'S PROLOGUE:
INTO THE BREACH

"I've found that sometimes the things you believe in become more real than all the things you can explain away or understand."
— Tommy Albright (Gene Kelly), *Brigadoon*

My heart pounds beneath my chest armor as sweat slithers from under the steel dome of my helm. Across the field they wait, 800 strong and menacing, a killing machine ready to chop us down with swords, spears and polearms.

If we don't kill them first.

The army of the enemy East Kingdom lets out a giant roar and its warriors smash their shields with weapons as a warning of what is to come. My compatriots in the Middle Kingdom army thump their own shields back in defiant answer. My sword gives a sharp crack as I bash my own shield emblazoned with the arms of the Kingdom's finest fighting house: Darkyard.

"Darkyard!" the house commanders bellow.

"Darkyard!" scream the other fighters. I just clench my teeth in determination.

I march forward with the other shieldmen. Our speedy, kamikaze shock troops hit a wave of oncoming Easterners with a churning of weapons. Bodies drop to the ground. The line of Easterners crashes into us, some lowering their shoulders into our wall of shields to bash through, others jabbing spear points into us. I deflect enemy blows with my sword and my shield as our spearmen reach around me to stab the evil Easterners in their faces and bellies.

I never really see the blow.

I see the Eastern warrior's eyes lock on me and I freeze. I lose track of his polearm for a fatal instant and it comes at me in a blurry, looming rush to smash into my helm. I reel a moment, trying to regain my balance, but simply sink to my knees and keel over. My head hits the grass as boots stomp, bodies sink into the turf and blades swish and crack around me.

I am dead.

My journey to this battlefield in western Pennsylvania began in the summer of 1996 when I first encountered the thousands of everyday Americans who try to bring the Middle Ages to life amid this modern world. Across the country, there are people—probably in your town, your neighborhood or maybe even next door—who go to surprising lengths to re-create an era separated from their office cubicles and subdivision cul-de-sacs by thousands of miles and hundreds of years. At the start of 2001, I set out on my own mission to learn not just the ways, but also the whys, people make this pur-

1

suit a focus of their modern lives. Fighting in the giant battles at this, the annual Pennsic War, was just part of it.

The Middle Ages clearly strike a chord with the masses, beyond inspiring corporate identities like Burger King and Knights Inn. The ultimate teller of fairy tales, Walt Disney, made castles the centerpieces of his amusement parks. Movies like *Henry V* and *Braveheart* made millions. And when I started my journey, the mother of the mix of Middle Ages and fantasy, *The Lord of the Rings*, neared completion and box office success. Though I always knew that thousands of people took things a step further by battling orcs and ogres with dice rolls in games like *Dungeons and Dragons*, I never realized there are many who go further still to re-create the age of castles and sword-play. A growing crowd seeks more than just watching from a theater seat, rolling dice for their paper characters or joining the paying crowds of renaissance fairs.

They want to do it for themselves.

Five years before my journey began, some new acquaintances went from talking to gushing as they told tales of some separate world called Pennsic. Every year more than 10,000 medieval enthusiasts turn a Slippery Rock, Penn., campground into a giant tent city and the biggest renaissance fair you've ever seen. But Pennsic goes beyond a fair by bashing through the envelope of audience participation with a mace. There are no spectators. Everyone who goes is both performer and audience. You don't just pay your $15, walk around in your Budweiser T-shirt and baseball cap, watch a couple of jousts, laugh at a jester or two, and leave in a few hours clutching a plastic sword for the kids.

You're just as much a part of the show as everyone else.

Start by leaving the T-shirt and cap at home. Everyone has to wear medieval costume—"garb" in the jargon of this subculture—just to get in the door. The rules ask everyone to become a medieval "persona," a character based on a historical period. Nobody collects a check for fighting in a show, for telling bawdy wench jokes to a crowd or even for organizing and managing the event itself. You and the 10,000 other attendees, instead of some movie director or corporate organizer fretting over his bottom line, make Pennsic the medieval celebration that it is.

Pennsic's host, the confusingly-named but world's-largest medieval history group, the Society for Creative Anachronism, has been giving medieval enthusiasts the chance to try out the Middle Ages for themselves since the 1960s. Pennsic is just its largest event. The SCA likely has a branch with meetings, handicraft work sessions and smaller events in your town. You may have even seen the odd figures in medieval clothes in the local park or coated with armor and wielding swords on the nearby college campus. The 25,000 SCA members and the 50,000 hovering on its fringes have Created 18 Kingdoms (The 18th, known as Northshield, was scheduled to become a full kingdom as this book was going to press.) that have their own Kings and Queens, officers and armies, Knights and Guilds, and have divided up the entire United States, Canada and even Europe and Australia. The local groups within these Kingdoms can hold feasts, sword battles and dancing in as many as 40 locations around the world any given weekend.

The Society for Creative Anachronism falls in the middle of a spectrum of other groups re-creating the same era in how it balances the difference between re-creation and recreation. The SCA uses real history as its starting point, though it takes some liberties in the name of fun and convenience. Other groups drift further into fantasy or add their own twists under names like Dagorhir, Amtgard, the Kingdom of Acre, the Adrian Empire and the Markland Medieval Mercenary Militia. At the other end of the spectrum, a community committed to more faithful re-enactment sets strict historical standards and shuts fantasy out altogether. By falling in the middle and pulling in enthusiasts from both sides under its big tent, the Society for Creative Anachronism is the 800-pound gorilla of the modern medieval world.

My first shell-shocked trip to the Pennsic War as a curious but skeptical reporter had given me a sniff of this subculture simmering under the noses of us "mundanes"—this group's term for modern clothing and people. Even after a few more short trips to Pennsic, I was still torn over what to think of this alternate world. The little boy in me that used to play Robin Hood with my toy bow and suction cup arrows couldn't wait to go back. My jaw had dropped at the 700-to-a-side battles, at the pageantry, the colors and the immersion of thousands of adults into this atmosphere. A part of my brain had the same reaction most of the participants in the hobby have when they first find it: *Cool! There are other people who love this stuff!* But the adult part was already scoffing and sneering, as many people do at this unusual group. *Get a life, losers! Adults don't dress up. They don't play make-believe. This isn't a real sport. It's kid's stuff.* The battle in my head mirrored that between the two main characters in the play *Brigadoon* after they discover a town from the past mysteriously appearing in the Scottish wilds. One wanted to go live there forever while the other railed against it being out of touch with reality.

"*What am I supposed to feel in a voodoo joint like this?*" the character yelled at his friend amid the confusion of this magical Scottish town.

"*Dream stuff, boy! Only about broomsticks and wishing wells! It's either that or a boot camp for lunatics.*

I don't know what goes on around here. All I know is that whatever it is has got nothing to do with me, and nothing to do with you. And anything that happens to either of us just doesn't count. How can it when you don't understand it?

And you want to give your family, your friends, your whole life for this? It's not even worth arguing about."

Which side was right, I wondered? Was this all just a silly game? Or is there more to this hobby than just play and escapism?

As 2001 hit, a few trivial coincidences sealed my fate. The Society for Creative Anachronism turned 35 that year. The great Pennsic War turned 30. And the start of 2001, as any SCAdian will tell you, was the true start of the new millennium. I decided to mark the occasion by journeying in both space and in time to see how this group of 21st century Americans tries to re-create and learn about the beginning and middle of the last millennium. I would learn this by doing it. I would attend the events, I would wear the garb, I would take the classes, sleep in the tents, build the armor and learn to swing the sword for combat.

The answer to all the how's and why's, I learned over the next two years, lies somewhere in the middle, just as the "Known World" of the SCA sits in a unique place straddling both theater and reality, while also bouncing between the modern world and the medieval one.

Umberto Eco, best known as the author of *The Name of the Rose*, points out in his essay *The Return to the Middle Ages* that stories of the Middle Ages can either make the medieval world their real subject or just use the period as its colorful setting. Authors can use their plot and the endeavors and struggles of the characters they create to teach lessons about the history of the period, or they can use the Middle Ages as simply a fantastic and attention-drawing backdrop for characters to play out very modern issues and plotlines. (Eco's *The Name of the Rose* largely fits his first definition while the movie treats the Middle Ages as little more than a setting for a Sean Connery mystery.) Even Shakespeare took liberties with history, molding the events in his historical plays into more dramatic tales that audiences could identify with.

Though the Society for Creative Anachronism uses the Middle Ages as the set for its ongoing serial drama, it has never made a definitive casting choice for the era. Instead, it lets its thousands of members decide on their own what role the medieval world will play in their own storylines.

While the Society tells the Internal Revenue Service it is an educational group, it also strives to serve "The Dream"—an amorphous concept of valor, virtue and glory, of which every member has a different definition. Everyone gets to be the star. Everyone gets to pick and choose, to highlight and downplay, the aspects of history that are important to them. Some use the "Current Middle Ages" to provide a physical context for the things they study in books, to help take things from the page and put them in concrete form. Others come for the themed costume party, to latch onto their fantasy fetish of the moment or to live "In Service to The Dream." It has room for readers (like you?) who actually read the entire masterfully-crafted *Henry V* prologue a few pages back to consider the analogies between a re-creation group and actors in bringing a version of history to life. And it can also welcome readers (like you?) who skipped right over all that burdensome blathering and went straight to the amusing bit below.

For the people that take this world seriously, their personal journeys carry an emotional weight in their real-world lives. The character in *Brigadoon* may have believed that "anything that happens to either of us just doesn't count," but deeds in this Society do "count" to its members. It may be as simple as finding a community where they are welcome, amid a "mundane" world where the best connection to others often comes through the Internet or television. It may come from having a venue to test themselves academically or as artists, fighters or leaders. The destination for still others is to sort out personal issues in a setting that lets them slide back and forth from the real world to a pretend one. This world lets ordinary people play heroes and gives flawed individuals a stage to grow into them. In treating itself as a separate world, apart from everyday struggles and failures, it borrows yet again from Shakespeare's *Henry V*.

"There is none of you so mean and base," King Henry tells his ready troops, "that hath not noble luster in your eyes."

With so many scattered views of what this world should be like, no one person—or even 10 people—can fully reflect this "society." Instead, I offer my own experience as a newcomer to this subculture to provide a glimpse for those who are on the outside. Those of you who are unwilling to put on tights or armor can just sit back and let me have that experience for you. I also offer the stories of a few people who help me along this journey and of many I meet along the way. In many cases, their efforts go well beyond anything I could experience in person and I let their "Tales" cover topics I can only hope to learn more about. To borrow from Eco, this account is more about the "Current Middle Ages" than it is about me, about the squire Valharic (who you will soon meet) or any of the other characters. Each of the portraits in this mosaic of stories is meant to illuminate a different aspect of this diverse Society.

When the new millennium hit, I picked up my notebook and pen, put on the costumes I had pulled together for my brief, curious trips to Pennsic and ventured into this "voodoo joint" and "boot camp for lunatics." To brace myself, I drew upon Shakespeare yet again and took to heart a command Henry V gave his troops.

Once more into the breach, I told myself. Once more into the breach.

THE SQUIRE'S PROLOGUE:
THE MAN WHO WOULD BE KING

If it be a sin to covet honor,
I am the most offending soul alive.

—Act IV, Scene iii, *Henry V*

"I'm going to be king," little Tommy Noble kept telling people. His parents. His friends. Even his friend's mother heard the boasts.

Some kids want to be astronauts when they grow up. Some want to be President or a fireman or even the guy who drives the ice cream truck. But the sword is what always fired Tommy Noble's imagination. Though the medieval weapon is obsolete today, it can still fuel dreams of dramatic and romantic adventure, of grand deeds and rescues. Of being a hero.

As a tot living in Italy with his Air Force parents, Noble watched Capitan Harlock, a swashbuckling Japanimation space hero with a cape and a scar across his face, on television. Even at four years old, Noble wanted to be the Robin Hood-like character at Halloween. On his first trip to the circus he picked a knight's costume with a small plastic sword, shield and helmet as his souvenir. In a precursor of things to come, it was Roman. His older siblings would tell him "get the saucy wench" and send him tearing off after his sister with the sword.

When he moved on to middle school back in the United States, now among the strip malls of suburban Cleveland instead of the castles and ruins of Italy, his desire to be king was a little over-enthusiastic but still amusing. By high school and young adulthood it might have been delusional. Nobody in America gets to be king, especially not a middle class Air Force brat, even if his last name is Noble. What is there to be "king" of?

But the friends he had chosen and the world he had decided to live in made that goal merely a bit boastful, not grounds for strapping him into a straitjacket. A few neighbor kids had invited him to a meeting of a group called Dagorhir (pronounced Dagger-Here), which gave him the chance to put his sword-wielding fantasies in a more tangible setting. Dagorhir plays at the fantasy of Middle Ages battles, by really playing at it. Its mostly-teenage warriors pick fantasy names, wear costumes and fight the battles themselves using foam-padded swords, spears and battleaxes. Dagorhir fights are not acting—though dramatic embellishments like battle screams and dying with a flourish are encouraged. They are real competition. Each side—whether it be an individual or an army—tries to beat the other by striking "killing" blows. If you are more skilled with your weapon in Dagorhir, you win. The big drawback is that the foam padding on the stick weapons swells them into giant puffy popsicles, about as close to real swords as a jumbo wiffle ball bat is to a baseball bat.

Until he hit 14, Noble was too young to fight under the group's rules. But he had found a home. "The Kid," as he was known, both affectionately and sometimes derisively by the wizened old high schoolers in the group, scooted around in borrowed costumes and was often drafted by fighters as a pack mule for their piles of armor. He signed up to fight as soon as he was old enough, despite parents who thought this whole hitting people with sticks deal was a little weird.

It wasn't weird for him, though. For Noble and his newfound Dagorhir friends, the normal puberty-powered pursuits of high school status seemed empty. Cooler medieval "garb" meant more than wearing the "in" clothes or the "right" makeup. Gaining positions of honor in the group meant more than being part of the right clique in school. It was better to be "king" of a band of fighters you could lead into battle, than to be homecoming king or queen, just to smile and wave to cameras. Outsiders could deride them as geeks or losers and laugh that they probably never went out on dates. But geek girls were there to go out with the geek boys. Many in this crowd were uncoordinated, gawky or overweight klutzes more comfortable at their computer than in a weight room. But many more skipped normal high school athletics just because they felt they could be more mythic heroes by the sword and in their coats of arms than in their school colors.

"It just seemed right," Noble said.

Soon he started hitting people in the battles more often than they hit him. His belief that he was destined to be a warrior and leader had found a stage.

He was still too young to drive when a friend's mother started taking him to Society for Creative Anachronism meetings, where the fighting and its setting cranked up a level. Dagorhir pads the weapons. The Society pads the people. SCA fighting looks much more real with its metal armor and helmets, despite the duct-taped sticks passing as swords. The Society also provides a much bigger stage than Dagorhir. With more than 20,000 members—plus an estimated 50,000 unofficial participants—in more than a dozen "Kingdoms" nationwide and in Europe, it has the critical mass to be worthy of its "Society" name. As soon as he was old enough at 18, he shifted to fighting in the SCA style. The stocky and young-looking warrior, a fireplug with dimples, started to build a name for himself in his new home.

He assumed a Roman "persona" as a fighter and mixed fantasy with history by adopting the name Valharic from Michael Moorcock's Elric fantasy novel series. He also became a squire to a modern-day "Knight" within this Society, who went by the name Forgan Aurelius. Noble joined the Roman-style fighting household that Forgan had formed and completed his new warrior persona by taking on Forgan's last name. The childhood goal of the newly renamed Valharic Aurelius had gained focus.

"I'm going to be King of the Middle Kingdom," he now said.

Often known as the Midrealm, the Middle Kingdom is one of the largest and most powerful kingdoms of the Society for Creative Anachronism's "Known World." It stretches from Ohio west through the Dakotas and it chooses its kings, as do the other kingdoms of this medievalist society, in a fighting tournament every six months. To win the Midrealm crown, a warrior must win the day over the best swordsmen from not just Cleveland, but over those from Detroit, from Louisville, Indianapolis, Chicago, Milwaukee, the Twin Cities and the web of suburbs in between. The Valharic Aurelius part of Tommy Noble would need to master the sword and other weapons to make both his defense and lashing attacks second nature. He would need to fight more and practice harder than the Kingdom's best fighters, who would make pilgrimages from city to city every weekend to hone their own abilities. It would take skill and effort, but if he won, Tommy Noble could be king of as real a kingdom as this modern world allows.

His dream now had a Kingdom for a stage.

Meanwhile, his life took several twists as he grew and gained all the adult stresses that come without a birthright to a real-world throne. He tried to hone his art talent at the Pittsburgh Institute of Art until a starving artist's bankroll forced him to quit. He learned to cook and prepare sushi, but could not find a job thanks to an odd form of racism: "White men can't slice," he grumbled after being turned down yet again. He put in a stint in the Michigan National Guard working on military strategy and amplifying his belief he was born to be a military leader. And while he never lost his dimples, he picked up a few rough edges that made him closer to the young Prince Hal than an innocent cherub. Like the young Henry in Shakespeare's tale,

"…his addiction was to courses vain,
His companies unletter'd, rude, and shallow,
His hours fill'd up with riots, banquets, sports;

Though the entire Middle Ages pursuit might fit that description on its own, the rest of his life fit it even more. "The Kid" worked security for a few rock concerts and helped manage strip clubs; his admiration of Capitan Harlock soon had a mate in the form of 1950's pinup Betty Page; and in between the names Valharic and Aurelius he added the middle name of "Caligula," after Rome's emperor of excess. After a string of bar pickup girlfriends, he met a woman through a Dagorhir party and Pennsic that he told friends was "The One." She had her own rough edges, but she was also a sword fighter. They hit it off and made a great pair on the swing dance floor.

She gave his dream of becoming king another driving force. He could make her his queen.

Nine months before I started my own journey across the modern medieval world, the couple made the drive to Davenport, Iowa, known in this alternate world as the Shire of Dark River. At the age of 26, Noble/Valharic would try to pull the Society's equivalent of the sword from the stone. If he could win the Middle Kingdom's Crown Tournament here in the spring of 2000, he would no longer be "The Kid," but the King.

It would be hard. A few dozen of the 1,000 other fighters in the Kingdom had the same goal and passion. Some of his opponents could fight so well and were so well versed in Middle Ages customs that they were no longer just fighters. They were

"Knights"—full-fledged, inner-circle, dubbed-by-sword Knights of this Society—not Knight wanna-bes like Valharic. He had a long way to go to prove himself worthy of that title. Some of the fighters had even won a Crown Tournament before and had taken a turn on the throne Noble cherished.

Among them was a 6' 7" giant who went by the name Edmund of Hertford. Edmund had won the crown before. Not once. But twice. And he towered over opponents with arms so long they could rain down stinging blows from improbable angles. Edmund loomed ahead in the tournament bracket, just as he loomed over the string of opponents he clubbed "dead" in round after round as the tournament progressed. Valharic kept his focus on his own matches and his sword tore through his half of the bracket. Fighting for himself and the glory of his soon-to-be wife, he felled foes with his bread-and-butter leaps and backhand chops to their helmets. He was good, but few people expected him to be this deadly. "It was as if," said one of his friends who watched amazed, "he had been touched by the gods that day."

In the semifinals, he dispatched one of the lofty Knights. He was one bout away from making 15 years of boasts come true.

All that stood in the way was Edmund.

Either Edmund or Valharic would spend six months serving as Prince before graduating from that understudy post to become King. The winner would have the honor and duty of traveling hours away nearly every weekend to rule the Kingdom. The winner would wear the crown and lead the Kingdom army into battle. He would be King and the loser would have to bow to him.

As they prepared to fight, the King of the moment, known in this Society as the Viking Dag Thorgrimsson, reminded the crowd that gathered in close—all wearing tunics, doublets and gowns to watch the heroics—that the fight they were about to see was more than just a battle between two men. Just like a sword, it would stand for so much more.

"My Lords and Ladies," he told his populace, "this is the first test of a true King. Courage, honor, veracity will be shown here. Watch these gentlemen, for one of them will be your King someday. Know their worth."

Valharic and Edmund moved to the center of the fighting ring. As is Kingdom custom, all of the Knights knelt in a circle around the ring to watch carefully. The combatants shifted their weight from foot to foot, sizing each other up from just out of sword range, before launching into each other with a blur of sword swipes, quick blade snaps and lightning parries. They split the first two duels, with Edmund swatting a clout to the side of Valharic's head and Valharic somehow, with a stretch of his arms, reaching almost over the top of Edmund's helmet to give it a smash.

As he readied for the third and deciding bout, Valharic bounced with anticipation, almost shadow boxing. His goal was within reach.

The fighters closed on each other. They swung and chopped, deflecting the hacks with their blades and shields. They managed only glancing blows until Valharic, with a quick slash, slipped a sword swipe below Edmund's shield and caught his leg. Edmund dropped to his knees wounded. With that one slash, the giant was cut down to size.

If Valharic could land one more blow, the lowly squire would take down the vaunted Knight. Little Tommy Noble would take the crown from a royal the Society held on high. David would beat Goliath.

Valharic backed up. He regrouped.

And charged.

Swords flashed. Shields shifted to block blows. The two collided. Each landed blows on the other as they toppled to the floor. The crowd held its breath. That jumbled and confused exchange held the futures of both combatants and the entire Kingdom for the next year.

Valharic and Edmund pulled themselves from their twisted heap in seconds. But that split-second crossing of swords had tied a knot of competitive drive, desire, honor, chivalry and fair play that would take almost two years to untangle.

Act I, scene 1
The Traveler's Tale: The Middle
Kingdom for a Stage

January 2001, Common Era
Anno Societatis XXXIV

> *...But pardon, and gentles all,*
> *The flat unraised spirits that have dared*
> *On this unworthy scaffold to bring forth*
> *So great an object...*

—Prologue, *Henry V*

The Oakland County Recreation Pavilion looks more like an airplane hangar than the castle it has to pass for today. Built of concrete and metal, instead of hand-hewn blocks of stone or beams of oak, it is surrounded by acres of fields for baseball, not for serfs to grow their crops. The parking lot's painted lines are the best stand-ins this modern facility has for stalls for travel-weary horses.

My journey into this unusual world has been a 3 1/2 hour drive from my home in Cleveland, past Detroit's suburban sprawl of malls and office towers to the tiny town of Davisburg, Mich. In the real Middle Ages, such a journey would have taken days or weeks. I could have fallen sick or died on the road. Dagger-brandishing highwaymen, not just the radar-brandishing highway patrol, could have set upon me. And more threatening figures than bored turnpike toll takers could have held me up for taxes at crossroads. In this version of the Middle Ages, the journey is an easy drive with no adventure or peril.

It is also short, by the standards of this Kingdom in the Society for Creative Anachronism. The so-called Middle Kingdom sprawls from Ohio to the Dakotas so its subjects expect journeys of a few hundred miles. I make the trip in one morning with Cat, the girlfriend who introduced me to these modern Middle Ages, thanks to the 100 horses under our hood. Others drove from Illinois or Kentucky last night and either paid for a hotel or sought quarter from other subjects. They will spend more time on the road than they will spend here today. For the diehards of this group, it is worth the drive to be among others who share the same passion, instead of stuck among those who look down on it. We pull into a stall among them and I dismount the car to take off my parka.

I wore my coat the entire way, less because of the January Midwest chill than for fear of being spotted in a tunic and a hood. Valharic Aurelius, the squire I will follow on his quest for Knighthood and the Middle Kingdom's throne, may want to be King, but I'm still unsure about this world he wants to be "King" of. My parka is my armor against the giggles I just know my costume will draw. When we made a pit stop at a Dunkin' Donuts, I zipped my coat closed tight before scampering past the counter and booths and ducking into the bathroom. I opened it only after looking both ways for witnesses. As I walked back to the car I could feel the clerk's jeers burning the back of my neck. I whirled around to catch him in the act.

It was all my imagination. He was just taking an order.

I climbed back into the car. Cat had her coat unbuttoned. She was shamelessly flashing the world with her medieval "garb." Her garb modesty evaporated long ago, as I'm told mine soon will. She has been part of this group for years and has no qualms about others spotting her in funny clothes. Veterans of the Society for Creative Anachronism joke about "freaking the mundanes"—"mundanes" being akin to the non-magical "Muggle" outsiders in the Harry Potter world. Today, the "mundane" I'm freaking the most with my clothing is myself. I remove the parka only when we arrive and I have safety in numbers.

I toss the coat onto the back seat and exchange it for a heavy wool cloak. Jackets, particularly Gore-Tex ones, do not qualify as medieval protection against cold. I pull on a pair of black boots and leave my sneakers behind. Reeboks do not come even close.

Today's event is my first step on a journey that will carry me through the "Known World" of this medieval society. Though I have seen some of how it operates at its massive, sprawling Pennsic War, with its 10,000 campers and world's-largest medieval-style battles, I want to see this world on a local level and learn its customs before I return to Pennsic and, hopefully fight in the giant battles at the War's 30th anniversary here in 2001.

We have trekked here on this January Saturday to what the Society knows as the Barony of Roaring Wastes—a medievalish twist of a name for a region responsible for much of this country's automobile pollution—to celebrate Twelfth Night with the Middle Kingdom. Twelfth Night marks the twelfth day of Christmas and the day, so tradition holds, that the Three Wise Men recognized the baby Jesus. Each of the kingdoms in the SCA's "Known World" will celebrate Twelfth Night, continuing its custom of linking some of its gatherings to historical holidays. The days don't always match up exactly because SCA events are almost always on Saturdays, thanks to the modern workweek. Here in the Middle Kingdom, often called the Midrealm, Twelfth Night sets aside the fighting that dominates most events to become a showpiece of courtly behavior, learning and the finest pieces of medieval garb people have managed to put together. With no fighting, no one gets too sweaty and dirty for their Saturday Best.

Recreation or Re-Creation?

Cat and I join the line of cloak-clad at the cinder block entrance. We pay a fee to cover hall rental and the night's feast to the "Troll"—a Society-wide play off of "toll" and the fairy-tale trolls that guarded bridges. Unlike admission to a renaissance fair, the fee only covers costs. All the labor to set up tables, cook the feast and serve it comes from volunteers. Nobody pockets a profit, except maybe the barony, which saves it to fund other events. We amble with the other travelers (Billy Goats Garbed?) into the center of the building, which has been transformed from a "Recreation Pavilion" into a Re-Creation one. In the 215-year-old United States, land of urban sprawl and home of Baby Boom cookie-cutter concrete school buildings, members dress the set with themselves, their clothes and their props instead of relying on medieval sites for atmosphere.

Old wool blankets, rugs and wooden chests piled with thick candles, blocks of cheese and wooden bowls line the rim of the hall in rows of day "camps". Flags the shape of giant shields hang from walls or on poles, emblazoned with coats of arms. I duck past a few women in long dresses with oversized hanging sleeves or with detailed, lace-up bodices. The men all wear virtual dresses: man-colored dresses of blue or green or brown, without any frilly bits. But they hang to the knees and belts are worn over them, not in belt loops the normal way. They call these outfits tunics here but they'd be considered dresses anywhere else. I don't even dress up at Halloween, but wearing an "attempt" at medieval clothing is required to even get in the door. I give in and wear a plain tunic—which definitely does not drop below the knee, mind you—that I grudgingly stitched together from rust-colored cotton fabric using a Simplicity "Renaissance Men" pattern.

Most of the crowd wants their medieval "garb" more ornate than my plain attempt, and has sewn wide strips of colored cloth at the hems of their sleeves. Others have splashed their outfit with ribbon-like decorations that would impress even a gift-wrapper at Christmastime. Some have Celtic knotwork, some have flower patterns and some have Mediterranean designs dating to the B.C. era. I duck past a couple, pausing to ogle a full Henry VIII-style Tudor outfit. It looks straight off a movie set.

I bite my tongue before that compliment escapes. In this Society, such a comment would almost be an insult. While Hollywood sets the Middle Ages image for most, some SCA scholars delight in de-programming misguided movie beliefs. I hardly notice Henry VIII's glasses, one of the less obtrusive anachronisms that give the Society its name.

The name "Society for Creative Anachronism," coined on the fly by too-clever-for-their-own-good hippies in the late 1960's, offers no real clues about what the group does. "Medieval Re-creation Society" would be easier to understand, but the terms "re-creation" or "re-enactment" do not accurately describe the SCA. Some label it "recreational medievalism" and many say the SCA's pretext is "the Middle Ages as they should have been," not as they really were. The stylized world of the SCA skips the plagues, forced labor and the Inquisition, even eliminating the most powerful force of the era, religion, altogether. The SCA adopts the Middle Ages world of Victorian historians and novelists, with far greater emphasis on chivalry and noble etiquette than the nasty, brutish and short realities of life. And it never fully re-creates any specific event. Where Civil War re-enactors will re-create specific battles with the outcome pre-determined (The North wins the war. Big surprise.), the SCA never does. Battles are more sporting events than plays. And the "personas" people adopt can be based on historical people, but they can't be that person. The costume of the Henry VIII look-alike may scream out "Henry the VIII, I am, I am." But he's not, he's not.

Real re-enactors ban anachronisms from their sites, but they remain a big part of getting by in this Society. It is how people justify sleeping in a nylon tent at medieval events and how I can travel 220 miles in one morning using directions downloaded off the Internet to see prescription glasses on a Tudor man. Even clothing is often inconsistent. SCAdians joke about their "explosion in a time machine" garb closet that borrows a little of this from the 10th century and a little of that from the 14th, plus underwear from the 20th. Even if several centuries are mixed, if it's all "period" it's good for most people. Underwear is excluded. If you're in position to take close note of someone's underwear, you've got other things on your mind.

Newcomers like me mistakenly lump all of history into an amorphous, catch-all "Olden Tymes" that covers very different eras. Though the Society narrows its time period into pre-1600s and shuts out the Cavalry, Confederates, Redcoats and Laura Ingalls Wilder, it includes everything from Roman centurions and Norse raiders to the patrons of Shakespeare's plays. Other re-creation groups set themselves in a specific place and time. But in this Society, I can cross paths with a Tudor gentleman arm in arm with his Italian Renaissance wife as I seek the Roman encampment of what is perhaps this Kingdom's finest collection of fighters: Darkyard.

Though the fighters in this "household" do not actually live together, the members of Darkyard train together, fight together and party together. Its troops boisterous shouts of its name—"Darkyard!"—ring across the entire campground of the Pennsic War, surpassed only by the wave of close to 100 of its fighters that rolls into and over the enemy in battle. On one of my forays to Pennsic, a fighter from the enemy East told me his best moment on the battlefield came when a Darkyard commander gave him a quick nod and salute mid-battle for nice fighting, even though he fought for the enemy. It had made his day, somehow outweighing the bad fortune of being slaughtered by the commander's men moments later. The Darkyard coat of arms featuring an outline of a leafless tree silhouetted by a full moon in the center is recognized across the Kingdom and the entire Known World.

In the back corner, I spot a cluster of black and white Darkyard flags and head toward them. Before I get there, a call rings out.

"Oyez! Oyez!," comes the bellow. "All commanders of the army of the Middle Kingdom should report to the commanders meeting."

In a corner, just off the passage between the snack bar and the bathrooms, the Kingdom's military commanders talk strategy. Omarad the Wary, the Midrealm's general, overwhelms a flimsy plastic chair. Like Edmund the King, Omarad is a giant but he brings another dimension to the Kingdom leadership. Wide instead of tall, he delivers a pep talk to his charges circled around him. As he talks, he shifts from "Wary" to Omarad the Intense.

"Start winning these Wars..."

Build your forces by the spring, Omarad urges his commanders. Recruit people. Teach them to fight. Start working as a unit. Across the huddle I catch the eye of one of Darkyard's lesser commanders, and he gives me a nod. His full SCA name is MaelColuim MacFlainn, but everyone just calls him Flynn, mixing the spelling with his old name from Dagorhir. Everyone in this crowd seems to have about a dozen names—a real name, a nickname, a "persona" name, their old persona name, their name from another group, and on and on. Keeping all these alter egos straight is going to be tough. In three days I will meet "Flynn" and other fighters at his house after work to sort out my plan for learning to fight. I will soon either be part of Flynn's solution to Omarad's charge, or the albatross that keeps him from it. Flynn turns back as Omarad talks about new archery rules this year.

SCA fighting mostly consists of close sword combat, two guys or rows of guys "swinging stick"—their rattan swords, spears, axes and polearms—at each other face to face. Fighting takes that format in one-on-one tournaments, but melees—the wars between groups—add a few other twists to it. You can be shot with arrows, not just bludgeoned with a stick. The arrows are safe, with tennis balls or an approximation of a halved super ball as heads instead of piercing metal points, and the bows are low-powered. But the strategies for using archers lag well behind the ever-expanding tactics for sword, spear and polearm ranks. Archers that don't confine themselves to target shooting on the range, safely away from those nasty swords, spears and maces, often tend to hang back and float arrows into the enemy lines. That is changing, but Omarad wants the change to come faster.

"We don't want them lobbing. We want combined arms. We want them up close," he tells the group, chopping his hands in the air to lay out where he wants his lines of fighters. "Shield. Shield. Spear. Archers."

One fighter suggests making a siege tower. Pennsic will have a fort for the first time this year. Battles normally have piles of cushy hay bales as obstacles, but Pennsic will have battles this summer on a wooden-walled fort that will be a huge step toward a simulated castle. A tower, the fighter suggests, could help attackers get over the fort walls. Omarad lights up. Fighters use towers at Gulf Wars, another large event in the south each spring, and he can figure them out when he goes there in two months.

Another commander, know as Sir Felix the Just of Ramsay, jumps in and tells the group they need to start practicing.

"We've made a decision in this Kingdom to start winning these wars," he lectures. "We need to start attacking the enemy with overwhelming force and in depth."

Omarad and Felix outline an army structure that had slipped my attention the first battles I watched. Pennsic battles are like the climaxes of *Braveheart* or *Henry V* playing out live in front of you. Just watching the masses of forces colliding, with shields slamming together, swords slicing the air and bodies piling up, is impressive. To an outsider, it looks chaotic. On my trips to Pennsic, where a tag like "The Wary" could have been slapped on me, I just saw two giant crowds surging into each other haphazardly like two runaway herds of sheep. But there is some strategy. In more than 30 years of fighting these battles, people have developed tactics for taking ground, different ones for holding it and a whole hierarchy of commanders and troops. Darkyard is known in the Kingdom for better teamwork than most in using oversized shields they call "war boards" to create a wall for spearmen to jab over and around.

Omarad steps up.

"You guys remember the Abbey Battle at War?"

One of several during the week of the Pennsic War, the battle scenario combines field fighting and the ability of armies to capture a series of 'buildings"—normally a rectangle of hay bales—on the field. The Middle Kingdom crushed its arch enemy the East, grabbing the buildings early and holding on to the end.

"How many of you guys were at Pennsic?" he asks. Hands go up all around.

Of course.

Pennsic is the focal point for the Middle Kingdom. Unless you are one of the few fighters challenging for the crown, Pennsic is the climax of your Middle Ages year. It is a vacation, a convention, Opening Night, Prom and the Super Bowl rolled into one. In the west and in the south, people focus on closer major events, mostly the Estrella War outside Phoenix and Gulf Wars in Mississippi. Around here, if you talk about "War" you mean Pennsic.

"Did you sense a different feeling this year? Did you like running over people?"

Omarad interrupts the laughter. "Take that feeling. Take it to every battle."

"A real man does whatever he wants…"

In another hall of the Pavilion, several women hunch over parchment, or their anachronism of the moment—paper that can pass as parchment. They slowly paint their own versions of medieval illuminated manuscripts for Edmund to give out as awards tonight. Sometimes they use period paints but most often use modern materials. They copy or base their designs on books of surviving medieval documents and they decorate the "scrolls"—actually single flat pieces of paper—in keeping with the time and place of the recipient's persona.

I walk the rows of tables set up by merchants in search of armor so I can start fighting. I have no idea what I am looking for. The most armor I ever used in gym class was a goalie mask. Do I want leather armor? Do I want steel, a Tin Man suit? And what are all these pieces called? I don't know spaulders from Spalding and greaves only mean grief. At least I know I need a helmet. I find a few leather belts and gloves but not the heavy metal helmet I need most. Cat and I wander the tables looking at pouches that serve as purse-on-a-belt and necklaces made of chunks of amber. Fantasy has snuck into this supposedly pure history event in the form of *Lord of the Rings* action figures. How precious.

The high ceiling and clatter swallows the high-pitched songs in Latin and English from a group of 10 carolers moving from camp to camp. The University of Michigan students belong to the Musicum Collegium of Ann Arbor's SCA branch called Cynnabar. The song, called "In Dulci Jubilo" is a Christmas Carol written in 1630 by Michael Pretorious.

"That means, "With Greatest Rejoicing," explains Elsa Von Heillbran, who goes by Katy Kreig in her studies at the university. "It's pretty late period."

It's actually a tiny bit post-period. But I'm in enough of an anachronistic mood to overlook that.

Von Heillbran wears a white net called a wimple over her tied hair and a plain, sleeveless dress over her long-sleeved white underdress. The armholes of the over-dress, called a surcoat, drop nearly to the waist. She has pretty much shouted down her colleagues in her zeal to explain the piece, but they laugh about it.

"No, I didn't write a five-page paper on this," she fibs. Her class load at Michigan apparently left her plenty of time to document the history of the song so the group could enter it in Society arts competitions, which are judged partly on skill and per-formance and partly on research.

While volunteers clear the other wing of the complex hall for feast, a few cooks load a table with goodies made from period recipes and ingredients. Next to marzipan of walnut, hazelnut, almond and pistachio, a few period surprises—saunders, fennel and black pepper—have made their way into the recipe for tiny gingerbread cubes rolled in sugar. Hais, made from dates, almonds, butter, breadcrumbs, pistachio and sugar, is like little balls of ground and mushy granola. The cooks then add tarts of apple, rose petal, pomegranate, peach and honeysuckle to the mix.

Soon the crowd files back into the hall clutching bags and picnic baskets stuffed with "feast gear." Plastic dishes and tumblers are not period and the family china or brightly glazed plates from Super K don't add to the medieval atmosphere. So most new SCAdians head to the Salvation Army for clunky wooden salad bowls and plates and someone's discarded high school reunion tankard, hopefully with the inscription "L.H.S. Class of 1971" faint enough to be overlooked. Despite plastic bottoms, the tankards have become a staple, though people routinely chug cans of non-period soda from very non-period aluminum cans (emblazoned with non-period, non-heraldic logos to boot). Many trade up to fancy and expensive leather mugs or fine goblets of metal or glass and replace their wooden bowls with metal. A few, unashamed at being practical instead of historical, set paper cups and styrofoam plates on the table.

Our table companions go the practical route but nobody will call them on it. Omarad the general, who heads the group at the end of the table, is the stoutest man in the room with credentials to match. Clearly, if the man wants to eat with a plastic fork, nobody's going to tell him any different. Then again, nobody would want to. Despite his responsibility to inflict carnage on opposing armies, he is as genial a fellow as you would want to meet. He cracks a wry smile as he inspects his chair before he sits down. "I broke one earlier today," he says.

Later, when a server asks if he wants more meat, he declines. "It's OK," he jokes. "I'll just waste away to normal."

Paul Newton, 33, spends his SCA time pouring his energy into molding and encouraging the Kingdom army. As its general, he ranks just behind the King in commanding the army and is its prime off-season pep-talker. But on weekdays, he plows away in his pursuit of a master's degree in education at the University of Kentucky. When not leading his troops, Omarad/Newton student-teaches at Scott County High School just north of Lexington, where he sneaks extra lessons on the Middle Ages and heraldry into his world civilizations classes. When an English class at the school studied Chaucer, he came in to the class wearing armor. At the start of each semester he writes his list of "Newton's Laws" on the blackboard, starting with Sir Isaac Newton's laws of physics before morphing into his own classroom rules.

A meld of good-ol'-boy and scholar, Omarad once served in the Army at Fort Knox. He would either hitchhike to medieval events or ride on his motorcycle, his armor piled on the back with a tent on top. He soon learned to fight with a polearm—the equivalent of a heavy sword blade on a long spear—instead of the standard sword and shield.

"A shield on the side of a motorcycle is a sail," he says. "The first time I did that, wind hit me and I changed lanes without wanting to. A polearm doesn't catch wind on a cycle."

In college he took medieval-related classes like The Role of Family in Medieval History, the Role of the Printing Press in the Protestant Reformation, and the Philosophy of Political Thought. Along with "manly" pursuits like trying to brew and making armor, he has learned to do calligraphy and illumination in the SCA, how to make period soap and even took a class in how to make lace.

"A real man does whatever he wants," he explains. "That's what I say."

"Groaning from the abundance of the food…"

Cat and I assemble our own motley feast gear—a wooden thrift store tray and a leaf-shaped wooden snack bowl. Instead of the roaring fireplaces, growling dogs roaming underfoot and sturdy wooden tables that movies have trained me to expect, the hall is filled with standard issue rec hall particleboard tables that volunteers have disguised with tablecloths and evergreen garlands. We fill our thrift store wooden goblets from a pitcher swimming with lemons and break chunks off huge wedges of cheese as we await the feast.

Then it comes. And comes. And comes again. Over the next 90 minutes come three separate waves of stuffing food. Each course contains about a half-dozen different items, all period recipes, all prepared as closely as possible with period ingredients. Like a restaurant with ethnic food you've never tried before, each feast can mean trying something new. Since the labor of preparing and cooking is free, it costs a fraction of what a restaurant would charge.

I knew going in not to expect potatoes. As much as the earthy tubers look, taste and feel like they ought to be a big part of a royal feast, they never were—at least not in this Society's time period. For all of the talk about the Irish and potatoes, it turns out my ancestors and the food met only a few hundred years ago. But we never miss them in the bombardment of food to come.

Our server lays a platter of small chunks of venison with a thick, tangy brown sauce on the table and collects our bowls to fill with lentil soup. Then comes a bowl of wedges of parsnips—a potato predecessor and carrot clone—in a sweet wine sauce, then pears cooked in cinnamon and wine. As I spear pieces of venison, which someone helpfully calls "dead Bambi," with my awkward, oversized wooden fork, I vow to figure out period utensils and buy a proper set. If I'm going to be doing the rubber venison circuit for a year, I ought not to slum it.

Since I have paid for the "Above the Salt" feast, which gives me the status for access to salt, a precious commodity in period, I just grab a few pinches from the small cups of salt on the table for my lentils. I down the whole bowl. Big mistake. These feasts are so new to me I have no warning of what is still to come.

I am already full enough to walk away when the second course comes with salad, more bread, a platter of half-inch thick cutlets of "Roast of Beef" and then a bright pink puree of crabapple called "Apple Muse." It also has two new items for me. The mushroom pasty is essentially a mushroom pie. The "seed cake" is a dense, slightly crumbly, mildly sweet cake with a garnish of rose petals and a leaf on top. We plunge in anew as two new companions join the table.

A curly blonde woman with a circlet on her head and a low-cut black and purple dress hurriedly sits down with her escort, a thin, long-haired, mustached man in a bright red tunic and black vest. He could be a brother of the magician Doug Henning. Harried and late, they sped at the last minute from Dekalb, Ill., about five hours away. The woman's two grade-school children, garbed and bearing a staff with a gargoyle glued to the end, sit off to the side for the "Low" or "Below the Salt" feast of cold cuts. Their expensive garb hides the fact this is just their second event. They still don't know if the SCA is the place for them.

It probably isn't.

The Empress of the Essence, and Lord Carybarb the Ogar are web-site fantasy personas. The new couple met online and hooked up by comparing their web sites and stories of their real world selves and their invented characters. They bought garb to attend renaissance fairs and are now test-driving the SCA in the hope of carrying their fantasy personas further into the living world. "This is what we were meant to do," explains the Empress as she tells Cat about her life as a wizardess.

"Don't spread that around or you'll get burned at the stake," Cat tells her, softening the blow with a smile.

Fantasy characters make their way into SCA events, but mostly at Pennsic where some people flat-out ignore the group's historical bent. Even there, the elves and vampires walking around draw some scorn and spark some debate. Our new friends are fast learning they may have to adjust. They have to drop the fantasy titles. Titles of

King, Duke, Baron and Knight all have such specific meaning in this Society I am surprised they are not trademarked like brand names. In this world, you can't just be an Empress or an Ogar, whatever the hell made-up thing that is.

"The thing that bothers us," the Ogar complains, "is that we're both descendents of royalty."

"My next big challenge is to take all of my fantasy gowns and make them period," says the Empress. "We just need to get away from zippers and modern fabrics."

"We're learning," adds the Ogar.

This feast, a culinary tour of the Dark Ages, set the first course in the late Roman era, the second in Dark Ages Britain and closed with Saxon and Viking food from around 1066, the year of the pivotal Norman invasion of England.

"The frame of mind I kept myself in," explained menu planner Urien Vitalis, a big bruiser of a fighter from Darkyard, MKA (Mundanely Known As) Ken Slamka, "was poorly lit smoky halls, 'peasant' style hearty, earthy foods, and an abundance that could make even myself full."

"We wanted things going out big. We wanted the tables AND the feasters groaning from the abundance of the food."

He succeeded.

I now understand the practice of feasters disgorging the excess with a feather tickle at the back of the throat. Binging and purging in this world is not an eating disorder. It's a survival tactic.

One noblewoman sums up the feast when, amid a parade of toasts that are a tradition at every feast, she declares, "I'd like to raise a glass to our most excellent chefs who made us break our New Year's resolutions."

The transformation of the hall begins again. Volunteers fold the tables, sweep the floor and set the chairs in classroom rows. In a half hour, the crew converts the hangar-turned-feast hall into a royal court. They replace dinner chairs with thrones at the head of the room. The Middle Kingdom does not have the money for thrones of gold and jewels but it has spent hours of human capital on carving and painting them with the green dragon and red and white stripes of the Kingdom coat of arms. At a shout from a herald, the belly-bursting subjects all stand.

Had Valharic not fallen just short in his bid for the throne at the Kingdom's Crown Tournament last spring, he and his wife would be marching in as King and Queen to preside over this court. Instead, by defeating the squire in the tournament's finals, Edmund of Hertford and his Queen, Katryn Bronwen of Gloucester, MKA (Mundanely Known As) Donald and Katrina Strubler of Delaware, Ohio, have that honor.

Heads drop and chins lower to chests as Edmund and Katryn lead a short procession to the front of the room. This deference to a banker and housewife raises my eyebrows. People take their royals seriously here, the lack of beheadings notwithstanding. Even royals like these, whose spot on the throne comes with a touch of controversy. A few who bow before them believe, rightly or wrongly, that Valharic should have that seat. Even nine months after their fateful duel, some of Valharic's friends still scowl at its result.

"Making people feel it..."

Donald Strubler, 34, lives in the Columbus, Ohio, suburb of Delaware and commutes every morning to his job at a regional bank. He comes home to his wife Katrina and two boys, two and one. On weekends, he and Katrina sometimes drop the boys at her mother's or pack them into their van with toys and a television to watch, then head off on their progress across their Kingdom. Once they arrive at events, they shift from being the ones the boys look up to, to the ones a whole Kingdom looks up to—not just because Edmund is 6'7". Because he is King.

While the SCA world has many different pursuits and features, at its core sits an idealized medieval structure in which royal ceremony, finery and regalia fire the imaginations and passions of participants. Here in the U.S., the Kennedys come closest to filling the role of royalty, just ahead of movie stars, rock stars and sports heroes, each fueled by either political power, athletic prowess or the cult of personality. The SCA splits the difference, giving political power to those that have seized it with athletic prowess and then adding all the trappings and glitter of celebrity. Instead of a lifetime on the throne or 15 minutes of fame, most SCA royals get six months. In return, the King and Queen must play the part and set the tone and atmosphere.

"The SCA was my chance to kind of be a medieval person, to do all the stuff medieval heroes did," said Edmund/Strubler, a longtime Richard the Lionheart fan. "I had my armor. I was fighting. I liked the mysticism of it, the different age, the romanticized version of the Middle Ages.

"Being King is about making the game for other people. That's your entire job, to make other people feel it. You can do cool things but it's really a time to give everybody else their due."

As he rose through the ranks over his 15 years in the group and changed gears from his role-playing roots to learn more of the actual history of the Middle Ages, he began to appreciate the SCA version of the era more than the real one.

"The Middle Ages weren't nearly as Romantic as we make them out to be. They were pretty awful," he says. "Honestly, I would not want to accurately re-enact the Middle Ages. It was a time of might makes right. If you were the baddest dude on the block, you could win. That's just not fun.

"I was taught by my mom not to be a bully," he said. "I'll use the advantages of the height because I have the disadvantages, but I don't go around trying to intimidate people or stare people down. I'm not really into that macho BS. It's a game of skill."

He met his wife—"it sounds corny, but it was love at first sight"—at the first SCA meeting she ever attended. For their 10 years together she has endured with patience all the hours he spends on the battlefield. He repaid her—in the currency of this hobby—in October 1995, when he won his first Crown Tournament to make her

Queen. After six months as Prince and understudy, then six months as King, he won again to start the cycle a second time.

His third Crown win—the one over Valharic nine months ago in the spring of 2000—was the only one that still had lingering issues. Nobody openly questioned Edmund. That would be bad form. But anyone who saw the bout, or even heard about it, knew it was a close call. A few friends of Valharic griped, away from SCA events, that Edmund "stole" the crown. Their fight had put this Society's long tradition of treating its fights as an honor sport to the test. It also involved rules I have yet to learn. It would make more sense, I hope, once I started fighting.

Tonight Edmund and Katryn fulfill a major duty as King and Queen—handing out awards. Although it reverses the true medieval habit of extracting excessive taxes from subjects, it can be the highlight for the royals and the person called before them.

"Until you sit in front of somebody and give them their award they really deserve and really means a lot, you can't understand," said Edmund.

As the two sit on their new thrones just unveiled tonight, two guards with spears and a group of heralds with a stack of scrolls to award stand at their sides. Some court sessions run long, with entertainment and speeches and lengthy announcements of Kingdom business. This one mirrors a Pack meeting to give Cub Scouts their Wolf badges, aside from the courtly vocabulary and bowing.

Edmund works down the list. As the herald calls people for awards, they go to the front, bow to Edmund and Katryn and then kneel on a cushion at their feet for Edmund to hand them scrolls for research, for garb-making, for leading an SCA-sponsored charity drive. Most are the most basic SCA award, the Award of Arms. Arms are granted by different standards in each kingdom but are recognition for scholarship, serious efforts at reproducing history or service to the kingdom. The people scrubbing dishes in the kitchen may be bucking for their arms and the title of Lord or Lady it carries.

Edmund and the heralds then call up a young man who hops up the step and kneels awkwardly. Instead of the standard kneeling on one knee, he settles on both knees with both feet behind him. Edmund leans forward as he speaks.

"It has come to my attention that you have done significant work on Norse research. You have outfitted yourself well and done excellent work in shoe-making."

The young man blushes and looks away. His two soles staring back at the audience have deep black treads. Store shoes. Modern shoes. Not hand-made Norse ones. The audience laughs and Edmund cranes his neck around him to see for himself. The trapped subject squirms in a hopeless attempt to draw the evidence under his haunches. It is too late. He is busted. Edmund reaches back for the award and turns to face him brandishing a wooden paddle, bringing more laughter, mixed with a few gasps as Edmund raises it in mock threat. With a flourish, he flips it over. The paddle is carved with a Norse-style horse head and the award inscription carved like runes on the front. The flustered subject sheepishly accepts the award to great applause.

In the back, the merchants have departed. Others scurry to pack chests and trundle children to cars. But a few people huddle in the back and I can hear the thump of a drum and a singing voice. A guitar, drum and recorder muddle their way through a song by the contemporary artist Loreena McKennitt, a favorite of SCA musicians for playing Celtic and Middle eastern-tinged songs that evoke the mood of SCA events.

The woman singing and adding guitar wears a complicated tan and brown, late 1400s Italian Renaissance gown. She made it herself, along with the Henry VIII outfit that caught my eye earlier. The Lady Antionette la Rouge d'Avignon, MKA Toni Nurnberger of Jackson, Mich., is married to the Henry wannabe, who goes by Lord Albyn Buckthorne. Lord Albyn stands up from playing the drum at the conclusion of the song so I can see his garb in all its glory. With his wife's prodding, he tosses back the cape, puts his hands on his hips and thrusts his pelvis forward. "You have to do that to show the codpiece properly," he tells me and a few passers-by.

He sits back down, grabs his drum and slips the toe of a boot into the rim of a tambourine to stand it up. The tambourine jingles when he lifts and drops his heel to the beat. Lady Antoinette takes up her guitar again and launches into a song she wrote herself. "It's the story of my beginning in the SCA," she said. "People really like the chorus. That's what it's about for me, the magic of the SCA." The words fly by too fast to record as the hall empties, but the chorus is clear:

"They said, "Take my hand and follow me
To tales of dragons and grand chivalry
And to moments of glory and friendship so rare
Let's travel through history and be who we dare."

Act I, scene 2
Do You Feel Like a Real Fighter?

He was not in the least bit scared to be mashed into a pulp,
Or to have his eyes gouged out and his elbows broken,
To have his kneecaps split and his body burned away
And his limbs all hacked and mangled, brave Sir Robin!

His head smashed in and his heart cut out
And his liver removed and his bowels unplugged
And his nostrils raped and his bottom burned off
And his pen…

—Monty Python and the Holy Grail

It all starts with the smashing in of my head.

"You're going to need a helm," says Sean O'Toole, the Flynn from Twelfth Night, pulling a basketball-sized mass of metal and foam from a gym bag.

"That's my old one," adds Rob Radcliffe, known in the SCA as Talon. "It's not great, but it works."

Not great? This helmet looks fittingly sinister to me. Dark gray bands of steel riveted together encase the head, with just a narrow open band for the eyes and cheese-grater air holes over the jaw. A foe will only see the eyes, glaring out with intent and searching for something to hit. If I saw this coming at me my fear might unplug my bowels for me. But since I'll be the one hiding behind it, nobody will ever see my panic.

I pull it over my head and can feel the weight on my skull and neck muscles. I sympathize with the Elephant Man. Suddenly, I can understand crushing your windpipe by losing the balance of your hefty head. Inside this world of muted sound and letter-box vision, I feel untouchable. And blind. With no peripheral vision I'd be helpless to an attack from behind. I turn to locate Sean in my viewfinder and the helmet wobbles around my head.

"It's a little loose," I tell him

"We can fix that with padding."

Padding is good. Very good. I'm going to need it.

Members of the local branch of Darkyard have gathered on this freezing January night at Sean/Flynn's house in the Cleveland suburb of Lakewood. Flynn and his cohorts started the meetings under the name "SFU"—"Something For Us"—so they could team on SCA projects even as most of Darkyard lives a few hours away in Detroit. Sean, 34, a lawyer for a firm specializing in bill collection, opens his house for a few hours every week as the group scarfs down Wendy's takeout, works out car pool arrangements to events and makes lists of projects to complete. Suiting me up in armor and somehow making a passable fighter out of me is this year's project.

In his basement, Flynn, like many sword and armor junkies, has saws and a drill press to make his gear. He jokes that one of the partners in his law firm told him he could be a judge someday if he spent his nights studying cases instead of making armor. But he would rather strike a balance. After a full day of sifting through volumes of case law, his hobby helps him recharge. As things have worked out, the basement "Armory" has become the boy's hangout while upstairs is the lair of the women in the group who focus on sewing and embroidery. With a few exceptions, members of this Society fall into a very traditional (or backwards, depending on your politics) idea of gender roles. Flynn, who can be very focused and direct, as those who measure their time by billable hours must be, takes charge of the Armory while his wife Erin, who is stretching her sewing and garb-making skills as an apprentice to a sewing expert, takes charge upstairs.

The men all fight with Darkyard or its expanded version, its Roman-styled Legion, which lets newbies and less-serious fighters into the mix. Most of Darkyard's Cleveland branch started with the foam weapons of Cleveland's Dagorhir chapter of Pentwyvern. It has become a minor league stop and pipeline for Darkyard as fighters graduate from boffing others with mushy foam to smacking people in the head with sticks. Darkyard is my passport into the elite of the fighting world. Valharic, one of Cleveland's big links to the household, sometimes comes to these SFU meetings.

While the women in the group hang back in the living room to embroider a dress, the boys—and Cat—head to the basement. Sean/Flynn has stacked bags of camping gear, garb and armor in a corner. Darkyard war boards, each marked with the silhouetted tree coat of arms, lean against a post along with a display shield bearing the arms of the house's founder and the Knight that Valharic had chosen as his mentor, the late Forgan Aurelius. Tools cover two large workbenches and part of a table in the middle of the floor. Sean/Flynn grabs a can of Coke from the small refrigerator against the wall and starts rattling off the list of armor I need.

As he starts running down my body, from the neck armor gorget to shin-protecting greaves, my shopping list of leather, plastic and metal sword-repellant grows. He keeps adding pieces—elbow protectors, bracers, kidney protectors—and I wonder if all this should scare me or comfort me. Is all this equipment going to keep me nice, cozy and safe from harm? Or am I about to step into some hell where being "mashed into a pulp" is a real danger?

For most people, the Middle Ages evokes images of knights—sword-swinging, steed-riding, shield-toting and jousting warriors rushing into peril to rescue damsels in distress. People think of castles—big hulking military fortifications with drawbridges, moats, arrow slits and towers to dump hot oil on attackers. And they think of duels, of Robin Hood and the Sheriff of Nottingham flashing blades at light speed as they jump over tables and leap up and down staircases. Minstrels, pretty clothes and great leg-o'beast feasts can be part of the picture, but much of the romance and myth of the Middle Ages comes from the great battles, of the clash of good and evil, of pure knights vanquishing the wicked villains to save the day.

While scores of Society for Creative Anachronism members spend years in the Society without ever taking up arms, combat is a central part of the Current Middle Ages experience. It is how Kings of this world are chosen. One-on-one tournaments form the core of most events, and the great events—the Pennsic War, Gulf Wars, the Estrella War—share a common thread: war. The merchants, the classes, the music, the theater and games all operate under the pretext of being the support community of the war.

"The tournament provides the focus for everything else the SCA does," one of the group's original members, who goes by the name Frederick of Holland, later tells me. The two-time Crown Tournament winner, now a staff scientist at the University of California, has had as much time as anyone to reflect on the phenomenon since he was an awestruck college student at the backyard party that started it all.

"The tournament is filled with high testosterone levels," he said. "It's the perfect opportunity to display all the medieval virtues with bright colors and loud noises, which we know is attractive to the human animal."

Another of the SCA's pioneers and the first promoter of a now-basic fighting blow, Duke Paul of Bellatrix, MKA Paul Porter, 57, of Mill Valley, Calif., calls it "the glue that holds the SCA together."

"Any real successful activity needs some sort of glamour," he said. "You need something exciting. The women that want the romance are as attracted to the fighting as the men are. They fight or they hang around the fighters."

After standing on the sidelines at Pennsic watching two armies charge each other, I realized I could never fully be a part of this group without diving into the fray. The only trouble is, like Brave Sir Robin, when danger has reared its ugly head, I have bravely turned my tail and fled.

I am no athlete and I have seen the war wounds from these battles. Though in nearly 35 years of fighting nobody has ever been truly killed in battle, there are broken bones. One fighter was carted off the field at Pennsic last year on a backboard. I hear of pancake-sized bruises that last weeks. I hear of broken hands, of knees that give out and of guys being picked off their feet by spear blows. When I tell an old-timer I'm thinking about fighting, he warns, "Wait until you get your helmet creased by one of those big guys and see what you think." Having your helm "creased" is holdover slang from the SCA's early days when aluminum freon-can helmets would dent with a good blow. The SCA banned those helmets years ago and big helm dents are rare, but more because the helmets have become harder, not because the blows have grown softer.

Flynn also issues a warning on par with the "See you in court" he tells debtors.

"I'm not going to shit anybody. You're going to bruise. You're going to get some doozy, show-off bruises."

Although the sight of some of the Goliaths on the Pennsic field makes me waver, my own doughy body resembles that of many of the computer programmers out there. This sport also has several levels of seriousness. As Edmund explained, there are fights where "I'm having a good time just playing, then there's sort of competitive fights, then the really competitive ones in tournaments."

I forget those serious fights. I just want to take the field for the charges at the great battles of Pennsic. People are rarely hurt by blows in those battles, though a spear can sometimes jam a facemask into your nose. They're hurt by being trampled, of twisting the wrong way in a pigpile or by having their sword or shield stepped on at an odd angle while their hand and arm are still attached. You have a better chance of getting hurt while lying dead than by being killed.

I have qualms but I think of Jocelyn le Jongleur, a bouncy and energetic young woman I met at Twelfth Night who just beat 13 guys in a tournament. Women make up a minority on the battlefields, but several fight—and fight well. I look at SFU members Mike and Jen Detmar. When Mike is not doing SCA activities as Logan mac Gavin, he's fiddling with his Palm Pilot and CD burner and while Jen can belly dance with coordination and grace, she's no hardbody workout warrior. Jen, who goes by Fionnhuala in the Society, is a schoolteacher for gifted and talented seventh- and eighth-graders. Her students would probably never believe the sight of her beaming through the grille of her helm at Pennsic last year as she marched off to battle. When she came back from battle still smiling, complaining of nothing more than a mild bruise, I realized I could probably hack it. In the deepest, darkest, misogynist recesses of mind I tell myself, "If a girl can do it…"

Sean, Talon, and Hobbs, a goateed bundle of enthusiasm who started fighting just last year, run down the basic rules for me and the confusion I saw on the battlefield at Pennsic starts to make sense.

"I should have taken that…"

Re-creating real medieval fighting with complete accuracy is basically impossible. Dead and dismembered participants would mean literally short-lived participation, so all medieval groups must decide where to make their compromises, where to give up accuracy for safety. They all must decide whether to fight for sport, fight for show or try to somehow walk the fine line between them.

Actors fight for show in movies, where special effects crews provide the wounds, or on stage, where they themselves sell it to the crowd. If you fight for show, you can use real metal blades (if you dull them) because you fake or pull your blows. You can make your armor light, pretty or comfortable without worrying about protection.

Fighting for sport adds some real dangers. The SCA avoids jousting or any combat with horses in the belief that steeds running down foot soldiers on the field would lead to impalings and tramplings. Real weapons—"live steel"—are also out. Nobody wants to take a blow from a real sword with a real blade swung with real intent. Instead of sacrificing competition, the SCA makes its big sacrifice in look and materials by making its weapons from rattan. The resulting patio furniture swords will take out opponents with hits somewhere between a touch and a bludgeon, not with slicing and dicing. Since an SCA sword may break your arm but not hack it off, fighters wear armor to stop a blunt impact, not to prevent a cut.

Combatants don't really die. They don't really lose limbs and they don't lose so much blood they have to yield to their foes. Something less concrete has to decide who wins. Different re-creation groups use different standards, but SCA rules say that any blow to the head or body strong enough to break real chain mail if struck with a real sword counts as a kill. If a blow that solid hits an arm or leg, the limb is "disabled" and its owner cannot use it in the fight anymore. That standard has very real pluses and minuses.

It avoids the complications of a *Dungeons and Dragons* system of hit points and armor class. But while steel plate in real history may have protected better than chain mail, which protected better than leather, none of it offers any competitive advantage in the SCA. If you have to run through the woods in a two-hour battle at Pennsic in August, that plate (don't even think about a +5 suit) may simply be dead weight and a heat stroke machine. It also leaves much open to interpretation. Since almost nobody who fights has ever tried to cut anything remotely close to armored flesh with a sword, fighters have to develop a sense of what counts as "good" by experience. That standard can evolve and varies from place to place.

Most importantly, SCA fighting is an honor sport without referees or judges. Every fighter must decide which blows hit hard enough for him to yield or fall dead. Nobody gets into yelling matches with officials over bad calls and nobody fakes making a good move in the hope a referee will call it for them. Many fighters find this system appealing because it places chivalry and fair play over winning. It allows even the loser to do so with honor. Fighters can take the field to fight for the honor of their lady and fail to win a bout but leave with some pride. They can make an impression about their character if they take all their blows with grace.

But that system can deteriorate into the "I got you first" bickering of cops-and-robbers cap gun fights when fighters do not "take blows." Sometimes the disagreement is honest, a difference in judgment in a subjective matter. Sometimes it's an overdose of adrenaline. Sometimes it's flat-out cheating. "Rhinohiding"—behaving as if your skin was as tough as a rhino's and not taking your blows—is the dirty little secret of this honor sport. Fighters reserve the most venom for those who don't take their blows.

"We're close knit," Omarad, the Midrealm general, had explained at Twelfth Night. "If you get a reputation, it will follow you everywhere you go. Guys will talk. So you're very cognizant of your reputation and that's very medieval too."

Sometimes fighters don't feel a blow as solidly as it looks just because they are pumped up for the fight. "Everyone will joke about getting into the shower after fighter practice, sudsing up and seeing this blue bruise and thinking, 'Hmm. I should have taken that,'" Omarad said. "You wonder what your opponent thought when you didn't take it."

Other times, blows that look bad to outsiders are not so hard after all. At one tournament, Omarad said, he hit an opponent just as his opponent moved away. "It looked brutal. Five different people came up to me that day and said 'You really knocked the shit out of that guy.' But he and I both knew it was nothing."

Then the dispute can come up at the worst possible time, like it did between Edmund and Valharic.

"In 90 percent of our fighting it doesn't matter," said Edmund. "In Crown Tournament, in Crown Tournament finals in particular, you're on the brink of making your lady Princess and then Queen and you get a little more fine-tuned about what is good."

The Squire's Worth

In their jumbled third and deciding clash, each had thrown sword blows as they collided and toppled. Valharic got to his feet believing he had struck Edmund well in the abdomen. Edmund disagreed and thought he had struck Valharic in the back of the neck. But both were falling the same way as the blows that hit them, reducing their impact. With no blood and no real injuries to help sort out the truth, it was one person's word against the other.

"I know what I feel in my heart was the truth," Valharic said. "And it's very difficult when both people feel they know the truth."

"If the two fighters disagree, it can be a real tricky situation," said Edmund. "It's so hard to say. You can't definitely say any blow was good from the outside. It's all up to the guy in the armor and the guy who threw it."

Though there are no referees or judges, a few officials called "marshals" are on hand to sort out and enforce rules and to step in if there is an injury. After a lengthy debate with the Knights serving as marshals for this crucial fight, Edmund and Valharic refought it. Edmund landed a blow and Valharic toppled to the ground a loser. Valharic gave Edmund a congratulatory bear hug after the loss, picking the giant up off his feet, before falling into a condoling embrace from his fiancée.

But even if Valharic voiced no complaints as he left that day, the final had failed a basic test everyone wants important bouts to pass: that they are clean, with no disputes. It also left Valharic feeling cheated. He had felt pressured into backing down from the argument by the marshals. He was just a squire fighting a two-time King. Who were they more likely to believe? Several other issues with his standing in the Kingdom—issues that I did not fully understand yet—put him on even more shaky footing.

Edmund still believes the final bout was handled right. To his credit, Edmund had not been hesitant to accept blows and face defeat that day. As late as the semi-finals he had accepted blows as killing and toppled to the ground dead three times, only to have the fight continue because he had landed almost- simultaneous killing blows on his opponent. "Double-kills" count as draws. But each time, Edmund had to make an instant and irrevocable decision to fall, without knowing what his opponent would do.

Once he fell, if the opponent had shrugged off even one of the return blows, Edmund's day would have ended.

I am beginning to understand that for the elite fighters there are more levels to this honor sport than just what the rules say. When the King had told the crowd to watch Edmund and Valharic to "know their worth" he had not been kidding. For a clueless newcomer like me, though, there are more tangible things to worry about.

I pick up Flynn's sword from the floor. The basket hilt, the weave of metal at the handle that protects the hand from blows, all but encircles my right hand. The blade is light, but solid. Sean has wrapped it in silver duct tape, with two black vertical duct tape stripes added to mark the edges. I touch the blade and press down on the tape, half hoping the layers of tape would provide padding. Nope. Beneath just the slightest cushion I feel the hard, solid wood. The blade is a club, a nightstick with a hilt. In a dark alley, you could beat someone to death with this.

"Getting you armored up is probably going to be the most difficult issue," Sean explains. I put the sword down. "You want to borrow everything and make sure you like this before you shell out $400."

After the helmet, Sean says, we will need a gorget, a combination of collar and neck brace that encircles the neck in metal or leather and protects it from blows. For my sword hand I could buy gauntlets, the full metal jackets, for my hands. Those can either resemble mittens or gloves depending on how many metal joints, called lames, I want to pay for. But the hemisphere of a basket hilt can protect the hand. I can make half-gauntlets for my wrist and the back of my hand from leather. For my shield hand, mostly protected by the shield, I can get by with a hockey glove. Many participants cut corners and use modern items like hockey gloves to save money. Many fighters have leather and metal shoulder armor, but others like Mike/Logan sacrifice looks for safety and cost and wear football shoulder pads under their tunics. If I take those shortcuts, I'd become one of those that authenticity sticklers deride as a "Wal-Mart Warrior" or "Plastic Paladin."

"You can wear plastic," Sean says. "But I don't want to see it on the field. Cover it with a big tunic or a tabard, but don't let it show."

Since elbows must be covered with something hard over a soft padding, I could go either way. I could try skateboarding pads or make some from leather.

"We have a pattern for wax-hardened leather, which is period and really cool," says Hobbs. "I made my whole kit from one hide for $85. When it hardens, it is like wood."

I will also need something to protect my short ribs and kidneys, either a steel plate, armor scales or hard, wide belt.

"We can make him the next member of the Big Belt Club," Hobbs suggests.

Although not fully historically accurate, Hobbs, Flynn and Talon all wear belts with giant, wax-hardened panels over the gut and small of the back, with smaller ones covering the love handles. Cinched together with leather straps and buckles, they protect all the vitals—save one.

"You're going to need a cup," Flynn says. Clearly, this is a purchase, not a borrow, item. "My cup is the least comfortable part of my armor. Get one that feels right if you have to buy four to do it."

Cat cackles as we debate the merits of wearing the cup over or under underwear or bicycle shorts. But she is not exempt. She'll have to hunt down the more elusive female cup and a chest protector, probably one designed for female fencers.

Rock 'Em, Sock 'Em Robots

A week later I pull into the parking lot of the Shore Cultural Center, a former school in the Cleveland suburb of Euclid only a good bowshot from Lake Erie. As I troop through the hallways, my boots clacking on the tile floors, I hear the cracks and thumps of sword on shield in a room at the end of the passageway.

About 30 fighters practice in a former classroom turned into a miniature gym at this weekly meeting of the Barony of the Cleftlands, the official SCA chapter for the Cleveland area. They practice inside all winter to avoid snowdrifts but, come spring, they will take their swords and spears outside. More than a dozen squat or stand in half of the former classroom, strapping on leg guards and wiping sweaty brows after a bout. The other half of the room is divided into two fighting rings by a rope sagging between flimsy and tottering stands.

Two fighters, buried behind armor and shields, lunge into each other like two grappling crabs. Sword fights in the movies are a flurry of clangs and chings as swords bash into shields and armor. Here, with wooden swords and shields, the dominant sound is "Whump!" I watch one of the fighters take a blow to his side and retreat, defeated, after just a 20-second flurry, not a ten-minute movie duel. Few fights last beyond a sequence of quick and sharp sword strokes akin to boxing combination punches. The long, arcing strokes of movie fighters stray far from historical and SCA reality. They may look showy and impressive, but such telegraphed blows rarely land. Stage combat comes about as close to competitive fighting as ice dancing is to hockey. Being able to skate or handle a sword helps, but the moves do not translate well.

The winner remains and a tall, slightly gawky opponent steps in. I take stock of the armor. The fighters here protect themselves much better than what Sean suggested. Armor practices vary all over. Some groups, like Darkyard, wear very little. Others, like Cleftlands, hit harder and wear more. The longtime baron of Cleftlands sets the armor tone for this group as close to the 14th century style of knights and fighters—the "Knights in shining armor" most people think of—as possible. I see scalloped layers of leather or metal over shoulders. I see full metal breastplates. I see several chain mail hoods, called coifs. I see arms and legs fully encased in metal, with separate pieces called copps at the joints. Everyone's shins and thighs are covered with leather at a minimum. Back at SFU, Sean teases Mike about the amount of armor he wears and how bulky he looks. After seeing this group, perhaps Mike and Jen are more normal than cautious.

The gawky fighter wades toward his opponent and swings. He has full metal shin and thigh guards with metal kneecaps and metal elbow pads. His chest is covered with a heavy leather vest with metal rings sewn to the outside. His swing is a little awkward, more telegraphed and deliberate than the others, a bit of a lunge. His feet do not move fast enough to keep up with his long limbs. He looks confident but a little off. He blocks several shots before he catches a blow to the ribs.

His opponent is Valharic. Perhaps only the superior competition makes the other guy look a bit slow. But he thanks Valharic for the fight and says he has not yet "authorized"—passed the test of safety, rules and basic form the Society requires of all new fighters. He is still a beginner.

Behind me, one man straps another into armor. The older one, thin with a brownish red beard, has a bib of sweat darkening his pale green linen shirt. Calum MacDhaibhidh, a veteran fighter and marshal, has received awards for his work in the SCA and tonight he is acting as a teacher for a brand new fighter. His pupil, Craig Tome of North Ridgville, Ohio, is known as Bastian Eychener in this setting. A week ago, Bastian had a basic lesson in holding and positioning a shield. Tonight he gets to put on armor, starting with Calum's sweaty gambeson. Stained by dirt and sweat, the quilted and padded overshirt has seen better days. But tied across Bastian's chest, it is welcome protection. Onto his legs, Calum straps two metal shin, knee and thigh guards, like metal catcher's equipment with thigh pads attached. Calum made them himself in the eighth grade from a pattern a local armorer lent him.

Bastian then pulls on a coat of plates, often called a brigandine. It is a common SCA piece of armor to protect the body. Metal plates the size and shape of cigarette packs are riveted to the inside of a sleeveless leather vest to create a scaly lining up the chest, along the ribs and on the lower back. Bastian grunts.

"I'm not used to carrying this much extra weight around."

The sleeves of the gambeson hang down well past Bastian's wrist. He is shorter than Calum. So Calum grabs a leather bracer—a laced leather wristband—and lashes it to Bastian's forearm, pinning the cuff of the gambeson in place.

"Wow," Bastian says.

"Feel like a real fighter?" Calum shoots back. "Now you've got to lose the glasses."

Bastian pulls a black stocking cap on his head and Calum eases the helmet on. It is very closed, a tin can with small vertical air slits. There are several big dents in the crown. Somebody—probably several people—has been hit hard in that helmet.

"Oh boy."

Bastian puts a leather guard on his sword hand and a metal gauntlet on his shield hand. Calum leads him out to a roped-off area. Calum is not armored but carries a sword. This is just a drill.

"On guard," he commands. Bastian wobbles under the weight to spread his legs and turn his feet. Calum spreads Bastian's feet to about shoulder width and Bastian hoists his shield in front of his front shoulder.

"Do not swing," Calum orders as he swings his own sword at quarter speed at Bastian's head. Bastian lifts his shield to block it. Calum swings and swings, forcing

Bastian to raise and drop the shield to block the long, arcing swipes. Even at that speed, the concept is overwhelming. Blows find their way through and glance off the top of Bastian's helmet. It is normal, I see, for newbies to struggle, to be confused about when and how to react—to simply not react even as a blow meanders straight toward his head. Another swipe clips the top of Bastian's head. He did not watch the blow closely.

"You just kind of lifted the shield up and hoped," Calum tells him. In about five minutes, the lesson is over. Bastian is exhausted, his shield arm throbbing from holding the giant sheet of wood at his shoulder.

"I got to the point where I'm trying to lift this shield and I'm going, 'Oooh, ooh' and I just can't get the shield up," he says.

"Nothing works the muscles you use for the shield like using a shield," Calum counsels. He advises Bastian to learn the stances and moves, then visualize them between practices. "Even if it's in the middle of the shower and you're lathering your hair, think, 'This foot goes here, that foot goes there.' Even that little bit will make a world of difference."

The group breaks for a business meeting and to prepare for an event the Barony is hosting that weekend. When they return, the crowd has thinned and the gawky fighter is back, still not fluid but holding his own with others and landing a few blows. He rotates in and out of the line for another hour before I can pull him aside. Bernard Ruple, 33, a divorced father of two young children, is a new addict to fighting. In August, while working as an engineer at a local rubber company he overheard co-worker Ted Bouck talking about his trip to Pennsic. Ruple bombarded him with questions.

"When I was a little boy I used to play swords and battles," he said, unbuttoning the scale-mail vest. "I was amazed there was anything like this, that you can actually do this."

Ted turned out to be Sir Theodric Von Rostock, one of the Middle Kingdom's Knights, and the head of a fighting household. Sir Theo brought in pictures from War, then loaned Bernard a tunic, belt and boots for a feast in the fall. Bernard then started coming to fight practice and strapped on armor.

"They showed me what it was like to get hit and let me hit them," he gushes. "I was like, 'Wow, do it again.' It really gets your adrenaline going."

Four months later, he has not missed a weekly practice. He fights with loaned armor while he makes his own using tools he and Theo made by hand. He just bought a workbench, drill press and bench for $500.

"My sister said, 'You probably could have bought the armor for that,' but I'm having so much fun making it," he said. "My children love it. I have two—12 and 8. They get really excited when I start talking about it. I'm going to bring them to an event when it matches up with a weekend I have them."

He has had a few struggles. He needs a forearm protector after being clubbed there a few times. He has received one bad rib bruise and he was once hit hard in the head with a pole axe.

"I got hit so hard I was going to go down on my knees. I was like, 'Whoa!' But to be able to go somewhere and play Rock 'Em Sock 'Em Robots is really neat. I love it. It's the most exciting thing I've ever done."

His gear is packed up and the hall is about ready to close. Bastian hangs around by the door, leaning on his sword and smiling despite his struggles, bantering with other fighters. He is about to join them at a local bar, already part of the group.

"I can't wait to come back next week and get into armor again," he says, as the lights are turned out.

Act I, scene 3
The Tailors' Tales: It Just Fits Medieval

Helen Shaffer's house is filled with fabric. So is her attic. So is a friend's garage. Six sewing machines cover tables. All to feed her medieval clothes habit.

"Our dining room is now my sewing room," she says.

Shaffer, 33, of Pittsburgh, uses Lean O'Connor as her medieval name but is much better known by the name of her business: The Bored Housewife. She is a medieval clotheshorse and part of the growing crowd of medievalists who churn out set after set of yesteryear's fashions to sell from period-style tents at events. Medieval-style clothiers also sell their handiwork using the latest blend of modern and medieval: hundreds of web sites and catalogs—each welcoming Master Card and Lady Visa—peddle Middle Ages fashions at all levels of prices, quality and authenticity.

Shaffer, who was hooked into making—and wearing—medieval garb right from her first SCA event nine years ago, spends about 35 hours a week cranking out sturdy and functional, but not often fancy, clothing for SCA members and renaissance fairs. She started her business to raise the cash to feed her own garb habit. As it grew, she began sewing costumes for medieval weddings for mundanes. The business is now big enough that she says she could support herself on it if she needed to.

From April to October, she packs her van to sell her clothes at events and fairs most weekends. Her biggest sellers are heavy cloaks that go for about $100 each, then washable cotton dresses at $35 each which she calls "my Wal-Mart line of renaissance dresses."

I will not meet "The Bored Housewife" for another few months in my journey across the Current Middle Ages, but the issue she solves with her "Wal-Mart" dresses is already weighing on me. How "medieval" do I really want to be?

Clothing is the first thing—and the most immediately visible thing—anyone has to sort out as they join this culture. The medieval garb that O'Connor latched onto at her first event stands for much more than the "pretty clothes" she saw them as. Garb is the primary battleground between modern ideas and true medieval authenticity. It is where most have to make their first choice between comfort and authenticity, between accuracy and cost, between simplicity and real effort. And it is the first place where people must decide exactly where and when they are trying to re-create.

For her off-the rack Wal-Mart dresses, the Bored Housewife makes small compromises to save time and make fittings easier. She admits her changes give the dresses a more mundane look to avoid clashing with modern preconceptions. She will not use modern fabrics like rayon or polyester and her color schemes are accurate, but her off-the-rack clothes, she said, sell much better with a few mundane concessions than if she were a stickler. When she tries to be accurate, she runs into resistance.

"I've been doing this a long time and I know what things should look like. People say, 'This fits funny,'" she said. Her usual response to those customers zeroes right in on their confused desires.

"No it doesn't," she'll say. "It just fits medieval."

The Traveler's Dilemma

I rummage through my closet with no success and sigh.

I have nothing to wear.

After the armoring session at Flynn's, I search my old sporting goods for items I can cannibalize to put me on the practice field. As I dig through gear buried in the back of my closet, I grimace when my gaze shifts to the clothing rack. Compared to the standards of Twelfth Night, the few pieces of "garb" that I have assembled look a bit inferior.

I really have nothing good to wear, not out on a Saturday.

I catch myself mid-thought. Guys aren't supposed to worry about clothes, especially not costumes like this. My foray into the Current Middle Ages is threatening to drag me into women's territory. Next thing I know I'll probably start sewing and wearing dresses and jewelry.

Shudder.

Some people latch onto the SCA and renaissance fairs for the clothes, for the chance to parade around in costumes even when Halloween is months away. But I do not have that drive. I have to make the adjustment from Mundania and I'm not doing well. It just *doesn't* feel right.

I draw upon my travels to other countries for reassurance. Clothing and styles have no objective standard, I remind myself. Your time, place and culture determine clothing styles and what gender roles clothing plays. Men in Marrakesh wear hooded and ankle-length djellabas, stores in Scotland rent out kilts like tuxedos and men on Bali wrap sarongs around their waists like skirts to go to temple. It all depends on the norms of where and when you are. If a Middle Age fashion sense or dress code steers me toward wearing a virtual dress, I decide, so be it. If Omarad, a general, can handle a lace-making class because a real man does whatever he wants, I'll take the same stance. I just draw the line at makeup.

Well…unless it's woad.

I catch myself again, but this time for real historical reasons, not because my mundane sensibilities are threatened. The blue body paint that put warriors on a high for battle would be inaccurate unless I want to be a crazed Celt from a particular time. I am quickly realizing this garb thing is hard to do right.

Though it is simple to put together a medieval-ish outfit, it takes serious effort to make a perfect one. Clothing shares a few problems with almost every aspect of re-creating this era: The time period is incredibly broad and the surviving examples are limited. For starters, the Middle Ages spanned several hundred years and many cultures.

What might be right for people living in (what is now) England in the 5th century differs dramatically from what 14th century Italians wore. The Society for Creative Anachronism's period ends 400 years ago in 1600 but it stretches back more than 1,000 years before that. Far less time has elapsed since the SCA era ended than is included in it. The difference between the 9th century and the 11th century may seem insignificant, but those 200 years equal the time between the American Revolution and today. Imagine going to work in knickers and a tri-cornered hat along with your shirt and tie today. Mixing garb from even long-past centuries can be just as jarring.

Other re-enactors have more artifacts to help push their authenticity standards a few notches higher. Civil War enthusiasts have photographs, family heirlooms and museums that let them try to match their uniforms to the very unit they re-create, right down to the exact styles and colors of the buttons. But medievalists fight about whether buttons even existed at a given time and place. Some World War II enthusiasts, like the curators of the U.S.S. Cod here in Cleveland, want to do more than re-create bedsheets for their WWII submarine. Their ultimate find would be an actual pillow from that very submarine that they can study before returning it to the very same bunk it came from. Middle Ages re-enactors have to extrapolate from surviving scraps and fragments, from statues, from carvings in ancient churches and graveyards and from illuminations in books.

For casual participants, clothing that evokes impressions of the Middle Ages is good enough. Anyone who challenges their clothes and bothers their "Dream" is an "authenticity Nazi" on par with the teacher's pet who ratted out classmates in first grade. The distance between fantasy garb and museum-quality clothing is vast and each step along the path toward authenticity requires a little more effort than the one before it. Most people, like me, need to start with the very basics: a simple tunic with a belt over it. The equivalent of a T-Shirt is the T-Tunic, a garment that takes only moments to sew using any of the dozens of simple patterns that circulate in the group. The rough equivalent of a long-sleeved T-shirt, just a little bigger and made of different cloth, the T-Tunic matches lower-class clothing for most eras closely enough to get beginners by.

Most of those who meet in Flynn's basement in the Something For Us group muddled their way through first garb attempts in the more forgiving culture of Dagorhir. Some people converted their fathers' old shirts and just cinched a belt over the top. Years before Flynn learned to be a Roman and he married Erin, who now makes stellar items for him, even the Dagorhir crowd sang songs about being blinded by his neon green polyester cloak. Talon for years relied on converted karate uniforms and Hobbs admits he made his first garb for a Dagorhir campout by buying nine yards of "crappy green wool—not even plaid" that he tried to pleat into a kilt. It wasn't just the cloth he picked that was in error. Kilts fall out of the SCA period, according to many historical accounts. People wear them anyway.

Flynn's approach changed 14 years ago at Pennsic. He spent a day wearing Native American moccasins, a satin bathrobe-style shirt and a hat with a feather. He topped it all off with rose-tinted red-rimmed sunglasses. Elton John would have been proud. Some SCA members were not.

One of the Knights at War confronted him. Flynn's get-up needed help. He had made a common mistake for newcomers. He had tossed aside modern conventions without really shifting to medieval ones. The SCA is about the Middle Ages, not any culture and style that differs from the establishment. Events are not just for wearing funny clothes, Flynn was told. Just because clothes are peculiar or out of style doesn't mean they are medieval.

Flynn snickered, shrugged it off and went about his teenage business. But it gnawed at him over the next few days and his attitude about his costume changed.

"There wasn't one thing medieval in any of it," he eventually realized. "It was the same garb I now look at and think, 'These people should be removed.' We often hate what we once were."

Almost everyone in the SCA can tell a funny story about their first garb attempt. Ask even a Knight or another "Peer"—someone who has earned this Society's highest rank for artistic work or study (Laurel) or service (Pelican)—to wear their first garb to the next event. They won't. They'll give a stream of stammered excuses to avoid the humiliating truth. Unless they admit their first garb was embarrassingly bad or that they put on too many pounds to fit into it anymore, they're probably lying to save their reputation.

Today, there are ways for even struggling college students and those unsure they want to sink lots of money into this hobby to do better than Flynn's early abominations. Lady Aurora deVie, MKA Catrina Kolesar, has spent years sorting out quick and easy ways to get by without any neon green polyester disasters. She has carved herself a niche within her Cleftlands home by teaching how to be a "Thrifty Anachronist" by mining thrift stores for treasures.

Aurora has harvested almost every piece of her SCA wardrobe from thrift stores and yard sales. She has converted second-hand mundane items into Tudor and Elizabethan outfits for a fraction of the cost and effort of buying fabric and patterns and starting from scratch.

"Nothing that I show you here was over $10," she tells her classes as she sets out laundry baskets packed with examples. "Some of it was under $1."

The Thrifty Anachronist

"What section are we going to go to at the library?" Aurora asks the students sitting in a semicircle in front of her.

"The 390s," the class calls back.

"Right!" She has asked three times in the last 20 minutes just to reinforce the point. If the students take advantage of the Dewey Decimal System and how it collects books of the same topic together, they can find guides to medieval clothing just by skimming that section. She passes out pages photocopied from two books plucked from the 390s with drawings of clothing samples from multiple eras. The simple line drawings give the minimum information that people need before they hit the thrift stores.

"Pick your time and area. And decide what level your social climbing has taken you. Then, memorize the silhouettes," she tells the class. Worrying about details and color is far less important at this stage than understanding the basic style and cut of the clothes.

"It takes a discerning eye. If you can visualize the concept, then sew a seam or two, you too can look just like in the books. We're not shooting for perfection here. We're just getting over the hump of 'I can't do anything.'"

I have already taken the next major plunge for men under her method: shopping in thrift stores. Taking Cat with me for cover, I have gone even further down the Thrifty Anachronist's path and shopped in the women's department. That section of a thrift store often has tights or drawstring pants that can pass as medieval trousers far better than anything in the men's department. Blouses and dresses often can be turned into tunics. Aurora holds up a very basic brown dress with no frills. It amounts to a very long T-shirt clone, but of better fabric.

"I got this in the Ladies Department, but I would pop my son into it in a New York minute."

The next stop is the housewares or bedding section, which often has decent cloth for far less than at a fabric store. Although cotton was hardly common through much of the Society for Creative Anachronism's period, sheets can be sewn into comfortable undertunics or passable beginner garb. Aurora has made several items from table-cloths. Back in the women's section, you can often find shoes that can pass as medieval and long skirts that with a little seam ripping can fill in as a cloak. Plain pocketbooks can be converted into pouches and many belts have buckles with enough personality that they can be cut off and used as clasps to close a cloak at the neck.

Aurora launches into her area of greatest expertise: women's clothing. She will rip legs off thrift store pants to use as sleeves, to turn into pouches or to use as headbands. She also fashions decorative sleeves from panels of skirts or vests by seam-ripping them apart. She adds them to previously sleeveless dresses by pinning one end of the just-detached panel to the dress' shoulder. By adding a few laces she can tie the new decorative sleeve together over her blouse at the wrists and forearms. When she needs shoulders to have a bit of a puff to them, she uses covers for sofa arms. Hair "scrunchies" become garters for both the legs and arms. And large doilies and table skirts can easily become the oversized collars used in some periods.

Whole dresses or blouses can also be transformed, she tells the class, with a few alterations like camouflaging distracting seams with trim, pulling off sleeves or ruffles or ripping out any zippers in the back then sewing the back closed and adding a notch in front to fit your head through. Or, Aurora suggests, simply remove the zipper, punch holes and lace the back up. If a blouse is correct in part, but wrong in other parts, wear it so only the good part shows. Learn the types of lace that were common in your period so you can identify blouses that can work.

"Sometimes the trim costs me more than the whole ensemble does," she says. So she raids January clearance sales for Christmas ribbon. Sometimes the ribbon can survive a washing, but she does not count on it lasting and will use it only for temporary stylings.

Aurora also re-works hats, which many eras almost require. One outfit she worked on needed a hat with a crest across the top of the head, much like a crescent moon toppled on its side. For 50 cents, Aurora bought a plastic tennis visor, covered it with cloth and ran ornamentation around the edges. She shows the class the visor. Instead of wearing it over her forehead she flips it upright and sets it atop her head.

"Underneath here," she tells her class with a grin, "it says Ford."

For an outfit in the style of the Burgundy section of France, she converted a thrift store dress. For the cylindrical hat that she needed to complete the outfit, she took a butter tub and covered it with press-on velvet from a craft store.

"I'm walking out in this configuration and a gal came up to me and said, 'I know exactly the reference number of the dress you took that from,'" Aurora recounts. The woman had worked at a museum and the dress matched one she had catalogued. "Part of me is glowing and thinking that this is really cool, but inside I'm saying, 'I faked it! I faked it!' If she only knew I had a butter tub on my head…"

Sometimes, though, she misses the mark. She will have friends inspect her before events to see if they can recognize the items she converted. If they do, she goes back to work or tosses it into the trash. If not, she has a victory.

"So, what section are we going to look at in the library?" she asks yet again.

"The 390s."

"Good!"

Time Traveling Though T-Tunics

Alina Meraud Bryte, MKA Patricia Hoge of Cedar Rapids, Iowa, used to have a problem.

She knew the appropriate garb for the time and place of her persona, but sometimes she wanted to be somebody else. Somebody else, that is, apart from the somebody else she already plays in this world. Sometimes events might have a theme from the Viking or Byzantine era, or an incoming King would plan his coronation to match his own period's style. What can a loyal subject do but try to fit in?

Changing to a different era within the Middle Ages usually forced Alina to make a new outfit, but the costs in time and money grew too large. So she learned to get by and cut a few corners, just in a different method from the Thrifty Anachronist. Now a Laurel from the Kingdom of Calontir, which covers Kansas, Missouri, Nebraska, most of Iowa and parts of Arkansas, she teaches students at events across her kingdom her method of "Time Traveling Through T-Tunics."

"I try to achieve the look for the least amount of fabric and time," she says, conceding that she does not teach authentic construction of the garments. Her class gets you close to authentic, she says, but more research is needed to do it really right.

Her class has more costume changes than most plays, all done right in front of her students. She keeps it from becoming a strip show with the key to her entire method: the basic T-Tunic.

Start with a T-tunic that drops to mid-thigh if you are man, Alina tells her class. Women should start with one that drops to dress length. Make it long-sleeved, strong, sturdy and comfortable, but not too baggy because everything else goes over it. It should also be of a neutral color and have no trim so that it can match many different pieces and times. That start can give you an undergarment—an undertunic or underdress—that is key to time traveling. The undertunic fits history because Middle Ages outfits usually had several layers of clothes. In the SCA context, a good under-layer makes your life easier. A good, comfortable undertunic will keep your sweat and body odor away from your decorated and showpiece overtunic. The basic undertunic can take all the washings and you can save your overtunic the wear and tear. You also avoid the scratchiness of the most-period fabric, wool, against your skin.

From that start, Alina whips through several costume changes right in front of her class by changing her outer layer over and over while sticking with the same undertunic. The lesson that follows is heavy on details. It makes a good overview of the evolution of major styles and reinforces the idea that the Middle Ages were not one monolithic and homogenous period. But Alina breaks the class into sections, so students seeking details about one era only have to pay close attention to that one.

Alina begins with 5th century Britain, starting right after the Roman occupation of the island ended. That immediately catches my attention. Darkyard borrows from both the Romans and the post-Roman British Isles. Though the enemy Romans had left, clothes still retained a Roman influence and many outfits resembled a Roman garment called a peplos. The peplos and its kin had two large rectangles of cloth as their main body pieces—front and back—fastened together in a single point on each shoulder. Alina takes two pieces of plaid cloth, each a little wider than her body and about her body length, and pins them together at each shoulder with brooches. Without brooches, they can be sewn in a spot on each shoulder to replace the pins. The fabric then dangles as an overgarment below her knees like a shirt with no sleeves or seams, held together only by the brooches at the shoulders. To add a little style, fold each of the rectangles over about a foot from the top before pinning them at the shoulders. That lets the foot-long swath dangle as an extra layer at your front and back.

Wool or linen are good fabrics to use and work best in natural colors. Plaid can also work if you are careful. Plaid is a major historical sticking point. Hobbs' story of making a kilt of "not even plaid" wool may contain yet another error. Preconceptions (and *Braveheart*) notwithstanding, the tartan patterns assumed by many to date back into Scotland's ancient history were not common until the 1700s. While a tartan can get you by, it might be completely inaccurate. And when choosing a plaid, Alina tells the class, know that many kingdoms had so-called "sumptuary laws" that reserved the finest clothing for royals. The kingdoms in early Ireland and Wales had limits on the number of colors someone could use, depending on their status. Kings and chieftains could wear many colors at once, lesser nobles could wear fewer and wealthy land-own-ers even fewer still. The lower classes needed to keep their clothes plain and simple.

Alina then shifts to the clothing of Byzantium, the eastern half of the Roman Empire. Byzantine garb shared several Roman influences, but had a richness and sumptuousness unsurpassed by many cultures. For women, the key accessory to wear over a dress is the oversized and jeweled collar called the super-humeral. Bordering on being a mantle, the flat doughnut of cloth goes from the neck to the shoulder points on each side and drops down the chest below the shoulder blades. Alina advises using good, not rough, cloth and not cutting and sewing it as a full circle. Leave a gap in the back or it will ride up on the shoulders.

"You'll look like a Klingon," she warns.

The super-humeral goes over a "supertunic," an overtunic made from more sump-tuous fabric than the undertunic. This very loose tunic with squared shoulders can be made from a brocade. Alina's example is made from black fabric with a gold paisley pattern. While many Byzantine outfits created in the SCA's Known World have a wide vertical stripe down the front of the dress from collar to hem, she advises not to use one. Those were only for the empress, she says, though members of her court some-times had it.

Men's Byzantine clothing is similar to clothes from the later years of the Roman Empire with decorations called clavi—vertical bands—running down the body from over each shoulder. This style matches exactly what the Darkyard army wears for both court and the battlefield, so I listen closely. The meaning and styles of clavi evolved over time. At first, they were signs of rank or status. Later they became simply a fashion choice, but some historians consider them and the circles—roundels—that appeared beneath them or on shoulders the predecessors of today's military epaulets.

Known as Coptic tunics since they were popular among a sect of early Christians known as Copts, Darkyard and other Roman-styled SCA units use them as their basic dress. Though the clavi and roundels were usually woven right into the tunic's fabric in period, modern warriors satin stitch the clavi and roundels onto basic tunics with a sewing machine so they do not fray.

For Viking clothing, do not even think about the horned helmet. That was made up years later. Though Norse clothing has a basic style, it could have several different influences since the trader and raider culture mixed with early Russian settlements and even Byzantium. From 750 to 1000 the clothes borrowed distinct features from other styles of the time. Women mostly wore "tube dresses," which as the name implies were little more than cloth tubes with a hole for the legs at one end and a hole for the head at the other. These would have plain straps running over each shoulder from back to front, where they were usually pinned with brooches. But it is unclear, Alina says, whether two pieces of cloth were sewn together to make the body or whether one larger piece was simply wrapped around the body before fastening with the brooches. She says there is no evidence of Norse women wearing belts so just let the dress hang.

Jewelry—amber and bead necklaces—helps complete the look along with bracelets of gold and silver, which served almost as money. Women wore them to carry wealth around for shopping.

Men often had sleeveless tunics—alone, or as overtunics. And they had a rectangular cloak clasped at one shoulder—normally their sword arm shoulder so the cloth would dangle on the other side and out of the way of the weapon-wielding arm.

Anglo-Saxon women had dresses with bell-shaped sleeves. And both men and women embroidered and decorated their clothing at necklines, at cuffs and at the hems at the bottom of tunics and dresses. Although embroidery was very valuable in period, she skips embroidery for this class. At major events, needleworkers teach whole series of courses of medieval embroidery. Proper Saxon women should have their hair covered and men often wore leggings—strips of cloth wound around the shins—below long tunics that often had a slit up the front to near the crotch.

The Normans, who beat the Anglo-Saxons at war in 1066, became a major power with that victory. As Alina puts it, "Costuming does not follow the fallen. It follows the victors." The clothing of England changed. Men saw only minor changes in their typical knee length overtunics. But women's clothing changed dramatically. Women start showing their hair, often in bunches of braids, and started wearing veils held around the top of the head with circlets. Sleeves shifted from form-fitting to oversized in a shift from function to fashion. The cuffs of an underdress did not peek out from under the overtunic any more and the height of style, "angel sleeves" like wings, could extend so much at cuffs that ostentatious royals could tie the sleeves into several knots or into one behind the back to keep them from dragging on the floor.

"This was their idea of conspicuous consumption," she said. All that extra and costly fabric was the Norman's idea of bling-bling.

From here on, fashion mostly changes over time more than it does by place. With improved communication, styles travel from region to region.

"We have gotten beyond a distinctive cultural look," she said.

Around 1250, a form of the old Greek cyclas returns, but as an overgarment, not as the only clothes people wore as they did centuries earlier. For women, the dress-length garment hangs on the shoulders, but has no sides or sleeves. The underdress clearly shows through a wide opening from the shoulders to the waist. Men wore wear similar items, but their cyclas stops shorter at the knees so leggings are visible.

Alina cuts her class off here because fashions after that do not fit her T-tunic method. As time went on, clothing in general became more form-fitting. Men's tunics and vests became very short and tight. Women's underdresses grew tighter. And the sideless surcoat, a cousin of the cyclas, grew popular. The arm holes curved far further into the body than the cyclas and the holes dropped a little below the waist but still above the hips. From there, clothing became more and more complicated. Tudor and Elizabethan clothing, though it can fit many people's image of the Middle Ages, is not simple enough for Time Traveling.

Alina has one other piece of advice for students struggling to make sense of all the styles on parade in the all-inclusive culture of the SCA. Copy what you like. Steal ideas from people you see. Even if the result is not exactly accurate, the process is in keeping with a true medieval practice. Throughout the Middle Ages, she says, cultures would co-opt pieces and styles from other cultures if they intermingled, even if they did not know what the decorations or styles represented. For years, many Normans decorated their tunics with bright cloth bands sewn onto the upper arm sections of their sleeves. It looked good to them. But the bands were copied from their foes from the Crusades. The crusaders never realized—or cared—that each band—called a tiraz—had blessings from the Koran written on it. All they knew was that it looked good, not that it carried the very message they were fighting.

"It's a very period concept," Alina explains. "'That looks neat. I want to wear that.' They didn't research. They just wore it."

The Contessa's Tale

Tonessa West Crowe snapped at the friend who had the audacity to ask her to a renaissance fair years ago.

The renaissance had always had a place in Crowe's life. Crowe's mother had taught her about the masters of renaissance painting she loved so much, inspiring the daughter to study art at the Massachusetts College of Art and at the Tufts University Museum Fine Arts School. This era was far too important to trifle with.

"I've always loved the renaissance," she hissed at her friend. "I'm not going to see you bastardize it."

But Crowe somehow relented. The experience changed her life.

"The moment my foot set down I felt like I was transported back in time," she remembers. "I was blown away by the magic of it."

So she set out on a mission to not only join the world where the people on the street could look like Shakespeare or Queen Elizabeth, but to lead it. Rather than dismiss the atmosphere and costumes, she set out to surpass them. Today, after becoming a well-known figure in fair circles, she is a star in the Society for Creative Anachronism as well. Not just because her adopted persona of Isabella, Contessa of York, sits as Queen of the SCA's East Kingdom. Not because a black woman with an Elizabethan persona stands out in this mostly-white Society. But because she is one of the finest costumers in the Known World.

Beyond earning her Laurel for costuming in the SCA and founding The Gilded Pearl, a group that shares research on the renaissance, she designs and makes clothes semi-professionally. She has made costumes for the major figures in the New York Renaissance Fair and has had items showcased in the window of Greenburg and Hammer, the oldest theater and sewing shop in New York City. Her creations, she said, cost $3,500 at the low end and can reach the $9,000 to $10,000 range. Combining some previous acting income with her pay as a legal assistant and her costuming income, she now buys yard after yard of fabric easily costing $160 a yard. She spent $4,000 just on her jeweled Elizabethan dress for her Coronation as Queen of the East Kingdom, most of it on 16 yards of silk chiffon.

As much as she loves the Elizabethan era, she refuses to cut corners and warns anyone who wants to try that time to make sure they can afford it. Just like in 16th century England, your finances determine your fashion.

"It's expensive to create," she said. "They wore their wealth on their sleeve. Take a look at your pocketbook and decide what you can afford."

For someone that loves the period but does not quite have the money, skip portraying royalty and go for a simple and modest costume fitting a townsperson or merchant.

"Select something that's not so high."

Or so heavy.

Her coronation robe, she said, weighed 87 pounds.

She started with a corset she made using a design by clothing researcher Janet Arnold, who she considers "the mother of all late period costume junkies." She used two fabrics, costing $28 and $38 a yard. She made a bum roll herself, then lined the gown with a canvas interfacing. She imported trim from Switzerland to complete the three-month process.

Her main concession was sewing in stays to replace the bones or reeds that would have been used to hold its shape in period. The only other shortcut, one only the most serious authenticity junkies would care about, was avoiding natural dye for the fabric because it can run and fade in weather extremes. That's one shortcut she always takes.

"I don't spend that kind of money to watch that happen just because it makes me feel more period," she said. "I think that's kind of dumb."

The dress, though, takes her an hour and a half to change into or out of—with help.

"I can't get out of it. It's impossible to get out of that dress alone."

When Isabella started trying to make dresses worthy of this period, she knew how to sew and she already knew a great deal about the Renaissance. But she did not know the details or the exact pieces and parts of Elizabethan clothing. She spent a month holed up in the Fashion Institute of Technology library in New York City researching Elizabethan and Renaissance garments. She learned that elite women of that era wore hoop skirts. She learned the style of the corsets of the time. And she learned that a farthingale was a support for the giant cone of the skirt.

The research took time and care, but that challenge helped drive her. Some people describe the different approaches to the Current Middle Ages as a constant balance between "fun" and "authenticity," as if the pursuit of authenticity is a hardship incompatible with fun. Isabella rejects that concept and considers those two supposed polar opposites to be the same thing, not opposites at all. She immerses herself in projects to satisfy her "basic need" to learn new skills and create things. She thrives on going the extra step to do things right when crafting dresses or brewing her many varieties of mead, a medieval honey-based drink.

While some can dismiss the SCA and other Middle Ages groups as pure escapism, the setting encourages Isabella to learn new skills then put them to practical use. She contrasts it with reading novels, a favorite pastime of her husband, an English teacher in Suffolk County, New York. Just reading, she says, only offers a vicarious experience and is far more escapist than doing things yourself.

"He loves books to zone out and take himself away," she says. "I zone out through books that tell me what I can do."

After all her research, her first costuming effort won first prize at the New York Renaissance Festival. She moved on to the SCA and attracted attention at her first event as a newbie. She goofed and used her renaissance faire name "Contessa Isabella of York," the same mistake the Empress and the Ogar made in assuming titles. A Contessa in the SCA would not only have a Spanish persona. She would have served once as Queen.

But her costume was impressive enough that she won an award that night.

Of course, just traveling to the meeting had given her one of those jarring moments of mixing time periods. Not wanting to show up in modern clothes, she changed on the bus on the way there.

"If you've ever tried to put on a farthingale, a hoop skirt and a corset in a little Greyhound rest room, you'll know how tough it was."

Act I, scene 4
Forged in Forgan's Fire

We went to find a Noble Chief
to lead us into battle
To teach us, train us, lead us on,
and slay the foe like cattle.

(Chorus:)
We'll go, we'll go and meet the foe
And swing the blade and swing the glaive
Hew and slash and hack and smash
And slay the Eastern Army.
So up and join our Noble Chief
Our banner's brought us so far,
And come what may we'll win the day
For Forgan and for Darkyard

We march across the battlefield,
Like a sable forest.
Our foemans' hearts are filled with fear,
They scatter all before us.
(Chorus)

We're off to join our Noble Chief,
We love the man so dearly.
When Forgan's back is tae the wall,
We see our duty clearly.
(Chorus)

And when the battle is o're and done,
And all the household kills are counted,
More Eastern dead have left the field
Than ever walked upon it.

(Chrous—slowly on second half)
And come what may…
We'll win the day…
For Forgan!
And for…DARKYARD!!!

Flynn and Valharic stand in front of the television in Sean/Flynn's living room, with Urien, the menu planner of the Twelfth Night feast at their side. They would be blocking the screen if the television were on. But the more than 30 Darkyard members jamming Flynn's house do not need to live through pre-packaged dramas and comedies tonight.

Flynn, Valharic and Urien command the living room stage on this January evening in the black and white Coptic tunics that stand as the Darkyard uniform. The other Darkyard members fill the couches and chairs while others kneel or stand behind, also in garb. A wooden carving of the household arms, with different-hued segments of wood forming the tree with the moon behind, hangs on the wall behind them. It hangs there always, as proud and prominent as Sean/Flynn and Erin's wedding photos.

The O'Toole home may have an armory in the basement, but the absence of battleaxes or the all-but-obligatory Pre-Raphaelite poster make it a departure from the normal SCA home. A few photos of Flynn in fighting gear sit on end tables, but the prominence of the wooden Darkyard arms as the only reference to the SCA or the Middle Ages speaks volumes about his view of the SCA. Darkyard is his medieval home. Its tree is a point of pride. Cleftlands and other issues in this Society come a distant second to the household. Flynn's SUV in the driveway announces his allegiance even more clearly. Next to the "BUSH" bumper sticker, his Army license plate spells out "DRKYRD."

"We call Talon to the front."

Talon, wearing a wry smile, ambles forward. He is the latest in a long line of Dagorhir converts to Darkyard. Unlike Valharic, Talon stuck with Dagorhir until he became King of Pentwyvern and spent a year commanding Cleveland's chapter of foam-wielding teenagers. For the last few years, he has focused on the SCA. Tonight, he's poised to take a big step toward being part of this powerful SCA fighting household.

"We like Talon. We really like Talon," comes a shout from the crowd.

"Welcome to the House of Pain," another shouts.

Talon cracks a slightly nervous grin. He trusts them, but has no idea what they have in store for him.

Darkyard normally meets in its base of Detroit, but holds a couple meetings in Cleveland each year, usually on the eve of events like the one the Barony of the Cleftlands will host tomorrow. The Detroit crowd can make the drive down for a 9 p.m. household meeting and crash with local members for the event. If they don't know the way to Flynn's house already, they can spot it the same way Darkyarders always find their household brothers: by the Darkyard "warboard"—a giant battle shield—left out front like a beacon on his front porch. Most members make the drive. Those who earn the right to wear the household's arms with a tree and a full moon will want to see their friends—their "brothers" as they call each other. If they miss a meeting—or several—the household usually forgives them. "Once a tree, always a tree..." a household saying goes.

Talon, MKA Rob Radcliffe, has worked hard to make the transition from fighting with the foam sticks of Dagorhir to the rattan swords of the SCA. Flynn and Valharic, his former roommate when both attended the Pittsburgh Institute of Art, brought him to Darkyard a few years ago. He is now more concerned with turning out SCA armor than with "foam-smithing" for Dagorhir. He also now makes the Coptic-style tunics of Darkyard—the ones used by Romans and Copts ornamented with vertical stripes called clavi running over each shoulder and down the front and back—instead of the low-standards garb mix of Dagorhir. He still needs work on his name, though. He adopted a historically accurate name for use in the Society, but it has the same problem as almost every ancient Gaelic name. Tighearnan O'Seaghdha looks too unpronounceable and is not catchy enough to supplant his Dagorhir name of Talon. Outside of work as an instructions writer for a medical supply company, he helps Flynn run SFU, spends time with his fiancé Wanda, who Middle Eastern dances in the SCA under the name Ileana de la Cuenca, and tries to bring his SCA fighting up to Darkyard standards.

Darkyard has many members skilled in the arts, but it is a fighting household. Everyone must fight or be an archer to become a member. Most of the women arch. Most of the guys fight. So do some of the women. One of Darkyard's main goals is to achieve the dream of the late founder Forgan Aurelius of fielding a whole army at Pennsic.

"You have been recommended as a candidate..." Urien tells Talon.

"Aye," Talon replies.

Urien shifts into drill instructor voice.

"Say it like you mean it!"

"Aye!" Talon barks back.

"And...?"

"Darkyard!" Talon shouts as the other house members join in the boisterous call.

It is a good thing it is still early or Flynn's neighbors would complain. The bellow serves as the household's calling card. Almost no one can make it through a Pennsic without hearing the group cry of "Darkyard!" at least once. Most will hear it a dozen times or more. Besides continuing a group tradition, it closes "The Darkyard Song" which the army sings at war every time it marches—for opening ceremonies, for court, and to battle. The lyrics proclaim the household's vigor for fighting and its goal for War—"Hew and slash and hack and smash and slay the Eastern Army." And the song is just one of many continuing tributes to Darkyard's founder, Forgan, whose loss the household cannot seem to move past.

The Imago of Darkyard

Real Roman legions on campaign far from Rome sometimes carried at the head of their ranks a golden image—an imago—of their emperor who was not with them. A cousin to the Virgin Mary statues that zealous Catholics march through the streets for festivals, an imago would display the golden bust of the emperor set in a precious-metal box atop a pole. The imago would remind the troops of their loyalty and give them a partially divine leader to follow, even if he was absent. Holding up an imago helped drive the troops to glory in the emperor's absence.

As Darkyard members confirm Talon as an official candidate for the house, members have one very symbolic question for him.

"Are you willing to swear fealty to the lord of the house?"

That means swearing loyalty and obedience to Forgan. Members of the entire Society swear fealty to their kings and queens all the time in this hobby. In a culture that mixes play-acting with very tangible deeds, vows of fealty sit in a strange no-man's land. Is it just the medieval alter-ego swearing to take orders and be loyal? Or are the real people behind the medieval personas swearing loyalty to the real person playing the role of King or leader? Usually, it's a little of each. Like most other things in this Society, the vows have as little or as much meaning as individuals choose to give them.

Swearing fealty to Forgan adds another complication. Forgan is neither here tonight or back in Detroit, the household's equivalent of Rome. He has been dead for more than four years, since he was killed in a workshop accident in his house in late 1996. Though Darkyard may not have a tangible imago of Forgan to stand in for him, the house holds up his memory much the same way.

Darkyard followed the normal pattern of SCA fighting houses by gathering around a local hotshot fighter making a name for himself. Forgan, the household's first Knight and founder, was still a young pup when he gathered several other young members together in the early 1980s. They all made their teenage and young adult mistakes, both real and SCA, in the company of their friends and they all hit the battlefield with the same level of enthusiasm. Even Valharic, who joined as a teen and was even younger than the group, described the house as "like a high school club" with a Middle Ages bent. At the least, it was and is much like a fraternity that picks its members and sets its own atmosphere and goals, slightly apart from the rest of the Society.

Forgan would spend nights in his armory turning out gear for fighting prospects and had a knack for making almost anyone he worked with feel important. A company commander and military strategy expert in the National Guard, he had the house apply real military tactics to the SCA. Somehow, he convinced everyone that fighting as a cohesive unit would bring success on the battlefield—no easy task in a Society in which everyone wants to play the hero. He convinced fighters to concentrate on shield work, to block for spear-wielding killers, and not just "swing the blade" in search of kills and glory. The idea took hold and shieldmen soon took as much pride in plowing over Easterners and fouling their blows as a college offensive line takes in blocking for its Heisman Trophy running back. The fighting was not exactly an accurate Roman style. The Darkyard warboards have grips in an upper corner instead of the center like true Roman scutums. Real Roman fighters also would rarely "swing the blade" but stab foes from the sides of their shields. But a key for the Romans was teamwork, not individual freelancing, and Forgan instilled that mindset into his troops.

The house's name came from the backyard fight practices in Forgan's yard that would stretch into the night. The coat of arms represents the silhouette of the tree that dominated the yard in the moonlight. As the headlights of cars lit up the yard, the silhouette would be cast onto the garage door. A few household members even keep pieces of that long-gone tree as relics. As the fighters pushed each other to improve, some even began to surpass Forgan's skill. One of his prize recruits, Matthew Muller, converted his Korean martial arts training into medieval fighting might that earned him the Middle Kingdom crown. A year later, the gaming buddy who joined with Muller the same day, who now goes by the name Tarquin the Red, also took the crown.

Forgan took on a few other stellar prospects as squires. One, Jon-Erik Jacobson, won the Crown in 1998 as his Viking persona Ragnvaldr Jonsson after Forgan died. Another, headed for leadership positions, went by Calador Quinnicaine. And Forgan also took on Valharic. At the age of 21, Valharic moved in with Forgan in Detroit when his money for art school ran out. As Valharic worked a stint in the Michigan National Guard, he had Forgan's help in understanding the military. The two spent hours reading military strategy books, wargaming with miniatures and dueling on computer war games. Then they would shift eras, hit the practice field and hone their skills with shield and blade. Forgan would command his growing legion with the same style he used in the Guard, even ordering his fighters to do pushups when they failed to meet his standards. That military style bothered some recruits, but it appealed to many former Army people like Flynn, who had served two years in Korea. Besides piling up honors for its fighting, Darkyard turned into almost a family. Members literally break bread together at feasts by gathering in a circle to all pull pieces from the same loaf.

Since Forgan's death in 1996, rather than grieving then moving on, the household has dedicated itself to trying to polish itself to Forgan's standard. Darkyard is like an orphan that struggles to live up to the standards, both real and assumed, of a departed parent. Members sometimes wear black armbands embroidered with Forgan's name. They display shields painted with Forgan's arms. They can spend hours embroidering banners, not just of the living and vital household's arms, but of Forgan's too. Each year they march to a tree planted in his memory at Pennsic. The ceremony pays homage to him with stories and songs that proclaim that they, as a house, "were forged in Forgan's fire." And because Forgan wanted to field a full Roman legion at war, the house has shifted from a Romano-Brit focus to an almost entirely Roman one. Members have increased their efforts to do things more like the Romans with better Roman-styled armor, better Roman garb and better Roman displays on the field. When push comes to shove, a What Would Forgan Do mindset can win out over new ideas, even when the household has leaders whose renown in the Kingdom surpass what Forgan ever had.

Today, 15 years after Muller joined Darkyard, his SCA persona, Brannos O'Irongardaill is considered by many to be the best fighter in the entire Midrealm. His reputation defies the SCA's normal pecking order set by the number of crowns someone has won. Brannos has won a Crown Tournament only once, but fighters across the Kingdom, even other counts (ex-kings) or dukes (ex two-time kings), believe he could have the throne again if he wanted it. Spotting him here for the first time tonight, I am surprised by his size. Perhaps because of a photo I saw of him on the Middle Kingdom's web site that makes him look like he has a linebacker's neck and shoulders, or possibly just because of misguided preconceptions, I expected him to be a hulking and burly monster. Instead, he is no bigger than anyone you'd pass on the street. And his close-cropped hair and beard are sprinkled with a bit of gray. The hours he spends in the gym build muscle tone, not bulk. His reputation, I learn, is built not on sheer bludgeoning power but on his technical and clinical approach to fighting. I will get the chance to see his work with the sword tomorrow at the Cleftlands event. All I know now is what other fighters tell me. The Kingdom's current prince, Bardolph, considers him the toughest challenge he has ever fought. Even the man in charge of running the mass battles at Pennsic considers him the best.

"I've never beaten him. Ever," said Sir Pieter Van Doorn, now a Knight for eight years. "He's got maneuvers I can't even see, much less execute. He can hit you from all different directions all at once."

Within Darkyard, he has such standing that Flynn and Talon both talk about time spent with him as if they have rubbed elbows with a celebrity.

I hear two fighters from the house talk about taking beatings from him as if lucky for the privilege.

"How may times have you hit Brannos?" one asked.

"Maybe twice."

"That's about right. I hit him once pretty good. He just gave me a nod, then spent the next half hour beating me in retaliation."

"Yup."

"Did he give you an ass wrap?"

"Oh yeah."

While Brannos has handed out more than his share of those stinging blows—a snap of a sword blade into an often unarmored posterior—he and his wife Rebecca (Rebekah in the SCA) have given more meaningful contributions to the household and to the Middle Kingdom by devoting much of their lives to it.

The Tale of Brannos' Keep

Mathew Muller, 35, now works in information technology as a contractor for a typical Detroit company—Daimler-Chrysler. But in his early 20s, he was attending community college and technical school while learning and teaching Tang Soo Do, a Korean martial art similar to Tae Kwan Do. A classmate told him about the SCA, then gave him another nudge when he ran into Muller at an arcade.

"I hate to use D&D as a reference," Brannos said. "But everybody has fantasies. The Middle Ages was just a bonus to start. I did not come in with medieval ideas, but thought, 'I'll at least have a small idea what it's like to put a sword and shield on and actually fight.'"

Rebecca, his future wife, now 38, did not have much interest in history. In the couple's awkward first SCA meetings, the odd crowd bothered her. "I was just the girlfriend that came along for the ride," Rebecca concedes. Muller laughs.

"I brought her in kicking and screaming."

A few months later, she became Rebekah MacTiernan, a 14th century Irishwoman. She started archery and helping out with some of the feasts. It was the start of the pair pushing each other on SCA projects.

Brannos and Rebekah's home in Warren, Mich., right outside the Detroit city limits now fills much of the role Forgan's did. Known to the household as Brannos' Keep, the house has an armory, a library of medieval-related books and a backyard for fight practices. With no children, they can dedicate themselves to the SCA and have become the power couple of the household. Rebekah, who eventually became such a convert she outranks Brannos in landing the SCA's lofty peerages two-to one (Laurel for her sewing and Pelican for her service vs. one—Knighthood for Brannos). She now has closets packed with more cotehardies than she can ever wear or keep track of. She estimates she now has 28 of the late-period dresses that button up the front and have tight long sleeves.

"They're damned comfortable to wear," she says grinning, then turns serious. She had to go through a period early on of researching the 14th century and Elizabethan garb she built her reputation on, right down to underdresses and socks.

She now teaches and mentors a stable of sewing apprentices. All of the apprentices, including Erin from the SFU group, aspire to become Laurels in their fields of embroidery, herbology or cooking. Rebekah gives them annual assignments in their fields.

"You don't really take them on to teach them their skill," Rebekah said. "It's already there. It's to help them, guide them along their path and make them a better peer."

While Rebekah sits on the sidelines or back in camp at events, Brannos fights. And fights. And fights. House members joke about how hard it is for her to pull him off the fighting field.

Part of his success comes from endurance and the willpower to outlast everyone else on the fighting fields at events and at practice. His experience in Asian martial arts also helps as it has helped many other SCA fighting stars, most notably Jade of Starfall, King of the pecking order by winning the Crown of the West Kingdom 11 times. Those disciplines teach body control, balance, agility and technique. In 1993, after five years of fighting, Brannos rose to the rank of Knighthood. A year later, he won the Crown and he and Rebekah served as King and Queen.

Since then he has fought in Crown Tournament just once, reaching the finals on the fifth anniversary of his win. He has not entered Crown Tournament since, partly because his experiences as King strained some of his personal relationships.

"For a year, I met lots and lots of new people," he said. "But I unfortunately tended to drift from the people I cared for."

The title of King means less to him now than before and far less than it means for some others. None of the accolades and ranks of this Society carry any real weight in the outside world, which is normally oblivious of Kingdom dramas. Just like the fealty people choose to give them. He is secure enough as a fighter to not need a second Crown. While winning another Crown would increase his status within the group, Muller takes a different philosophical approach. Testing himself and pushing himself as a fighter against a standard he sets in his mind can be as rewarding as winning a fight on a bigger stage. Commanding the army of Darkyard and its expanded Legion is now more fulfilling. Like many former Kings, his most challenging fights come against other top fighters on quiet practice fields with nobody else watching. He took the same approach years ago to Tang Soo Do, skipping his black belt test for years, even as students he had taught grabbed the rank.

Brannos says he will only seek the throne again to make Rebekah a Duchess.

"Maybe someday," he says. "I'm never going to say no to anything."

Snoop Lupus Lupus

Tonight Talon does not have the choice of saying no. He has to withstand the barrage of good-natured hazing a candidate for Darkyard membership must endure.

Flynn hands him a polonian cap, a pillbox hat clone which many historians believe was a common item in post-Roman Britain. But Flynn makes a crack about it being Talon's "homeboy" hat.

"What's your homeboy name?" Flynn asks.

Talon drops into Latin and repeats the Latin word for dog.

"Lupus, lupus."

"You are now Snoop Lupus Lupus. Every time you are asked your name you will say, 'Sir! Snoop Lupus Lupus Sir!'"

He must also wear the hat every time he is in garb for meetings or for events. Valharic hands Talon a toy sword of stuffed satin and tells him he now has the task of using it against a "lost" member of the household.

"You will learn who it is at a later time," Valharic says. "We will call you again when you are ready."

The call to become an actual member, Valharic tells him, could take days, weeks or months. He will have to prove himself a worthy member of this family. But that task has no clear timetable or course of action. In some ways it mirrors Valharic's frustrating bid to become a Knight.

The Squire's Knot

Valharic is easily a good enough fighter to be named a Knight.

He has fought in the SCA for eight years, from the moment he turned 18. He made his own armor—a coat of leather scales called lamellar—and developed his fighting style using a center-grip shield. He draws on his mundane boxing experience for the counterpunching skills that help him overcome his lack of height. He sizes up opponents to find their weaknesses, sometimes by studying their armor for dents that suggest spots they routinely leave open. He has even won many tournaments in this Kingdom, if not the one he desires the most.

But Knighthood, the recognition by his peers that he is one of the best, has eluded him. Becoming a Knight in this Society is different from how it was in much of the Middle Ages. Knighthood then could simply mean owning a horse and armor. Being named a Knight here is almost like being named to the Round Table.

Standing in Valharic's way are the amorphous "peer qualities" that many SCA Knights look for before welcoming a new member into the Order of the Chivalry. There is no real definition of how a squire should act to earn that honor. Knights just know it when they see it. And the Knights of the Middle Kingdom have yet to see enough of it from Valharic.

Valharic started in the SCA young and the immature first impressions he made on people linger. His "gung-ho" military attitude also turned a few people off when he was given command opportunities. Then losing Forgan, his mentor who he considered his "best friend ever," deprived him of the role model that most Knights serve as for their squires. Just like with fealty oaths, this relationship has one foot in the real world and the other in the Middle Ages gameworld. Knights and squires take this relationship so seriously they even track the lineage of Knights back to Grand-Knights and Great-Grand-Knights. In this case, Forgan had taught Valharic, as the song goes, to "slay the foe like cattle." But Valharic could still use Forgan for the "teach us, train us, lead us on" part.

Though Darkyard's other Knights try to fill that role, they face the same awkward situation as a stepfather or godfather. They want to honor Forgan's commitment to Valharic, but are uncomfortable assuming his place. Valharic recently broke with tradition by reaching outside Darkyard for guidance from a Duke, Finn Herjolfsen, who had also served in the military. Finn, in addition to being a Knight, holds a second peerage, as a Laurel for glassblowing. Valharic will never be a squire of anyone but Forgan, but Finn took him on as an apprentice in the arts to fill some of that void.

Despite Finn's efforts, the knots of opposition to Valharic have tightened since the Crown Tournament loss.

His wife had come to the SCA through the Tuchux, a group considered on the extreme fringe by even the counter-culture SCA. Based on John Norman's *Nomads of Gor* fantasy novel, the Tuchux are not part of the SCA but use similar enough fighting rules that they join some SCA battles, including Pennsic. Playing a tribe of barbarians from the planet Gor—with their spiked and fantastical leather armor and with scantily-clad "wenches" following along—their game does not always fit well into the SCA value system. Every time they join SCA battles, an us vs. them mentality takes over for both sides. At the start of Pennsic in August, 2000, just a few months after Valharic's Crown Tournament loss, a flare-up between the Tuchux and his then-fiancé—the former "wench" that had almost become Queen of the Middle Kingdom—brought a wave of accusations and threats that meant hassle for Kingdom leaders.

Then Valharic was passed over for Knighthood at that same Pennsic in a way that hit home harder than ever before.

After a battle, as often happens, the fighters of the Middle Kingdom all gathered for a battlefield court at the foot of the King. Valharic had watched earlier in the War as a Cleftlands Knight nominated his squire for Knighthood. After the battle, the three Darkyard Knights who had taken over Forgan's squires went to the front to "beg a boon" from the crown. "Beg a boon" ranks right up there with "And the winner is…" or "Gentlemen, start your engines" as a signal that something is about to happen. It almost always means someone will become a Peer—either Laurel, Pelican or Knight. Here, on a battlefield, it could only mean a Knighting.

Valharic's heart leapt. It was about time. Surely, all the long talks he had been having lately about Knighthood were a sign. Today he would finally be recognized as a full-fledged member of the club. It would make something of a consolation prize for not quite winning crown.

Standing toward the back of a crowd of kneeling fighters, Valharic tensed as they offered a nomination.

The Knights asked for Knighthood for Calador de Quinnicaine, one of his Darkyard house brothers, instead.

Valharic blanched. He had been blindsided. It was like Crown all over again. The sight of the three Knights begging a boon had dangled the coveted white belt of Knighthood in front of his eyes, only to snatch it away.

He smothered his disappointment until the post-battle court ended. Then his hurt escaped in wails and snarls. Valharic was a better fighter than Calador. Valharic was a contender for the crown. Calador was not. If the Chivalry was a martial order, why did people keep making his candidacy a morality play?

But there is more to being a Knight in this Society than fighting ability. Calador had years of service to the Middle Kingdom that made a difference. He ran Darkyard and helped outfit fighters of the house and looked after them. Valharic's disappointment interfered with celebrating for his household brother. Even worse, his open disappointment did not help his cause. Others noticed he was more upset than he was happy for Calador. It was not what many expect of a Knight.

Since Pennsic, his case for Knighthood has taken a few more hits. Both he and his wife will later realize their marriage is a mistake. It has become a frenetic series of breakups and reconciliations, and it is hard to tell if this hobby is helping or hurting them. They often argue over time he spends at Society events and time she spends with another male friend. Rather than start more fights, Valharic now skips events and has failed to live up to some of the vows he made to Kingdom leaders. Though the oaths are often flowery and melodramatic, they carry weight in this group. The Thomas Noble part of him cannot be held to them. But his Valharic Aurelius persona, the very part of him that wants to be named a Knight, loses honor if he does not live up to his promises. He started missing more Kingdom events when his wife became pregnant with twins right after their fall wedding. The pregnancy scuttled his plans for the Middle Kingdom's last Crown Tournament in October 2000, and he began working two jobs to prepare for the twins' arrival. Though he will fight tomorrow and sometimes come to the "SFU" meetings in Flynn's basement armory, he will all but shut down his Middle Ages pursuits for the next several months.

By the time I started my journey through this world, Valharic's predicament had become as tangled and binding as a Gordian knot. As the layers of honor and chivalry at play in this group unfold before me, it becomes clearer that it will take more than Valharic's sword to cut himself free from this knot.

The Tale of Pierre

Tonight, Valharic's temper at being passed over has cooled. Earlier tonight, he and his brothers joked about the twins. Mike Detmar kept calling them Romulus and Remus. And Valharic announced that an ultrasound showed one was a girl. They couldn't tell about the other, he said with glee, because the girl kept kicking it.

The group calls up another candidate for the household who goes by the name Cydrych Autorix. Valharic steps forward and tells Cydrych he must take charge of the long lost member of the household. He whips out a sock puppet.

"His name is Pierre," Valharic says.

"Darkyard!" the puppet cries out from Valharic's hand in a horrible French waiter accent.

"Whenever any member asks to see Pierre, you must bring him out, place him on your hand and help him orally," Valharic continues.

He is smiling, but keeps control. The double entendre breaks up the crowd. "For the rest of tonight, you are without voice. Your voice is Pierre."

Cydrych looks stricken. Valharic turns to Talon and points to the satin sword.

"If you fail to strike him when Pierre speaks, it's pushups," he says. Talon brandishes the sword.

"If you," Valharic says to Cydrych, "fail to speak with the puppet, it's pushups." The other members are in tears. All they have to do is make Cydrych talk and they either get to hear the ridiculous puppet voice, or they get to watch pushups or sword swats. Every time. All night. Valharic has boxed Talon and Cydrych in.

"If you lose Pierres's hat," Valharic continues. "You will *wish* it was pushups." He thrusts the puppet out to Cydrych.

"Have fun."

Cydrych slips it on his hand. He'll be a good sport.

"Merci!" Pierre says and Talon bops him with the sword.

In a moment, though, they catch Cydrych speaking in his own voice. "Pushups!" comes the yell. Cydrych drops to the ground, the puppet still on one hand.

"Um. You can't do pushups on Pierre's face," Valharic yells, standing over him. "He'll have to go on your belt."

Cydrych slips the puppet under his belt and counts off his first pushup.

"One. Tw…"

"Where's Pierre?" someone shouts. Taking Pierre off so as not to mash his face into the rug broke Rule No. 1: Cydrych must wear Pierre all night, no exceptions. Cydrych is caught again. With no way out, they let him off easy and as he counts out pushups to complete his allotment, Talon smacks his rear end with the sword at each number.

"You guys are going to be best friends," someone tells them.

"Oui," says Cydrych/Pierre.

Smack.

Act I, scene 5
Being a Knight

Early on this January Saturday morning, about two hours before the first swords cross in combat, Sir Alaric LeFevre bustles around the basement of the function hall. As one of four Knights in the Barony of the Cleftlands, and a newly-minted one at that, Alaric must help play host with his barony for today's event—a tournament, classes and feast. Alaric, MKA Tim Miller, was the Cleftlands squire "elevated" to Knighthood at Pennsic only five months ago even as Valharic was passed over. At 29, he is one of the Middle Kingdom's younger Knights, and one who feels obligated to play the part.

A few other organizers help out as fighters straggle in and strap on armor. New fighters, including Bernard, who I met the other day, will seek authorizations before the tournament. As a few marshals begin an authorization bout, an older and very befuddled couple pulls Alaric aside. Cub Scout leaders, they have never seen an SCA event before, but they need advice on how to run a Middle Ages event for a scout camp. A few minutes before, the heavy-set scout leader named Joe had struggled to pull a loaner tunic over a ratty Ohio State University sweatshirt and his ample belly. They had come without garb or a clue and needed both. Who else to step in but the new Knight? Alaric patiently explains his armor.

"This," he says, pointing to the band of metal buckled around his neck. "Is a gorget…"

"It's like being a Boy Scout…."

Tim Miller would make a good poster boy for an SCA Knight.

He is a Knight of the Round Table wanna-be.

The whole idea of knighthood has fascinated him since he devoured the tales of King Arthur as a child. In college he took biology classes for his career but also took medieval and Renaissance studies courses for his minor in Arthurian literature. The romance, the nobility and the ideals of the Arthurian period all appealed to him. When he learned about the SCA, he leapt at the chance to be a knight in shining armor.

"I was one of those people that walks in and sees what it has to offer and it hooks you," he remembers. "The SCA provides a place for living the ideals—the outward representation of the ideals—that are missing in today's society. This provides us with a modern-day venue to portray those ideals you want to be."

And after watching a Knighting at his first trip to the giant Pennsic War in 1992, he wanted the rank of Knight in this society, not just to be a regular fighter. He soon became a squire to Sir Theo here in the Barony of the Cleftlands and Miller, now under the name Alaric LeFevre in the SCA, started using his black belt in karate to move up the fighting ranks.

As I talk to Alaric/Miller, it becomes clear that only a small percentage of fighters ever become squires. Some fail to become good enough fighters. Some are unwilling to put in the effort to hone their skills. And there are those who never build enough of a relationship with a Knight for the Knight to take them on as a student. Even if the two lack the chemistry of Valharic and Forgan, the Knight and a chosen student swear oaths to bind their new relationship. The new squire generally swears to be a servant and student of the Knight. The Knight gives the squire a red belt—the SCA's standard symbol of squires—and swears to teach the squire about fighting, about the SCA and how to be a role model. Then it should work that way in practice.

Ideally.

More than a few stories circulate in each Kingdom about squires essentially becoming lackeys for their Knights. The student-teacher bond can often deteriorate into a series of work orders: fetch me water, fetch me food, clean my armor, pack my car, set up my tent, watch my kid. It often sounds like the 2 a.m. pizza runs that fraternity pledges endure. In Alaric's case, Theo and the other members of Theo's household were more evenhanded, more like a family looking out for each other.

"Being a squire is both a privilege and a responsibility," Alaric explains. "It's kind of like hanging a sign around your neck saying 'I'm available for anything.' But Theo was not the kind of Knight that said, 'Here's my armor. Go polish it.' If he had, I would have lost respect for him."

Instead, Theo taught him to be a better fighter. Just as importantly, Alaric believes, he taught him lessons in humility, always gave him suggestions on his next step to improve and taught him a few other skills Knights of the SCA should have: period dance and courtly manners.

"Being a squire is like being a Boy Scout," Alaric noted. "It's the same level of expectations. Be prepared. Be courteous, thrifty, brave, clean and reverent."

As Valharic is learning, becoming a squire is no guarantee of becoming a Knight. Without a checklist of requirements, it mirrors in some ways the PhD. Alaric is pursuing in molecular biology at Case Western Reserve University in Cleveland. Universities can list the basic steps for a PhD. on paper, but intangibles in the quality of research and analysis often spell the difference. Some never make it.

At Pennsic last year, Alaric received the call.

Throughout the war, he noticed Knights glancing down at his squire's belt. It should have alerted him that something was up. But he shrugged it off. After a major battle, Sir Theo went up before then-King Dag Thorgrimsson at a battlefield court and "begged the boon" of making Alaric a Knight. The Order of the Chivalry of the Kingdom knelt in a circle several rows deep around the King. They all agreed with Theo.

The next day, at the Midrealm's court, King Dag dubbed Alaric a Knight with Oathbinder, the Midrealm's sword of state. Alaric received the white belt of a Knight, a chain around his neck and a set of spurs. The white belt is an SCA-invented symbol and SCA Knights do not ride horses in battle like their historical predecessors, but the spurs are a symbolic link to that history.

The ceremony was both the fulfillment of a goal and a passage to another phase of life. The novelty of being a Knight has not yet worn off from Alaric. His Knighthood feels a little, he says, like a brand new pair of sneakers whose squeak on the floor has yet to wear off. He is growing accustomed to the constant responsibility, realizing that his position of power can draw people into the group or drive them away.

"Just because they put a white belt on you doesn't mean you get to go into retirement," Alaric explains. "The goal isn't to become a Knight. It's to *be* a Knight."

Fighting Tests

I leave Alaric to sort out the Cub Scout people and watch as a young woman I saw at the meeting the other day steps into a section of the basement roped off for fighting. Though I need to watch the legendary Brannos fight today and am still sorting through the different perceptions and visions of Knighthood, I have more basic concerns. I want an idea what the fighting authorization test is like and I need a better sense of how this fighting actually works in reality.

The woman stepping into the so-called "list field" for her authorization is no bruiser. And she's not packed like a sardine into a metal can of armor. With a few pieces of metal on her knees and elbows, she relies on a large purple gambeson cinched at her waist with a belt to protect her. She steps forward beaming, a ponytail streaming out the back of her helm.

Lyonnete Vibert, MKA Marie Vibbert, has a twin sister also in the Barony. Unless you know them well, it is nearly impossible to tell them apart or sort out their persona and mundane names. Milesent Vibert, MKA Grace Vibbert, does artwork, the baronial newsletter and bounces gleefully into period dance sessions at Cleftlands weekly meetings. Lyonnete, who is trying to become an expert in Burgundian garb, used to join her. But for the past few months she has skipped the dance revels for fight practice, inspired by lessons from the Cleftlands' Baron, Duke Sir Laurelen Daksbane.

When Lyonnete first watched SCA fighters she though they "looked darn stupid."

"They were covered in crap and they were hitting each other with sticks," she scoffed. But one of the swordsmen, who wore a "scary black gray helm" with a gold cross on the face looked impressive. "They all looked stupid except for that guy."

When she asked about him, she learned that he was a Knight.

"Well, how does he get to call himself a Knight?" Lyonnete asked.

"He earned it," she was told.

So she sat in on a class Sir Laurelen taught at a baronial meeting in which he outlined all the virtuous qualities of historical and SCA Knights. Laurelen stressed qualities like courage, generosity, nobility and humility. When he took questions from his audience, Lyonnete asked him if someone could become a Knight if they were good at those things, but could not fight.

When Laurelen told her that "prowess at arms" is required, she decided she would have to learn to fight.

For her test today, a very beginning step toward Knighthood, she fights against Rutgur von Stuttgart. He is a member of Darkyard but is just as active in the Cleftlands. The two trade blows. This bout, as I had been assured, is not a beat-down, so Rutgur pulls his shots, even though he is strong enough to leave bruises with each blow. Lyonnete calls out "Good!" each time Rutgur tags her with a sufficient blow. Rutgur also lets a few shots slip through to hit his helm.

After a few minutes of sparring, Rutgur calls "Hold!"—the sign to stop—and huddles with other marshals looking on. Lyonnete waits as Rutgur and the marshals talk for a few moments. They discuss her weaknesses and what to test next. When the fight resumes, Rutgur tries to bully her a bit, crowding in and pushing her with his shield. Lyonnete gives ground without backing down and swings back. Rutgur takes a cut at her leg and connects. Lyonnete takes the blow. A head blow would have killed her. This blow was strong enough to disable her leg under SCA fighting rules. Since she can't use the leg anymore, she drops to her knees.

Rutgur could fight from his feet and have a clear advantage. Instead, he offers Lyonnete a "point of honor," a sometimes-followed SCA tradition. To make the rest of the fight more even, Rutgur drops to his knees as well.

"Hoobah!" the few fighters watching the test shout in acknowledgement of Rutgur's chivalric act.

Fighters debate this tradition endlessly. Some view it as showing honor to your opponent or making a more fair fight, especially when one fighter is clearly superior. Other fighters consider it an insult, a dismissal of an opponent's chance to overcome the disadvantage. Still others see disabling a limb as an advantage won through combat and never yield it.

Rutgur, one of the Kingdom's better fighters, clearly is superior to the not-yet-authorized Lyonnete. His move makes the fight more even. That lasts only for the moments it takes for Rutgur to swipe at Lyonnete's sword arm and connect. With her sword arm now disabled, she cannot use that arm now either. Lyonnete drops her shield and switches the sword to her off hand. Rutgur parries a few awkward blows before the marshals are satisfied she can at least try to fight with that hand. Lyonnete may still need a lot of practice, but she is passing the test of rules and basic safety.

The marshals order them to stand up and start over, fighting close to full speed as the final test. Rutgur eases enough for Lyonnete to give him a solid bop to the helmet and he keels over "dead".

"Congratulations. You've authorized," a marshal tells her.

She hops up and down in her armor, beaming.

"Thank you," she squeals, still hopping.

"I love it," she tells me later. "It's so much fun and I can't stop. There's this invulnerable feeling when you're wearing 60 pounds of armor and someone hits you as hard as they can—and it doesn't hurt."

More fighters pour in to register for the tournament and have their armor inspected by marshals to make sure it meets standards and is safe. I spot Bernard, sweaty but grinning. He, too, has passed his authorization.

A few heavy hitters will fight today. In addition to Brannos, the three-time King that Valharic chose as his mentor, Finn Herjolfson, has traveled from Cincinnati to fight.

I watch as Brannos and Valharic challenge one another in warmups, fighting hard but laughing as they do it. Brannos may not be a big man, but he is a compact package of muscle, intent and confidence. He wears little armor, but each piece fits him so perfectly that he could drive back to Detroit fully armored and hardly notice. Fighting has become second nature. Opponents rave about a few of his habits. In melees—the big group battles—he takes the old *Dungeons and Dragons* concept of initiative to a new level, darting around and engaging people in fights with lightning speed. In a one-on-one bout, he goes the other route, often taking the idea of counterpunching to unnerving levels. He is like a predator laying in wait until unawares prey walks by. He can wait opponents out until they make the first move—and first mistake—often out of unease.

"You have all day to kill your opponent," he tells his students.

Though he is not waiting out Valharic in these warm-ups, I see another of his skills that makes him the envy of the Kingdom. He has an uncanny ability to slip blows simply by backing up. Other fighters usually lose their balance if they jerk their head or shoulders back to avoid a sword. Brannos' legs always catch up with his head's retreat. He will backpedal right out of a fight if he feels off, then reset and start again. When he stands on guard, if you take away the sword and shield, his hands are in the same positions as a boxer's. Cleftlands fighters, who mostly use the style promoted by their Baron, Duke Laurelen Darksbane, almost always hold their swords with the hilts back by their shoulders unless actually swinging, Brannos and his Darkyard acolytes hold theirs far more in front. Brannos teaches that the fastest way to a target is a straight line. A sword blow that approximates a punch beats a swing.

"If I were boxing and threw a big old roundhouse punch, I've got a good chance of being knocked out because the inside lines are opened," Brannos says.

A roundhouse swing also expends energy to the curve of the swing, not right at an opponent.

"I try to use as little energy as possible at first, then explode at the end, just like martial arts. It can be very powerful without having a lot of strength."

For those who do not know him, his armorer has hammered a brass crown outline along the temples of his helmet. SCA kings and ex-kings will do this to proclaim their rank on the field where sword swats would ruin a real crown. The brass crown on his helm announces to all that he is somebody. His body language announces it louder.

So naturally Hobbs, the relative newcomer to Flynn's "SFU" armoring group, wants to fight him.

The Broken Newbie's Tale

Hobbs is a scrapper.

Just like almost every Cleveland-area member of the Darkyard community, the goateed Hobbs started with the Dagorhir chapter of Pentwyvern—meaning five dragons—and their battles in the woods and fields of the local parks.

Hobbs, MKA Craig Hatfield, 28, a Lotus Notes expert for the paint manufacturer Sherwin-Williams, became an instant Pentwyvern legend at his first event. His earlier dabbles with fencing gave him the habit of lunging forward with his head as he fought. With one lunge, he moved his face right into a blow. Though blows to the head are illegal in Dagorhir, this one caught him flush in the nose, breaking it.

"I was just gushing blood," he remembers. "Breaking the newbies is kind of a joke, but in this case it really happened."

Worried he might end up with a crooked nose, he wrenched it into place himself even as other fighters rushed over to help. Still, he was hooked. He paid his Dagorhir membership that day with bills stained with his own blood.

Hobbs/Craig came to medieval hobbies later than most. Though he took courses in old English and Irish literature at the University of Dayton, he looked down on the campus SCA group as "just like the dorks playing frisbee golf." A small renaissance fair near Cleveland hooked him a year and a half ago. The Baycrafters Renaissance and Fantasy Fayre in the Cleveland suburb of Bay Village caters to a Labor Day crowd of children looking for puppet shows, women who want to buy pagan jewelry and guys in search of knives with blades big enough to rival those in fantasy novels. It is the kind of place that sprinkles gratuitous extra "e"s on random words—stolen from Hobbs' name?- to make Ye Olde Shoppes of Junke seem more medieval. Unlike Hobbs, who found a real medieval name spelled without the extra vowel favored by philosophers and cartoon tigers, most of the vendors and entertainers at the "Fayre" have only a passing idea of history.

Hobbs, who knew little more than the vendors that day, looked right past a stodgy display and demonstration by the Cleftlands. He latched onto the flashier, rough-and-tumble Pentwyvern clash with its exaggerated swings of giant foam axes and dramatic writhing collapses by those who were "killed."

"I liked the crazier guys throwing themselves around," he remembers. "Compared to the antique show the SCA set up and guys with rusty armor, this looked like more fun."

Talon, though, nudged him into attending a full SCA event called Baron Wars that used the colonial Fort Meigs outside Toledo for its battles. Watching those SCA battles with their "real armor and arrows and siege weapons" around the spiked log walls of the fort convinced him to make the switch.

"It seemed more serious and Dagorhir seemed kind of fake. Once I saw the SCA, I had to try it. It would seem like college as opposed to high school."

It was then mid-May and he had about six weeks to learn fighting basics and make armor to fight at Pennsic. He started going to Flynn's house several nights a week as the whole SFU group scrambled to finish projects for War. At the last minute, the group drove him to Detroit to a Darkyard practice, always attended by several marshals, so he could authorize. If he had failed, he could not fight at Pennsic. He received his first real bruise in his authorization bout with a swat to his rear end, but he passed. He camped at Pennsic for two weeks, fought in the battles and grew so sure he loved the SCA he dropped $400 on a new helm.

"I had no question, no doubt. There was too much to do that interested me. My family always accused me when I pick up a hobby of being obsessed. I'd jump into hobbies, I'd buy stuff and I'd quit. This I want to do until I'm old and gray."

It didn't hurt that at Pennsic he met his current girlfriend, Amanda Morlocke, a belly dancer and member of WulfDen, a small, close-knit group of SCA and Dagorhir members that has close ties to Darkyard. Now living together in one of the far rural suburbs of Cleveland, the pair attends events together, Hobbs fighting by day, Amanda dancing by the fires at night. Slowly Hobbs has improved as a fighter. Only about 5'9", he is solid with strong shoulders and forearms from weightlifting, but he is not bulky. In recent months he has started to feel competitive about the sport and wants to improve. Today is his first tournament and his first real chance to test himself. So he maneuvers for a shot at Brannos.

Poor Hobbs. Poor deluded Hobbs. He has no chance against Brannos.

Someone to play with…

As it turns out, I need not have worried. As tournaments go, this one is low key, with a format that takes pressure off of individual bouts. Some tournaments can mirror the NCAA basketball tourney with a brackets system. One loss and you're out. Others, like Crown Tournaments are double elimination and losers can re-emerge into the field if they can beat all the others in a losers bracket. Another style lumps people into groups for round-robin bouts, with only the top couple advancing. Some are more creative at their groupings and at the scenarios behind them. Today's tournament, though, gives as much credit for effort as it does for skill. Cleftlands has set no order or structure of whom to fight. Fighters simply pair up, have a bout, then go to the marshal's table and report results. The winner receives points, the loser none. Then they get back in line and pair up with someone else. The winner will be the fighter with the most points at the end of the day. You can fight as much or as little as you want, limited only by time, stamina and tolerance for pain.

Hobbs, Flynn, Talon and Mike/Logan all join the line. With several bouts going on at once, I soon lose track of them. Fighters keep streaming into the rectangular fighting area, roped off just as at the fight practice, and lunge at into each other, swords flying. I am a long way from discerning the strategy in the flurry of blows. But I can tell one thing—sportsmanship is alive and well.

As fighters line up to seek new opponents, they ask, "Do you need someone to play with?" I note the choice of words: "play." Today this is just a game. And fighters actually argue to accept borderline blows.

"You got me," one says after a shot to the side.

"Are you sure? I thought I got mostly shield."

"No. That's good."

"Really? You sure?"

"Yeah. Good match."

I watch Alaric fight in a few bouts. His speed and intensity changes, depending on his opponent. Some fighters, he rips into. Others, he ratchets it back a notch or two. I spy on Brannos and on Valharic's mentor, Duke Finn. They do the same. After fighting Valharic, Brannos takes on an endless string of fighters, moving first at half speed and often stopping a few seconds into the bout to give a lesson. Instead of knocking them out in seconds, Brannos gives them ten minutes of instruction. The fighters in today's tournament are vying for a prize. But neither Brannos nor Finn need a win here for either their egos or reputations. They never go to the scoring table to register their victory points. Today is about being a Knight, being a teacher and mentor.

"That's why we're out there—not only to bring honor to our Kingdom, but the primary responsibility is education," Brannos says. "If I were to go out and win every tournament or hold a field all day long, it's no longer fun for other people. After a number, you become what other people view as arrogant."

"I really don't have a lot to prove on the tournament field," added Finn, MKA Kevin Griggs. "If I can raise the mean quality of fighting, it forces me to get better. The better they get, the better they force me to be."

If Alaric could be a poster boy for Knighthood, Finn meets the same test. If his three Crown wins did not qualify him on their own, Finn also has an intimate understanding of Alaric's comparison of Knighthood to the Boy Scouts. Finn is an Eagle Scout.

"I think there's a lot of carryover," he says. "Scouting tries to build well-rounded men that are active participants in multiple facets of the community. That's the same thing the SCA is trying to do."

I also watch for Jocelyn, the woman from Twelfth Night who regularly beats guys at this game. Jocelyn, MKA Jessica Keeslar, is a music teacher for schools outside of Detroit. She moved back to the Midwest a few years ago after going to school in Florida and has immersed herself in Darkyard's fight practices with her boundless enthusiasm. Darkyard has boosted her fighting skills, but Darkyard's minimalist armor concept has yet to win her over. From head to toe she is covered in metal like an armored tank, ready to grind over anything. She is impervious to blows, at least those struck with rattan blades. As I watch her prepare for a bout, I expect her to be anchored down by the armor.

Then she swings her sword and I do a doubletake.

Despite her full plate armor, Jocelyn practically springs into the duel, bouncing and dancing on the balls of her feet, like a boxer dancing around the ring. Only later do I learn the secret: it's all aluminum. It would cut like butter if hit by a real sword, but here it is legal and protects her amazingly well. Instead of making her a plodding heavyweight, a George Foreman in a helm, she can be a nimble-footed Sugar Ray Leonard. Dance. Dance. Thwap. Thwap. Opponent dead.

A few days later our SFU group is still buzzing over her.

"She just bounces around out there in full plate and it's bounce, bounce and then Ring!" Flynn says, tapping his head. "And you never see the shot."

"She's so quick," adds Hobbs, miming a sword swing. "She does this thing where she starts to swing and then stops. When you look to see what she's doing she just…"

Hobbs completes the swing with a snap. "…rings you up."

Hobbs creates a little stir of his own. He finishes nowhere near the top of the standings and is unnoticed by anyone outside of Darkyard. But the fighters there see him go out bout after bout after bout, throw some good blows and never back down. Hobbs, they note, has some potential. Of course, he probably overdoes it. He takes one wicked blow to the buttocks and suffers a giant purple bruise he is only too happy to drop his pants and show us a few days later. And he calls in sick on Monday, too exhausted even after resting all day on Sunday to drag himself from bed and go in to work. Hobbs closes his day with Brannos, maneuvering in line for half an hour for his shot.

He is rewarded with a free pass to land a dozen blows to Brannos' head.

Brannos allows every last one of those hits and even tells Hobbs to hit him in the head as part of the lesson in blow mechanics. Since the head is the best-armored body part, most fighters would rather be hit in the head than anywhere else. After about 10 seconds of fighting, Brannos stops the fight to position Hobbs' sword hand, then stands unflinching as Hobbs strikes the blows. It's about the only way Brannos could be hit today.

When I head upstairs to check out some merchants, Hobbs is starting to pull off his armor. Jocelyn is still out on the field, swinging with Alaric, who still hasn't run out of gas. She's still bouncing, still flying around. For the day, she is the tournament's runner-up for winning the second-most bouts.

About 90 minutes later, I sit down to feast. The Barony, just to be a little different, has shifted the time period of this event a little later than normal and has cooked a "New World" feast. Darkyard cleared out to have dinner as a group elsewhere. As the food is served, I spot Alaric among the wait staff. He has ditched his green and black fighting gear, showered and changed into his dress garb, a red and white tunic and a matching hood. Throughout the meal he brings course after course to the guests.

As the meal winds down, the group's Baron, Duke Sir Laurelen Darksbane, emerges from behind the head table. Laurelen, MKA Howard Fein, is not a large man. He's actually fairly small and slight, with his longish but bushy hair sometimes wider than the shoulders it drapes over. He has virtually no chance of overpowering with brute force somebody like Finn. But a little over 20 years ago years ago in the adolescent years of the Middle Kingdom he was as good a fighter as any in the Kingdom. In 1978 and 1980 he won the Kingdom's Crown Tournament, which earned him the title of

Duke. His prominence and efforts also earned him the title of Baron, the lord in charge of the Greater Cleveland area.

He also earned his white belt of Knighthood without ever serving as a squire. He made his impression on the Kingdom all on his own.

Tonight, he has a few observations on the Knight-squire relationship he wants to share with the guests.

"You will all see something special," he tells the seated crowd. Alaric will take his first squire.

The Elvish Knight's Tale

Laurelen is a product of the less formalized times of the SCA. His baronial subjects alternate between respect and puzzlement as they refer to him either as a "rocket scientist" or "The Elf."

Howard Fein, 50, was born in Nuremberg, Germany. Like Valharic, he was a military brat. After a few years in New York, he came to Case Western Reserve University Cleveland in 1970 where he studied French, astronomy and physics. The science stuck. Today he has a laboratory in suburban Cleveland where he runs tests with lasers for his own business.

"When I was a kid, if you asked me what I wanted to be, it was a tough choice between a scientist and a Knight," he remembers. "Fifty years later I'm both."

He studied fencing under a master fencer while in New York and was on Case Western's nationally ranked varsity team. His private lessons with the master started him on the path.

"I learned not only fencing but a great deal of insight into the martial way of life, the way of the sword."

Just like with Alaric, King Arthur stories and mythology books were childhood favorites he kept reading to become a disciple of the Arthurian legend. But the SCA does not force an Arthurian view on anybody. It does not force a strict historical view either, though it keeps nudging people that way. Instead, it often borrows from Laurelen's greater inspiration: J.R.R.Tolkien.

Laurelen/Howard, a self-described "Tolkien purist" considers *The Lord of the Rings* "as much a meaningful piece of literature as King Arthur." He has studied Tolkien's Elvish language for 25 years, putting Tolkien's languages into a dictionary and lexicon. He can rattle off an Elvish poem from the top of his head. And he has tried to work Tolkien influences into his persona and the entire Middle Kingdom, imbedding many of them deeply before the SCA started blocking fantasy aspects from the game.

The name Laurelen means "Golden star" in Elvish and describes his coat of arms, an eight-pointed star that he says has Buddhist and pagan significance. Even in high school, before he heard of the SCA, he would use the star as a pseudo-signature to mark property and would use the name Laurelen with his friends. When Laurelen made the Middle Kingdom's sword of state, named Oathbinder, he etched Elvish writing into it. He also borrowed heavily from *The Return of the King* when he was a Middle Kingdom leader and was writing much of its ceremonial language. When subjects swear their fealty to the crown, the King and/or Queen responds:

This do We hear and will never forget,
Nor fail to reward that which is given:
Fealty with love, service with honor,
And oath-breaking with vengeance

It is nearly identical to how Gondor's lord, Denethor, responds to an oath of service by the hobbit Pippin in *The Return of the King*:

"And this do I hear, Denethor son of Ecthelion, Lord of Gondor, Steward to the High King, and I will not forget it, nor fail to reward that which is given: fealty with love, valour with honour, oath-breaking with vengeance."

Laurelen is also one of the Kingdom's main protectors of Knighthood standing as a measure of character, not just fighting ability. To earn the white belt of a Knight, you must be both a good fighter and a good person, forever aspiring to noble ideals. Valharic may resent how the Order of the Chivalry seems fixated on moral issues and overlooks his skill with the weapon. But Laurelen sees the morality play as the whole point. His personal last name, Darksbane, is just one expression of it. He hates the Dark Side, he explains, using the Star Wars analogy. Obi Wan Kenobi, he says, taught that the Dark Side is not more powerful but is easier and more seductive. People need to fight against such influences. He says he also quit competitive fencing because he saw too many people cheating. He chose SCA fighting instead because it offered real competition without sacrificing his values. He tells fighters in the barony that fighting reveals your heart. How you react in the split-second after a blow hits you—whether you fall, whether you accept it or whether you slough it off and fight on—speaks volumes about your character.

"I'm a creature of the light," he says. "I believe in the infinite perfectibility of man. There is light and dark in everybody. It's up to us which one we tread."

A few residents of his barony, though, snort at such statements from him. Though Laurelen was a major factor in organizing Cleftlands, critics believe he has not quite lived up to the ideals he promotes. Named permanent baron for his work years ago, some view his organization as a closed shop. Darkyard gained many of its Cleveland members from Pentwyvern because Cleftlands did not welcome them. Even people who would persist and achieve things within the SCA believe the barony that Laurelen ran gave them the cold shoulder.

One, a high school Spanish teacher who goes by the SCA name Alys Katharine, is both a Laurel and a Pelican for her work. She is also the friend's mother who drove Valharic to his first SCA meetings. Now in charge of organizing and scheduling the more than 1,000 classes on history, performance and crafts taught at Pennsic each year, she believes the barony ignored her as a newcomer and discouraged her from intense participation. She had wanted to use her experience running a newsletter for another organization to create one for the barony, but the Old Guard of the Cleftlands rejected the idea. Newcomers, she felt, were forced to sit back in the background for a few years before gaining acceptance. Energy for projects was often interpreted as ambition for awards and looked down upon. She stuck it out, often traveling outside the barony, but many did not.

As active as he was years ago, Laurelen's once-frantic activity for the SCA has slowed. His wife, Baroness Ithriliel of Silverlake, is virtually nowhere to be seen. As they have aged, Laurelen has grown more concerned with his own laser business and his son's piano recitals. But he can still show even good fighters a trick or two out on the list field.

And he still holds his post as baron of the Cleftlands as a life position.

"Make it part of me personally..."

Today, as Baron, Laurelen introduces the very busy Sir Alaric and his squire-to-be Stephan von Lubeck, MKA Steve Kerg, 26.

Most of the activities of the SCA, Laurelen tells the crowd of feasters sitting at rows of tables, are total fantasy or historical recreation. We are not actually in the Middle Ages, he says. But in some ways the things we do *are* real. Artists who make something medieval have actually created art. A fighter on the field may not have fought an actual medieval battle, Laurelen says, but he is truly practicing a martial art. The Knight-squire relationship has several real aspects, he announces, beyond the training in a martial art. A Knight should teach his squire things with a real world application. Chivalry, courtesy and the willingness and confidence to be on public view and open to both public criticism and admiration are steps toward full maturity that will carry over into the real world. Following through on duties to your Knight makes you a more responsible adult.

Alaric is eager to take Stephan as a squire tonight. Alaric had been a Boy Scout, like Finn, and a camp counselor several years ago. Teaching people is not going to be a problem. He has known Stephan for several years and was the one who talked him into fighting. They have already unofficially slipped into their roles. This makes it official.

Alaric fastens a red belt around Stephan's waist and gives him a quest to start his work toward Knighthood: Talk to at least 15 Ladies of the Rose—former Queens—and ask each of them what they consider the most important chivalric virtue and why. He must then find out which of today's Knights they believe most embodies that.

In return, Stephan offers a pledge. Before tonight's event, he roughly translated into the German language of his persona the same pledge that Alaric had made when he became a squire to Sir Theo. In halting German, he pledges before the crowd to uphold the five key points in the old French code of chivalry: fighting prowess, largesse, courtesy, humility and noble bearing.

"The end of the oath," Stephan later explains, "was to do it in my daily life, to make it part of me personally, not just act that way in my hobby."

As the event comes to a close, I pack up to head out. Even as it grows late, both Stephan and Alaric still carry out their roles. At the close of the feast, one of the kitchen workers called out a request for help with dishes. Since Stephan had just taken a vow of service, all heads turned his way and the crowd let out a bellowing beckon of "Stephan!" He had virtually no choice but to graciously head to the kitchen.

Off in another room, the post-dinner session of period dancing has started. A circle of people, mostly women, skip to the center of the circle and back out, tightening and widening it as the medieval music blares from a boom box. Very few men join the dance but Alaric has stepped in.

Milesent Vibert, the head of the barony's dance guild and sister of Lyonnete who authorized to fight today, says Alaric's Knight, Sir Theo, teaches all of his squires period dance.

"Even Laurelen has told young hopefuls, 'If you want to be a Knight, you're going to have to learn to dance.'"

With a shortage of men in the dance hall as usual, it matters not that Alaric's day started 12 hours ago setting up the list field. No matter that he fought all afternoon. No matter that he carted trays of feast around at dinner.

This is all part of the job. It is just part of *being* a Knight.

Valharic broods at the Pennsic War (left) after being passed over for knighthood. Duke Edmund (above) has a Saxon persona but his heraldry reflects a later period because of his previous persona. The "Big Belt Club" projects group (below): Logan, Hobbs, Flynn and Talon at the Cleftlands January event.

Brannos leads Darkyard's Legion to battle at the Pennsic War, follwed by the banners of House Darkyard and the Barony of Roaring Wastes.

Ragnvaldr (bottom left) and Brannos and Rebekah (bottom right) lead both House Darkyard and the Middle Kingdom.

Clockwise from top: Cleftlands Duke Laurelen Darksbane, Bastian Eychener, Squire Stephan von Lübeck and Sir Alaric le Fevre

Time Traveling Through T-Tunics:
Alina Meraud Bryte shows different styles of basic garb: Post-Roman Britain (top left), Byzantine (top right), Norse (bottom left), Anglo Saxon (bottom right.)

Clothing styles shifted after the Normans defeated
the Saxons in 1066 (above). In the 13th Century the
former Greek cyclas returned (right). The sideless
surcoat (below) came soon after.

Act I, scene 6
(Two) Arabian Nights

The crowd that packs the tiny firemen's hall in rural and remote Bellefonte, Penn., stares as the young dancer puts on a show of twisting and shimmying beneath the Bingo scoreboard nailed to the bare plywood walls.

Dozens of eyes scan up and down her body with each move, each arch of her back, each thrust of her hips. A few moves draw a chorus of whoops and hollers.

Kimberly Minardi, 24, just beams. Dances like this are her passion.

Today, smack in the center of Pennsylvania, in the shadow of Penn State University and amid acres of snowy woods and diners with signs that say "Welcome Hunters," an oasis appears. Minardi, known to this gathering as Narah bint Durr, is among al-gamat—"the community" in Arabic—a growing community of SCA members who choose to set their personas and pursuits in the ancient Middle East. Minardi/Narah has traveled here from Huntington, W. Va., to revel in re-creating traditional Middle Eastern dancing. Her dance moves—officially known as hip snaps and chest pops—are part of a long tradition of dance that is very different from the sleazy image that belly dancing has been stuck with. The cheers are a sign of admiration—not lust—from the other dancers that her fully-clothed, buttoned-down attempts are working.

Twice a year, more than 200 devotees journey to this rural community to celebrate the dance, music and food of the Middle East. They come in true nomad fashion, caravanning with friends from hundreds of miles away, loaded down with Persian rugs, exotic spices and fine silk clothing. For an afternoon, their costumes, music and spirit transform this tiny hall into an Arabian oasis from Appalachia, Mundania and the Eurocentric bias of the SCA.

This hafla—Arabic for party—is an extension of the nightly haflas at a Pennsic encampment called Orluk's Oasis. Started 11 years ago to gather Middle Eastern-inclined SCAdians around one campfire, the camp and its leader, Baron Durr al-jabal, a civil engineer mundanely known as Dale Walter, have served as a catalyst for a proliferation of Middle Eastern dance and music across the SCA. At night during war, musicians and dancers flock to the camp and play and dance in a sweaty, joyous frenzy until the wee hours, luring passers-by with layers of rhythm from a pack of drummers, the flash of bright costumes and scores of women—and men—in the throes of sensual dance. Year-round, they trade information on dance seminars and concert tours by Middle Eastern musicians and teach classes for newcomers in dance and drumming.

They also have their own battles to fight against three common enemies: Americans' knee-jerk dismissal of the Middle East as crazy, the SCA pinning everything to European history and the widespread belief that Middle Eastern dancing is little more than a T&A display.

"It's something we all create..."

Icy snow crystals nip my cheeks in the ripping, chill wind as I pull the door to the hall open. So much for the desert effect. Here in a western Pennsylvania January, we get blowing snow instead of blowing sand. The night before the hafla proper begins, many have already arrived for set-up and a henna party. This typical rural function hall, with light blue institutional floor tiles and plywood walls has huge Bingo boards reading, "Number Not Valid Until Called." Already, people have staked out floor space by spreading carpets and pillows along the walls and tacking rugs, huge bedspreads and tablecloths with Arabic and Indian designs on the walls. Toward the back, a dozen people, some in robes, some in T-shirts, sprawl on the floor painting designs on their hands and feet by squeezing a dark green puree from the corners of plastic bags like frosting. Photocopied patterns—spirals, florals and curlicues—are scattered on the floor with books like *Henna From Head to Toe* and *The Henna Body Art Book*.

Hobbs, who took the day off to make the drive, has traded in his armor today for a flowing tunic of peach silk and is painting designs on his hands. The stain will last several days and he relishes "freaking out my office" on Monday. His girlfriend Amanda, a dancer with a closet full of gorgeous tribal dance garb she bought off eBay, waits for her already-hennaed hands and feet to dry. The longer she lets the henna sit undisturbed, the darker and more pronounced the designs will become. Both she and Wanda, Talon's girlfriend who goes by Juana Ileana de la Cuenca in the SCA, hold their hands out, careful not to smear their handiwork. Wanda/Juana takes a cup of lemon juice and a Q-tip and begins dabbing it over the design. The juice is one of the tricks to make the henna dye darker and last longer. She can try to keep it warm, blow it dry or even wrap it with Saran Wrap to keep it from smudging overnight. Some people put sugar, rosewater or eucalyptus oil in the paste like alchemists. Another girl in the circle on the floor shows off the triangle designs she has painted on her feet and hands. She has cemented the henna with Nuskin, the skin glue designed to help cuts heal. It has become the latest and expensive rage among serious henna artists. Wanda sticks with lemon juice.

At the other end of the hall, a young woman named Genevieve de Loire, directs the half-dozen people who scurry in and out of the kitchen preparing 200 meat pies and 200 feta cheese and spinach pies for the next day. Genevieve, MKA Lynne Powell, trekked here from Arlington, Va., to cook the hafla feast. She has been in the SCA for about 10 years, but only found her niche as a cook in the last 18 months. As her name suggests, she had a European persona until delving into the Middle Eastern community two years ago. After serving as an apprentice under two excellent cooks in her home Kingdom of Atlantia, which covers much of the mid-Atlantic region, she prepared a local feast last year for 50 people. Now she's heading a large one.

A delivery of $1,000 in groceries came today and huge boxes of Pita Folds (120 to a box), 20-pound bags of couscous, and pouches of basmati rice, whole dried limes, mustard powder and coriander powder are stacked on tables. Already, Genevieve has prepared giant bowls of carrot dip, fava bean dip, a cucumber dip with mint and vinegar and plates of stuffed eggs.

In the kitchen, some of a 10-person, three-car caravan from Hamilton, Ontario, churns out meat pies in assembly-line fashion, dropping spoonfuls of spiced meat onto ready-made puff pastry, folding the pastry over and smearing it with olive oil. The pies are stacked in layers inside boxes awaiting cooking tomorrow.

"We come down every year for this," says Viscountess Moria Black, MKA Michelle Moll. "It is an overwhelming experience to be totally immersed in Middle Eastern culture with hundreds of people who feel the same. It's not the same as going to a restaurant or a festival because it's something we all create and participate in."

"Middle Eastern dance is my passion," adds a man on the other side of the counter. Stocky and of Jamaican heritage with bushy hair and a ponytail, Rob Galbraith, 34, is an editor at the *Toronto Sun*. With the paper scrapping to survive among bigger papers, the job means erratic hours, but Galbraith, known in this world as Valizan Rakkas Al Bassim Ra'ee al Saleh, or just Valizan for short, has made belly dancing his main activity outside of work.

"Some fighters will spend nine hours driving to go to events," he says. "I'm the same way. This woman from Chicago saw me dance at Pennsic and asked me to teach a class. So I got in my car, drove for nine hours overnight, slept for two hours and taught the class. And I had fun. I just like it. It's cool. It makes me feel good."

"The dancers all want a rhythm..."

By noon the next day a sea of rugs and pillows has packed the hall. Merchant tables line one wall and create a row down the middle of the hall. Textiles from India, Pakistan and Iran blanket a swath at least 15 feet wide the whole perimeter of the room, leaving only a few feet of walkway. More textiles cover the walls and block out the Bingo signs. Durr and Genevieve have set up a meze—finger-food—table with trays of pastries, triangles of pita to smother in dip, carafes of coffee and mint tea and a turkey stuffed with couscous, spices and sliced almonds. Huge brassy plates about a meter across lie off to the side to be used in the feast later. I bring some tea back to my pillows, ease to the ground and garb-gawk a while.

The hafla version of the T-tunic is a long, flowing robe tied with a sash around the waist. Sandals and a turban of rolled fabric wound and knotted together finish the basic package. I make do with a long pullover navy nightshirt that is close enough, to my eyes anyway, to the djellabas of Morocco. I had dressed with the other members of the SFU projects group back at the motel room we all rented. I had to have Amanda tie a turban for me because I don't know how. People here know, though. With the Middle East their primary focus in this Society, most surpass the just-get-by garb I have and have showpiece outfits in this style. Many of the women wear cholis, far more ornate and Indian-style sports bra clones with tight sleeves added on. Those are splashed with black, red and green embroidery and tiny oval mirrors. I see oversized coats with long earth-toned stripes over black and tan tunics. Several women have tight-fitting jackets buttoned only at the midsection, some of which are tight on the forearms while others open into wide, open sleeves. Belts with bright dangling tassles or coins are often beaded with cowrie shells. Turbans and caps are garnished with jewels, pendants and delicate chains. With the globs of henna now flaked off their hands and feet, the women have virtual tattoos of dark brown and red lines.

Musicians have gathered in a circle in the back. Several drummers have the SCA drum of choice, the dumbek, which is shaped like a mushroom with a flat top. Mass-produced by the Middle East Manufacturing Co. and a few other suppliers, merchants sell them by the hundreds at Pennsic and other large events, making the drums both revered and loathed. Aluminum drums with synthetic heads make virtually indestructible training models for novices that can withstand the weather swings of camping. Their cost and hardiness make it easy for anybody to buy and try out a drum. That's the good news. The bad news is that it is also easy for people with no rhythm to buy a drum. And they do. And they play. Loudly.

The tapping and thumping of drums at Pennsic makes a constant backdrop to nightlife, easy to find if you want it, impossible to avoid if you've tired of it. Many new drummers play at a volume that exceeds their skill level and repeat the few rhythms they know for hours. Over and over and over, driving neighbors crazy. The Orluk's crowd has a reputation as drum snobs for its approach that louder is not always better; that the interaction of drummer and dancer is key; that a stable base rhythm gives good drum players room to improvise in subtle ways.

This crowd of "drum snobs" treats the music and dance as a serious art form. But one drummer at Pennsic explained it a more hormonal way: "The dancers all want a rhythm they can dance to. If you give it to them, they will like it. They will come over and dance…" he said, pointing only a foot or two in front of his drum as a grin spread across his face, "…right here."

"Now that's not a bad way to spend an evening."

One woman sits within the circle with an oud, a string instrument with a bisected teardrop for a belly. Another puts what looks like a recorder aside and sets up a speaker for another stringed instrument that she later describes as a "pot bellied banjo." It is actually a cumbus, a Turkish instrument much like the oud, and Melissa Kacalanos has played it about a year. She has learned Middle Eastern music from her Greek father and can also play several wind instruments. The "recorder" is actually a mauixaphoon, which has finger holes like a recorder but uses a saxophone reed in the mouthpiece.

Kacalanos picks away at a long, meandering intro to the Turkish folk song "Bir Demet Yasemen"—"Bouquet of Jasmine"—and unwinds a series of twanging notes as the drummers quietly tap a simple rhythm called chiftitelli. They add fills to the basic rhythm and a handful of dancers snake their arms as the melody unfolds. Kacalanos sings the mournful Turkish lyrics in a deep voice. Translated, they read:

A bouquet of jasmine is the only reminder of my love
Our separation does not end; the pain of my heart does not go away
Yet my crying and my groans won't wash away bad fortune…"

When the song ends, I follow the oud player to learn a little about the instrument. I end up learning about dance as well. Rhianwen o Entys Disberod, MKA Linda Krecker-Schlered of Morristown, N.J., bought her oud three years ago for $350, but has been slow to learn songs, largely because she has no teacher. A precursor to the European lute, which in turn is a precursor to the guitar, the oud has five sets of double strings and an 11th single string.

"It adds a really unique sound," Rhianwen says as she hands the instrument to her friend Denis, another Orluk's regular. "If you play it next to a guitar, even if you're playing the same song, the sound is so much richer with the other strings."

Rhianwen is trying to learn a Turkish song called Ayezein—"Oh Beautiful"—and has Denis play it. I look at the lyrics in a songbook while Denis strums the tune: *"Oh beautiful, Oh beautiful, O most beautiful believer, Oh blossoming flower, Best among all the flower gardens."* She is grateful for a few pointers from Denis, which will have to last her several months until she sees him at another event.

On the dance floor, three women, two in cholis and one in a coat called a yelek, start swaying to the next song. One's arms ripple and flow in the air. The other two pop their hips out from side to side, in unison. Galbraith/Valizan, who helped with cooking the night before, joins them in baggy olive pants, no shirt and a short vest, standing on one foot and pointing with the toes of his other as he twists and waves a scarf like a boa.

Observers learn fast that dancing at Orluk's is not like the belly dancing they have seen before. The crowd at Orluk's and at this hafla shudders at the reputation that Middle Eastern dancing, often just called belly dancing, has among the general public. Though the general public sometimes regards belly dancing as harmless and a little silly—*I Dream of Jeannie* stuff—some view belly dancers as "Arabic strippers and prostitutes," as Narah put it with exasperation. SCA dancers separate themselves from the sleaze factor by dividing the field into two styles—cabaret and traditional. They avoid cabaret, which includes many modern styles in its mix and often becomes Las Vegas-style glitz and glitter. The costumes are exaggerated, if there's much of a costume at all. Traditional dancing is more historical, more of an art form. It is about grace, style and balance. The message is more sensual than sexual, of coy seduction, of suggestion and flirtation, not raunchiness. It is an attempt to re-create period court dances where excessive flaunting would have been considered rude.

Serious SCA dancers have their own little epithet for the sweet young things who flock to War every year, squeeze into halter tops or chainmail bikinis and a coin belt and bump and grind aimlessly by the campfires: "belly bunnies." To be a belly bunny because you're new and haven't learned yet is forgivable. Many of the best dancers have been there before. To know better and persist earns you icy stares.

Belly dancing, Rhianwen explains, has several basic moves that all beginning dancers learn. As they progress, they will piece the moves together in different orders, with different accents and speeds to create their own style. Beginners often start with five hip moves—lifting a hip, dropping a hip, making a circle with a hip and giving both a full shimmy. They can also make a figure-eight with their hips and do each of the same moves with their chest or shoulders. "It's the same thing on the top or the bottom," she says. There are also basic foot patterns, the undulation of arms sometimes called "snake arms" or "Persian arms" and moves in which the dancer lowers herself to her knees. Fluidity, balance, strength and poise all separate great dancers from mediocre ones. A novice will drop to the floor by first sinking to one knee, then dropping onto both knees. An expert will lower both knees simultaneously in one motion at whatever speed she chooses. The ability to isolate a particular move and do it perfectly also sets experts apart.

Rhianwen wants to see Middle Eastern dance better accepted within the SCA. She bristles at what she considers a lack of awards for Middle Eastern dancers and the routine complaints from European personas that the subject does not fit into the SCA or is not period.

"There was this lady who would not allow Middle Eastern dancers to come and dance in the hall they had rented for the barony dance classes," Rhianwen complains. "She said it was not period. She said, 'Prove to me it's period and I'll let you do it.' Specifically, she said, 'Prove to me it's period in Europe.'"

Dancers immediately posted on the internet message board created by Orluk's. Within days they presented the woman with evidence of Middle Eastern dance performances at European courts. The message board, of course highly non-period, has been amazing in creating a network of people with interest and knowledge in the subject. Their ability to share information has improved tremendously.

At the same time, it is difficult to prove what is period and what is not. Without videotapes and films of dance from period, dancers have to derive their costumes and moves from period descriptions and paintings, often painted miniatures. They also have to weed out accounts from Western travelers who embellish their tales to create a romanticized and often lurid picture of dancers and harems. Often, movements are based on a combination of today's belly dancing and the extrapolation of possible movements from the body position of women in paintings.

Minardi/Narah is working on an 11-page paper on dance she plans to enter in her kingdom's Arts and Sciences competition. Citing a series of books and studying several figurines, miniatures and paintings from period, she explains the origin of the dance from fertility cults and religious rites. Her paper traces its evolution and the blending of styles due to the migration of Romani culture (most commonly known as Gypsy) from India to the Middle East, central Asia and Spain. By studying Egyptian tomb drawings, prints of a painting on a ceiling in Palermo, Italy, and some 11th century drawings, she outlines how certain poses in the art suggest certain steps and spins.

The Dancing Daughter's Tale

Kimberly Minardi was just 17, a junior at Poca High School in suburban Charleston, W. Va., when her first belly dancing class moved her—both physically and emotionally.

The music and its rhythms instantly meant more to her than the grunge and hip-hop her classmates blasted from their car stereos. Even trying her first few moves was a spiritual experience that brought what she calls an "indescribable energy change." She bounded home, giddy to tell her parents about her discovery.

"I said, 'Dad, guess what I'm going to do?'" she remembers.

Dad, wondering just what his daughter was about to get into, shot her the stern look every teenage grand plan draws from parents. He asked in a tone of voice to match, "What?"

She paused. Even at that age, Minardi knew the reputation of belly dancing.

'Oh, nothing.' she said, having reconsidered. Then she just practiced behind his back.

"Every time I walked in front of a mirror I was practicing," she remembers. "It was instant obsession and it has only gotten to be more of an obsession. I dream about dance. I daydream about dance. If I'm not dancing, then it's likely I'm thinking about it."

As Minardi's dancing alter ego, Narah moves among a mass of other dancers at the hafla, the distinction between vulgarity and art becomes clear. Some of the dancers wear skimpy costumes. This hall has an ample supply of bare tummy and cleavage. But the dancers do not flaunt themselves, and Narah is proving that exposed flesh is no prerequisite to being a good dancer. Unless she added a ski mask to her costume, she could not be more covered.

While her arms unfold and weave through the air, her body remains perfectly poised and balanced. Each movement is precise as she lifts and lowers hips in turn, deliberately and often slowly, but always evenly and in total control. They all end with a sharp snap while still flowing easily into the next. The movement of a finger or turn of the wrist sends a delicate wave through her body until it ends at her hips. Watching her dance is as sensual an experience you can get without crossing the line into sexual.

"True, it started out as a fertility dance and naturally has movements which emphasize the hips and pelvis," Narah says. "Sex is part of the life cycle, and is a part of the earthy elements of this dance. However, lust is NOT."

"This dance is so natural to me, that I have to be reminded that other people may see it in a different light."

Her wedding last November was nearly a hafla in and of itself. Minardi skipped the whole white dress and train routine and went tribal. She put together a Rajasthani outfit with a 10-yard skirt, a choli and an embroidered Indian turban with silver and pearl jewelry. Her husband, who has a 15th-century German persona, wore his own garb and the couple rented the same hall in Huntington, W. Va., where their barony holds events. They danced to German medieval music and recordings of period hurdy-gurdy music performed by two well-known SCA musicians, drummer Kevin Hartnell of Cincinnati and hurdy-gurdy player Paul Ash, of New York City. Also performing was the Pittsburgh-based belly dance troupe Ghawazee, which draws many dancers and musicians from the SCA.

Her father, won over long ago, was proud.

"He tells people I'm a dancer and shows people pictures of my wedding now."

"Listening until you get it…"

When the song finishes, the musicians pick up the tempo and start banging away at a frenetic pace. In the middle sits Jeff Senn of Pittsburgh, the drummer for Ghawazee, the troupe that danced at Narah's wedding. Senn, known simply as Jas to the Orluk crew, joined the Society for Creative Anachronism in the mid-1980's. He describes himself then as a "typical goofy, geeky teenager who played D&D and didn't have a real defined social group." He tried fighting and some arts through the SCA but latched onto drumming at a Middle Eastern event in Pittsburgh about 10 years ago. He received a few drumming lessons from Baron Durr, today's host, but Middle Eastern personas were rarer then and he mostly sorted out his drumming by snapping up tapes and listening to others.

"I had no music background at all so it was kind of a challenge," explained Senn/Jas, 33, the chief of technology at a Pittsburgh product design firm. "But I'm naturally analytically minded. I picked it up in the folk music style: You just hang around listening until you get it."

Like the dancers, drummers have trouble researching period rhythms. Very little writing about drumming survives, Jas said, with almost none in English and even less in a form that can help him.

"When they wrote about things like music they didn't treat them technically. They were very descriptive, like 'He played the song and it was beautiful like leaves falling.' But they didn't break it down. It's a very oral tradition. People just do it. Finding sheet music is incredibly difficult because everyone just knows it."

Instead Jas dug up dance music tapes from the 1970s belly dancing fad and began listening. Surprisingly, much of the music was traditional despite the cheesy sexpot album covers. He has since written down dozens of rhythms in a notation others can understand. In the true spirit of techno-medieval anachronism, he built a web site that lists rhythms, has sound files and even a program for playing them on a Palm Pilot.

As the drumming starts, Valizan and Alixia Aurora Ariel, MKA Marley Kent of Sunnyvale, Calif., take sabers and balance them on their heads. They drop to their knees to the music, then lean back and forth, the swords balancing on the dull edge of the blade the entire time. Alixia has spent $350 of her Christmas bonus to fly here after Valizan talked her into coming. She has been dancing for 18 years as she bounced from Arkansas to the suburbs of San Jose. She picked up her mix of Persian, Turkish, Indian and North African styles from a string of teachers and colleagues. Now 39, she wears a North African style conch shell belt, an Egyptian style coat and an Afghani choker. And she has the sword dance down cold. Still keeping balance she shimmies her hips, then tosses them far out past the line of her body to each side. Then placing her hands on her hips, she slides her head from side to side without tilting and losing balance.

"Very nice," Valizan says. "I love the spin under the arm and the tuck and the twirl."

The Tale of the Manly Men

Valizan's first taste of Middle Eastern dancing came at Pennsic as he wandered the pathways between encampments at night, hearing the drums and eyeing the dancing in the flickering campfire lights.

"I thought I'd like to give it a try," he remembered. "Hey, I was far from home, knew nobody and had nothing to lose if I looked silly."

"Standing off to the side I tried to do what they were doing. A lady saw me and pulled me out for everyone to watch. I guess I didn't do too badly, because four hours later I was still there and very popular."

The next day he took a class at the War called "Middle Eastern Dancing for Manly Men." It was taught by a woman—a woman in drag, in men's Middle Eastern garb with a mustache painted on her upper lip. She used the men's dismissal of the dancing as girlish as a motivator, pushing them hard since none dared to back down in front of other guys in such a sissy endeavor.

Helping with that class was Viscountess Moria, who teaches local classes in Toronto. She persuaded Valizan to come to a few and his interest took off.

Also taking the classes was another novice, Ren Woodwarth, 33, of Hamilton, Ont., known in the SCA as Roak of Ealdormere. The two, Valizan said, engaged in a contest of one-upmanship in training, with sit-ups and exercises, each practicing moves that made both of them better.

It culminated at a Pennsic when both dueled in a courtship scene of a dance. Roak's character was trying to steal the girl away with dance. Valizan's would not let him.

"He and I one-upped each other in dance conflict, trying to impress the girl with our ability to isolate assorted bits. People cleared away to watch this piece. The drummers went the whole distance with us. People didn't realize we hadn't choreographed what we were doing. We were living in *that* moment."

Both Valizan and Roak were mobbed with congratulations after the dance. In Roak's case, his participation sent a message that dance is not just for sissies. Roak, a stick-jock, was one of the best fighters in the Kingdom. When Ealdormere was still just a principality of the Middle Kingdom, Roak twice won the principality's crown with his fighting. At this hafla he was the sitting Crown Prince, due to become King in four months.

Just as women dancers are often lumped in with strippers, male dancers have to battle the stereotype that they are gay, or at least a little swishy. The perception is so obvious that the "Manly Men" course description proclaims, "Yes, it is possible to appear manly while wiggling!" In fact, some are gay and many are not. And several, like Roak, are successful in more testosterone-laden pursuits. Valizan has seen the stereotype and is often bothered by it. But he thinks people who refuse to try miss out.

"North America seems to be the only place on the planet where a man dancing puts his masculinity in some kind of jeopardy," he said. "A lot of men change their minds when they see the reaction women have to men who can dance."

"Try to dance to this…"

Valizan pulls out his own sword, sets it on his head and begins strutting, leaning his body far out over bent knee with each step. He drops to his knees and leans forward and back. Alixia does the same and they step past each other still practically on their knees. The drummers play a basic rhythm that beginners learn on their first or second lesson. Called Ayoub, it simply alternates a big "Dum" bass note with an accent note "ka" and repeats, Dum ka Dum ka, Dum ka Dum ka. The dancers work to keep up with the driving beat, which is often used to boost the energy of a song or dance to its climax. The simplicity of the beat provides no relief for the dancers. It just gives the better drummers plenty of room to improvise "fills," the accents and counter beats between the beats of the main rhythm. Jas takes full advantage, ripping off machine gun fills between each "Dum." Valizan knows what Jas is doing: upping the ante, seeing if the dancers can keep up. He later translates Jas' rhythm message into words for me: "You think you're so hot? Let's see you try to dance to *this*." And he does. With each of Jas' finger-tapped flourishes, Valizan's feet and arms move faster until he is dripping with sweat and Jas is grinning. Tension builds as the two match each other.

Finally, the sword wobbles and Valizan snatches it. Point for Jas. Valizan now simply holds and twirls the sword until Jas catches him again and Valizan's footwork breaks with the rhythm. Jas has struck the killing blow. Mercifully the song ends.

Valizan bends over, hands on his knees as he sucks in air.

"That's why I drive six hours," he pants. "For that moment when the drummers and you are on the same wavelength. That's what it's about."

The Host's Tale

Durr parades up the aisle a few hours later, one of the great platters perched atop his head. He lowers it, then raises a hand. The crowd quiets.

He is in a plain robe, tied over an ample belly. His rumpled white hair and long, pointy white beard are perfect for his role as patriarch of this gathering. The guests have not seen much of Durr today. He has sometimes been up at the front door, sometimes manning the meze table, but he has not partaken of the dancing and drumming, even though he himself taught many of the drummers there. Instead, he explained to me, his role is to be host, to provide the hall and the food. It is his guests' duty to be entertaining.

Dale Walter's early SCA days gave little hint he would become a leader of this Society's Middle Eastern contingent. He joined the SCA in 1970 at the age of 14 as a science fiction junkie and Trekkie. The honor and chivalry appealed to him and he stuck with the SCA as he bounced from high school to high school across the country. By the late 1970s he spent his Navy shore leaves making helms and teaching people to fight. Since the SCA was still in its infancy, he was at times the only authorized fighter in a four-state region. He became a fight instructor and organizer of many local groups stretching from Charleston, S.C. to Myrtle Beach, N.C., to the suburbs of Detroit. As he did so, he churned his way through several personas. He started as a slaver.

"That was what we call today a Human Resources Director," he said, ending his quip, as he ends many of his sentences, with a chuckle. "Of course I was instructed very quickly that was an inappropriate persona to have."

He then went to "Frank the Friar" and "Brother Dexter" before becoming, as he puts it, a "Danish Merchant of Opportunity," better known as a Viking. He joked that he sometimes called himself "Munn the Dane." By 1976 or so, he was known as "Durr of Hidden Mountain." Around that time he became interested in the relationship between Vikings and Arabs and finally settled on an Andalusian persona in 1992. He made his persona skilled in architecture, particularly building fountains, to dovetail with his mundane career. Durr/Walter has degrees in electrical engineering and computer science from Penn State, has worked as a civil engineer and now works in information technology for a local firm.

He is now known as Durr al jabal al-mustarib.

"Al-mustarib," he explains, "means 'the guy who is mostly Arabic but not really.'"

Over the course of his SCA life, Durr has been the head—the "Khan"—of the Dark Horde, the Mongolian-based branch of the SCA. He ran a now-defunct landmark called the Pennsic Inn, and has served as aide de camp for several kings. He inherited the Middle Eastern contingent at Pennsic from David Korup, one of the SCA's drum gods. Durr is a major player in the SCA's Middle Eastern community in the east. In the west, the Kingdom known as The Outlands, which covers New Mexico and Colorado, has had the most influence. With many Outlands events held in the desert, a large portion of its members wear Middle Eastern clothing that fits the climate. The Outlands has produced some of the Society's major drumming forces. A drumming household called Rolling Thunder is based there and it is home to a drummer named Sylvanos, the Society's first-ever drumming Laurel. Sylvanos and David (pronounced da-VEED) are considered Johnny Appleseeds of drumming, leaving drums and new drummers in the wake of their travels from kingdom to kingdom. David and Sylvanos sell a drumming instruction CD they made together and David is well-known as the drummer of Turku, a band of SCA and mundane musicians that plays traditional music from Turkey and the Silk Road. For the last two years Turku has performed at Pennsic and drawn a giant crowd of dancers. David used to teach most drumming courses at Pennsic but gave most of them up to Durr several years ago.

Middle Eastern personas have taken off in the last few years to become an increasing part of the Society. For a while, though, the group struggled for respect, fighting with SCA leadership over space, class fees and their legitimacy in this Eurocentric group. It also must struggle against the hostility most Americans have against Islam.

On the eve of the first Gulf War in 1991, Durr remembers, a former King told him, "You know, being a towelhead right now is not a good idea."

"I said that's more of a reason to do it."

Looking back, he says, the Gulf War may have actually generated more interest in Middle Eastern culture. As we talk, September 11 is still eight months away and the invasion of Iraq even further off.

"The mundane media, I think, tried to play both angles. Over here is Saddam Hussein but over there are the people we are trying to help. This is their culture. It introduced a lot of people to the existence of these cultures."

Within the SCA, part of his persona is that he is the adoptive father of 12 dancer daughters, Narah included. That whole idea, he explains, chuckling at himself, has two stories behind it. The persona story draws on the Hadiz, the stories of the life of Mohammed. In one story, Mohammed says that if a man wishes to enter Paradise he should adopt three daughters. In that historical period, Durr explained, Mohammed was fighting the Meccans and there were lots of widows and orphans. Men were taking in sons, but not widows and orphan girls, so Mohammed started adopting the women.

"The whole concept of adopting daughters was to make sure they were provided for."

In today's Current Middle Ages the story is a little different. Durr says he made the adoptions part of his persona schtick a few years back after it became a little awkward to be the male head of a group of largely female dancers.

"People kept coming up and calling them my harem and my ladies, but they were just my friends. I figured I'd stop this nudge, nudge, wink, wink, thing and make them my daughters. I can give support to them, just like in the story, and it allows me to have a close relationship with a member of the opposite sex without any other overtones thrown in."

"They are in need of husbands..."

Tonight at the hafla, the host has some fatherly duties with one of his 12 adopted "daughters." Perhaps, Baron Durr warned me beforehand, he might even agree to give one away in marriage. But first, he has a few other matters to attend to. He stands at the head of the room and the crowd quiets.

"When the food is brought out you will see many wonderful things. Meanwhile, would you like to have a tale?"

He calls up a slight man with graying beard and moustache. Called Chengir, he is both a personal friend of Durr's and a regular storyteller at hafla and Orluk's Oasis, where his tales provide much-needed catch-your-breath breaks for the dancers and drummers. Brian Woodruff of Rochester, N.Y., has been telling Middle Eastern tales in the SCA for 15 years and has been developing his Chengir persona—a Norseman dropped into a 13th century Persian empire—for even longer. His persona even has its own voice. As the mundane Brian Woodruff, his voice is no Barry White but sounds as smooth as anyone's. As Chengir, it rises in pitch and rasp, and he all-but barks out a story for the hafla in short, punctuated bursts.

When he finishes, Durr and his assistants begin serving. It takes two people to balance the great trays from all the food. Dodging pillows and rug folds, they set the tray before us on stands.

In the center of the tray sits a foil platter, stuffed with rice and covered with flaky and peppery fish. Around the edges are heaps of lentils, chickpeas, salad and meats. To truly follow tradition, we would all just dig in with our hands—right hands only—and eat straight from the tray. But in mixed company and with the tray too wide for easy reaching, we scoop with spoons onto our own plates. Most eat with their spoons. Others pinch bites out of their bowls between pieces of pita or just between their fingers.

A half-dozen meatballs encircling a mound of cous cous disappears instantly and only scraps remain of the salad of spinach leaves, walnuts and mandarin orange slices. Big chunks of chicken stewed in coriander and cumin go great over the remaining cous cous, but the big hit is the heap of tiny cubes of eggplant, dusted in flour and fried until just crisp on the outside. On top of the pastries and dip earlier, the food has everyone overstuffed.

Durr claps his hands above his head at the front of the room.

"There are important things to be said."

"One of the themes of this hafla is romance and marriage," Durr continues. "I am the father of 12 jewels of my eye, my daughters who would come to me at this time."

Narah heads toward Durr with four of the other "daughters" who made it here this weekend as they all play along with being part of the same persona family. It is all just part of the game.

"They are so beautiful." Durr pauses. "So desirable…Yet they are in need of husbands. The number of suitors has been dwindling. This has been a cause of great concern because how else will my family increase?"

A man steps forward. He is about 40, wearing a coat over his flowing sleeves, two giant feathers rising out of his bulbous black turban.

"You know me," he announces.

Durr gives him the evil eye.

"I have seen you…hanging around," Durr snaps. "Behind the wall of the harem."

Durr waits for the laughter to die. "So, you have come before me?"

"So I have," the man says, stepping forward. "I want to express my suit for your daughter Ciera."

In this world, the man is Savatakh Tousai Bouse, the only son of a rich Mongol businessman. His family was among the invaders of Baghdad in the mid 1200s and he now hangs around the conquered city, aiding the occupation and increasing his family's fortune. Mundanely, he is John Alexander, a network security engineer from Washington, D.C.. Ciera is really Kathy Stroud, already his real-world wife of two years and a graduate student studying Geographic Information Systems at the University of Maryland. A persona wedding would make something fun to build another hafla around.

But despite Savatakh's business acumen, others have helped him with the dirty work of this proposal. Tradition dictates that a marriage is as much a business contract as a declaration of love. Ciera has no right to marry without her father's permission and Savatakh would never negotiate directly with Durr. It would be too easy for either to lose face. Savatakh has had his cousin negotiate this marriage over the last two years with Durr's representative, Chengir.

Durr explains to the crowd that it is customary for a marriage to be settled with a contract. When such contracts are signed, he says, all the men of the village gather as witnesses and the small boys run around as spies, checking to see if any of the men stand on one leg, cross their fingers or tie a knot during the signing. All of those actions would jinx the marriage and prevent it from being consummated.

"It is also part of the agreement that there should be dowry for the bride and dowry should there be a divorce—which today we call alimony."

Chengir takes the agreement and growls it out:

"In the name of Allah, the compassionate, the merciful, he who bestows all blessings, do we proclaim a celebration during the feast of al-hafla. Let it be known that in accordance with the Koran and the traditions of the prophet that the good Emir Durr al-jabal, father of many daughters and a good shepherd to all, agree to the most beloved and cherished daughter Ciera joining the family of Seti Savatakh Tousan Bouse. The agents of the bride and groom have met and agreed how the good character of the groom…"

At the words, "good character," Savatakh bows and mugs for the audience. "He is a character all right," someone shouts. Chengir continues:

"…may be determined. They find that the groom has shown himself to be generous, good-natured and well-versed in the codes and responsibilities of a husband. They swear before Allah and the whiskers of their beards that all has been done according to law with-out bribe, falsehood and deception."

"Do you find this acceptable?" the cousin asks Durr.

"I'm considering…" Durr hesitates.

"You have *twelve*," a daughter jumps in, admonishing. There is no need to be stingy.

"True," Durr says. He signs the agreement with a flourish. The wedding is sched-uled for November or December in Washington, D.C., the cousin announces.

"It should be splendid," the cousin says. "There will be much merry."

Savatakh steps forward to give Ciera a kiss.

"Not yet," Durr commands, stepping forward and putting his hand up. Savatakh retreats glumly as Ciera flashes him an exaggerated and sweet smile and bats her eye-lashes.

"I forgot to fix the hole in the garden wall," Durr laments.

Then he smiles and raises his index finger to a point. He stabs the air with it for emphasis as he gives a pronouncement that continues the party into the night.

"Let us now celebrate the signing of the agreement!"

Act I, scene 7
University

At the sound of the bell, students stream into the hallways of the Armory, an impressive Georgian brick building on the University of Maryland campus. Clutching notebooks and dangling bags from their arms, they bustle past the soda machines and school newspaper kiosks to their next class. As I join the crowd of eager students on this brisk February Saturday, I match room numbers with my schedule and ease into a painted cinder-block classroom. I pull out a pen and notebook as the instructor writes his name on the board.

Thomas Longshanks. Research Methods.

His long ponytail and wispy beard might have fooled me into thinking he was just another 1960's radical turned professor. But the name is a giveaway and the long green tunic with birds and leaves embroidered around the brown collar clinches it. I might be in a 20th century classroom but I am about to receive a lesson about another century altogether.

Today, this building at the University of Maryland has become the University of Atlantia, the SCA Kingdom covering Maryland, Virginia, North and South Carolina and part of Georgia. Twice a year, the Kingdom gathers its finest researchers, heralds, brewers and fight instructors along with its best leatherworkers, seamstresses, calligraphers and cooks for a one day college to pass on their collective knowledge to newcomers.

Informal lessons, like the ones I am receiving at the SFU projects sessions, are common across the Society. Teaching takes place every day in local barony and shire guild meetings that form the backbone of this hobby. Local experts teach a few classes at most weekend events. And major wars have extensive class schedules. But today I will see a more structured Kingdom "university" system that gathers a critical mass of teachers and students at one event and brings the best instructors from hundreds of miles away to solely increase knowledge of the Middle Ages.

"This, more so than any of the rest of what we do, is the purpose of the SCA," explains Lord Richard ffaukes, who holds the lofty title of "Chancellor" of this university. Over the course of the day, broken into five one-hour class sessions, students can pick from more than 70 classes ranging from "The History of the Celtic Church" to "Early Tudor Clothing" to "Lighting a Viking Home."

"This is where we really learn how people did it back then. If you do it informally, you might reach people around Washington but you won't reach someone in South Carolina," adds ffaukes, MKA Bobby Jones of Raleigh, N.C. "This way, we'll have a big university then someone will go back to their barony and they'll teach it at the local level."

Today is the Kingdom of Atlantia's 52nd university session. Atlantia has hosted two or three a year since 1971 and this Kingdom's system is one of the few so formalized it even offers degrees. At most SCA events, people sign up for classes only to reserve a seat. Here at Atlantia's university, you enroll for course credit. You even sign an attendance sheet in class. Students who complete 26 hours of classes receive a bachelors' degree. Instructors who teach at three separate universities are named "fellows" of the university. And the university awards masters' degrees to those who earn both a bachelors and a fellowship. Ffaukes recalls one student who took Atlantia's university so seriously he cited his degree on a graduate school application.

Meridies, the Kingdom covering much of the south, has a similar system of degrees. The Royal University of Meridies goes a step further, dividing its courses into different areas of study and requiring students to take core courses in each area to earn a degree. Transcript forms and teaching instruction are available online and the university typically draws about 200 people. In the Midrealm, my home territory, it is much less formal. Nobody keeps track of who takes what and there are no degrees.

Today in College Park, known in the Society as the Viking-laden Barony of Storvik, 320 gentles have stowed their winter coats and feast gear in a huge lecture hall and scattered to classes. I am about six weeks into my travels through the Society for Creative Anachronism's Known World and still worry how others will react to my costume. Though the Bored Housewife looks at medieval garb as "pretty clothes," it's still just funny clothes to me. Just like with my trip to the hafla, I do not have Cat for cover or moral support. She will be too tied up with her own mundane university pursuits until spring. I am on my own. I keep my garb hidden in a duffel bag for the 30-minute subway ride from Washington, D.C. much as I did for Twelfth Night. This time though, even without Cat's support, I am less worried about stares and jeers than the clothes drawing the attention of ghetto passengers looking for a target.

Arriving at the last minute, I stuff my jacket into my bag, pull out a tunic, and strap on a belt with my pouch and mug holder already attached. I am becoming a master of the quick change. Rather than haul boots around, I am slumming it in black high-top sneakers. At least I'm not in white tennis shoes. Today I have no agenda other than to sample a variety of classes and to make sure I meet Longshanks. I read his course description on the university's web site a few weeks ago and immediately targeted his class. In three days he will fly to Spain to study the original manuscripts of a 15th century Catalan cookbook he is trying to translate. How does somebody latch onto a project like that, I wonder? Why would somebody go to such extremes?

While waiting for his class, I enroll in a few morning session classes. One, on decorating garb, teaches me a few basics of embroidery and ways to paint designs on tunics using stencils as a shortcut. I also take a basic course in how to pick a period name for myself. I have been getting by with my mundane name, but I will need to choose a historical SCA name soon. I gather notes in class to ponder at a later date. From there, I sample a quirky little class called "Stupid Food Tricks: The Games Cooks Played." It has drawn more than a dozen SCA cooks, mostly veteran feast masters. Genevieve, who prepared the hafla feast just last week, is now back in her home territory and joins the class. It has also drawn a few curious and intrigued laymen, like myself, who can't help but wonder about a class that promises to teach "how to make two pigeons out of one, how to make a cooked stag look alive and the proper method for preparing 'The Holy Piglet, Roasted Inside Out.'"

"Everything but the squeal of the pig..."

"The time of the Middle Ages was a time of conspicuous consumption," explains the instructor, John Le Burguillun, MKA Les Shelton of Columbia, S.C., a planning and data analyst for the South Carolina Department of Health & Environmental Control. As both a Pelican and a cooking Laurel, he is one of Atlantia's better cooks.

Medieval feasts, Le Burguillun tells the class, were a way to show off wealth and often to glorify the host through extravagance.

"One of the more stupid legends of the Middle Ages was that food was heavily spiced because it was covering up the fact that the food was rancid," he says. "That's foolish. Rancid meat will kill you. If the meat was rancid, putting sugar and cinnamon on it won't change the fact that it was rancid."

Students interrupt with their snickers.

"Like you're going to kill a cow and let it sit there a week before you eat it," one scoffs.

"Oh, at least," adds another.

"They have no accounts of mass poisoning at feasts, like...'King Louis had a feast and half the people died,'" Le Burguillun continues. "It was conspicuous consumption. Spices were expensive. They showed off."

In addition to using spices, cooks were sometimes pushed to create foods as much for effect as for eating, foods he calls "illusion foods" or "spectacle foods."

"They had a lot of pageantry, a lot of spectacle," he continues. "A lot of it was very lavish and some of it was a little on the ridiculous side."

He passes out photocopies of translated period recipes to the class. As Le Burguillin gives an overview of some of the most outrageous items, we giggle over the absurdity of the recipes and the mindset that gave rise to them. The Holy Piglet, it turns out, is a pretty tame recipe in this company. It is simply a whole piglet split open, turned inside out then sewed shut with stuffing packed into the new insides made by the former outsides as it is grilled. We read an old English recipe for "Great Pies," struggling to grasp the size of a pan needed for a recipe that says: "Take capons, hens, mallards, coneys and parboil them clean; take woodcocks, teals and great birds and plump them in a boiling pot; and then put all this fowl in." The recipe then helpfully tells us to bake the pie "enough." No elaboration. Just "enough."

We read a recipe from 1395 Paris for meat jelly and feel queasy as it tells us that after chopping up and cooking a pig, calf's feet and two rabbits we should "take for the best plate the feet, snout and the ears."

"They ate everything but the squeal of the pig back then," Le Burguillun explains.

We learn that we can create a giant hardboiled egg by separating the whites and yolks from 30 or 40 normal eggs. The yolks can be cooked into one big ball of yolk in a small pig's bladder, then dropped into a larger bladder with the uncooked whites. When boiled in the bladder, the recipe tells us, "The whites of the eggs will boil around the big yolk, and there will be one big egg. You can serve it with a sauce of vinegar."

We also learn we can costume a roast peacock so that it looks like it is living and breathing fire by ramming rods through its legs to stand it up. The cook should then put a little ball of wool soaked in spirits in the beak and light it.

"In this way it will breathe fire for a long time," the recipe states." To make it more magnificent, you can cover the peacock with gold leaf and then cover it with its skin."

But of course. Why didn't I think of that?

We learn how to make a mock pitcher out of meat—a useable meatloaf pitcher that will actually hold liquid—and how to prepare "Eggs in Lent," the medieval equivalent of a Cadbury creme egg using almond milk. At this point, the class morphs into more of a discussion than a lecture. It is a pattern I soon find to be standard. Classes are filled with a range of students, some total newcomers, some novices and frequently experts on the subject. Sometimes the students even know more than the instructors.

Ffaukes said he does not verify the knowledge and accuracy of teachers. That is up to the class, which often will have experts sitting in just to test the teacher. If you want to move up in rank in this Society, you had better look good in front of the Peers. At some point in nearly every class, somebody asks for documentation on a key point. Instructors better have sources that back them up, or explain why they don't, or they risk losing face. Inventing an answer to cover for yourself is even worse. With experts around every corner, instructors know to teach what they know and no more. And when they don't know, to say something. Expertise in the ranks of students can sometimes be helpful. Instructors routinely admit they have been stymied on a point, only to have a student chime in with a solution or a source to check.

"There's a Laurel in every class just about," ffaukes said. "People aren't going to stand up in front of their peers—or in front of The Peers—if they don't know what they're doing. They're going to wait until they've learned enough that it's worthwhile."

In this classroom, the interaction stays in the spirit of sharing, even if only because the idea of using pig parts as pots has turned stomachs enough to suppress the combative edge. Today's students start sharing their own attempts at food tricks. The class hears of how other SCA members created "armored" chickens for feasts by using puff pastry as plate armor or cooked multiple birds as one by de-boning the smaller birds and stuffing them into the larger ones like matrushka dolls.

In another class today, a student becomes the hero when the instructor fails to show up for Mead Making 101. Student Jehan Yves Dechateau Thiery stepped up and taught the class the basics in making the honey-based alcoholic brew right off the top of his head. As the head of the Brewers, Vintners, Mazers and Cordialers Guild in the neighboring Barony of Lochmere (Anne Arundel County, Md.) Jehan Yves came stocked with a large supply of tupelo honey and maple mead to give out as samples. Students left raving about the mead, including one very influential one: Princess Mary-Grace of Gatland, MKA Nancy-Ellen Gatlin. At the feast later that night, after Jehan Yves makes a dash to his home to replenish his mead supply, she gives him a small award and vows to make him a Laurel if he can provide documentation of his research and methods.

Le Burguillun closes this class with a list of "Dishes you'll probably never see at an SCA event." We head off to lunch—or maybe not, after all—with visions of Pie of Cocks Combs with their Testicles and of Glazed Kids Heads with their Pluck (stomach, pancreas and guts) stuck in our heads. What timing. Maybe I'll just have some Pop-Tarts from the vending machine. We leave as ffaukes marches down the hall ringing a hand-held bell to mark the end of class.

"There's so many things…"

I wander down a main hallway, edging past several tables and shelves packed with books. The hallway has become a one-day medieval book fair, perfect for a medieval university. I browse titles like *The History of Underclothes*, the *Pirotechnia of Vannoccio Biringuccio: The Classic 16th Century Treatise on Metals and Metallurgy* and a collection of old brewers recipes called *A Sip Through Time*. As befits a Viking-style barony, a woman who calls herself the Viking Answer Lady shows examples of Viking clothing and artifacts and answers questions on Viking history at a table outside the main hall.

Inside the hall, a woman in Viking garb—a long tubular dress held up with large metal brooches—sits working on a loom of sorts. Moirin Fionn, MKA Maura Pfeifer of Takoma Park, Md., and her husband Lord Sylvanus Perin, MKA Brian Pfeifer, are active in the barony here with Perin helping to teach new fighters and Moirin serving as the arts and sciences minister. Today she has signed people up to attend the Kingdom's next coronation in April. She has attended several universities and last fall drove eight hours to Wilmington, N.C. for one. This morning, for a $24 materials fee, she has learned to make bobbin lace and she is spending her lunch hour winding thread along long wooden bobbins.

"There's so many things for me to learn and try," she says. "Where else can you take a class on bobbin lace in the morning and illumination in the afternoon? If I did that elsewhere it would cost me $150."

Some, though, do not want an overview of many different things. They want to know one aspect of history intimately. Thomas Longshanks, the man I want to meet today, has made it his personal quest to dig deeper and deeper, one level at a time, back to as primary a source as he can find about his chosen craft.

Mundanely known as Thomas McDonald, 39, of Richmond, Va., Longshanks is a graduate of Culver Military Academy, an Illinois prep school, and holds a Bachelor of Science from Virginia Commonwealth University. By day he works as the Business Analysis Manager for the City of Richmond Department of Public Utilities.

At night, he plops down on the family room couch, cracks open a giant binder and begins decoding medieval Catalan in an attempt to complete the first English translation of the *Libre de Sent Sovi*, a cookbook written by an anonymous author, he believes, in the 1300s.

It is also an attempt—one many other Society members can understand and perhaps look up to—to be a true scholar of the Middle Ages without the trappings and title of a university position to prop him up.

"I work with computers all day," he tells me. "I'm not a professor. I don't have a background in medieval history. I didn't even have a good background in medieval Spanish. But I intend to make it the best amateur effort I can. And I'm doing it...I don't know...because it's there. It's a chance to break new ground.

"It's an obscure little area, but if somebody doesn't beat me to it, I'm going to produce the first English translation of this cookbook."

The Translator's Tale

As Thomas Longshanks talks, his words are measured and controlled. Some people bubble as they talk about their hobby. Longshanks hides his passion behind an earnest but incredibly poised facade. I soon learn why: Librarians don't give out 500-year-old manuscripts to people who don't mean business. And sometimes it takes a lot of work to convince outsiders that you are not simply playing at history.

Being part of the Society for Creative Anachronism has been a double-edged sword in his pursuit of medieval knowledge. It opened many doors for him when he was learning basics. But the higher up the ladder of learning he went, the more it became an obstacle.

Longshanks started in the SCA 20 years ago, adopting the name Thomas Longshanks to keep his mundane first name and build a medieval name off his long legs. He spent most of his early years in the Society volunteering as a herald or as kitchen help. Over time he developed an expertise in brewing, in heraldry and in the cultivation and use of herbs both in cooking and in medieval medicine. His volunteer work earned him status as a Peer—a Pelican—and he concentrated more and more on cooking.

Then in 1984, a "little project" he took on turned into "what is basically a 17-year quest."

He was apprenticed to a Laurel, much the same way as fighters become squires to Knights. His Laurel had just received a coffee-table cookbook called *La Cocina Medieval* when she decided to test him on his earlier claims that he had studied medieval Spanish for three years in prep school. Just as a student of English history often reads Shakespeare for insight into his times, Longshanks had to read medieval Spanish in school to better understand early Spanish history.

His new assignment from his Laurel was to translate a recipe for "pollo armada"— "armored chicken"—from the cookbook. He finished the translation but did not stop digging. It took several steps of tracing the origin of *La Cocina Medieval* to bring him to his current quest.

The lineage of the recipes was a lesson in the ways information was recorded and passed down in previous centuries: *La Cocina Medieval* had copied the recipe from a

1529 cookbook called *Libro de Cozina*, which was no original work but a medieval Castillian translation of yet another cookbook—a Catalan cookbook called the *Libre del Coch*, dating back to about 1520.

Longshanks and his Laurel went even another step further back. With more research, he learned that many of the recipes in that book came from a medieval Catalan cookbook called the *Libre de Sent Sovi*.

"Our desire," he said, "was to push our knowledge of the cuisine as far back the timeline as we could get."

The two of them found that a professor, Dr. Rudolph Grewe, had published a critical edition of two copies of the book in 1979. As far as they knew, these two copies, one in Barcelona and one in Valencia, were the only copies in existence. The original, he believes, dates back to 1323 but is lost. The Barcelona manuscript—Barcelona MS 68—is the one he is using as his primary source and dates to around 1450.

He and I sit in the hallway as SCA students hurry between classes. He has already taught two classes today, but his energy for this topic is not flagging. He still considers every word carefully but he is starting to get a little excited about his progress.

He pulls out a binder and opens it up to pages of gothic script. All of the pages in the binder are photocopies, but Longshanks treats the bundle like gold, encasing each page in plastic sheets. I don't blame him. It took him 10 years to get this copy of the cookbook.

"This is an introduction here," he says, pointing at a bit of the script. "It says 1024. But look at this…"

He flips to another page that demonstrates the difficulty of determining the age of something. Despite the 1024 claim, other pages mention a King Fernando of Naples and to being a cook for an English king. Those references suggest that the original was written in the 1300s. Many of the foods in recipes also raise doubts about the 1024 date because they were not around in the 1000s, Longshanks explains. The author might have just exaggerated the age in his introduction.

"A certain amount of puffing certainly does occur in medieval books. It's sort of like slaying 10,000 on the battlefield."

He learned of a third surviving manuscript in 1995 when a short paper was published outlining a collection of four cookbooks in the Library of Catalunya. Catalunya MS 2112 seems to include an even older version of the *Libre de Sent Sovi*.

Longshanks tried to obtain a copy of the manuscripts from Spain but his attempts were futile.

"I spent 10 years writing letters to libraries in Spain and getting no response back. There is a bias against people from America. It is an obstacle you have to overcome.

"If you're talking to an English-speaking country, it is not too bad. Otherwise, you should try to deal with them in their language and show you are respectful of the material. You must also be specific and give them manuscript and folio numbers. It's only when they think that you know what you're talking about, that you get results."

His big break came when he ran across a used book dealer on the Internet with a shop south of Barcelona. The dealer, Dr. William Cole, is also a professor at the

University of Barcelona in literary iconography. He was sympathetic. He was Longshank's proverbial foot in the academic door.

"He talked to the librarians and got a copy for me—from a librarian who was doing it for him, not for me," Longshanks says

Since then he has been working on his translation using the photocopies. Although he understands medieval Spanish, the cookbook presents another challenge. It is not written simply in Spanish, but in Catalan, the dialect of northeastern Spain. The dialect has its own vocabulary and grammar and, as Longshanks puts it, "It's close enough to Spanish to throw you off." Luckily, unlike English which seems to change every day, Catalan has remained stable. For example, he said, there are 50 varieties of fish mentioned in the Barcelona manuscript. All of these fish have a counterpart with the same name still caught by fishermen in the area today. Otherwise, he muddles his way through.

"My experience is not Catalan. It's medieval gastronomy. But in working my way through the Catalan I'm using my years of studying medieval cuisine. If you look at these recipes and (compare them to) English recipes, they're similar. It's the same language—the language about food, the words are the same foods, the treatment is the same treatment, only in another nationality's language. Your challenge in translation is to keep the subtleties."

In *Libre de Sent Sovi*, several recipes tell the cook to "caress" a sauce or to stir a sauce "gently, gently." The distinction between that and "very gently," he said, is important to preserve.

"He chose the word for a reason. He could have said 'very gently' but he didn't. He said 'gently, gently.' 'Caress the sauce.' What a phrase. It conveys an attitude toward the food. There's a shading that could very easily be lost."

He is fairly sure the cookbook is a working book—not a monastic one—because it has no references to god. And it's not fancy: It has no illumination and the Valencia edition has ornamentation only for the first letter of each section. The Barcelona edition, which perhaps was never completed, leaves space for ornamentation that was never done. Ornamentation or no, the recipes themselves, he said, are special.

"The kinds of things that gotten written down back then were remarkable—worthy of remark—either remarkably good or remarkably bad, but rarely in between," he continues. "You don't find many recipes for toast or the medieval equivalent of a peanut butter and jelly sandwich. The *Sent Sovi* recipes are, in my opinion, remarkably good dishes that someone wanted to preserve, and very representative of dishes that would become known throughout medieval Europe. This was not the cuisine of the poor. Nor was it the everyday cuisine of the wealthy. These were special dishes someone wanted to remember and be able to reproduce from time to time."

"You can lose yourself in time..."

With about 70 percent of the book translated, Longshanks has started adapting the recipes into polished and useable ones. That involves testing and tasting. His favorites so far:

Limonea: a spit-roasted chicken with a sauce of almond milk, lemon juice, sugar, ginger, and saffron.

Salsa a bolets: pan-fried wild mushrooms with a sweet onion salsa.

Mató: sweetened fresh cheese curds with orange blossom water.

Porch ffresch ab mostaya nostrada: spit-roasted pork with sweet-hot mustard.

And, he adds, a poached monkfish with white garlic sauce.

He is still trying to translate the book's name. "Libre" means "book," but he is not sure what "Sovi" or "Sent" means in this context. The title could be something like "The Cookbook of Saint Sophie." Or "Sent" could mean 100 and "Sovi" could mean sauces and the title would be "The Cookbook of 100 Sauces."

At least, as he puts it, "I'm in good company" on this count. Others with scholarly credentials have also foundered on that rock. He has started correspondence with some of those experts and seems to have won some respect, but he fears that respect could vanish. When I ask if I can talk to these professors about his work he balks.

The SCA, he explains, sometimes has a poor reputation in the academic world. Documentation in the SCA world rarely reaches academic standards, and its culture of anachronisms falls well short of historical accuracy.

"None of these professors knows that I am in the SCA, and I would prefer that they not know until after they have had a chance to see the quality of my work," he explains. "The bottom line is that I don't want the poor academic reputation of the SCA to cause a knee-jerk rejection of my work, regardless of its quality, and I don't want to lose their cooperation."

Three days from now he will fly to Barcelona to see the manuscript in person. After years of dealing with photocopies, he finally has a chance to inspect the real thing. He is anxious to see the variations in color and pen strokes on the words he has trouble reading in the photocopy. The copying process has evened out some of the strokes. He is also excited to put his hands on it, amid the historical context of the city.

"I will be staying in a Gothic guest house, walking two blocks to a Gothic library building to study a 15th century manuscript, then walk along Roman walls surviving from the 4th century," he says.

"In my food I'm trying to help others taste history. Now I'm going to be immersed in it and that's exciting. In the SCA sometimes we talk about moments when things go real. We're all playing here, but for a moment you can lose yourself in time. I think I'll have that opportunity in Barcelona."

I turn irreverent for a moment.

"You said this is a working cookbook. Will you get to see food stains?"

His impossibly earnest facade cracks. His eyes flash a wild gleam and an impish grin escapes.

"I hope so," he gushes. "That would be really cool if I could."

Act I, scene 8
The Squire's Tragedy

Valharic has been scarce at the "Something For Us" armoring and sewing gatherings at Flynn's house the last couple of months. Since the entire Darkyard household met here in January, he has only popped in at the weekly meetings a few times, in between his jobs doing maintenance for a hotel chain and working at a grocery store. When he does come, he usually hurries home or in search of his wife after heated cell phone conversations.

Neither his marriage nor his wife's pregnancy are going well. Both he and his wife suspect each other of cheating. Valharic worries about the young man his wife hangs out with when he is at work. Then she creates a scene at a SFU meeting when a situation common in this insular subculture sets her on edge. Geek girls may be around to date the geek boys, but there are fewer of each. Running into ex's in this small community is unavoidable. Valharic once dated Amanda, the current girlfriend of the goateed newbie Hobbs. When Valharic comes to a SFU session and Amanda also comes with Hobbs, the wife's alarms go off.

Even Valharic's friends, who once felt he had been wronged at crown, are glad he did not win. Both for his sake and for the Kingdom's. This group that meets at Flynn's can shrug it off when Valharic's personal stresses spill over into informal work sessions. But being King and Queen right now would only add pressure. If his problems surfaced at an event, it would ruin the game for everyone.

Then Valharic's situation becomes even worse.

Several members of the projects group plan an all-night drive from Ohio to Mississippi for the giant Gulf Wars, the event that Omarad had raved about back at Twelfth Night for its use of arrows and siege weapons. As we sort out which of us can ride in Flynn's SUV and which need to make other arrangements, we get the news.

Valharic's wife has given birth to the twins. After only 20 weeks, they will not likely survive.

The entire Darkyard household shifts into family mode and the army mobilizes into a support network. Former roommate Ragnvaldr is on the road to Cleveland within hours after receiving a call. A few house members in Cleveland cook food for Valharic and his wife. Outside of Darkyard, other Society members flood the couple with well wishes. Even the wife of Valharic's mentor Finn, Countess Tamara diFirenze, treks up from Cincinnati to help out.

None can help with what matters most. Neither can the doctors. The boy, named Gabriel, dies just as we depart for Mississippi. The stronger girl, Paige—the one who had kicked at her brother in the womb—dies shortly after. Those of us heading to Gulf Wars miss the services but several Darkyard members come down from Detroit. The children are cremated in the standard modern fashion. But one of Valharic's household "brothers" memorializes the loss by heading into his workshop. Kynar Augustus, who had made probably the best-looking set of Roman armor in the house, takes on a project to honor Valharic and the children.

Centuries ago, Vikings used different ceremonies to honor their dead than we use today. If the deceased had real status, they would often use a ship in the ceremony. For many kings, the Vikings would load the body and immense wealth into a ship and bury it whole. Other times, they would put the bodies on a ship and set it both afloat and ablaze. This Society borrows from that tradition at the Pennsic War every year when attendees push a mock ship into a lake on the campsite and set it afire as a memorial to people they have lost.

In his workshop outside Detroit, Kynar will craft a model ship in Viking style. He makes one major style change by giving it a below-decks area instead of leaving it open at the top like many Norse vessels. He will top the ship with a sail embroidered with knotwork that approximates Viking designs.

"It was amazing the love and care he put into that," Valharic tells me when I return from Gulf Wars.

The ashes of the twins will rest inside the handmade urn of a ship. They will sit on display in Valharic's house.

Until things grow worse for him yet again.

Act I, scene 9
Gulf Wars

...Suppose within the girdle of these walls
Are now confined two mighty monarchies,
Whose high upreared and abutting fronts
The perilous narrow ocean parts asunder...

—Prologue to *Henry V*

A roar rises up from inside the fort.

"Ansteorra!" comes the cry of hundreds of armed and bloodthirsty fighters.

While the Kingdom of Ansteorra and its allies gird themselves inside the fort, the armies of the rival Kingdom of Trimaris and its own allies, spread out outside the gates, preparing to lay siege. For three days these two sides have fought several battles. Today they settle the war.

Behind the ranks of soldiers, archers haul boxes and barrels of arrows to the battle-field, then boxes of oversized arrows the size of harpoons to serve as bolts for ballistae, the medieval equivalent of rocket launchers. More than 30 of the chest-high versions of mounted and super-charged crossbows sit in menacing formation at the back of the battlefield. In a few moments they will fire bolts in an arc over the six-foot walls of the fort and onto the heads of the enemy. Archers already glare down from the fort's towers, arrows nocked and ready to fly in return fire.

Trimaris has two piles of wooden ramps and stepladders that sit ready for use in the assault. Once its archers and siege engines soften the defenders with the aerial barrage, troops will vault the walls with the ramps. Then the killing will really begin.

About 200 feet in front of the gate, the Trimarians have dragged the most powerful weapon on the field into position. The 1,700-pound Roman onager—an early form of catapult—is capable of hurling a rock 200 yards. Made of six-inch-square wooden posts and iron reinforcements, it is here to batter down the fort's gate.

The onager's operator, a bare-chested gladiator with scales of armor plates running down just one arm, barks at his crew to ready the weapon for battle. He climbs the beast as if it were a set of playground monkey bars, checking the tension of ropes and the sturdiness of the supports. It will take three shots at the door to take it down. They will need to act fast, before the enemy takes the weapon out.

"I don't care what else happens," Lorcun Attalus yells as the cheering of troops grows louder and louder in anticipation. "We need three shots. Let's get that door down."

I half expect Lorcun to turn to his crew, steely and resolute, and pull a *Gladiator* by saying, "At my signal, unleash hell."

"All right," he says instead. "Let's power it up."

As he turns a crank to set the level of rock-hurling tension, a yell comes up from atop the tower.

"Prepare for war. For honor and for glory. Lay on!"

A last giant roar thunders from each side and a flurry of missiles arcs into the air and over the castle walls.

The battle is on.

Dashed Expectations

"...Pierce out our imperfections with your thoughts..."
—Prologue to *Henry V*

The SFU contingent pulls into Lumberton, Miss., at 7 a.m. on a March Wednesday morning after an all-night blast south from Cleveland. The four of us packed into Flynn's DRKYRD SUV had a very mixed mood as we traded four-hour shifts behind the wheel for the 16-hour drive. Valharic was at the hospital and the twins still fighting for life when we lashed Flynn's two rattan spears to the roof after work the night before. Joining the trip is a woman named Bobbie, who normally sews at the SFU project meetings and is also an archer. Like Talon, Bobbie is a candidate for admission to Darkyard. She and I share the back seat while Flynn sits up front with his wife Erin. The dire situation with the dying babies might have been reason to stay home, but Erin carries a major reason to go. She is pregnant with a child of her own. The baby is due in September and she and Flynn have planned this trip as their last fun excursion before pregnancy becomes difficult.

Flynn is excited. He hopes to meet—to learn from and get some exposure with—the Kingdom's bigshots. Away from home, with a small contingent of Midrealmers, he won't be dwarfed by the sheer number and prowess of his house brothers. Being a member of Darkyard has its plusses and minuses. Simply wearing the household coat of arms and carrying the shield lends a mystique. But standing out from that crowd is tough. It is the classic small pond/big pond dilemma. Flynn has also wanted to see Gulf Wars for several years. The Pennsic War is the largest and grandest of all SCA events, but Gulf Wars is gaining fast. It may already be the Society for Creative Anachronism's premier fighting event. Started 10 years ago—just months after the real-life war that inspired its name—this war between the Kingdoms of the Gulf states has grown each year from a small camping event into a major war drawing about 5,000 people from as far away as California and, well, Cleveland. For me, this event will be a prime opportunity to see how others outside of my home kingdom play this game.

As we sped down I-59 through Hattiesburg just after dawn, downed trees and leafy branches were scattered along the side of the highway. Weather reports warned that we could have severe thunderstorms, a common problem for this region in March. Just before we left, I learned that high winds and even tornadoes have ripped through Mississippi, taking down trees and causing injuries. Even Brett Favre, the multi-millionaire quarterback of the Green Bay Packers had his house in Hattiesburg pulled apart by the storm. If the best house money can buy is destroyed by the weather here, what chance do all those nylon tents and canvas pavilions have?

Kings Arrow Ranch is a wooded campground tucked behind a lake—the "Loch," as the event map calls it—and a golf course where fighters needing a break from war engage in "Golf Wars." The "pine belt" of Mississippi looks different from the swamps I expected and Kings Arrow sits amid a patchy and sandy pine forest. I am grumpy from the long trip as we drive into the campground on a small road lined with painted wooden figures of knights, barbarians, kings and queens.

I grimace.

Medieval-themed lawn ornaments belong in a Cub Scout fair. I better not have driven 15 hours for Kitsch Wars.

The Troll area of "rustic" (to be polite) shacks with a bunch of cars parked around them isn't much better. But I pay my $30 for my site token—a metal medallion engraved with a horseman—that is my pass for the campground. I am entrant number 4,049.

It takes about two hours for the SCA's time warp illusion to kick in. I still wear the Dockers and fleece jacket I left Cleveland in, not medieval garb. I still notice the cars here more than the period items. For four days we will live in a nylon Coleman tent. Its green and tan earth colors blend into the woods, but it still looks nothing like a medieval tent. The yellow, red and blue domes mushrooming across the site are worse.

It takes a few hours for my bad mood to subside, for the garb, the people, and the events to gradually pull me along. But eventually, my eyes start skipping over the modern tents, dismissing them as irrelevant background, while I focus on the more medieval items. I start noticing the medieval-style pavilions, the giant white canvas tents with scalloped and dagged edges that look like they belong in the Middle Ages. Cars lingering on the site fade into the background. The color of the period-style items—the wonderfully carved campsite gates, the perfect and brilliant banners, the light of torches at night—takes over. I stop caring that the "swords" are duct-taped clubs and that they go "Thump!" instead of "Clang!" That shift of mindset is crucial for anyone pursuing this hobby. There will always be anachronisms. Members need to see the full half of the glass rather than the empty half. If that moment never happens, if you can't suspend disbelief just a little, you go home and dismiss the Society for Creative Anachronism as a waste of time.

One of Gulf Wars' main draws is its fort. None of the other major SCA events (until Pennsic later this year) has anything close to it, largely because the Society for Creative Anachronism owns no property and must rent sites. Dirt mounds, safety tape or hay bales become bridges, mountain passes and castle gates. The only exceptions are in the

SCA Kingdom of Drachenwald in Europe, which uses real castles a couple of times a year, and a few U.S. sites that have model castles or forts.

Gulf Wars' fort was built by the Hattiesburg, Miss., group known as the Shire of Dragoun's Weal with the help and blessing of Kings Arrow owner Larry Stanford. The fort has a wide gate and doorway, with a walkway and two towers above. The wooden walls to each side have crenellations—alternating high and low sections—to hide behind and fight through. I have heard so much about this fort that it would take a virtual castle to live up to expectations. When I spot it on the campground, it looks more like a fence with turrets. But as fighters approach the "castle" to practice, the scale begins to make sense. It is, as several war veterans describe it, "playable." The walls are high enough to make climbing over them a challenge, but low enough for fighters to thrust spears over the top. Any bigger would likely add danger without adding much more fun.

Don't consider it a castle, someone suggested later. Look at it as a fortified camp.

More importantly, I reminded myself, don't expect perfection. Volunteers, or people paid on a short-term basis, do everything in the Society for Creative Anachronism. The SCA as a corporation lacks the cash, staff or the proactive mindset to build the same kind of strongholds a real medieval monarch (with the plunder of war and thousands of peasants to tax) could construct. Big improvements come only when a group of people set their mind to doing it on their own. Not for profit. Just for the sake of it.

I trudge down a dirt campground road looking for a class on how to spin fiber into thread. I want to see the campsite hosting the class, the most authentic medieval camp at this war, before I return to watch the fighting around the castle. The forest around the road thins and "Queen's Highway" dead-ends in a nasty tangle of brush. A giant wooden gate with Norse runes carved into the poles announces a campsite. This must be the place.

"I do want to do one period..."

"We want to depict a pre-1066 camp," explains Master Erik of Telemark as he guides me through this camp of canvas tents. "Some of us are Viking. Some of us are Norman-Saxon. But we all want to experience the same thing across a weekend or a week."

Master Erik then touches on a goal that is almost universal in this world, regardless of exact time, place or pursuit.

"There's a major point in a camp where you look up to find you've lost the 20th century," he tells me. "That's what we're going for."

It is the same effect that cookbook translator Thomas Longshanks hoped to experience in Barcelona, that seamstresses seek with their authentic garb projects and fighters strive for when they carefully craft their armor and garb. Everyone takes a different route, but they all seek the same thing: to not have to suspend their disbelief, to see the glass as completely full for a moment, to really believe they are in the Middle Ages, if only for an instant.

Erik leads me about while his wife helps with the spinning class. Several women gather in a circle feeding wool onto drop spindles. The spindles are basically dowels that impale wooden discs at the bottom. They spin like tops as the women feed and pinch rough wool into threads that spiral around the spindles. Smoke wafts through the site from a smoldering fire pit as I hear clanging off to the side. The group has built a permanent blacksmith shop in the camp and assistants are pumping bellows while the smiths pound away.

"We're trying to get everything in camp period," explains Erik, MKA Ed Kreyling, 46, a software quality control engineer from Jackson, Miss.

This site takes the idea of primitive camping to a new level. There are no mundane tents, at least not in its main area. Instead, everyone camps in "wedge-style" tents of cloth stretched between A-shaped wooden supports. Across the camp, fires burn in small pits or above ground in iron pans supported by iron legs and chains. There are no mundane chairs, only wooden ones made by intersecting two planks. Aside from items brought in by the women taking the spinning class, I see almost nothing mundane. No soda cans. No wrappers. No mundane clothes or coolers.

"We're getting rid of modern chairs," Master Eric says, pulling back a layer of black sheepskin to reveal a plastic chair beneath. "If we can't get rid of a chair, we'll cover it with a fur."

"Or burn it!" shouts a passing campmate.

The camp is named "Bastarmark"—a combination of the names of the three households that joined to make it: the Bastarnae, Clan Prechain and Eric's group, Telemark. Named after a region of southern Norway, Telemark is made up of Viking personas set in the years 700 to 900 and is an arts household far more than a fighting one. The other two households are also set in the pre-1066 Dark Ages, which SCAdians usually just call "early period." Artists from the households have carved the name "Bastarmark" into their gate in an ancient Norse alphabet unofficially called "Futhark," after the "word" spelled by the first several letters of the alphabet.

Last year the group built a small house at this campsite for Erik and his wife using the basic design Vikings used at an althing, the giant clan meetings where they set laws and settled disputes. The households built a shack to enclose and protect the blacksmith shop they now call The Rusty Anvil Forge. This year they are building Kildonon Hall, a long house named for the man who will spend almost his entire Gulf Wars building it.

Brian Kildonon, MKA Bryan Moneyhun of Knoxville, Tenn., steps from under a particleboard roof on this longhouse-in-progress as Erik leads me over. This 5th to 6th century Celt, usually called "Mad Dog" by his friends, is scrawny and nearly as thin as his stringy hair. But twelve years of framing houses and five of roofing them before he became a "pixel pusher" behind a desk have made him wiry. They also taught him a trick or two about building.

The particleboard on the roof of this rectangular lodge, he hisses, is a waste. He does not need it. It costs time and money. And most of all, he says, it's not how they did it back then.

"That's just decking because a lot of people said it's going to leak," he says, almost apologizing. "I'm appeasing the people who think they'll have a wet butt."

Kildonon plans to thatch the roof in a manner much closer to authentic by taking hay bales, twisting them into bundles and nailing them to the roof. This is the part his campmates don't believe will hold.

"They insisted it will leak," he mutters. "No it won't. It will do just fine, but they have no faith. The next one, we'll do a thatched roof and they'll see."

The "next one"—if it ever comes about—will be the one that satisfies "Mad Dog's" main goal of doing something really, truly, 100% authentic.

"I do want to do one period, with period stuff," continues Kildonon, 45, the father of three adult children. "Even before joining the SCA I liked how people used to do it before they had Home Depot to go to, before they had contractors, before they had building permits. It's a challenge."

This long hall will be a start. It will be a meeting house, he says, much like the kind made famous in Viking movies. Kildonon read several books on the Vikings to study pictures before deciding to build the house 16 feet by 32 feet. That way the camp could buy wood and supplies in standard sizes. At this size, he guesses, the hall will seat 50 to 60 people for dinner and sleep about 20, "depending on how cozy we get."

"This will give us a focal point—a place where we can show off our stuff," Kildonon explains, just before I head back to the castle. "We can hold classes here, maybe inspire folks to build stuff in their camps that will be just as cool."

"I didn't even notice..."

At the fort, the crowd that has just finished a practice battle disperses in groups, chattering about their exploits on the field. Though Gulf Wars is a war between the Kingdom of Trimaris (Florida) and the Kingdom of Ansteorra (Texas and Oklahoma) and hosted by the Kingdom of Meridies, the kingdom covering a wide part of the south, a few unofficial battles before the real war mix up the sides. A few fighters stay behind and spar after today's practice.

At the edge of the field, two fighters duel. One fights without a shield, flashing his sword hand at lightning speed. He holds a crutch with the other. The bottom half of his right leg is missing, ending in a nub at the knee.

A white belt of Knighthood holds his Ansteorran tabard, with its black six-pointed star on a yellow field, in place. A figure of a lion is superimposed over the star. The fight takes only seconds before he reaches over his opponent's shield to hit him on the wrist. The puzzled opponent cannot figure out how the blow snuck through.

"I'm left-handed," the Ansteorran Knight blurts out. His opponent blushes and an "oh, duh" look crosses his face.

"I didn't even notice," he says embarrassed.

Apparently when your opponent comes you with just one leg, you can overlook little things like which hand he's trying to kill you with.

But Sir Kief av Kierstad does not need surprise to hold his own on the field. Sir Kief did not receive his coveted white belt through some chivalric affirmative action program. He got it the very, very, very old-fashioned way. He earned it. Three times he has advanced to quarterfinals of the Kingdom of Ansteorra Crown Tournament. One of those times, he was the only fighter to land a blow on the Society-wide legend Duke Inman MacMoore, as Inman breezed otherwise untouched to crown. Balancing himself with his right arm on his crutch while he fights, Sir Kief's left hand is fast enough to block blows and throw more than a few as well.

"With two good arms and two good legs all you people would be in trouble," he says, grinning out from under his helm.

Before gaining confidence in his style of fighting, he tried to compensate for not being able to use a shield—"Boy howdy is that a disadvantage," the native Texan says— by using an "SCA legal" crutch made of steel and rattan. Unsuspecting opponents would focus on his sword and then…wham! They would take a shot from his crutch. But Kief shelved his crutch weapon soon after when he rejected it as "kind of a trick thing."

Such tricks do not fit into his concept of honor and chivalry, the very values that convinced the mundane Lee Cockerham to leave a motorcycle gang for this world 17 years ago.

The Tale of a Lion of Ansteorra

In between hunting deer and squirrel as a child in eastern Texas, Lee Cockerham, now 48 and a resident of Huntsville, Texas, used to "haunt the bookmobiles" for adventure stories about the old west and Vikings. He loved the Viking sense of adventure and exploration, as well as their rowdiness of sacking and pillaging. He would have made a perfect recruit for the Society for Creative Anachronism, but even after graduating high school in 1971, he had never heard of the SCA.

"I was involved in a completely different world," he says.

In 1973 he joined a Harley-Davidson motorcycle club. He refuses to say which one. It is a part of his past he does not share details about. But he admits his main sport became "brawling." The club's camaraderie and adventure hooked him for 10 years and he stayed with the group while he served as an Air Force radar specialist in Panama City, Fla.

"It was like my fascination with the Vikings. We had freedom. We traveled. I had lots of other men to hang with and see how much trouble we can get into and get out of," Kief/Cockerham said. "It's the modern day equivalent of how I think of the Viking culture."

In 1978, his life changed when his club attended the National Harley Drags to watch one of its members race. As Cockerham rode out of the site with friends, another group of bikers came the wrong way on the one-way road. Four motorcycles with six riders hit head-on. Two people died and Cockerham was thrown from his cycle. His right arm was smashed and ripped, as he puts it, into "hamburger." He could not feel his legs.

"When I woke up I was laying face down on the ground. Bones were sticking out everywhere."

He spent nine months in the hospital. Although doctors tried to save his right leg, they had to cut it off at the knee a few months after the crash. The biker community was there to support him—collecting his belongings after the accident and getting word to his friends and family. And they were there for him as he recovered.

But over the next several years he became disillusioned. Some of the bikers remain his best friends but others were murdered or died of other causes. He also started to have ethical issues with the "lying and backstabbing" within the group. He quit and resumed college at Sam Houston State. In 1984 he saw the Society for Creative Anachronism do a demo on campus and the Current Middle Ages gave him a new stage to brawl on. This Society offered camaraderie like his biker club, but also had a real sense of chivalry his previous life lacked.

"Everyone I met had the same code they lived by. It was different from the rest of society."

Within a week he was attending fighter practice. He developed his persona as a member of the Varangian Guard, the group of Vikings that became elite guards of the emperors of Constantinople. Varangian Guardsmen, I soon notice on my journey, make up a far greater percentage of the SCA than they ever did in history. They are a popular choice for those who can't choose just one culture to set their persona in. The Varangians were one of the rare historical mixes of two very distinct cultures, combining both the Norse and Byzantine worlds. Cockerham's adopted name of Kief is an old Danish name meaning "stout" or "valiant" and "Kierstad" means "village by the marsh." He chose it because the lower 10 acres of his 17-acre wooded property outside of Huntsville is creek bottom.

He survives on government disability payments, by making and selling armor, shooting and selling nature photographs and working as a tattoo artist. He and several other SCA members with art backgrounds work out of a shop called Mystic Marks in San Marcus, Tex., south of Austin.

Because Ansteorra, like many other kingdoms in the SCA, requires fighters to start fighting using both a sword and a shield, Kief had to learn to fight with a sword in one hand and a shield in the other. He had no crutch to help, and he never used a prosthesis because it would slow him down. He eventually settled on his own single-sword style using the crutch that he calls a "shoulder forward, sword-forward saber style."

Kief was surprised when he became a Knight on a 1991 trip to Pennsic and totally stunned in 1989 when then-King Gerard and Queen Vanessa named him a Lion of Ansteorra—a special honor for people the royals believe best embody the ideals of the

SCA and the Kingdom. Royalty can select only one person per six-month reign to become a Lion.

"My ego will speak for me for just a moment," he says, chuckling a little. "People say I have an ego the size of, well, Texas. But I think the accident has prevented me from being crowned. I don't have the mobility a lot of folks have. It prevented me from doing an awful lot.

"But I may not have ever found the SCA if it didn't happen. It was one of those very strange happenstance things. And if I joined with all my limbs intact I might not have found the challenge that I did."

A war with one enemy

I wander off into the market area, a series of neat rows of open-faced tents packed with swords, hilts, shields, garb and trinkets. In this marketplace I can buy an amber necklace, tankards engraved with knotwork, heavy cloaks, full sides of leather and the ever-present dumbeks. Several armorers have set up shops offering fighting gear, from leather armor to steel plate. At least a dozen garb shops hawk dresses, tunics, bodices and doublets.

With guidance from Flynn and another Darkyard fighter here, known as Sulla, I will buy a long pole of rattan and a few basket hilts that I can convert into swords for Cat and I. The blisters that terrible footwear have ripped into my feet convince me to spend more than $30 on a new pair of boots. Shoes and hair, one of the Midrealm's Knights will later tell me, are the ultimate gauges of someone's commitment to authenticity. Almost nobody cares enough to change their hair, unless they can easily change it back when they get home. Shoes get even less attention. Many fighters take the field in their sneakers or combat boots. To avoid wearing sneakers, I had bought a pair of black boots at a thrift store. But the black biker boots are not much better than sneakers. Most of Darkyard's fighters buy pairs of used, lace-less and strap-less old East German army boots. The plain black boots I find go halfway up my calf, stand out less than my biker boots and, most importantly, stop gouging bloody holes in my toes.

At this moment, though, I am in search of a simple hat. The rain has started, and I am fast becoming drenched. The T-shirts for sale here read, "Gulf Wars: The War with No Enemies." But the shirts are wrong. Gulf Wars has one big enemy: weather. Any outdoor camping event endures weather hazards, but Gulf Wars has had more than its share. Gulf Wars veterans tell stories about floods, of thunderstorms, of lightning strikes and even tornadoes.

I head for the nearby dining hall in search of something warm to eat or drink. Although many camps arrange meals for their whole group at their campsites, Kings Arrow opens a dining hall during war that offers full meals three times a day. Shivering, I sit down. The hall has a giant anachronism, a big-screen television tuned to the Weather Channel. I watch the satellite images of giant clouds moving eastward across the Gulf. There is a tornado watch in effect tonight for much of Louisiana and southwest Mississippi, but not the New Orleans area. We might get clobbered by the storm. Or maybe not.

It hits that evening.

Wind and rain pound the outside of the tent where the four of us from Cleveland huddle for shelter. Lightning flashes light up the campground every few moments. They are close. Very close. A trickle comes in through the door. A second trickle starts at my end of the tent, but I ignore it. We're all too tired from the overnight drive. Hopefully it won't puddle and soak my sleeping bag. I am exhausted and cold. Sleep comes quickly, even as I wonder whether that stream bed two feet from my head will hold the runoff.

Let's Get Ready to Melee

Take heed how you impawn our person
How you awake our sleeping god of war...

—Act I, Scene ii, *Henry V*

The storm has moved on without inflicting too much damage by morning. The weather is bright, warm and near perfect when the royal leaders of the Known World ride onto the battlefield on horseback to declare their grievances and pick sides. The days of peace at Kings Arrow Ranch end now.

Several hundred subjects crowd the edge of the battlefield as Ailgheanan, the King of the host kingdom Meridies, rides in atop his horse with his Queen and a pack of royal greyhounds parading in front. Announced as the Shah and Sultana of Meridies because the Queen, Ilissa, has a Middle Eastern persona, they are surrounded by a swarm of animal handlers. Their attendants all wear black and white tunics or tabards displaying the Kingdom's arms, a crown with three stars above it. They march across the field and take their place by the gates of the fort. Gulf Wars is one of the few events in this Society that uses horses. Though the Society does not allow horses in battle, it does have competitions for riders to strike targets. This war also has a parade later in the week to show off barding—the heraldic garb of the horses. Today, the horses just add to the opening ceremony.

A barrel of a man in flowing sleeves and a hat bursting with plumage steps to the edge of the field. Modius von Mergenthein, an accomplished bard and officer of the Society, announces the King and Queen of the Kingdom of Ansteorra in a voice matching his size and reputation.

"Some battles are fought by men-at-arms," he bellows across the field. "Others by heroes. Today Olympus opens its stellar gates and out stride gods."

As the Ansteorran King and Queen ride in amid a flood of yellow uniforms with the black Kingdom star in the center, this 16th century Vince McMahon pours on the hype:

"At the head of the host of Olympus, rides Jason, the wrath of the sable star of Ansteorra. Beside him rides Aphrodite incarnate, his radiant Queen Saereid. Assembled warriors, do not flee in fear. For only then will you draw the gaze of the gods of Ansteorra. You are only allowed to tremble in complete and utter humiliation."

The mere lowly mortals who rule the Kingdom of Trimaris, Mittion von Weald and Dulcia MacPherson, are introduced next by their outmatched herald only as "Defenders of the swamps of Trimaris and protectors of the highlands and the lowlands." They just chuckle instead of trembling, though, as they ride across the field on horses bedecked in the Kingdom's blue and white symbol, three hook-shaped waves radiating from a center point.

"Vivat, Trimaris!" the herald calls. The populace of that Kingdom joins this equivalent of "Long Live!" on the "Trimaris" part.

"Vivat, Trimaris!"

"Vivat, Trimaris!"

One by one, the other kingdoms march out: Atlantia in blue and yellow with giant yellow seahorses on the barding; the Middle in red and white with green dragons; Calontir, which covers Missouri, Kansas, Iowa, Nebraska and northern Arkansas, in bright purple and yellow; Ealdormere, out of Canada, singing as its entourage comes.

After a brief introduction from Meridies' King, Trimaris' outdone herald, Baron Maredudd ap Cynan, takes the field. By most standards, his declaration of war is a grand and inspiring one. Normally, it would pose a serious threat to Ansteorra's King and Queen.

"Take warning from this wise counsel and touch not Trimaris! You have broken, between our two realms, the peace over which we, by right of arms and rule of wisdom, do command," he shouts. Trimaris must "proceed with due rigor against such presumptuous and criminal audacity."

"Blood will be drawn," Maredudd continues, and "bones will be crushed" if Ansteorra does not withdraw.

As he finishes, a shout of "Vivat!" comes from the crowd.

The shouter is quickly hushed.

Modius stomps to the center of the field, tears his hat from his head and flings it to the earth.

"You have heard the dronings of a feeble infant trying to incite the wrath of the heavens." Modius' voice rises with passion as he spits out the words angrily, shifting into human megaphone mode. "It has succeeded.

"Now does our purpose become grim, and our resolve steely, for before us stands..." Modius pauses before his voice turns icy and he growls. "...the adversary.

"We see that the upstart sons of lowly Neptune have crawled forth from their barren and desolate spit of land...to vainly try to block our path. Yet know that mighty Zeus.shall cast his fiery spear into Neptune's weak, watery rank and send him home in abject supplication."

Modius is in a frenzy, turning red, over-enunciating words as he shifts into herald overdrive.

"So say we Jason.

"So say we Saereid

"So say we An-ste-oooor-ra!"

Sucking in a breath, he snatches up his hat, clasps it to his chest, bows with a flourish and strides from the field. The score after Round One of this SCA Herald Smackdown: Ansteorra 1, Trimaris 0.

The royals of the other kingdoms ride one by one to the center and declare their sides. The East, which has enjoyed the alliance of Ansteorra at many Pennsics, declares for Ansteorra. "We do not forget these allies," King Andreas Eisfalke, MKA Andre Sinou of Toms River, N.J., proclaims. "This day we declare as allies and forever our brothers, Ansteorra." Andreas is joined by his Queen, the very Isabella of Elizabethan garb fame, who has somehow managed to sit atop a horse in a giant skirt fitting her period.

Edmund aligns the Midrealm with Trimaris. Aethelmearc, the Kingdom that hosts Pennsic, sides with Trimaris, as does Atlantia. The Kingdoms of Calontir and Ealdormere side with Ansteorra.

Ailgheanan, the King of Meridies, the Switzerland between the Axis and the Allies, steps up.

"We have heard the declarations and find we are at a crossroads," he says. Since the sides have declared more or less evenly, he offers to count the men on each side, then split his own up to make the battles even.

The crowd applauds the sportsmanship as he faces the crowd and cries, "I believe we've got ourselves a war!"

Colors That Bite

While the royals change from their court garb to their fighting gear, and other fighters suit up for the first official battle of this Gulf Wars, I dash back to the Bastarmark camp. I will return there several times this war for closer looks at how things really were done in the Middle Ages. The camp is a break from the stylized world I often see, separated from actual history by countless layers of stories and retellings, most recently in the form of movies.

About a dozen students already gather around a table by the time I arrive for today's class on period dyes. Instructor Marthe Elspeth of Oak Hill has already started outlining the dyes people used in the days before you could just buy a bottle of RIT at Wal-Mart. She runs down a list: the plant weld for yellow, madder for red and indigo for blue. Smoke drifts over the table from a fire pit as four large pots bubble away over the coals

Mistress Marthe earned her rank as a Pelican in this Society for her service in running events and for Meridies' unversty. MKA Martha Knowles, 46, of Oak Hill, Tenn., she works as a records manager for a Department of Energy contractor. Although she sets her persona in Henry VIII's England, she time travels today to looks more like the early-period Vikings and Celts of the campsite. Her olive dress has knotwork birds painted at the skirt, cuffs and across her shoulders and she has a straw hat to shade her from the sun.

"Solveig, will you check the pots and see if they're boiling over?" Marthe calls out.

Her assistant, standing over the pots, Solveig Ericsdottir is a late period Viking with a bit of traveling thrown in. MKA Duren Thompson, 34, also of Oak Hill, she has been in the SCA since her mid-teens, learning cooking, textiles, singing and how to paint woad. When she's not slathering on Celtic war paint, she does technology training and web site development for the state of Tennessee through its Center for Literacy Studies.

"No, they're not," Solveig tells Marthe. "They're just sending smoke your way."

Marthe continues. Indigo, the main source of blue, is the dye with the longest continual use, dating back 5,000 to 5,500 years. Red to purple dyes often come from cochineal, the dried bodies of a dead insect. It is not a true period dye, she concedes, since the bugs come mostly from Mexico and Guatemala—the New World. About 70,000 dried bugs are needed to dye a pound of fabric, but she says you can skip the endless bug hunt and just buy packages of dried dead bugs instead.

Turmeric, the kitchen spice, gives a good brown to orange tint. Onion skins can also produce a nice yellow color, darkening to orange if red onion skins are mixed in. Walnut bark makes a great brown, as do nuts. She has a pot of walnut on the fire, along with one of cochineal, one of onion skins and a green one of mimosa.

But the colorful soups need one crucial ingredient—mordant. All colorings, from dyes to housepaint, to even the paints that scribes in this Society use to make illuminated scrolls, need three basic parts. The pigment, the actual color, must go in a base that helps distribute and spread it. Then it must have some form of mordant, a form of the French word for "bite," to make it stick.

Different mordants and the time they are added to the broth create different effects. Alum, a common mordant, gives bright, clear colors. It is very safe and was used in period. Copper sulfate gives a blue-green cast to the fabric. It is somewhat toxic and may or may not have been used in period. Iron salts produce darker or "sadder" colors. Today we can add ready-made iron mordant. Or you can boil your dye material in an iron pot or throw in a few rusty iron nails. Tannic acid works well with oak and sumac for real dark browns or blacks.

Or you can use fermented urine, Marthe says. There is even a period essay on the types of urine needed for different results.

Marthe advises recording what you use, how much, how long you heat it and the type of mordant used in each experiment. Save a skein of yarn each time and add it to your records so you can reproduce what you have done later.

"Put wood ash in your list of ingredients because there's a lot of it," Solveig shouts over from the fire.

"OK. We're at the part now where we have to strain the steaming hot pots."

As Marthe notes the time the pots have been on the fire in her log, Solveig calls out the temperature of each pot. I help by pouring the pot of green dye into a straining bag as clumps of leaves slop out. Marthe dumps the strained dye, now a dark olive, back into the pot and I return it to the fire. Someone else helps dump the onion soup, which comes out a hearty orange, then the walnut and the cochineal.

Some people have brought fabrics they want to dye. Others will use little samples of yarn Marthe has brought. All have been soaking in water the entire class to open up the fibers and prevent shock to them.

While the fabric and yarn stew, Marthe sets her scrapbook on the table. It has a separate page for each type of dye plant and a separate sample of yarn for different mordants with that plant. I look at the page for turmeric. Using iron as a mordant, the yarn is a yellowish brown. With copper, bright yellow. With tin, the yarn is orange.

It is now just a waiting game. The materials will simmer about an hour, then have to be dried. I take off, knowing I will be back the next day for a blacksmithing class. I'll pick up my samples up then.

Melee Madness

At the shout of "Lay on," the two armies make an armored and awkward sprint across the carpet of leaves in the tree-spotted ravine

Two masses of bodies, spears and helms collide in the center of the ravine's bottom near a white flagpole stuck in the ground. A firecracker explosion of sticks on helm and shield rises up the slope of the ravine to my perch on one rim. Since nobody is really worried about being killed, nobody hesitates to charge into battle here.

Bodies fall as each army spreads out to form lines of troops up the sides of the ravine. Neither side wants to give the enemy a gap to cut behind them. Spearmen prod and poke across a no-man's-land between the two lines. The gap between them expands and contracts, from as little as sword length to as much as 10 feet as they charge, fall back and regroup. For the next 90 minutes, the fighters down the bottom will wrestle for control of the flag, the grail of the battle. Along the hillsides they will threaten charges and repel opposing threats.

Today is Thursday, March 15, 2001 in the modern world. Moments from now, the NCAA men's basketball tournament will tip off in Greensboro, Long Island, Boise and San Diego. Tomorrow, more contests will be played just 90 miles away from here in New Orleans. But here in tiny Lumberton, Miss., teams from Florida, Texas, North Carolina and Kentucky have just started their own form of March Madness.

Melee Madness.

Gulf Wars will have no television cameras, excited announcers or sellout crowds. But even without those trappings, the battles match the spectacle of the three NCAA tournaments I have attended. The water-bearing women, in their bright and flowing gowns, rushing bottles to their lords match up with cheerleaders. Ansteorran herald Modius has already outdone any furry or foamy mascot. And Kingdom cheers match the college chants of fans. Over the next few days, fans will shout in support of cheerleaders as they parade and wave flags with their college logos around the court during timeouts. Try doing that, I think, in full armor while a few hundred warriors try to beat you down with swords.

The sight of these battles resembles a football game more than a basketball game. But they are not like one team facing another. They are closer to the whole Big Ten taking on the entire Pac 10, all on the same field. If you don't know the pattern, strategy and flow of battles, the crush of bodies, shields and weapons looks like a pigpile. But the struggle combines brute force and leverage, as fighters maneuver shields for maximum protection so spearmen can reach above the shield blockers to make a kill. Amid the pileup, sticks chop and thrash over the heads of the combatants.

This particular battle is about taking and holding a key spot of territory—the pole. The side controlling it at the end of 90 minutes wins. Like some other SCA battles, this "resurrection battle" allows people who have been "killed" to return to fight once they go back to their side's "resurrection point" at the end of the ravine.

I settle back for the marathon stalemate when a blur drops a spearman to the ground.

Down goes another.

Suddenly arrows fly across the gap in the lines, catching fighters in the head and chest. Archers with bows and crossbows dart back and forth behind their lines, finding gaps and letting arrows fly at a furious clip. They are loaded with ammo. Most have taken Rubbermaid trash baskets and strapped them to their belts, stuffing them with arrows to fire at the enemy. They won't go to waste. Archers shoot down opponents at this close range every two or three shots. With dozens of arrows unleashed every minute, both lines spend half their time ducking for cover.

"Shields to the front!" comes a yell from the Ansteorran side. Something's got to stop this barrage of sniper fire before the whole front line is picked off.

Omarad, the Midrealm general, had told his commanders way back at Twelfth Night that archery battles here are a whole different game than at home. Back in the Midrealm, archers are second-class citizens, banned from most battles and forced to use the clunkiest, least aerodynamic weapons imaginable: golf tubes. The Society for Creative Anachronism has sought a safe alternative to real arrows for years. The challenge is to find one that flies straight, does not hit too hard and whose tip will not slip through the grille of a helm. Nobody needs to meet the fate of poor Harold at Hastings. The Midrealm's solution of using golf tubes, as big around as SCA rattan swords and topped off with old tennis balls, fools nobody that they are real arrows. They amount to bow-powered staves that do little more than wander through the air and flutter like knuckleballs.

But down here, the SCA's version of states' rights has let kingdoms like Trimaris and Ansteorra use normal arrow shafts that zip straight across the lines. They buzz like a swarm of gnats, making spearmen rub their shoulders and chest a little with each bite before giving a quick salute to the sniper and marching off dead.

A woman in a blue tabard with the yellow silhouette of a bear, troops up the hill, white arrow shafts fanned out in her belt against the blue of her tabard. The belt also stands out against the blue. It is also white. She is a Knight. She starts positioning archers as two spectators sitting next to me point her out.

"That's Sir Erika," one tells me. "She's the Goddess of the Bow."

Erika Bjornsdottir is an archery fixture in Trimaris and its mundane setting of Florida. Most weekends, if she is not off winning mundane target archery competitions, she brings her bow, archery armor and a briefcase filled with archery rules to SCA events to try to make combat archery a more regular part of melees.

"Sometimes I feel like one of the apostles proselytizing the word of combat archery," she tells me after battle. "There are times I'm the only combat archer out there, but I do it. The fact that I'm doing it every time, all the time, means people think of it and might come with a bow next time."

Her own household of archers, called Ice Bear, practices every week on her 10-acre property to hone their skills. When they come to events within their kingdom they bombard the combatants with arrows. Their fellow Trimarians leave bruised all over from arrow shots. But they know what Erika's work will mean.

"They put up with being shot all year long so that when they go to Gulf Wars the guys who have been killing them all year will be killing Ansteorrans instead."

The Goddess of the Bow's Tale

It is entirely coincidence that Sir Erika's mundane name is Linda Archer. It is even more amusing, but still coincidence, that she lives at the border of Archer, Fla., in suburban Gainesville. And off Archer Rd. to boot.

Even with a name like Archer, Erika, now 40, did not pick up archery until her late 20s. For her first few years in the SCA she was more apt to belt opponents in the face with a pike.

Archer joined the SCA in 1985. Fresh off of a divorce—she married at 19—she was so painfully shy that she would break out in a sweat if someone came into her office and said hello. She wanted to find an active social group to overcome her unease. She jumped at a chance to go to an SCA event with two women from her office.

Watching the tournament that day, the fighting drew her in. She had done judo and other martial arts and, despite being shy socially, hated softening her blows in those sports. Here, fighters in armor did not have to hold back.

"I turned to someone," she remembers, "and said, 'Can women do that?'"

Two women fought in that tournament and Archer talked to them afterward. She found the local group in Gainesville, gathered armor and started attending fight practices.

"People were so nice. The guys were always very sweet. They would never hit me very hard to begin with until they learned I could hit them real hard and take hits real hard. We had to go through this every time I fought someone new," she notes.

"I don't get cut much slack anymore." Her white Knight's belt has taken care of that since 1991.

She was the first woman Knighted in the Kingdom of Trimaris. And it wasn't for her archery skills but rather for her heavy fighting ability. Until she started having back problems several years ago, she believes she could hold her own with just about any fighter in the kingdom. Sometimes she would even beat Baldar, the five-time King of Trimaris, who she served as a squire at one time.

In 1989 she tried archery and began sorting out ways to use it in SCA combat. In battle scenarios involving bridges or portals like doors—battles with static lines of fighters—bows are potent weapons to pick off sitting-duck targets. She began using her bow to fire at the enemy until she ran out of arrows, then charged into battle with a pike.

She also attracted attention in the mundane target archery world by showing up at a tournament with a primitive bow, made from a single piece of wood—"a string and a stick" as she puts it—instead of the modern compound bow contraptions most used. The handful of traditional archers were thrilled to find someone using that kind of equipment, welcomed her and started teaching her. Today, she is one of the better primitive-style archers in the south. Last year she won the southeast regional traditional archery championship at a tournament in Georgia. Two weeks before Gulf Wars she won the women's primitive category at the Traditional Bowhunters of Florida championships.

Years ago, having always wanted a lot of land, she bought a 10-acre property and put a mobile home there. Erika, who works at the University of Florida testing orthodontics on the jaws of rats, now has a larger mobile home, a big field and a workshop. It is perfect for fight and archery practices, arrow making and, for her third husband—the gladiator with the giant onager—making and testing siege engines

Erika trains her bow archers to work with crossbow archers, having the bows loop high shots into the enemy to be blocked with shields. At the right moment, as the shields come up, the crossbows fire low at newly exposed midsections. She has taught her archers to rotate in and out of the prime firing positions—firing, then backing out to re-load and step back in.

For years the standard arrow in Trimaris was a modified version of one used by the Markland Medieval Mercenary Militia, a separate medievalist group in the mid-Atlantic states. The Markland arrows use a disc sliced off a fat dowel as arrowheads. But they flew, Erika says, "like a potato on the end of a stick." Another arrowhead called a Thistle Missile—a rubberized bulb-shaped tip that could be put onto the end of a shaft—was better. But when she showed those to Baldar, her former Knight, he said, "I could do better."

The result was the Baldar Blunt, the arrow tip now a near-standard across the SCA. The tip has made its inventor famous in this Society, while at the same time overshadowing what was already an impressive list of SCA accomplishments.

The Inventor's Tale

Alex Cooley was a bright young boy with a lifelong habit of reaching for—and often grabbing—the brass ring well before the establishment expected him to.

He had the credits to graduate from high school by the end of his sophomore year. He then took college courses at the University of South Florida, where his father worked. He also created a minor scandal in the SCA world by becoming a Knight ahead of the schedule that Trimaris' Knights laid out for him. He also won Trimaris' first Crown at the age of 19, the first of six times he would win (five to become King, once to become Prince before Trimaris had grown enough to be a Kingdom).

In his early teens he and his friends were rabid *Dungeons & Dragons* players and role-played through campaign after campaign.

"I was a total geek," he says. "I probably still am."

As a 15-year-old riding to class on his bicycle, he spotted a few guys fighting on the South Florida campus. They strapped him in armor and let him try the "living *D&D*." Soon he was making basic garb from two yards of black fabric, cutting a hole out for his head and belting it. And he started making armor. Even though the SCA was 14 years old, it had not developed armor standards and techniques close to those used today. The group on campus still used freon cans for helms and his first suit of armor, like that of many people in those days, was made by cutting and sewing carpet turned inside out. The simple concept of making armor was an epiphany for him. Growing up in an era where everything was store-bought and machine-made, the idea that he could make weapons and armor with his own hands was incredible.

"I was astounded that I could do these things myself. I was so proud of the first real piece of armor I made—a shoulder pauldron I made with a ball peen hammer and a piece of scrap metal on a stump in the front yard."

He started cleaning armor in return for rides and adopted a Viking persona because a local Laurel was making "cool" Viking items. He took a Viking history class at the university on the way to his dual degrees in chemistry to medieval history. He chose Baldar as his name, after the Viking god of beauty and resurrection, followed by Langstrider—Viking for "longstrider"—because even at that age he was 6'2". But he weighed only 155 pounds and was "the baronial whipping boy."

"I had no mass to me," he remembers. "But that's part of why I got good. I had to fight with my head."

When a Knight picked someone else as a squire, he poured his anger at being passed over into his fighting. For the whole next summer he would hit a pell, the equivalent of a punching bag for swords, an hour a day or for 1,000 blows. He ran two three-mile routes a week and attended three or four fight practices a week. He won his first tournament that summer and by 1984, when he was just 19, he became prince of Trimaris.

Trimaris was not yet a kingdom and still just a principality—a Kingdom in train-ing. When Trimaris held its first Crown Tournament as a Kingdom in 1985, Baldar won again, as a darkhorse at the age of 20. As he tells me about his struggle for respect and the fights he had over becoming a Knight, I am reminded of Valharic. Though Valharic is a bit older than Baldar was, the Middle Kingdom is far larger than Trimaris. And both were dismissed by the Knights as a "punk kid."

Today, at 36, Baldar is no longer a scrawny 155 pounds but a strong 215. He has won crown four more times and is the head of House Asgard, a fighting household of more than 70 active members. His men are easy to spot on the field with their giant matching aluminum shields that have a vertical bend in the middle. Etched with an eagle on the front, the shields are designed after Byzantine siege shields. His men are the ever-recurring Varangians, the mercenary Viking bodyguards of the Byzantine emperors. Instead of old carpet, he takes the field with a spear and an aluminum belt. Each of the panels on the belt has a drawing from Viking art acid-etched into it in relief. One is from a Viking runestone, another from the carving on the front of a walrus tusk box.

Mundanely, he has just finished his residency to be an anesthetist. He hopes to win crown again to make his wife of eight years a duchess and hopes to someday win for one of his daughters.

And, no longer a punk kid at 36, he's famous across the SCA. Not for any this. But for the arrow tips he and his father created.

When Erika, his former squire came to him with a problem, his knack for making things took over. He consulted his father, who had 27 patents and ran a plastics business out of his house. Though his father still believes the SCA is a phase his son will someday grow out of, he offered to help.

"I think he was just doing it to humor me more than anything else," Baldar said, but together they tried to build a better arrow.

The biggest problem, he said, was preventing penetration of the arrow. When an arrow strikes, he explained, it concentrates a tremendous amount of force on the tip. He and his father tried 11 different designs—each time with Baldar firing prototypes against a brick wall to test them—before they found one in which the shaft would not burrow through the head. The solution was to put a hard nylon disc—the same material Glock pistols are made from—in the center of hemispherical heads made of sanoprene, an injectible rubber.

"You could take one of these nylon discs and hit it with a hammer and it would stand that," he said. "It would deform but it would not shatter. When the arrow strikes, it puts pressure into the disc and the disc dissipates the pressure into the round front of the head."

The result was the Baldar Blunt, arrowheads that look like superballs sliced at the equator. Baldar believes they are the first piece of SCA weaponry mass-produced and machine-made with high-tech methods. His father's business, now called Dragon Jewel Plastics in Zephyr Hills, Fla., makes the heads for him in between doing short manufacturing runs of new plastic products for inventors.

Baldar estimates he has sold 32,000 of the Blunts. Selling for $2.25 each—or as low as $1.50 in bulk orders—the heads give archers arrows that simulate real arrow flight, although the heads drop far faster than real heads. The impact rarely causes injuries, though some fighters blame the heads for a few. Baldar is now testing a new version with a clear head.

"My ultimate improvement would be to take that same head and put a flash of black down the center so it looks like a broadhead arrow from 10 feet away," he said. "That would be ultimately cool."

"That's noble combat..."

Gulf Wars uses archery far more than other Wars. The push by both Trimaris and Ansteorra, some say, has been a sea change in how battles are fought in the Known World. In the past, fighters could move without fear of being hit by anyone not close enough to strike back. Troops could sit in one spot and not be killed from afar. Accomplished fighters could run around the field, dart in to attack weak spots or specific opponents, then retreat to open space. Not anymore. Individuals in the open are easy pickings for archers.

That change is a cause of a great deal of debate that will only grow more fierce after this Gulf Wars. In today's Ravine Battle, a Knight from the Kingdom of Calontir will suffer a bruised eyeball. An arrow tipped with a Baldar Blunt will ricochet backwards through the grille of her helm and the nock will hit her eye. That injury and other complaints will spark the Society to require 'Anti-Penetration Devices" to be attached to the back ends of arrows to prevent more unlucky bounces. Others will complain about overpowered crossbows sending bolts rocketing at them with enough power to knock them over and dent armor.

Combat archery also raises a more philosophical debate. Some believe SCA fighting should resemble the non-lethal, spectator-sport tournaments of the late Middle Ages, which had group fights called Grand Melees, but no arrows. Some fighters believe being shot by an archer ruins their game of face-to-face combat and chivalry.

"I've heard Kings tells their guys, 'We were beaten by the archer' as if it's an excuse," said Erika's husband, the gladiator Lorcun. "Some Duke will get pecked in the ass by an arrow and say 'I don't want it on my field.'"

Erika and Baldar look at the battles as re-creations of wars, not of tournaments. Medieval woodcuts and paintings of battles, Baldar says, show fighters covering their heads from the rain of arrows. Archers have been a key part of nearly every medieval battle and if the SCA wants to re-create history, he believes, archery should be included.

But even Erika believes archery should never be completely on par with standard fighting in some ways. Archery's biggest promoter bristles at the idea of someone becoming a Knight solely for archery.

"There is no such thing, nor will there be, if I have anything to say about it," she said. "Knights were the guys who went out in all the glittering armor and fought toe to toe. No disrespect to the archers, but that was noble combat."

At the bottom of the hill, the two sides continue to bash into each other and spear duel. The Midrealm is smack in the middle of it. I have only followed this Society for two months but I am already rooting for my home kingdom.

The Middle Kingdom brought more than 100 fighters to Mississippi. Most are Knights and squires, serious fighters, not the common foot soldier I aspire to be. They drove 900 miles to fight and they are ready for it. The numbers make the Midrealm Trimaris' biggest ally and Trimaris has given the Midrealm an important task—grab and hold that flag. Others would worry about the flanks, but Omarad, who made the trip down from Kentucky, needs his men to capture and hold the prize. Before the battle, the general and King Edmund huddled the troops on one slope of the ravine to rally them for their mission.

"Are we going to take that banner?" Omarad barked.

"Yes!" screamed his troops.

"Are we going to lose the banner?"

"No!"

"Are we going to keep that banner?"

"Yes!"

He and Edmund make a mismatched pair of giants, Edmund towering over everyone and Omarad, stuffed into his red and white general's tunic, a giant Midrealm wrecking ball.

Though the Midrealm controls the banner much of the fight, I watch as the troops for today's "enemy" Ansteorra snatch it in the final minutes. I see Flynn down in the ravine guarding the pole all battle, even when the Midrealm and Trimaris push the lines several feet away. Omarad knew that Flynn and Sulla, the other Darkyard fighter who made the trip, would follow orders and stay put, not go off freelancing. It wasn't Flynn's fault the pole was lost. The battle, Omarad later explains, lasted several minutes longer than he had expected. The amount of time added to deal with injuries, just like "extra time" in soccer games, caused Omarad to mis-time his final push. His troops had tried to drive forward, risking "death" at the last minute because they expected the battle to end. When they were marching to the rear to "resurrect," Ansteorra bulldozed the depleted line and grabbed the flag.

"It bothers me that I feel I failed," he says. "But the plan worked."

The Midrealm, he recounts, held at 90 minutes and still held at 105 minutes.

"We fought a great 105 minutes of a 90-minute battle," he says. "It was just 120 minutes long."

"It's good to be the bard…"

Down the road past the stables, a path dives into a gully with benches set into the hillside. A single electric light sends a modern shine onto a stage at the bottom, as the hill is cloaked in the damp dark of the Mississippi night.

With no televisions and radios, nighttime entertainment in this Society reverts back to the pre-industrial type. Drums come out. Guitars are pulled from tents. And songs and stories are exchanged around the campfire. A good bard—a singer and teller of tales—is the prize of every group.

Tonight it is more formal. Instead of entertaining for fun, the best bards of the three Gulf Wars Kingdoms will compete for the bardic championship of the war.

The first round of performers to take the stage as the night darkens is a blur of styles: a young man singing a war ballad, another man telling a fairy story, a woman reciting a tale of a girl pursued by wolves in the forest and a man singing a song about two ravens.

But a Trimarian named Lucan is the hit of the first round with a game he and his "clan brothers" created in drunken revelry 10 years earlier. Songs in the Society fall into several categories—completely period songs rendered in period manner, to songs and stories about Current Middle Ages events, to "filk," the hybrid of often-humorous lyrics set to well-known tunes. Filk includes the song parodies of Weird Al Yankovic at one extreme and the "Star-Spangled Banner," a serious filk of an old drinking song, at the other. Lucan gives the crowd on benches rising up the hill a category in and of itself.

Thin, with blonde scraggly hair running over a sheepskin slung over his shoulders, Lucan tells the crowd that we are about to make our packing list for the Pennsic War. With each item he names, we must call out all of the previous items in order. It's the "I know an old lady who swallowed a fly" deal, only tougher. Much tougher.

"One map!" he calls out and we repeat.

"One map, two ice chests."

And he goes on, through "Five washable tunics."

"Now we're done playing," he says with devilish glee. "Six boxes of pagan sisters' powder-coated funnel cakes."

We all laugh in the dark, our breath freezing into little round clouds at each chuckle.

"Normally I give the sucker—uh, the person who comes up—a chance to gracefully bow out. I'll string you guys along."

He pauses, then hits us: "700 spools of sticky silver double-duty duct tape."

Now we start tripping up. Starting from the beginning and muddling through is tougher each time.

"It's not that hard," he taunts, sitting cross-legged on the stage. "And we were drunk."

He keeps upping the ante, through "Eight blue baronial banners brimming with bad heraldry blowing in the breeze" and "Nine kegs of old froth and slosh, the pale stale ale with the froth on the bottom."

"Wait," he adds. "Pack it in the Pinto, please."

He keeps going and we are stumped. He leaves to great applause. He advances to the next round.

At the break at the end of the round, the contestant who started off with the war song is surrounded by an entourage. Freiman the Minstrel, MKA Dave Wilhoite, has attracted a pack of even younger admirers, mostly women. With long hair and puffy white shirt, he is Gulf Wars version of a rock star.

"I am surrounded by women and a guy who makes really good mead," he says, laughing. "Liam, come here."

Liam, one of the groupies, hands over a mead bottle and Freiman takes a swig.

"This is what honey would taste like if bees were not teetotalers," he says. "It's good to be the bard."

Wilhoite, 33, has been making music in the SCA and "walking the fires"—wandering from campsite to campsite with his guitar—for several years. Born in Biloxi, Miss., he mostly grew up in Germany with army parents. But members of his family have earned music degrees and worked in the music business. He describes his style as "early period campfire," borrowing styles and songs from the SCA period but often straying into modern folk that is traditional but hardly medieval.

"I just play what the audience wants to hear. It's their dream and if you give them a chance they'll dream you into it."

The groupies?

"I don't know how that happened," he says. "I just play my guitar and sing. They tend to follow me around because when there is music it seems like a party…I do like being around pretty girls."

He quickly adds, however, that he is married.

The first round has halved the field of 12 contestants as well as half the crowd. It is too cold tonight for the bardic to draw much more than those with a friend or spouse competing. Freiman and Lucan make the second round.

As they wait to start the next round, one of the judges starts a song, then trips on the lyrics.

"Oh, I forgot that bit," he growls.

"In Finland, we just fill in with Tra-la-la," one competitor chips in.

"Or, And a Down-Derry-Down," a British character chimes in.

Also advancing was Kief av Kierstad. I had not recognized him when he came on stage for his first piece, though the crutch should have been a giveaway. He had advanced with a Viking tale of explorers setting out from home in longboats in search of Vinland, the New World.

For his second round, he tells a tale of an epic battle at Pennsic when he was beside Duke Inman in support of the East. His unit was charged by Tuchux.

'They fell upon us like wolves upon a slaughter," he booms, then drops his voice and adds, matter of factly, "…and died."

"Then came the Great Dark Horde," he roars. "And against our wall they broke…"

"…and died."

At the end of the battle, only four of Kief's group remained, but his allies, the East, had won.

"We few withstood the charge of hundreds," he concludes. He advances to the third round. "I've always been able to spin a good tale and just do stuff around the campfire," he tells me later. "I always had trepidation about getting up before an audience, but I took theater speech in college to get over it."

"I do nothing by rote, by memory. It is all off the cuff. I may tell the tale many times, but it's never the same way twice."

He builds a tool chest for his tales by reading poetry, prose, and lots of science fiction and fantasy.

"I pick up imagery. Being an artist and photographer I look at things in terms of how things can be framed. It's a snapshot in my mind. Or a particular feel: How the trees moved in the wind, the smoke of the fire, the taste of blood in one's mouth. Then I expound on what I'm feeling so the audience can get a sense of what's going on in my head."

Freiman is paired against Lucan, who shifts gears and drops into a deep-voiced Irish ballad. As he sings, he picks up a candle lantern and holds it in both hands in front of his face.

"Red is the rose that in yonder garden grows
Fair is the lily of the valley
Clear is the water that flows from the Boyne
But my love is fairer than any."

"Oh, he's good," Freiman says and fortifies himself with another swig of mead before stepping up.

"That was wonderful," he says. "A salute to my opponent…That way it looks better if things happen to go badly."

He launches into a traditional song called "Mattie Groves" that dates to the tail end of SCA period or just after. Freiman, though, did not learn it from history books but from "a biker named Stonewall." Playing his guitar fast as he sits, he tells the tale of a Lord Arlen whose wife is unfaithful to him with a young Mattie Groves even as Arlen is off working in the fields for the family. Warned by a friend, the husband rushes home and finds Mattie in his bed with his wife.

When Mattie awoke, Lord Arlen
Was standing at his feet.
Saying how do you like my feather bed?
And how do you like my sheets?
And how do you like my lady
Who lies in your arms asleep?

Arlen, in a rage, kills young Mattie, then asks his wife whom she prefers. When she snaps back that she'd "rather kiss one dead Mattie's lips than you and your finery"

Arlen stabs her in the heart. The song has the crowd backing Lord Arlen and hating interloping Mattie. It is a winner. Freiman advances.

Kief steps up for the third round, paired against another bard with European connections. Galen of Bristol, MKA Paul Mitchell of Fort Worth, Texas, once won the Crown Tournament of Drachenwald, the Kingdom covering Europe. Kief decides to wing it this time, asking Galen to give him a topic on which to base his next tale. Galen picks "love."

"Love," Kief instantly begins. "Some say it is fleeting. But it is not."

The story that emerges is a dark tale of love, death and revenge: A young lady, a noble's daughter, watches her father and new husband fail in a desperate attempt to repel attackers from her castle. She watches them both die, then runs back deep into the castle, sets aside her fancy clothes and pulls on servants clothing all covered in soot. Thus disguised, she hides and waits as the attackers take the castle and drink and pillage.

She listens to the screams and burning and looting and waits until they drink themselves into an insensible state. Finally, she emerges and slays them all with her dead lord's blade, before taking her own life.

Everyone in hushed crowd is speechless from the emotion of the climactic suicide. Kief coolly smiles, walks over to Galen and whispers, "Pressure."

"It came out of the back of my head right there on the spot," Kief says later. "Everything just unfolded as I went. I didn't know how it would end until I got about 30 seconds from the end."

Galen, in a gorgeous blue and yellow cloak with a castle on the back displaying the arms of the Barony of Elfsea, the barony he heads back in Fort Worth, steps forward and croons a song about King Arthur. It is a tough call.

Kief sits back, awaiting the judging.

"As soon as this is done I shall go to the castle and I shall become…inebriated," Kief says. A torchlight party has been scheduled for the battlefield, promising "drink from our two-story tall War Funnel" and the opportunity to "annoy your friends, inebriate your enemies and fail to make it to the first battle in the morning." For rough-and-tumble Kief, who says "the only thing I do in moderation is moderation," the party may be a good time. He wins the round and advances again.

For his third round, Freiman is matched against none other than Master Modius, the booming herald from opening ceremonies. Modius sets the bar high, delivering a monologue of a soldier who wonders the night before a battle if he should set aside the soldier's life and return to his wife. He decides to give it up and return, but receives a letter that his wife is dead.

"Never leave your home with words unsaid," he concludes.

Freiman tries to beat him by shifting gears with a rollicking song he wrote called "The Bastard Children of Meridies" about a mercenary fighting legion that switches sides, often in mid-battle. "A real tankard swinger" as Freiman calls it, he plays it in "a bluegrass style 'chunk' rhythm that actually sounds a lot like a Bo Diddley hand-jive thing." It includes a new verse added today:

"Then again at Gulf Wars Ten
The legion switched their sides again
And killed our closest kith and kin
We're the Bastard Children of Meridies!"

Even with that crowd pleaser, Freiman loses, probably because the style is not period. The guitar itself, at least its current form, he explains, dates only to the 1800s.

"Musicians in period were discouraged from strumming their instruments," he says. "It was considered lazy and sloppy. I do it because the volume created is much, much greater than single notes."

The finals are anticlimactic. Modius goes with a goofy item he claims comes from "A Finnish Cookbook to Spellcraft"—a Finnish book passed on to his German persona, "so we have true passive aggression." Modius incants lines in Finnish, making odd hand motions in front of his chest, then face. The punchline is the translation to English: "The itsy-bitsy spider…"

Kief steps up with a tale of a Viking who fights hard with a great axe, but is killed for his efforts. Kief burned up his best effort in the semifinals. The group disperses as the judges confer. At the end of Gulf Wars, Kief av Kierstead will be named the winner.

Back at the battlefield, the torchlight party is in full swing. A giant crowd mills around the base of the castle, huddled in cloaks and downing booze for warmth. As parties go, this is on par with a medieval-themed frat party. The party flier circulating around Gulf Wars invited people to:

"HEAR—Real live drummers perform on *actual* drums!

SEE—Real live dancers perform *actual* Dances!

TASTE—Hunnydik, the Nectar of the Gods!

SMELL—Sweaty people from other Kingdoms!

FEEL—Sweaty people from other Kingdoms, if you're lucky"

Atop one of the towers of the fort a few guys man a beer keg with a long hose and funnel. From the tower they pour beer into the hose and funnel to a happy crowd of imbibers below. I walk back to camp and overhear a woman tell her friends, "I am hoping to have a great night with a man I am still to meet." The SCA party scene, with the rain over, is in full swing. I hear later that Trimaris, famed for its very anachronistic pudding wrestling matches at Pennsic, has a doozy this night. But the cold and sleepless night of driving still wears on me. I decide to sleep and pass on the chance to "Be the first on your block to fail to remember the previous night."

"Everybody does Ballistae and Trebuchet…"

Over the night and throughout the next morning, fighters drag their siege weapons to the battlefield where they stand in a great semi-circle at the edge. It is a rather jumbled assortment of weapons, with odd forms of ballistae making up the majority. A ballista in period was a large weapon capable of doing damage to buildings by firing giant bolts. The SCA has scaled them down to the size of a catapulta, a smaller Roman weapon of the same style. SCA ballistae use full golf tubes as bolts with tennis balls as heads. They will not affect the fort, but under the rules, should "kill" an opponent even if they hit a shield.

A few of the homemade ballistae launch the bolts in test shots today in a tight arc of a few hundred feet. Others do not work as well and flip the bolts into the air at awkward angles. Underpowered and askew, they flutter and blow off target in the light wind. They do not use the true period source of power—ropes twisted and turned to create an incredible force, along the lines of rubber-band toy airplanes. A "bungilista" on the field uses a rubber cord as its power. Baldar's household brought a set of six identical ballistae, each powered by two 35-pound bows strapped onto a heavy, squared deck post as the barrel. Because the posts look like bedposts, they are dubbed "Baldar's Bedpost Ballistas."

Gulf Wars has also become famous for "novelty weapons." Duke Sir Bytor Fitzgerald, the last King of Trimaris, has covered golf carts with barding so they looked like warhorses as he drove them around the site. He also built a replica Viking ship that operates on Flintstones power—the occupants' feet hitting the ground as they mock a rowing motion. One year, Bytor brought "war elephants" to the field—huge gray plywood elephants on wheels that archers could stand atop and shoot from. They were only "somewhat effective," Baldar said, in the attack on the fort but they had another, far better use. As Trimaris was about to take its turn defending the fort, Baldar recalls, Bytor wheeled the "elephants" into the castle doorway, made a show of slashing their "throats" to "kill" them and upended them to block the door.

"Needless to say, Ansteorra was not amused," Baldar said.

Ansteorra has also joined in with its "armadillo of Death," an armadillo-shaped battering ram. But that fell apart as the Ansteorrans pushed it.

But Lorcun's onager, of all the weapons on the field, is no toy. Since only true heavy siege weapons like catapults and trebuchet can take out the fort door now, Lorcun set out to create the most powerful weapon on the field—and power it an authentic way.

"Everybody does ballistae and trebuchet," Lorcun said. "I was told by countless supposedly enlightened siege experts that torsion engines are an engineering nightmare, more trouble than they're worth and innately hazardous to operate. After hearing all that, how could I refuse?"

The Gladiator's Tale

Lorcun Attalus, MKA Todd Johnson, 38, takes pride in trying to do things a little differently.

The SCA lets him try a new spin to his martial arts training. His gladiator persona is an attempt to zig when others zag. And he now is trying to make his mark with his weapons.

He has built siege engines before this onager—once using the graphite power rods off of a Bowflex weight training system as power. He then tried using twisted and tightened skeins for power in true period style, but that attempt failed when he took a modern shortcut: The polypropylene skeins stretched under tension and lost power. At Gulf Wars five years ago he tried another onager using the top of a lacrosse stick as the throwing cup. Though that weapon could be towed on a Jet Ski trailer, it couldn't withstand high pressure and fell apart over the winter.

Three years ago, he launched into his latest project by reading the book *The Crossbow* by Sir Ralph Paine Galway. Much of the book is devoted to siege engines and contains drawings from ancient manuscripts depicting a variety of design principles. From there, he figured out the rest by trial and error. The basic design of his onager is a frame about six feet long of six-inch beams of wood, bolted together with iron. The end of the throwing boom sticks into the middle of the tightly twisted rope. To fire, Lorcun and his crew turn a crank that forces the arm back. They load it, release the crank, and the arm snaps back to the upright position.

If the frame is not strong enough, the pressure of the rope can collapse it, "turning it into a giant mousetrap," Lorcun says. On a trip to Home Depot he spotted a sign for 6x6 pressure-treated "Super Timber".

"My wife sees this stupid grin coming across my face. There was my new catapult timber."

Even then, Lorcun went through several booms before finding one that did not break or damage the frame. Number seven is a 2x2 steel rod with a wooden core inside. The cup for the ammo is a former copper vambrace—forearm armor.

"I found that wooden salad bowls and dog bowls don't make good catapult cups," he said.

He has bolted an engraved metal plate to one post that reads: "This machine is Y1K Compliant." Aside from a few concessions, it is. He uses a boat winch to crank the boom back for firing, but plans to replace it with a period one by next year. The rope is manila, instead of the hemp which would likely be used in period. This is simply a matter of cost. After investing $1,600 for supplies and custom metal work for the braces, then $500 for a flatbed trailer to haul the thing around, costs had to be cut somewhere. Rather than using one thick rope as some do, he has used 100 smaller ones. This way if any break, as one already has, the onager only loses a fraction of its power.

The machine's greatest limitation is the ammo. He must use duct-taped tennis ball clusters, which he makes more aerodynamic by wrapping them with shredded dish towels before taping. The result is still something of a flutterball.

"Loaded with an actual spherical stone and powered to full—beyond what is allowed in the SCA—it can fire a five pound stone about 150 to 200 meters," he said. "This is like trying to speed pitch a cotton ball."

A Killing Cup

Shortly after siege inspection ends, both armies line up on opposite sides of an open field for the most straightforward of SCA battles: the field battles. Two armies meet in an open field. The last one standing wins. Because the scenario is so simple, it is easier for newcomers like me to watch battle strategies unfold. Today I will see a good example of a plan that works.

Unlike at Pennsic, where the Middle and East Kingdoms fight just one field battle, here it is best two out of three. Today's first two battles end in a split, with the Kingdoms of Ansteorra and Trimaris each winning one. For the deciding battle, arrow-inventor Duke Baldar and his squires modify the plans from a battle in 216 B.C. to try to take a victory for Trimaris.

On a greaseboard back at home with his squires before Gulf Wars, Baldar adjusted the plan that Hannibal, the ancient Carthaginian general, used to defeat the Roman army at Cannae. In that battle, Hannibal set a long line of troops across the field and drew the Romans into the center. Hannibal then backed up the center of his line as though the Romans were driving him back. Instead, the sag in the line was a trap. It let Hannibal curve the ends around to trap the Romans in the middle for slaughter. It was one of the most decisive battles in military history. Baldar read about the plan in *Medieval and Ancient Warfare: The History of Tactics*, written by instructors at West Point. But he realized he was unlikely to have weekend warrior SCA troops back up and achieve the curving effect he wanted.

So he starts the battle with all of the Kingdom of Trimaris' troops and her allies in a cup, a big U-shape across the field. At the least, that formation offers Ansteorra no flank to attack.

"I just invited them in. If they come down the center, fantastic. They'll die," he explains. If the Ansteorran foes attack one side instead, Baldar reasons, he can have his troops on the other side sweep across the field to trap them.

Although SCA field battles usually are mad charges and flurries, this time, when the marshals call, "Lay on!" both sides hold still, Trimaris by plan, Ansteorra trying to sort it out.

"In case you missed it, lay on!" the marshals call again.

Finally someone moves. As Ansteorra and its allies try tentative charges, they make no dent and the small groups of attackers are wiped out. A few Trimarians sally to the middle to try to induce Ansteorra into the full charge that Baldar wants. The Ansteorrans don't bite and they retreat. In front of me, Omarad, manning a wing of the U for the Trimaris side, steps out alone into no-man's-land with his mace and shakes it in the air, taunting the enemy to charge. He is out there alone, screaming, telling them, "Come and get me! There's only one of me! Come on!" A few guys come after him and almost pin him to a tree in the scramble but he retreats to the shield wall and both sides regroup.

Finally, Ansteorra moves forward and the two sides meet. The small charges have depleted Ansteorra. Trimaris and her allies easily surround Ansteorra's main group. The Midrealm pushes halfway across the field, then wheels back to the middle to help Trimaris win the day.

Omarad is even more giddy after the fight than Baldar, holding his hands over his head roaring and laughing.

"I'm sorry I got a little excited in that one," he laughs.

Edmund gathers his troops and calls them "melee monsters."

"We came down here with two missions—to have fun and to kick butt," he shouts. "We have clearly done number one to the best of our natural and unnatural ability. How are we doing on number two?"

The group lets out a roar.

Rodger fan Morvil, who commanded the Meridies troops fighting with losing Ansteorra, is disappointed. He and the other commanders did not anticipate Trimaris waiting them out. After losing too many men to unsuccessful charges, the others were trapped in what he called a "killing cup."

"They outsmarted us before we even crossed swords," he says. He will have another chance tomorrow, on the war's final day when the sides battles for the fort.

"Blacksmithing is a dance..."

"The only way you're going to learn," the Viking named Stilicho tells the dozen students gathered around his anvil, "is to pick up a hammer."

This afternoon is my last trip to the Bastarmark camp. This class, on blacksmithing, is just as hands-on as the others. A table in the "Rusty Anvil Forge" has an iron-lined hole at one end for a fire pit. Assistants use a black leather bellows bag to force air up through the fire pit to the pile of glowing coals in the center.

Stilicho, thin and wiry with a small beard and ponytail, jabs the end of a metal rod into the heart of the fire. He wears a black and red Viking and Celtic tunic, with knotwork designs painted on. MKA Steve Corn of Murfreesboro, Tenn., Stilicho has been working part time as a blacksmith since 1992. Just laid off from his job hanging lights for film and television sets, he now makes his living selling his work from his Stilicho's Anvil web site. His mainstay is knives, swords and silverware for SCA feasts but he also sells portable "firepits," like the ones used in this camp for $150 to $250 each.

Fritz der Rothirsch, the Baron of the Steppes in Dallas, Texas, and another film lighting man, joins him as co-instructor. For two hours the pair gives a full, basic lesson in smithing, from explaining the parts of an anvil down to how-to's of building our own smith and several techniques of working the metal.

And a chance to try it.

When I have my chance to "pick up a hammer," it feels like it weighs about 10 pounds. Each swing comes down with great force as I pound a glowing red rod the instructors are turning into a hook. I can feel the metal move and flatten with each strike, but only slightly. Fritz and Stilicho compare the softened steel to a hard clay—it moves and changes shape, just as clay does when it is struck, only it has to be struck a lot harder.

"It moves a little differently than you think it is going to," Fritz says. "You think that you'll pound it and it will move like hot butter, but it doesn't."

The glow fades and the metal gives less with each blow. By the time I put the rod back in the fire I feel like I'm hammering on an iron fence.

"Blacksmithing is a dance," Fritz says. "You know the saying, 'Strike while the iron is hot?' While the steel is heating you should be thinking about your next move. You don't want to waste time when your iron is out of the fire."

There are several basic techniques a blacksmith needs to learn, the instructors tell us. Fritz starts with a technique called "upsetting" in which a thin rod is turned into a fat one. After heating one end, he says, bang the very end, not against the table or anvil, but back into itself. It will shorten the rod and make the end a bulb like a mushroom. Fritz then reverses the process by "drawing" the metal out into a thinner piece. He hammers the glowing rod into a square then pounds each side against a flat surface, rotating after every few hits, to mash it thinner.

To make even bigger pieces, he says, we can weld two smaller ones together. Fritz bends the end of a rod over into a hook, then keeps bending until the hook point almost touches the rod. He tucks the metal back into the coals to soften it again before banging the two pieces together.

"You just have to hit it enough to get the pieces together. When it starts to cool, the pieces will bond and you'll end up with one solid piece of steel."

If we want to start our own smith, Fritz tells us, it's pretty simple: "You need something to hit with and something to hit on." An anvil is the usual first step. There are cheap anvils available from China but Stilicho calls them "disposables" and recommends a piece of railroad track instead. A decent-sized new anvil would cost about $400. Car brake drums make decent fire fits because they are metal and very resistant to heat. If you do not want a bellows, blowers are cheap. Coal is the best fuel source, but Stilicho's first forge used charcoal briquettes from a grocery store and a hair dryer as its blower. An old beer keg makes a good "quench bucket" they suggest, but do not use plastic barrels. Hot metal can melt holes right through.

"Once you know the five or six basic things—the drawing and the flattening and whatnot, that will give you what you need for everything," Stilicho says.

"Just do it. You've got to beat the hammer."

A notch in the machine

Lorcun cranks back the arm on the onager until it is level with the ground and slaps a "rock" into the cup. The marshals have just called "Lay on!" and the clock is ticking. My time at Gulf Wars is ticking too. It is now Saturday morning and the Cleveland group must head home right after this, the climactic set of castle battles that will end this war.

Lorcun yells, "Clear!" and hits the release.

The onager arm snaps upright, shooting the taped tennis balls in a high arc. The artillery hangs above the fort for a split second, then drops on the heads of the fighters inside. It probably "killed" a few people inside the fort, but that is not Lorcun's mission. The onager's arm, to borrow a baseball pitching description, does not get on top of the rock enough. Instead of firing on a straight line, it is lobbing. The rules did not let Lorcun and his crew test the aim before the battle, so they have to adjust the weapon's calibration on the fly. The ballistae are having no such trouble. One in front of the onager sends a shot on a line straight at the fort. With a quick adjustment, the ballista sends shots on a line over the walls and in. As soon as a bolt is fired, crews slap a new one onto the machines, crank it back and fire.

The onager keeps lobbing but Lorcun and his crew are refining the range while Erika's Ice Bear bowmen snap shots over the walls at turreted snipers. As bolts fly out of the fort, the fighters yell, "Bolt!" and shuffle as a group out of the way. Inside the fort, arrows and bolts from outside slowly pick off fighters who have little room to move and cannot see the bolts until they come over the wall. Out here, shots fired from the fort fall harmlessly in a ring of litter. I remember a fighter telling me the other day he was unimpressed with the siege ammo. "They're relatively large and you just see them coming," he said. "Oh, a rock. Move." It seems a waste. But the shots from inside do serve a purpose. They amount to suppressing fire that holds the Trimaris attackers away from the wall. The longer they keep Trimaris from mounting an assault on the walls, the longer Ansteorra holds the fort. The side that holds the fort the longest wins.

Ansteorra's trebuchet inside the fort is less effective. Huge shouts of derision come from Trimaris when the trebuchet lofts a boulder nearly straight up, only to have it crash down inside the walls and onto its own allies.

Suddenly, the fortress gate opens. Rather than make Trimaris take it out, Ansteorra opens it on purpose to allow its ballista to fire out the front.

"They stole my thunder!" Lorcun cries. The onager will not get to complete its mission.

"That was the dumbest thing they could do," Lorcun says at the end of the battle. "Rule #1: if you're inside the castle, stay inside."

The field is littered with spent bolts and arrows before the pace of firing slows and the troops gather tighter. Men grab the ramps for the assault over the walls. A few units cluster directly in front of the door and try to charge through. They pile up in front of the fort as the Ansteorrans plug the hole from inside. Others race to the walls with ramps. At first glance, the ramps look just like flat boards nailed as steps on 2x4 beams. But when troops set the top edge of the ramps onto the top of the fort wall, supporting poles just the right height drop down to brace them. These don't just lean. They stand on their own.

Spearmen charge up the ramps and leap over the fort walls into the Ansteorran defenses. A stream of Trimaris fighters and allies climb over to slug it out inside. Flynn, in the charge at the door, is killed when a friendly ballista bolt goes too low and hits his shoulder. Were it a real bolt, he would have been nailed to the fort.

It could have been worse for him. The assault is halted with screams of "Hold! Hold! Hold!" The yelling is more urgent than usual. Off to one side, fighters have pulled out a woman in armor. She lies on the grass, surrounded by frantic helpers. One foot dangles at a crazy angle. The leg is broken. Horribly.

Omarad, dead already, takes charge of clearing space and backing people away. SCA medics, called Chirurgeons, splint the leg with two swords as someone calls for an ambulance on a cell phone. Omarad grimly walks to the spectators and dead fighters and tells us it is pretty bad—a compound fracture. Multiple breaks. Details leak out slowly. She had jumped the wall and landed funny.

"When you go over the wall, you become a missile," one dead man says to another. "You become a lawn dart. But you know that when you decide to go over the wall. I signed my waiver. It's on me."

"I personally won't be sorry if the ramps never come back," says another. "Every year we have somebody get severely hurt."

He points out a man from his unit who dislocated his shoulder falling off the wall one year. It took a year, he said, before the shoulder was right again. The ambulance takes forever. The girl grips someone's hand and they cover her with blankets to prevent shock.

When the battle resumes, the marshals ban the ramps for safety reasons and designate new openings for an attack—just marking off open air with shields—at the end of the fort walls. These are now makeshift rules. The injury hold has been longer than the battle. It feels almost like a different battle when Trimaris masses at each new entry point and pushes into the fort. Eventually, the attackers kill all of the defenders and Trimaris raises its flag atop the tower.

"Vivat, Trimaris!" they shout.

"Vivat, Trimaris!"

"Vivat, Trimaris!"

I watch the second battle from behind the fort, where I can see the bolts come over in long, looping arcs, fluttering and curving in the air. Ansteorra tries to break in with a "battering ram" made of a giant cardboard tube with handles. Several fighters will have to carry the ram to the door, the rules say, and hit it six times to take the door out. Meanwhile, archers will shoot at them and other defenders will drop "rocks" on them from above. The door is eventually opened, creating a giant scrum at the entranceway.

"It's a damn meat grinder in there," one newly-killed combatant says as he walks off the field and pulls off his helm. "I swear I was being held up by two guys and my feet were off the ground and I was hit, Bam! Bam! Bam!"

Without the ramps and the door now open, this battle is one of attrition at the doorways. In the middle of the fort, Lorcun and his crew keep firing the onager, lofting rocks out of the fort. The onager is virtually impervious to anything on the field except Ansteorra's trebuchet, but its crewmen could be killed by ballista bolts. A few times they are saved by a small wooden shield hung in the middle of the machine when it blocks bolts bound for the machine or crew.

Ansteorra eventually pounds it way further and further into the fort as the battle become a mess, with combatants from both sides mixing in the confusion. I spot Flynn, his arm taken out by a shot, wander around the back of the fort looking for a single-hand weapon, then wade back in with his dead hand behind his back. I lose him in the scramble almost instantly. Lorcun, at the urging of Baldar, leaves the onager and heads to a spot where he has clear crossbow shots at several spearmen. As he sets up, he takes a ballista bolt to the head.

The Trimaris defenders thin out and the marshals call a hold.

"Are there any defenders left?"

A dozen or so raise their hands. They fight on for a few more moments.

"Are there any defenders left?" the call comes again. There are just two.

They are vanquished in seconds. But not fast enough. Ansteorra has captured the fort. But Ansteorra was four minutes slower—42 minutes to 38 minutes—than Trimaris. The day goes to Trimaris.

I pick my way inside the fort. It is in a shambles, with hay bales broken and scattered, arrows and bolts crushed, bent and in giant dirty piles. Ballistae are tipped over. One of Baldar's ballista clones has fallen and broken in half. But Lorcun and his crew are celebrating.

"Whose house?" they sing in unison. "Our house."

"Whose house? Our house."

It's not quite period, but they are having fun. They are happiest about their "first counter-siege experience." In the middle of the battle, one of their rocks took out Ansteorra's trebuchet. "We're going to put a notch in the machine," Lorcun says.

"This gun was invincible," he boasts. "You know what kept us alive?"

He points to a small white piece of cloth embroidered with Trimaris' coat of arms. It is the Queen's favor.

"It was the mysterious blessing of the Queen." He laughs. The group poses for photos standing on and around the onager. Lorcun lets out a deep breath and looks at the mess around him.

"All right guys, let's go pick up rocks and get out of here."

Act I, scene 10
One Piece of Metal Can Change Your Life

"I got it," Hobbs blurts out, bursting into Flynn's kitchen for the weekly SFU work session. "I had to. I was losing sleep knowing it was out there and someone else might get it."

He has just paid $500 for a new helm. For the last two weeks, ever since spotting a For Sale ad on an SCA Internet newsgroup, he has agonized over an early-period Viking helmet with brass inlay decorations and a brass goggle-style visor. The posting had fighters across the country gushing over the helm.

"Wow!! That is f***ing gorgeous," one wrote.

"I have only one thing to say," posted another. "DROOL!"

Hobbs has only been doing this hobby less than a year but he has been pining for this helmet the last few days. He already had a helm, of course. He had justified the $400 he spent on that—a late-period French style called a bascinet—as a onetime expense. "I'll never have to buy one again," he had told us. But the Viking helm really hooked him. He had sent us all e-mails as it sat on the market so we could see it and share his lust for it. Finally, last night, unable to resist, he plunked down the $500.

"It's a lot, but I had to have it. I know it's a lot of money but I'm not married and I don't have a house or kids so this is the time in life to do this stuff."

Of course, in addition to the price tag, the helm presents a few new problems for Hobbs. First of all, he had been working on a later-period persona, shooting for the 14th century "Knight in shining armor" look. This helm, though, is Viking, a few hundred years off of that goal. But it is a showpiece. With an investment like this, he starts to realize, he'll have to change his persona and re-order his SCA life around it. Within a few weeks, the mundane Craig is no longer Hobbs. He becomes Ulfr. And as his surname he adds Forkbeard, after the braids he has been creating out of his goatee.

"It's amazing how much a piece of metal can change your life," Craig/Hobbs/Ulfr Forkbeard says.

"I looked like garbage…"

I have been trying to finish my own armor through these SFU sessions for the last few months, completing a little here, a little there. The others were also plowing through projects or just enjoying the locker-room banter of the basement Armory while the women upstairs churned out new banners for the household. Though some groups make banners by painting silk, most Midrealm groups use appliqué. That technique involves cutting shapes out of bright-colored fabric, setting them down on the banner base and then stitching the edges by hand or satin-stitching them by machine. Using this method, the women completed their assignment from Mistress Rebekah back in Detroit and turned out banners of the Darkyard tree and Forgan's arms to display at Pennsic.

As I cut out sections of leather for my "Big Belt" and half gauntlets, the others would run down their fighting exploits from the past weekend's events. They would brag about guys who "opened up a can of whup-ass" on opponents and griped that they needed a can opener to get blows through the armor of some foes. The group also has fun using the medieval world as a perfect straight man for jokes or riffing off of medievalish pop culture. Hobbs'…sorry…Ulfr's latest tongue-in-cheek plan is to make a foam rubber head that appears as if it was chopped off at the neck. He could then bring it to battles, hold it aloft and bellow at the other side before battles like the grungy, bearded Germanian behemoth in the opening battle of *Gladiator*. Flynn would sometimes fire up his laptop in the basement to download music while everyone worked, or to show the crew his latest amusing find. The group buzzes when he discovers a gem in an animated argument between *Dungeons & Dragons* players. On screen, it features characters from the video games *Summoner* and *Red Faction*, with the voices and dialogue of the comedy troupe The Dead Alewives.

"The pungent stench of mildew emanates from the wet dungeon walls," the Dungeon Master tells his friends in an ominous voice. The other players bombard him with requests for Cheetos, to fire a magic missile to combat 'the darkness,' and to make sure a character is really getting drunk and hitting on girls while waiting in a tavern.

Until now, I have been happy to take my time assembling a set of armor while I survey how other people do it by borrowing it, buying it, making it or converting it. But the trip to Gulf Wars has me more anxious than before to move the process along. I am still not sure this sport is worth spending $500 for just one piece, but the camaraderie that Kief av Kierstad talked about, the exuberance of fighters who won battles and the color and atmosphere started tugging at me at Gulf Wars. I have no armor to wear on the field and no idea what to do once I get there, but I found myself caught up in the moment a few times. I wanted to reach out and help…to be part of the action.

But the task of piecing together an armor kit, a task that had looked so easy a few months ago in January, had more barriers—both practical and aesthetic—than I expected.

Flynn and Talon had advised me to wait until after I pass the authorization test and find out if I like this sport before spending serious money on armor. "After you authorize, you can go for style all you want," Flynn told me.

"I looked like garbage," chimed in Ulfr, who was then Hobbs. "And you will, too."

With that in mind, I had hoped to just borrow an extra set of gear someone left behind. But I quickly learned a lesson about armor. One size does not fit all. Clothes can be worn a little tight or belted in when they're too big. But not steel. The same rigidity that offers so much protection means you can't push and pull and stretch it to the proper size. I tried several too-small helmets and steel leg pieces that were not only god-awful heavy but designed for someone both shorter and slimmer than me. A set of full leg armor even a half-inch too long can catch in odd spots and give you "armor bite" bruises. I luck out and find a few pieces: the neck-protecting gorget and a set of leg protectors Flynn used years ago. For the rest, I would either have to buy it, convert sporting goods into passable gear or make it from scratch.

After my first session in Flynn's basement back in January, I spent hours perusing armor sites on the Internet. Hundreds of metalworkers earn a living—or at least a few extra bucks—making and selling armor to SCA fighters and other re-enactors for $80 to several hundred dollars per helm. Other pieces of leather or metal armor can be ordered online in minutes. Sometimes it is shipped to you in days, but special orders can take months. I skimmed web page after page of helms, slowly learning the types and styles of helms and their period of use. All were more or less "medieval" and fit the SCA's broad restrictions. But styles from different centuries look dramatically differ-ent, often in such basic ways as whether the face is left open or blocked by a faceplate. I quickly learned to distrust any style claims on eBay or some web sites without doing more research. Many advertising claims do not stand up to examination or just slap labels onto items because they sound good. The same thing happens with weapons. A "Gladius-Claymore-Naginata" I saw listed on e-Bay turned out to be neither of those completely different styles of swords.

Because different languages, cultures and periods often called the same thing by their own names, sorting out the right name for something is difficult. Armor, just like any other crucial product, evolved with the needs and technology of the time. It also evolved at varying speeds and sequences in different regions. Early period helms, for example, were usually open-faced. Romans (with *Helmet Version 1.0?*) had the metal equivalent of sideburns often extending over their cheeks, but rarely had anything blocking the mouth or eyes. Normans and Saxons (in *Helmet 2.0* or *Helmet 1066*), often wore metal caps with a nasal guard. Hobbs'/Ulfr's new Viking helm goes one step beyond, with a goggle-shaped guard for the eyes and a chain mail veil shielding the lower face. By late period, the number of styles has exploded. Barrel-shaped helms with a completely flat top would encase the entire head, leaving just slits for the eyes and mouth, while a popular French-style helmet called a bascinet had a smooth and slightly peaked dome. The point and curve of a bascinet—the most common helm in my part of the Midrealm—would deflect the force of blows and guide a sword to skip off the surface. Historically, the bascinet would cover the top and sides of the head but unless the fighter attached a faceplate or a peaked face with a point—a "pig face"—it would be wide open in front.

For the SCA, however, any helmet style that does not cover the face is modified by adding a grille of metal bars over the face. The metal bars that form a cage over the faces of SCA fighters are a wholly modern invention designed solely for safety at the expense of authenticity. A cage of bars is added with the bars no further than an inch apart, regardless of what the helm looked like in period. Most bascinets have a totally different profile in the SCA, with their hemispheres of cage in front of the dome, than they had in period.

New fighters also have to make decisions about the accuracy of their other pieces of armor. Some fighters set their goal when starting to fight on doing it right even at the start. They can match their armor to the place and time of their persona and use only accurate and authentic materials. But that can take months or a giant outlay of cash. Others go the other extreme and do whatever is necessary just to get on the field. Their haste, low budgets or laziness leads to the armor suits cut from bright blue plastic pickle barrels on the field at Pennsic. And at Gulf Wars, a company called Egg Armor sold full suits made from Kevlar.

Andre Sinou, of Toms River, N.J., is part of the crowd of armorers selling suits of armor and their parts to SCA fighters. Sinou offers full suits of armor for between $1,300 and $1,800. Though some armorers can do better work for higher costs, and others specialize in different styles, Sinou specializes in one stylized design. Known in the SCA as Andreas Eisfalke or Ice Falcon, he also has intimate knowledge of what works in the SCA and what doesn't. Andreas was King of the East Kingdom at Gulf Wars.

"We're the best bang for the buck," Andreas tells me, slipping in a quick plug. "Seriously. Most armorers know what they are and know their place. We all fill a different niche. It's not a cutthroat business. We all help each other. I'll send people to other shops that do what they need and they'll send people to me."

The Tale of the Ice Falcon

Andre Sinou's first set of armor looked nothing like the armor he makes now.

Andre was a senior at Toms River High School when he saw his first SCA battle. The varsity football player who somehow played both the offensive and defensive lines at just 175 pounds decided he had to try this unusual sport. He bought a $75 mild steel helmet, cut a shield from plywood and spent a night making body protection from old carpet.

His armoring skills have improved dramatically since then. Today his distinctive, late period, gothic style and mirror-finished armor is available at events across the country from his company, Ice Falcon Armory.

"I'll go anywhere in the United States," he says.

He will set up shop at every major SCA war—Estrella, Gulf Wars, Lilies, Pennsic, Great Western War, even the West-An Tir War, often shipping chest plates, leg pieces and helms there a week in advance. From spring through the Pennsic War in August, he is on the road most weekends to both sell and to fight, often with members of the household of fighters he founded, Bloodguard.

His livelihood depends on it. Trained as a hydrologist at Stockton University in New Jersey, he started making armor to pay bills while still in school. When he finished school, he started making armor full-time while looking for a "real" job.

"Then I realized I was making a lot more money armoring than I would if I was just a hydrologist."

So it is now a business, as much as it is a hobby. Along with his pay from weekends with the Marine Corps Reserve—he served in Kuwait during the Gulf War—he makes enough money to pay his bills and to finance his last reign as King. Andreas and two employees work full time out of a rented shop in a Tom's River industrial park where they produce armor pieces assembly-line style. Most of the work is done with Beverly shears, a Whitney punch, an electric-powered buffer, an anvil, leather mallets and a ball peen hammer. With the help of two part-time welders and a few others Andreas uses for special jobs, the group works on 10 to 30 pieces at once. They will make a pile of lames (articulations for joints), cuisses (upper leg protection) or knee cops, then assemble the parts together in the end. All of the workers have a specialty. One cuts metal, one assembles the parts, one prepares pieces for the polisher and another does little but polish.

"It's not easy to get a mirror polish on stainless steel. If you came to work for me, we'd test you on everything. You'd find the thing you'd do better than anything else."

The "mirror polish" he works hard to produce both wins Andreas sales and costs him some as well. Andreas calls his later-period armor "knights in shining armor" equipment. That style inspires some fighters. Others hate it. A few of the Darkyard guys snicker at it—sniping at the pretentiousness of the shiny finish. But the Darkyarders are all early period personas—guys with leather armor, hidden armor or more rough-hewn metal. They don't question Ice Falcon's basic quality. It's a matter of taste. But Andreas openly admits that some other armorers make higher quality equipment. It's all about the segment of the market they aim at.

Most shops, he said, charge appropriate prices for their product. High cost means high quality and there are usually few big bargains on lower end items.

"You always get what you pay for with armor. If you find a suit for $100, that's what you get."

"Start light"

Thanks to Hobbs/Ulfr and his seeming slip off the deep end with his Viking helm purchase, I solve a major problem when he offers to let me use his "old" bascinet. No matter that I'll be fighting with a Roman unit. Almost everyone starts in this sport as a walking anachronism.

Ulfr, though, is quickly chomping through his checkbook like a veteran. Less than a year into the SCA, he's probably dropped $1,000 on armor. Ulfr has also placed an order over the Internet for a kit to make a coat of plates. Also known as a brigandine, the common piece of SCA armor and offers some of the protection of plate but less weight and better mobility. In period, plates of metal about the size of a cigarette box would be sewn inside a leather vest to provide protection. It is what the Cleftlands fighter I saw training back in January was using. A coat of plates is a historically accurate piece of armor, most designed from archaeological finds in Wisby, Sweden. Though some people cut corners and use pickle-barrel plastic instead of metal, Ulfr has ordered a full set of already-cut metal plates with holes drilled in them for rivets. He'll then buy a big piece of suede, cut it to make a sleeveless shirt and rivet the plates in a layer over the body.

He also ordered a gambeson, a quilted and padded undergarment, to put under it. He purchased it for $100 over the Internet two months ago, and it just arrived. But it's too big. He ordered a medium. But SCA sizes, it seems, run on the big side. Particularly with fighters, many of whom are just simply large and overweight, sizes have little correlation to real-world standards.

"In SCA sizes, I guess I'm a petite," Ulfr says, grinning as he eyes the rest of us to see if we would fill it out better.

His new helm, though, will make a big statement. The inlay is, at least at a distance, very similar to the kind that Counts, Kings and Dukes, proudly wear on their helms.

"People will be like, 'Oh, there's a Duke. Let's get him,'" he says. He can't stop grinning. "I am going to get killed *so* fast. People are just going to come after me. I have to decide if I want to fight a while or if I want to look good and get killed right away."

Not sure I want to pay hundreds of dollars quite yet, I started lower down the armor food chain. I spent a week rummaging through piles of sweat-stained, scratched and worn gear at Play It Again Sports, a chain store of used sporting goods. I turned bins of gear inside out, stacking prospects in the aisle, blocking other customers as I tried things on, singly and in combination, mixing and matching. I inspect lacrosse, hockey and football shoulder pads, testing for arm movement and protection for the shoulders, breastbone and upper arm. Hockey goalie chest protectors, lacrosse flak jackets, rollerblading and lacrosse elbow pads and hockey and baseball shin and knee guards were close, but not perfect.

"Can I help you find something?" a clerk asked, no doubt dreading the re-shelving work I had created.

Oh sure, I thought. I'd like a set of used beginner plate armor. What do you have in cuisses?

"Well...," I said instead, before launching into a convoluted explanation of how I was doing medieval combat with clubs. The clerk just smiled and nodded.

I settled on a Santa Claus sack of stuff—two sets of shoulder pads (I would return one), the flak jacket and a couple of youth goalie chest pads so cheap I couldn't pass them up. I lugged the lot into my apartment and put on the shoulder pads. In the context of the store and all the other gear, they hadn't looked so big. Here they seemed gigantic. When I pulled a big tunic over them I became a hunchback Frankenstein. Discouraged I stuffed it all back in the bag. I'll let Flynn sort it out, I decided.

Flynn wasn't thrown a bit. The shoulder pads were just fine.

"But they look huge," I protested.

"As compared to what?" he said. "Do you see what some of those guys have out there?"

Minimum standards were working in my favor. We made one alteration that made a huge difference, snipping off the scallop-shell plastic layers that cupped the shoulders.

"Oh yeah, that's much lower profile," Sean said, before giving it a few test whacks with his sword.

We try the same test with a helmet, one of the late-period helms in SFU's loaner pile. I pull the helm, lined with blue camping foam, over my head.

"Start light," I ask. Talon nods.

He pulls back a sword and measures the distance to my temple. Tap. Not bad. He raps me harder. I feel a bit of a jar along the side of my face and jaw. He snaps a harder shot. The jar is harder but no pain. He takes about a dozen shots, mixing them on both sides and on top. None are big blows and they only move my head and neck slightly.

"Don't close your eyes," Flynn tells me.

"Actually, he's doing all right with that," Talon says.

Good. I have been blinking, but only involuntarily at contact. I am fine as he swings, surprisingly so, as the blade rushes at the side of my head.

"Don't you need to hit me harder?" I ask. I almost want to take a dizzying, eye-watering hit just so I know and won't be scared.

"Nope. Those were good shots."

"Really?"

"You shouldn't get hit much harder than that very often."

"Well cool, then."

Talon has also been hard at work on his own armor. He is shooting for a style much the opposite of what Ice Falcon makes—all leather. As part of his bid to become a full member of Darkyard, he wants an armor "kit" that matches the Roman or post-Roman style of the household. He has also ordered replica Roman swords and belt decorations for his "dress" garb to wear to court and ceremonies.

The last few weeks he has tinkered with a leather torso he made and first test-drove at the Cleftlands tournament. From big sheets of black and brown leather he cut out small rectangles, punched holes in them and laced them together. The result was a suit of leather scales that overlapped their neighboring scales on all sides. This process, using either leather or metal, has been documented back to the earliest reaches of SCA period. Called lamellar, the scales are reasonably cheap—scales can be cut from scrap—and the overlap helps distribute force across a wider area. Even though the leather is not particularly thick, it dulls blows well enough for him.

I am fast learning all the fun you can have with leather in the SCA.

I decide to make at least a couple of pieces of armor myself. I will likely make a leather bracer (forearm protector) and elbow protector combination in a few weeks. For now I need hand and kidney protection. Sean and Talon give me a shopping list and I head to the leather shop for a whole hide and a plate of sole bend, stiff leather about 1/4 inch thick that will go for my half gauntlets.

I immediately feel out of place in the workshop. The members of this projects group have years of experience making armor and weapons from foam, leather and metal. They are also used to sewing their medieval clothes. But like many people, I have not made anything by hand since high school art class. The division of labor of today's economy is more efficient than the methods of the Middle Ages, but it often disconnects people from the origins and production of items they use every day. Few people know how to sew their own clothes, grow their own food or make and fix the things they need. That's the job of factories and machines. But trying to re-create an earlier time forces you to learn many of the steps involved in creating goods. While you might not go all the way back to the beginning of the process—actually mining the ore to smelt for a sword or planting the flax to harvest and weave into linen—it takes you several steps closer. With every step you do yourself, you gain a better understanding of the item and a greater feeling of ownership in the finished product. Duke Baldar had told me at Gulf Wars about his epiphany that he could create something of value, on his own, when he make his first armor piece. I had a similar feeling as I started improving my medieval garb. *I made a shirt! I never knew I could do that.*

But each new task also has a learning curve that poses a challenge. Here in the workshop, I have no clue how to make anything from leather. The idea of even cutting the hide intimidates me. *What if I ruin it?* I feel as if I'm on shaky ground at every step and need assurances from the others that I'm not way off track. I need lessons in cutting leather straps, in attaching a buckle to the straps and in riveting it on. I even need guidance using modern tools, like Flynn's band saw and sander. This hobby is fast exposing my inadequacy at tangible, hands-on tasks, so different from the paper-pushing jobs that dominate the workplace.

I muddle through my shortcomings to complete my first armor project, protection for my sword hand. There are several types of hand protection for fighting. Some fighters buy expensive full gauntlets of metal. The more lames, layers to a joint, the more expensive. Sean bought a new set at Gulf Wars for $250 from an armorer he and Darkyard fighters regularly use. I'm going a different route. At Gulf Wars I spent $40 for a basket hilt—about two-thirds of a globe of steel bars with a slot for rattan to slide down the axis. When I reach inside and grab the rattan going through the center, my fingers and front of my hand are enclosed. But my wrist is vulnerable. Leather half gauntlets, a staple armor item, protect the hand and wrist with two loops of hard and thick leather sewn together at the wrist. The loops each look like round cross-sections of a cone, with one end wider than the other. Half gauntlets are made by sewing two cone cross-sections together at their thinner ends to create something of an hourglass shape, only less pronounced.

Cutting the leather is slow until we reduce the time to a fraction with Flynn's power saw. Thick and stiff, the sole bend cuts like a slightly softer wood. With a small bit on the drill press, Talon and Flynn help me drill holes about a quarter centimeter apart to make sewing the two leather pieces together easier. After soaking the leather in water for a couple hours, the once-stiff leather becomes pliable. I can now mold it and shape it to the form I want. Using an oversized needle made for sewing leather, I easily pull waxed thread though the holes to make the oversized cuff of leather. Once dry, it bends slightly if I try to crush it, but just knocks like a door when I rap it with my knuckles.

Because I used such thick leather, it is hard enough. But there are techniques to make softer pieces of leather harder. Immersing it in boiling water makes the leather shrink into stronger protection. For my "Big Belt" we use wax. Leather, like a lot of materials, will absorb just about any liquid. Molten wax is no exception. As a liquid, the wax is easily absorbed into the leather, infusing all the gaps and spaces between fibers. When the wax cools, it hardens, making the leather practically as stiff as a board. There is some debate within the SCA about whether this would have been done for period armor since a cutting weapon like a real sword might cut through a stiff piece of leather faster than it would a tough and stringy one. Against a club of a sword, it works fine. Several people recommend putting the leather and wax in a pan in the oven to heat it up and let the wax soak in. Talon and Flynn though don't want to fool around. They sprung for a cheap electric wok, then drop in big blocks of paraffin and beeswax at a 60/40 ratio.

Talon takes my leather pieces and heats them with a blow dryer.

"It opens the pores," he says. "Leather is skin. It has pores and the heat makes them open."

Once the wax turns to liquid, we dip about a quarter of my belt into the wok at a time and ladle the liquid over much of the rest. Using an old rag to avoid burning his fingers, Talon pours ladle after ladle onto the leather panels. The leather sucks the wax in like a sponge. The black-dyed front looks no different, but the rough unfinished back grows darker. Little white spots appear on the surface and leave little bubbly, gurgly trails, like clam air holes at the beach, as the wax runs down.

"That's air coming out. The wax is replacing it."

He hands me the ladle. I keep ladling wax and turning the leather until the trails stop forming. Then I ladle some more to saturate the leather. If the wax hardens before seeping in, we just pull it out, turn the dryer on and the wax grows shiny and slick again.

We have stir fried my first piece of armor.

Now I need to learn how to use it.

Act I, scene 11
Controlled Multiple Personality Disorder

Most years, the classes at the Pennsic War include one on Middle Eastern history. Students come expecting handouts, a lecture and an instructor who drops the pretense of persona for the sake of teaching.

They get Chengir.

With his turban, beard and growling and snapping voice, Chengir abu ben Said will begin, "I will tell you a story…" For the next hour, the students will never get a straight or direct answer. The lesson will jump around. But with an organic, flowing, stream-of -consciousness series of narratives, the storyteller I met back at Baron Durr's hafla will reveal the secrets of history.

David Woodruff, owner and puppet master of this persona, never appears. He almost never does at SCA events. Once Woodruff dons his garb and hits Troll, he is gone and Chengir is all that remains. For him, that's the best part of the SCA.

"Persona has really become a lost art in the SCA," he explains. "I am so disappointed that persona has become such a lost thing. It's hard to do. I think as adults we grow up being taught that if you're an adult, you can't be someone else.

"But to say things you would never say, and be things you're not, is incredible. It helps us decide who we want to be next and who we don't want to be. As adults we get away from that. You get trapped in jobs and life because you lose your ability to dream. I like the freedom to reinvent myself whenever I wish."

"Who are you…?"

Way back at the first projects session that I attended at Flynn's, he pulled out his laptop and began taking down information from everyone. He went around the room asking for weapons authorizations, talents and awards. And personas.

He finally worked around to me.

"What are you?"

I turned a little red. I hesitated.

"I don't know what I am," I finally stammered.

"None of us do," Bobbie had jumped in. Everyone laughed and Sean moved on. I had plenty of time to pick a name later.

When I first encountered this group, people seemed to have about eight names each, all of which they would use interchangeably, even within the same conversation. It took months to match names to faces, with all their SCA names, Dagorhir names, gaming names, nicknames and real ones. When I finally started keeping names straight, Craig/Hobbs shifted to Ulfr. Then Flynn and Talon began researching Roman names to change theirs. I will have yet another set of names to remember.

Parents and roommates unfamiliar with persona names can be puzzled when friends call asking for Olaf, Elspeth, Thorvald or Lothair. Even today, mail arriving with unfamiliar mundane names on the return address can be a head-scratcher. Couples that meet each other as their personas will often call each other by their persona names even after marriage. Milesent Vibert, the woman in charge of the Barony of the Cleftlands Dance Guild, met her husband Mark Doblekar as his persona, Edward of Brackenburye. She uses both names interchangeably. When he left messages for her under both names when they started dating, her mother had a talk with her. Dating two men, her mother warned, was a bad idea.

The concept of using a different name and behaving as a different persona adds both authenticity and fantasy to this world. Picking a name can force people to narrow the time and place they research. It can focus their garb and armor choices and push them to better understand life in that culture. But playing someone else can also offend modern sensibilities. It also takes effort most members of the Society avoid. In practice, the majority treats their personas like a crazy aunt they left at home in the attic. They shop for it, make things for it, refer to it in the third person, but never bring it out in public. They certainly don't act like it, talk like it or live like it.

Many build detailed persona "backstories," mapping out all the twists and turns of their persona's lineage and pursuits, none of which ever come into play in the Known World. Omarad the general said his name has a history, but he never put together a persona history.

"People say, 'What is your persona?' and I say 'I'm a first century SCA Knight,'" Omarad said. "I am myself. I don't really have one. People are who they are with some flavor thrown in."

Thomas Longshanks takes a similar approach. When I asked him what his persona was, his response started, "That is a tough question.

"If by persona you mean a developed life story of an individual set in a medieval location and time in real history, like 'My name is Thomas Longshanks. I am the son of a brewer near Aconbury in the north of England in 1423.' Then I don't have one.

"If by persona you mean a developed fantasy story that explains disparate clothes and interests, like 'My name is Thomas Longshanks of the Misty Lake of the Unicorn. I was abducted by gypsies who then fled to the Steppes of Mongolia and only recently returned to England via Persia and oh, by the way, I am a half-elf.' Well, I don't have one of those, either."

Instead, he said, he spent several years working behind the scenes at events, often dealing with the mundane logistics of making them happen. So he is just Master Thomas Longshanks of Atlantia who studies food history, medieval food and cookery.

I decide to just start with a name.

A "Problem Name"

Eogan macAlpein, a bushy-haired Scot with a screaming hatred of the English, had laid out the basics of picking a medieval name for a class back at Atlantia's University in February.

"This is a journey, not a destination," he told the students. "I don't want you to think that you're weird if you struggle to find a name. I would rather you find something you like and that is historically accurate. I would like you to find something that fits you, rather than trying to please other people."

It is a challenge to officially satisfy the Society for Creative Anachronism, however.

The SCA requires names to be historically documentable to a particular time and place. Your *Dungeons & Dragons* name may count in groups like Dagorhir, but not here. You can go by it. Your friends can call you that. But the Society rejects it as an "official" SCA name if it was never really used. This Society fights the battle between fantasy and history with names, just as it does in other areas. The SCA welcomed both fantasy and history when it started, but has drifted over time toward history. It allowed Duke Laurelen Darksbane's elvish name years ago but would block it now. I will have a chance to investigate the origins of this world when the SCA turns 35 years old in a few weeks.

Unlike today's names, Eogan continued, which almost always use the father's last name as the surname, period names are broken into four categories: locative, occupational, descriptive or patriarchal. Instead of Patrick O'Donnell (patriarchal), I could be something like Patrick of Cleftlands (locational), Patrick the Chronicler (occupational) or Patrick the Red (descriptive, for my red hair). Likewise, all of the Viking "—ssons" and "—dottirs" use patriarchal Norse names, Edmund of Hertford is a locational name, Omarad the Wary is a descriptive name and Freiman the Minstrel is an occupational name. In period, villagers would likely go by just one name until someone else also had the same name. Then one, or both, needed a surname to distinguish him from the other. The same might occur when he left town, Eogan said, with the surname changing based on the circumstance.

"If I was going to go from my little village to Edinburgh, I would tell them I was Eogan, son of Alpein, and they would say, 'Oh, I know Alpein. He fought with the King at such and such battle. He's OK.'"

Forms and pronunciation change dramatically over time. Originally, Eogan was spelled Eog and pronounced "On" with a silent "g." Then it became Eoghan, pronounced like Ewan.

"Then the English got involved…" Eogan said, snarling, "and it became Eoghann, still pronounced like Ewan. The 'h' says the 'g' is silent."

"I should have everybody call me 'On.' I tried it…for two days. But everyone looks at it and says Eogan. It's a reasonable enough pronunciation and I don't want to educate the whole barony."

The most common error is trying to mix too many cultures for the chance to play several roles. The Varangians are one common fallback. The other is merchants.

"Merchants," sneered Eogan. "Oh God. If you listen to SCA people, Europe was seething with merchants and travelers. But 95 percent of the people lived and died within 25 miles of where they were born.

"If you pick a name like Abdul MacGregor there is no story you can tell to get those cultures together. You might get Olaf MacGregor because those cultures did intermix."

The class skipped over the Mongol personas in the "Dark Horde" or the increasing number of Japanese personas in the Society. Dozens of people wear Japanese clothing and Japanese-styled armor under the idea that they have come into contact with European explorers. The Baron of Roaring Wastes (where I attended Twelfth Night), the mundane Don Walli, has a Japanese persona as Munenori. Also pushing the boundaries is Midrealm Knight Sir Ix Cacique, MKA Bo Ring, who plays an Aztec warrior who has run across Conquistadores. In what is either an inspired attempt to take this persona the distance or an exercise in absurdity, Sir Ix fights wearing a full body suit of leopard-print cloth over his armor and an imperfect leopard head with ears that sit atop his helm to match Aztec warriors who wore real leopard skins.

In the end, I choose what seems like the simplest route—an early version of my real name. But like any other task in this arena, doing it right turns out to be anything but simple.

I set off expecting to use a form of my mundane name, like Padraig, with little trouble. But the earlier I wanted the name to fit, the more changes I needed to make. The heraldic group Academy of St. Gabriel, whose members study primary sources from the Middle Ages—rosters, old town records, period histories—for names has categorized "Patrick" as a "problem name."

"Some names that many people think of as common to the Middle Ages or Renaissance are either purely modern or otherwise problematic," the group's web site notes. "For example, some names which were used in one medieval culture are now mistakenly believed to have been used in others. Other medieval names are mispronounced, or thought to be feminine names when they were only masculine."

Patrick joined its list of "problem names" that also includes Amber, Ian, Garth and Megan. St. Patrick, it turns out, is to blame.

"The name *Patricius* first made its appearance in Ireland in the 5th century when the future saint arrived to evangelize the Irish," St. Gabriel's web site explains. "Throughout the Middle Ages and Renaissance, the Irish considered the saint's name too holy for normal use. In the early Middle Ages, starting in the 9th century, he was commemorated with devotional names like *Gilla Pátraic* 'servant of St. Patrick' and *Máel Pátraic*, 'devotee of St. Patrick.' In late medieval Gaelic spelling, the same names became *Giolla Phádraig* and *Maol Phádraig.*"

Flynn's official SCA name of MaelColuim suddenly made sense. Malcolm is a form of "servant of" St. Column. The "O'" in my last name took several forms over time too, based on whether it was meant to show clan affiliation or connection to parents. After several revisions, I ended up accepting Mael Patraic macDomnaill, even as its resemblance to my modern name became fleeting.

Others, I soon learned, took on entire personas, not just names, with only a passing resemblance to their real selves.

"They're not going to believe you..."

"This is what I think is one of the most fun parts of the SCA," Lady Lucia Borromeo tells her students from beneath her Gulf Wars class tent.

Lucia is a member of the Order of Justinian, a Meridies-based group that pushes persona within the SCA. The SCA has two extremes on persona, she explains, with "authenticity mavens" who look at persona to the point of questioning, "Does your name match your garb which matches your pavilion?" On the other side, the "fun mavens" simply say, "It really doesn't matter, Give me a name. I don't care what my garb is. It's just a tunic."

"Take it to whatever level you want," she tells the class. "There's no requirement that you sit down today, write a five-page paper on your history and your name and you're stuck with your persona for life."

Although some just pick a persona that goes with the household they fall in with, like Roman Darkyarders, she herself was so interested in the Italian Renaissance she started with a 14th century name because she had a beautiful dress with dagged sleeves. The clothing you like can often drive persona decisions as much as historical interest. People who do not enjoy elaborate clothing should avoid the high Renaissance and Elizabethan eras.

"Anything before the 13th century you're getting into your comfy clothes," she said. "What would I look really good in? What makes you look like you want to feel? It's nice to have a Tudor persona but if you're still running around in 7th century T-tunics you can tell people all you want but they're not going to believe you."

The more research you do on your persona's setting, the more you can behave like such a person. When she attends events with People of Persona, a group started in the SCA's southern California and Nevada Kingdom of Caid, she does extra research so she can keep up. But talking like such a person does not mean reciting your persona backstory.

"Don't exchange autobiographical info," she said. "Nobody really does that in real life. Bits unfold in conversation."

Her husband also offers a few hints on speaking "forsoothly," the form of Elizabethan English many renaissance fairs require their employees to use. Avoid mundane topics and stick to real history or Known World events, he says. The quotations in the King James Bible offer a decent model for such speech. Or try the *Wayne's World* approach of attaching "not" at the end of statements to indicate a negative. And push not others to talk that way.

Lady Lucia needs no push. Taking her persona to extremes is the gateway to the ultimate goal that so many in this group seek.

"You can be transported for an instant," she said.

The Tale of Chengir

David Woodruff does not have to try to become Chengir abu ben Said.

After playing with him as an alter ego for 20 years, the storyteller Chengir just comes out sometimes.

That's what can happen when you mix history and the modern world the way Woodruff has. It's what happens when someone pours their energy into building an alter ego in detail, learning a whole life story instead of making it up by imagination and by playing out the things that inspire your own imagination with a persona puppet.

"It's easy to drop into him," Woodruff says. "He's such a well-defined character he just appears."

The distinctive voice, which some say is similar to an Irish accent, also just appeared.

"I think the voice decided on me," he remembers. "I hear actors say characters sort of spring forward from them. I'm not sure at what point he appeared, but he appeared as a character, his voice came with him and that was that."

The birth of Chengir is an example of how many seek the safety of an invented world to escape an unhappy mundane life. When Woodruff was in high school in Basking Ridge, N.J., in the early 1970s his father bickering often with his mother on the way to a divorce. His mother, he said, wanted to use him as a "bludgeon" against his father.

"I made it a point to not be around," he said.

School wasn't much better. His grades were bad and teachers looked at him as a problem student. He failed to memorize multiplication tables because "I just couldn't see the importance" and he could figure the problems out on his own.

Though Woodruff now has has three degrees from Allegheny College and works in Internet operations, it was hard for his high school self to envision his situation changing. He latched on with local theater groups, and was typecast as old men in community productions because he was thin and gangly. Some of the New York actors took him to an SCA event in the city. He went, believing it was a theater event. Instead, he found a perfect mix of theater and history.

"The play-acting of a persona was a great thing for me," he said. "Here was a bunch of adults who were pretending, and in my family, adults didn't pretend. The concept that it was O.K. for adults to pretend was fascinating for me at the time. It was a whole new way of not only learning about history but experiencing it."

Woodruff declines to say what his first persona was—"I buried any evidence of the early mistakes that I made"—but learned the best way to pick one is to think about the stories you enjoyed as a child.

"The things that always excited me were Sinbad and Aladdin. You've got to think of it like a little kid growing up in New Jersey. Arabic culture is about as far apart from New Jersey as you can get. For me, the Sinbad stories were impressive because here was a person who traveled places and saw things and did things that were extraordinary."

As he started researching, he grew more excited about Arabia. While Europe was in the Dark Ages, Arabia was flourishing. Medieval Arabic culture was more cosmopolitan than Europe, had more respect for women, and was the world's storehouse of knowledge. While Europe was burning books, the Arabs saved Greek philosophy and the history books that provide our only links with the past. The process of researching triggered his interest in storytelling. He found the big historical details—dates of wars, names of rulers—in history books. But the best information came from stories.

"The very important things—the way you understood their feelings, their prejudices, their ideals—were from the stories they told about themselves. If you read enough of them, the way of life comes together."

The name Chengir is a Persian corruption of Genghis. Chengir lives in Khwarazm, an empire that controlled Baghdad, Afghanistan and parts of India and the Soviet Union from the 1000s into the 1200s. Woodruff liked it because that culture let non-Muslims hold high positions in government and an account of the time reports that a mere four of every 10 citizens were Muslim.

"It was accepted to have multiple religions in the same country to that was a pretty extraordinary thing," he said.

Most of Chengir's stories come from two sources, *A Thousand and One Nights* and *Travels With the Caliph*. There are few English translations of the latter, written in 910, so Woodruff collects portions printed in other books. He skips the famous Sir Richard Burton version of *A Thousand and One Nights* for a more original version. Though it has just 300 of the stories, they were all recorded by an Arab. English translators, he said, change too much. Woodruff often translates on his own, using a copy of same manuscript that Burton translated for his version. Translating helps him memorize. He now estimates he knows 930 stories from memory. He hopes to someday translate the stories of a Turkish folk hero called Kuroghli, who might be the inspiration of Robin Hood, because many of the tales are similar.

On Woodruff's only trip to the Muslim world in 1994, he spent a week learning enough Turkish to ask for a copy of the book. He wanted to see an original to compare the stories to Victorian translations and learn if Kuroghli and Robin Hood are the same legend. He went from shop to shop in Istanbul, but had no luck. The answer to his question still eludes him.

Instead, Chengir's most-used character is named Abunuwas, a true historical character who was the chief poet of Caliph Harun El Rashgeed. The Caliph also had a clown in his court. Over time, stories of Abunuwas and the clown were merged.

Woodruff said Abunuwas is much like Chengir and Chengir takes his last name—Said—from an Abunuwas story.

Woodruff even designed his armor from images on pottery recovered from Khwarazm. He uses metal leg armor and a chest piece made from small rounded leather scales. He wears a coif of chain mail like the fighters on the pottery, and his helmet is specially made from a period drawing. He also has inlaid a decoration on his helmet in brass, much like crowns that star fighters use to proclaim their rank. Woodruff measures his worth in this Society by a different standard, the completeness of his persona, so the brass just reads "Chengir" in Arabic. It also has an Arabic message based on a verse in the Koran inlaid in the back.

"It says, 'If you can read this you're a coward,'" he said. "It's more flowery than that, but that's what it means."

Chengir is well armed for helping Woodruff in another arena: social situations. He can be more free to say things as Chengir and, he says, "if Chengir makes a faux pas, it's not me.

"He goes up to women and says, 'Your appearance is so lovely you force Muslims to think about things they're not supposed to think about.' But I would never go up to someone and say, 'Gosh, I like the way you look.'

"I think it's tremendously freeing to do that. I look at Chengir as a controlled multiple personality disorder. I hear people say how free it is to be a ventriloquist and have a dummy say things. Well I know Chengir says things I would never say. It's a freeing experience.

"There's a joy in doing that that most people never have."

Act I, scene 12
The Squire's Wall

Come home with me little Mattie Groves, come home with me tonight
Come home with me little Mattie Groves and sleep with me tonight

Oh I can't come home, I won't come home and sleep with you tonight
By the rings on your fingers I can tell you are Lord Arlen's wife.
'Tis true I am Lord Arlen's wife, Lord Arlen's not at home
He is out to the far corn fields, bringing the yearlings home.

Little Mattie Groves, he lay down and took a little sleep
When he awoke Lord Arlen was standing at his feet
Saying how do you like my feather bed and how do you like my sheets?
And how do you like my lady, who lies in your arms asleep?

Oh well I like your feather bed and well I like your sheets
But better I like your lady maid who lies in my arms asleep.
Well Get Up! Get Up! Lord Arlen cried, get up as quick as you can
It'll never be said in fair England I slew a naked man!

So Mattie struck the very first blow and he hurt Lord Arlen sore
Lord Arlen struck the very next blow and Mattie struck no more.
And then Lord Arlen he took his wife, he sat her on his knee
Saying who do you like the best of us, Mattie Groves or me?

And then spoke up his own dear wife, never heard to speak so free
I'd rather kiss one dead Mattie's lips than you and your finery.
Lord Arlen he jumped up and loudly he did bawl
He stuck his wife right through the heart
And pinned her against the wall.

—Anonymous, written 1600-1650

Under the official rules of the SCA, the King and Queen are required to attend only three events in their reign: their coronation, the Crown Tournament to select their successor and the coronation where they step off the throne and hand it over.

By late spring, the relationship between Valharic and his wife has deteriorated to the point that nobody wishes he had won Crown anymore. If Edmund had taken one of the borderline and disputed blows, and Valharic had become King, the six-month reign would be a failure in both the spirit and the letter of the rules. By late April, the end of the period that Valharic and his wife would have been King and Queen, their marriage has ended in a nasty fight. They could not even go to coronation together to turn over the crowns.

The relationship comes to a violent end after Valharic hears a few too many reports that his wife's "friend" is more than that. Police have to break up the fight between him, his wife and the "friend" playing Mattie Groves to Valharic's Lord Arlen. Though Valharic threatens to kill the other man and has ample weapons to do it, nobody is stuck "right through the heart." On the day he would have handed over the crown to a new King, Valharic has already spent a night in jail. He has been charged with domestic violence and the almost-Queen has moved in with the interloper. She will live with him for at least the next three years.

The plans he had set for his life have fallen apart. He should be heading to coronation with his wife to hand over the thrones after a glorious reign as King and Queen. He is supposed to be a Knight by now. He is supposed to be a father of a baby boy and a baby girl. And he and his wife, 27 and 24 respectively, are supposed to be lovingly feeding them and putting them to sleep.

When he is allowed back in the house to clean up and move back with his parents, all his belongings have been thrown around the house. Slices from his wedding cake, saved to remember the big day, rot and collect mold in the disconnected freezer. A belt his wife bought at Pennsic that spells out in ornate letters, "VALHARIC MY TRUE LOVE ALWAYS" lies discarded and tangled in a corner. He hauls the mess back to his parents' house, stacks it in the garage, and collapses, sobbing, onto his mother's lap.

He has hit bottom.

Three weeks later, when he travels to the SCA event called Baron Wars he will decide what he has to do.

Gulf Wars
Kildonon Hall under construction in the
Bastermark camp (top left); Fritz der Rothirsch
(above) teaches a blacksmithing class; Mistress
Martha Elspeth gives directions in her natural dye
class (below); Sir Kief av Kierstead (left) a Lion
of Ansteorra.

Middle Kingdom General Omarad the Wary and
King Edmund (top) talk to troops before a Gulf
Wars battle; Duke Baldar Langstrider (above
and right) on the sidelines and in a one on one
bout.

Fighters start their siege (top) of the Gulf Wars castle; Lorcun Attalus
(left and above) prepares his onager and ammunition for battle.

The view from I-79 of just a sliver of the Pennsic War. (top) Some from the crowd of 12,000 explore shops at the War. (left) Clothes and armor are for sale at one of the more elaborate temporary booths at Pennsic. (right)

Darkyard's Pennsic War camp entrance. (top)
Roland Kein sells hats, socks and baskets at
events across the Known World. (right) The
Bored Housewife shows off her line of
"Wal-Mart Renaissance Dresses." (bottom
right) Some of the hundreds of yards of
medieval-styled trim for sale at Calontir Trim.
(bottom)

Middle Kingdom King Bardolph and Queen
Brigh at the Pennsic XXX opening ceremonies
(above); The Clan Tynker practices juggling
(right); The Tynkers lead the Kingdom of the
Outlands in the procession to Pennsic opening
ceremonies.

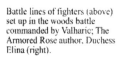

Battle lines of fighters (above) set up in the woods battle commanded by Valharic; The Armored Rose author, Duchess Elina (right).

Act II, scene 1
Learn by Doing

April-May 2001, Common Era
Anno Societatis XXXV, XXXVI

> *"Sword and shield in bloody field,*
> *doth win immortal fame."*
>
> —Act III, scene ii, *Henry V*

"I will tell you this is what works for me," Bardolph Odger Windlauffer says to his class. "Take it with a grain of salt. If it works for you, use it. Or use just the parts that help."

Just a week after ascending the throne from Edmund, the Middle Kingdom's new King teaches a class of about 20 students at the Royal University of the Midrealm (RUM) how to throw basic SCA sword blows. For an hour, he explains his system of using footwork and body positioning to put himself in the right place to make killing shots and avoid being clobbered.

Bardolph, MKA Illinois state trooper Jonathan Purviance, takes his history seriously. Though he started in this Society caring most about Tolkien fantasy, he has focused increasingly more on his late-period German persona. "Bardolph" is Germanic for "Bright wolf" and his clothes—with giant flowing scalloped underarm wings—and armor meet his ever-developing persona. His helm is an "onion top" shape and he has a visor style used only in German regions.

"At first you just play," he tells me after class. "Then I decided to get things that were period. Then I wanted things that were 14th-century period. Now I want things that are late 14th-century German period."

But unlike the keynote speaker of this university, who is here to talk about the Society for Creative Anachronism's own history, Bardolph does not cover history, SCA or otherwise. Most every fighting class here at RUM and at other SCA events across the Known World has instructors who teach form and skills designed for SCA combat, an odd and ever-evolving hybrid of history and sport. But they almost never teach how fighters actually fought in the Middle Ages or how today's SCA styles compare to the historical ones.

SCA fighting, said Frederick of Holland, one of those present at this fighting style's birth, "is related to" medieval sword fighting. But he adds, "Note that its not 're-creation of,' but 'related to' medieval sword fighting."

"The amount of thought (to consult old fighting manuals) wasn't there," he said of the SCA's early days. "We based our techniques on the weapons: I am trying to beat my opponent and I am developing my technique in a way to beat my opponent."

Though those techniques have developed to fit the style, critics rip the SCA for the many ways it skirts around real history. The Society as a whole has never had the will and drive to make the same transition Bardolph has from "play" to "period" with its fighting. People disagree over whether that change is really necessary. Just as with anything else in this hobby, it all comes down to the same question: "How medieval do you really want to be?"

"At first you just play…"

BE IT KNOWN TO ALL
who may be lovers of
CHIVALRY
that there will be held on the first of May
12:00 to 6:00 p.m.
an
INTERNATIONAL TOURNAMENT
—for that it is spring
all knights are summoned to defend in single combat the claims of their ladies to
the title of "fairest," signified by the crown which will be awarded to him who the
judges deem fights most bravely. And for the increase of joy both to them who
fight and they who watch, there will be both singing and dance. All guests are
encouraged to wear the dress of some age of Christendom, outremer, or faerie, in
which swords were used.

Henrik Olsgaard hands photocopied pages with this message to the dozens of gentles packing the bleachers of the Hamilton High School gym in Sussex, Wisc. When Henrik was a student at San Francisco State University back in 1966, another student gave him the original of this invitation, mimeographed in purple ink "on low grade, full of fiber, cheap offset paper." That party beckoned him, as it now beckons close to 25,000 SCA members around the world. The party will hit its 35th birthday on May 1, 2001, just three days from now.

Two assistants fumble with the movie projector as the bleachers fill up here at the Royal University of the Midrealm (RUM). The projector looks more than 30 years old, about as old as the film it will—hopefully—project. This projector falls into an odd no-mans-land for this Society crowd. The engineers and computer technicians jamming the bleachers could instantly fix a new one. Others here could likely sort the projector out if it were from the 12th century, but because it's just 30 years old—obsolete but not yet antique—it is a quandary. A multi-colored divider has been pulled across the gym length-wise, cutting it in two. On one of the far walls the mascot of the Hamilton Chargers is painted in black and red. It is a Knight on a horse, lance pointed and shield raised.

As the projector starts spinning film of the first SCA event, Henrik wears a suit of chain mail. He made it himself in the late 1960s from 550 coat hangers he scrounged up while a student. Henrik, known in the Society as Duke Henrik of Havn, was the second Knight ever in the SCA and the first crowned King. The Norman helm he wears is the first helm made for SCA fighting. He developed the basket hilts that most fighters use. And, still active in local events in San Rafael, California, he has seen the Society grow from a small backyard party to the international organization it is today.

That first event, he tells us—though many in the crowd have heard this story already—started as a going-away party for a graduate student in Berkeley, California. Diana Paxson, later an author of several Arthurian-era historical novels, was finishing school, Henrik tells us, before she was to head off to Peace Corps training. In addition to being a science fiction fan, Paxson had a few friends who dabbled in medieval weaponry. They had made wooden swords and 16-gauge steel shields—the same weight of heavy metal as the minimum now required for SCA helms—that they covered with leather and practiced with in Paxson's backyard.

Paxson always had an interest in the Middle Ages. Her specialization in her masters program was medieval literature and she had spent two months the previous summer tromping around England, Scotland, Ireland and France taking in the castles and the history. Paxson was not at Henrik's presentation. But the day after the SCA turned 35, the woman most credited with founding the Society explained that her fighter friends had hit on a novel concept.

"They were trying to learn by doing," said Paxson, later known in her group as Diana Listmaker. "I had been in academia, which was all about scholars talking—'Dr. So and So wrote this' and 'somebody wrote that.' It was all very, very detached. It was either that or fiction—people imagining. But it hadn't seemed to occur to anyone to try to learn by doing."

As she watched her friends spar, she thought others might be just as interested. She began planning a tournament with other medieval activities included. Paxson kept it small enough to fit in her modest backyard jammed between neighbors' homes. She found dancers at Mills College who knew Middle Ages styles and some other people to sing medieval songs. She and other medieval literature students planned readings. And, she pointed out with a bit of pride, everyone had been "encouraged" to come in costume.

"It was a participation event from the beginning."

The lights dim and the projector rolls. The faded and silent footage opens with shots of maidens in dresses skipping around a maypole that has long white ribbons flowing from the top. There are no elaborate outfits, though one woman wears a ruff around her neck. Others have passable T-tunics or tabards pinned at the shoulders. A slender man with a shaggy beard wears an oversized brown robe with a hood. A few excessively bright or shiny fabrics seem out of place. Otherwise, the errors of experimentation are covered up by the film quality.

The fighting between combatants wearing fencing headgear and carrying wooden shields draws laughter from the crowd. One of the fighters wears a motorcycle helmet.

They are all virtually unarmored, with nothing to dull the blows. But even unarmored, they smack each other nearly full speed. Some wield maces made from sticks with a ball of rags at one end. Others swing swords cut from plywood or made from aluminum tubing hammered flat.

"It wasn't flattened completely, but it was flattened enough to hurt your knuckles when it hit you," Henrik remembers. "There's me with a mace in my hand and my back to the camera."

A young man on screen in a white shirt and black tabard is lunging at his opponent, horribly off-balance and awkward.

"You can see my form is exemplary."

Most of the fighting is a little out of control. Combatants charge at each other. They swing wildly in crazed and looping arcs. They lose their balance, lunging and falling to their knees, scrambling around the yard. A good fighter today would crush them. Then again, today's fighters have 35 years of experience from which to draw.

The other activities that day also went well. Paxson had time to do a reading in Old French and watch the fighting. In an article in a fanzine called NIEKAS published shortly after the event—and reprinted later in Society publications—Paxson describes processional marches from the Play of Herod, readings in Anglo-Saxon and performances of scenes from a Cervantes play. She recounts costumes ranging from a "14th century dress of blue and gray satin and gold brocade" to fantasy ones like "Queen Lucy of Narnia in a red velvet dress with a bird on her arm" and a gentle who "in a russet cloak, was a hobbit."

The film continues to a few later gatherings in Bay area parks. The fighting is still furious but more controlled. Swings are tighter and less roundhouse. The fighters shuffle and bounce in a less frantic and crazy fashion.

"You can see the progress," Henrik says. "There's improvement. There's less running around, less wasted movement."

They have one endearing habit when they topple over dead: They end with a flourish by back-flopping and letting their feet pop up in the air to crash down for extra finality. Rules for fighting developed over the first few tournaments. Face thrusts were eliminated after Henrik took a bad blow to the face. That rule typified the governance of this embryonic club. The members only set rules after encountering a problem that needed solving.

Sword breakage, Henrik tells the crowd, posed one of those problems. After cracking too many plywood great sword blades, a tournament had to be finished with fighters using only javelins made from broom handles with crutch tips on the end. They found the solution—one that survives to this day—when they discovered 12-foot poles of rattan on sale at a local store for $3 each. While wood splintered into dangerous points, the rattan simply broke down and pulped. Armor quality improved. After breaking his thumb when a traditional cross hilt didn't stop a blow, Henrik devised the first protective basket hilt. And after fighting for a while in an old catcher's mask, he made the first-ever SCA helm—the Norman helm he wears here—by riveting and bending four triangles of steel together into a cap and adding a nosepiece. He fought in it for several years before adopting—on his own, not under SCA orders—a helm with a face grille.

"The SCA very quickly got into getting good stuff together," he remembers. "Just about everything we did in those days, you did it yourself because nobody knew how to do it and you'd have to just figure it out."

"It's all very human..."

As the infant club expanded and added more events, the group decided it needed judges for the tournaments. Members also wanted to prevent the same person from winning every time. They needed respected fighters as judges, but none of the good fighters volunteered.

"Nobody wanted to sit out," Paxson said.

It was time for some reverse psychology. The organizers decided to give the winner of one tournament the duty of overlooking the next, but added an honor as well. Once the organizers decided they would crown the winner of each tournament King, the rank became a status symbol. Then, as Paxson noted, "as soon as you had Kings, the whole feudalist feelings of loyalty and actions snapped into place."

Listening to Paxson, I realize that one bureaucratic decision had led to hundreds of fighters striving for a position created just to get them to do work. The squire Valharic, like so many others, had fallen for the Tom Sawyer trick and was paying to whitewash the fence with sweat, bruises, tears, anger and frustration. Part of that cost and desire falls into the medieval world, but Paxson noted that such striving for recognition and status is far more universal.

"Those needs are human psychological drives right up there with food and sex, with which they are closely, biologically connected," Paxson said. "Animals have a pecking order. The SCA provides an ideal environment to fulfill that drive, to express that drive. It sometimes gets out of hand as a result."

Then, she said, the SCA devolves like any other organization into a game of politics and power.

"It's all very human."

She advises members to play for playing's sake. Play because it is fun.

"Participate for love of the activity, not for hopes of rank and recognition. Second, if you help out, you will inevitably achieve recognition. Volunteer. You can endear yourself immediately to the powers that be by volunteering to clean up the hall after the revel."

About a year after the backyard party, the group had grown dramatically. Though many members kept trying to learn more history, the Society was also intermingled with the fantasy and science fiction community. The writer Marion Zimmer Bradley, who mixed fantasy and the medieval world in her later *Avalon* novels, had attended the first tournament and started what is now the East Kingdom when she moved to New York. On the 4th of July, 1967, just after the June tournament, the group attended a large science fiction convention in Los Angeles and staged a tournament in the park across from the hotel. At the end of the summer 1968, they boosted membership again with a tournament at the Science Fiction World Con at the Claremont Hotel. Today, World Con draws 9,000 people. Then, it drew 2,000, a huge crowd at the time.

"That's where the population explosion really began," Paxson remembers.

The idea spread to Chicago through people like David Friedman, the son of Nobel Prize-winning economist Milton Friedman, and others. Friedman became Cariadoc of the Bow, the first King and one of the founders of the Middle Kingdom. Later he started the Pennsic War. The early membership was filled with writers beyond Zimmer Bradley and Paxson, including Poul Anderson and Mary Monica Pulver. Pulver set a murder mystery at Pennsic called *Murder at the War,* later renamed *Knightfall.* Writer Robert Asprin helped found the SCA's Mongolian group, The Dark Horde, under his persona name "Yang the Nauseating." The author Peter S. Beagle, perhaps best known for writing *The Last Unicorn,* built his book the *Folk of the Air* around an alternate version of the SCA called the League for Archaic Pleasures.

Paxson has watched with interest as the society has shifted away from its roots in fandom to become more of a history-based organization. Clinging to the Society's fantasy roots may be natural, she said, but she believes it no longer needs to continue.

"In the early days when fandom wasn't so developed, maybe. But over the years fandom has increased so you get 9,000 at World Con. Now there's an environment for people to explore that without the SCA."

As the fighting developed, winning the day's tournament became more of a goal than strictly testing what people did centuries earlier. Duke Paul of Bellatrix, who developed and popularized what is now the most basic of SCA blows—the "flat snap"—joined just a few years after the group started. He quickly rose to the top. Paul says he bases his style on asking the question: "What makes the end of your blade move faster?" not on what really happened in history.

Paul, a project manager for Electronic Data Systems, had an easy adjustment to SCA fighting at the age of 25 because he found the timing and application of power to blows to be similar to judo. He started playing with different swings and soon stopped using any of the baseball or tennis-style cuts that led to the roundhouse swings at the earliest events. Cupping his sword hand by his ear, he learned to whip his hand—and the tip of the blade—around using his elbow and a turn of his hips.

"It added a whole lot of speed and power to the game," he said of the "Snap." "It required modifications in footwork and defense to deal with it."

But Paul does not know whether the blow mimics actual historical fighting. "To tell you the truth, I don't even care," he says.

The blow spread quickly across what became the West Kingdom and gradually to the other, newly forming Kingdoms. By some accounts, it was a first step toward SCA fighting becoming its own sport, rather than a true re-creation of actual medieval fighting.

As a result, SCA fighting has several critics who deride it as "stickfighting" and scoff at how its rules tread a no man's land between reality and make-believe. The

Association for Renaissance Martial Arts, formerly the Historically Accurate Combat Association, can point out inaccuracy after inaccuracy in SCA combat—and frequently does. ARMA bases all of its fighting moves off of translated historical fighting manuals as members try to recreate those to the letter, unlike SCA fighting which simply evolved.

"My view is that the SCA has done as much to harm and retard the study of European martial arts as it has to promote research into the subject," says ARMA's Executive Director John Clement.

He and ARMA bristle at the belief among some SCA fighters that the SCA way of fighting is historically accurate, or even that it's the closest anyone can come to real medieval fighting without actually hacking your opponent into pieces.

"The SCA has a legitimate martial sport," he said, emphasizing "sport" as the distinction. "It's just not historical."

"Keep the play version separate…"

"A lot of times we get so far away from the historical starting point, what people actually did with the weapons," ARMA's Executive Director John Clement starts a lecture. "We're out there doing anything and everything."

To Clement and ARMA, that historical starting point is key. It is the same core issue that comes up over and over among medievalists. How medieval do you want to be?

ARMA's goal, Clement says, is to recreate one-on-one medieval combat as accurately as possible using the extant texts as the starting point. As its base, ARMA uses the surviving old fighting instructions, the fight books or "fechtbuchs" as the Germans called them. Its web site and lectures are packed with excerpts from renaissance fighting manuals, translations and summaries of the choreography and combinations of blows that the masters taught.

"Here's how a guy in the 1300s says how he fought," Clement said.

ARMA's approach differs dramatically from the SCA. It skips trying to be a "society" and ignores feasts, clothing, pageantry and arts. ARMA also ignores wars. It has no siege tactics, no battle strategy or unit combat, only bouts of one fighter against another. For even that combat, it ignores competition, even the period tournaments that form part of the SCA system. Its goal is to be an Ace of its single trade, not a Jack of all.

The books handy to SCA founders in the 1960s, Clement tells me, fell short of fechtbuch translations available today. The books then only "perpetuated Victorian-era myths" that over time became the SCA's version of true combat. Right from Day One, at the first event in Diana Listmaker's backyard, precedents were set that skewed things. The first, he said, was competition, the tourney to crown a woman "Queen of Love and Beauty."

"As soon as you start trying to score points, you turn it from a martial art to a martial sport," he says.

Some of the SCA's fighting shortcomings are obvious, but others require a little study. Using sticks instead of a sword can change the way a basic blow is delivered. Because SCA blows are delivered for clubbing force, not cutting, the sport downplays the need to have the thin blade edge at an almost perfect angle as it connects. Eliminating the area below the knees to be a target, as it would in real combat, changes both the targets of the attacker and the areas a fighter must defend. It also means fighters duel at much closer range than in history. Grappling, a common a tactic in history, is banned in the SCA, as is "halfswording," a technique of wielding a sword with two hands, one on the hilt and the other on the blade. And SCA fighting puts far less of a premium on footwork and movement than historical fighting, Clement said.

Then there is the whole business of dropping to your knees when legged.

"That's got to be the most absurd thing we've ever seen," Clement said. "There's not a single account of anybody getting hit in the legs and then sitting down and fighting. A man gets hit in the leg, he doesn't sit down and keep fighting."

If a fighter can stand with his injuries, he will rise and keep fighting. If not, the fight's over.

"Get off your knees and allow people to hit your foot. That would change everything."

Fighters in ARMA's period, the 1300s to 1700s, had to learn effective methods under threat of far more serious consequences than sword-fighters today. Masters would teach systems that married the moves of attack and defense and taught methods that would approximate wrestling more than the genteel fighting of the SCA. Hard slaps to the body would do little against a heavily-armored opponent, Clement says, so fights would often hinge on clubbing an opponent to the ground or ramming a sword into an armpit, eye-hole or under the chin.

Though SCA fighters must club with the duct-taped portion of rattan marked as a blade, real fighters had to worry far more about blade orientation. Being off slightly or turning the blade for a wrist snap, as in some SCA moves, can put the blade out of position to cut anything. Most period styles also stress blocking blows with the flat of the blade, never the edge, to save the edge from damage. Many counter moves are most effective after blocks with the flat.

The styles of fighting that ARMA teaches use both the period texts and more accurate copies of medieval equipment. Many of ARMA's members have handled surviving period weapons and armor and base reproductions off of them. The balance of a sword, Clement said, can totally change the mechanics for how you throw a blow. Real swords, he said, are so well balanced that they handle more easily than movies would indicate. "They're weightless," he said.

Armor can also change the way you move. Most SCA armor, even kits far more specialized than my pseudo-sporting getup, is thicker than real armor and often made all from one sheet the same thickness. Real armor has thin spots and heavier spots, to provide strength in key areas while reducing weight in others.

Then ARMA will hold "test-cutting" sessions where members slice sides of beef, reproduced armor and other objects with re-created swords to let its members see and feel how well swords cut. They do not have to guess, like SCA fighters do, whether a hit is strong enough to cut real chain mail with a real sword. They have tried it.

ARMA picked up steam under the name Historically Accurate Combat Association in the mid-1990s toward becoming recognized experts on true historical fighting. Clement said he hopes ARMA will set standards that form the basis of fighting systems for other organizations, whether they be computer game companies or re-creation groups. But he believes that coming up with a system easily accessible to the masses is probably hopeless.

"I don't believe you can have a play version that is anything more than a play version," he said. "We should keep the play version separate and have the real thing separate."

"Not modern either..."

Some SCA fighters enjoy ARMA's teachings and try both systems. Most believe both systems have advantages and disadvantages. Although ARMA members duel each other, they do not use full contact. Its fights establish no pecking order and though fighters battle "in earnest"—as Clement puts it—they never have anything on the line. None of its members train to beat anyone else. It also lacks the critical mass of people the SCA has.

Cariadoc of the Bow, the Midrealm's founder, believes the SCA has advanced knowledge of fighting, even with rattan swords.

"As long as the weapons are of reasonably accurate weight and balance, trying to hit someone with them who is trying not to get hit does give us some useful information about medieval combat," he said on an SCA newsgroup.

Frederick of Holland, like most SCA fighters, is satisfied with the accuracy of the fighting style. Photos of him fighting look enough like the etchings and illuminations of real medieval fighters to suit him. The armor looks reasonably close, as does his positioning.

"If the methods are not medieval," he says, "they're not modern either."

As I sit in on Bardolph's class, I easily buy into Frederick's view. The idea of wearing armor is new. Carrying a shield is new. Swinging a sword, even a rattan one, is new. It is a lot closer to swordfighting than any other sport. And the idea of willingly putting myself in a situation where others in armor will try to pound or stab me with sticks, shoot me with arrows or plow me over with their shields comes far closer to a real medieval war than I imagined. Even if SCA fighting is simpler and less sophisticated than real fighting, I still have to learn the basics of this Frankensport.

The King's Lesson

The lesson from newly crowned King Bardolph Odger Windlauffer at today's university fills in many of those fighting basics for me, along with details of his own personal style. While some fighters try to overpower opponents, Bardolph builds his personal style on light footwork and avoiding charges. He needs to. Though six foot tall, he weighs only 155 pounds.

The key, he tells the class, is learning how to move while keeping your balance. Many fighters put themselves in a tough spot when they back up when under attack. Very few fighters—Brannos is a major exception, he notes—can lean back away from shots and still have balance. Most, he said, "throw up their sword and shield and start backing away." That can block their vision, puts them on their heels and leaves the advantage with the opponent.

"I'll step off the line instead," he says, likening himself to a matador facing a charging bull. "I simply won't be there."

The legs are also the key to striking a blow solid enough to count. Many new fighters, particularly women, have trouble hitting hard enough for opponents to accept their blows. Big, long, swooping baseball swings are out. From a novice, they're telegraphed and will be blocked. And while some fighters with a lot of upper body strength can hit hard using mainly their arms, the vast majority generate power from their legs. It is no different in this sport than in baseball, where pitchers rely on legs to power fastballs, and basketball, where shooters use their legs to boost jump shots.

"Which muscles are stronger than the other—legs or arms?" Bardolph asks. "If you use just arms, I give you 10 blows tops and you're tired. Use your legs and you'll double that. My arms are there for guidance. It's my legs and hips driving my shot. My arms just become guidance for the sword."

In a typical swing, the sword-arm shoulder and hip turn into the swing at the same time. Body weight shifts into the shot, just like a baseball player or tennis player making a swing. But very few fighters are quick enough to take opponents out with one blow, Bardolph continues. Combinations of shots are necessary. After throwing the first blow, he notes, his right (sword-arm) hip is all the way forward. But it is not necessarily out of position. It is actually cocked to throw another shot—like a tennis backhand—on the recoil. The easiest two-count combination is to throw a forehand then a backhand, using the recoil of the hips to power the second shot. If you keep your sword-arm elbow in close to the body with each swing, the blow has less arc and it is easier to shift the swing's direction at the last moment. Keeping the elbow in close allows you to shift to the second shot faster.

As he demonstrates variations of a blow, his hands are empty. With no sword, his palms chop the air karate style. The blows and blocks could be struck just as easily with hands as with swords, the only difference being the distance. I am beginning to understand why other martial arts carry over well here.

Shots, he says, should be aimed for a few inches into your opponent instead of at his shell of armor. On a leg shot, aim to cut to the bone. On a head shot, aim to hit through the skull to the eyes.

He advises everyone to build a pell, the swordfighting equivalent of a punching bag, or at least make a siloflex sword and practice on street signs and light poles. Use the pell to practice throwing each of the shots, to work out combinations, to see where you go off balance or have trouble.

"You'll find if you start to work the pell a couple times a week—above your fight practice—you'll really improve. Pell work is where you rough out what you want to do, where you work out the bugaboos. Practice is where you polish your skills. Tournaments are where you want to shine."

"Find what's comfortable for you."

With about a week's worth of work left on my armor, I can't take it anymore. I need to start practicing. Flynn loans me a heavy wooden shield that is bigger than I would normally use. I need to become accustomed to carrying one. He and Talon give me an assignment: Hold it. Hold my stance. Hold my shield. Hold it up and in position. In front of the television. In front of the mirror. Do it until my arm's about to fall off. The more I get used to holding that weight, the better off I'll be. You droop, they warn me, you die.

I also take Bardolph's advice and make a trip to Home Depot and an auto parts store. I come home with a pole of PVC pipe and a hose clamp to hold the pipe into one of my basket hilts. I now have a practice "sword." Wedging my head into a borrowed helm so I can grow used to that weight too, I walk out behind my apartment building and turn a defenseless phone pole into a pell. As commuters return home from work, they stare at me as I pelt my pell with flat snaps. I pulp and chip the helpless pole as I fumble through the weight shifts, the wrist snaps and forearm twists for different blows. Carrying a big heavy shield throws my weight off balance. I struggle with trying to turn my right hip and shoulder into a blow without letting my left hand and shield turn too, which would leave me wide open.

I am also learning quickly that shields, while blocking swords from hitting me, can also block my vision and my ability to hit my opponent. My first tendency is to hold the shield squarely in front of me, with its top line parallel to the ground. But that can create all kinds of problems in SCA fighting, where head-shots are the most common killing blow. Blocking your face with a whole shield only blocks your vision. Flynn and Talon have me angle the shield so the inside top corner points into the air and the outside corner points down. The angle positions a corner of the shield so that it covers the left side of my face but allows me to look around it at my opponent. When throwing blows, I must swing over or around the shield, or else lower the shield and leave an area open.

On the first Sunday of May, about four months after Twelfth Night, I pull into Clague Park in Westlake, one of the far west suburbs of Cleveland for my first fight practice. I drive past ball diamonds and a pond with kids fishing, down the appropriately, but inadvertently, named Roman Road until I find Talon stretching in a parking lot. Reliable weather has just arrived for the Rust Belt. Cleftlands just moved its practices outdoors a week ago, and today the Darkyard wing in the SFU projects group has its first of the season. It takes an all-day session at Flynn's house the day before to pull my fighting kit together.

Flynn and Logan/Mike arrive after me but manage to put on all their armor before I even finish fumbling with my elbows.

"You'll get faster," Flynn says.

He lends me a sword and gives me a more manageable shield than the one I had used at the pell. The so-called "heater" shield, shaped like an inverted pear or the face of an iron, has a rim of rubber tubing laced with string around its edges. SCA rules require that anachronism to prevent splinters and to dull edges in case I stab someone with the corner. I lumber from the parking lot into a field feeling like the Michelin man. With shoulder pads that offer chest protection below the nipples and a solid belt up to my ribs, I can hardly bend my torso. I have weight in odd places on my body tugging me in crazy directions. Bending over to pick up my shield and half-gauntlet is an exercise in not toppling over.

I immediately recall the story Duke Baldar told me at Gulf Wars about his first try at this sport after spotting fighters on campus.

"They just looked like guys in tin armor bashing each other," he said. "They looked pretty pathetic. Then I put on the armor and realized it was a little more difficult with all this stuff on."

Flynn starts me with some stance lessons. While Bardolph uses what in baseball would be called an "open" stance and faces his opponents almost head on, others fight with a more "closed" stance with the shield arm forward and the sword arm back a bit. Putting weight on the back (sword side) foot leaves the other leg way out in the open. That stance plays off of one SCA rule that ARMA rails against: not allowing blows to the shins or feet. If the left leg was a target, the stance would likely fail. Instead, it leaves a non-target closest to opponents and can keep the head back out of harm's way.

"I'm not going to tell you this is what you have to do,' Flynn says. "You have to find what's comfortable for you."

Talon jumps in, showing a much more open stance, similar to Bardolph's, that other Darkyard members are experimenting with. "Try things. See what works."

I wobble at sparring partner Logan, barricaded in his own shoulder pads. He swings and I block it. I start swinging back first with just single snaps. I can do these just like at the pole. But I don't get anywhere. I need to put a couple of lessons to use. Throw combinations, I remember, and use both sides—left and right—and work both top and bottom. Getting an opponent going one way and hitting another is a key. I try going back and forth. High and low. I start puffing. Mike blocks most of them. My backhand and second shots are a little wild. After two blows, form is out the window and I am lunging the rest of the skirmish.

Talon stops the fight and offers a critique. I have read and listened enough to avoid one typical newbie mistake—trying to intercept blows with the middle of the shield. Instinct and baseball groundball training (Get in front of the ball!) tells me to get as much shield in the way as possible. But that can block vision or leave too much open. All that matters is that a shield stops a blow. An edge will do that just fine and reduce movement. I make one mistake by using my arms—the forearms and triceps—to move the shield. I can make my life easier by just turning the shield with my hand to block some spots or simply shrugging or sagging my shoulder to raise or lower it reasonable amounts. I can also crouch a little to put more of my body behind the shield, just as a baseball batter can cut his strike zone with a crouch.

I also almost punch at shots with my shield, thrusting the shield out to meet them instead of just blocking them as they come to me. This is also puts me off balance. When I start sparring with Talon I do not ever catch him with the sword, but almost injure him by (illegally) smashing him in the chest with the corner of my shield. Good thing for the tubing on the rim.

We start again and Talon quickly chops me straight down right in the forehead. With a pole for a pell, I have been thinking swipe, not chop. I have been holding my sword blade straight up, leaving myself open to being "slotted"—sliced right between my vertical sword and my nicely tilted shield. Darkyard sets the sword and shield in more of an A-frame—with the sword blade angled across the face and above the top of the tilted shield to cover that hole.

Talon tells me to try a few snaps to his head so he can test my power and form. He lets me smack his helmeted face several times. Normal blows to the head do not hurt, though a poorly padded and strapped helm will ring when hit. I am doing OK, he concludes. Though I hit hard enough, I let my hand fly out to the side more than I should. He has me come at him. He has told me marshals will leave openings for shots in my authorization and he is giving me that opportunity. But I don't fully see them as he moves. He stops me.

"Hit me. I am wide open."

"Where? I don't see it."

"All over."

His shield was low and a snap to the helm—if fast enough—could have hit him. His chest is open—his shield was too far off to the side. A hack straight down would slip through and hit his chest. Again—like with the slot hole—I have been thinking side to side, not vertical in the middle of the body. He had also seemed too far away, out of range where I would have to lunge. Not so. We reposition and he has me chop at his chest. I have six inches to spare when the tip hits his leather chest protection. We have not even touched the idea of using thrusts and jabs.

"OK, we're going to tell you a lot of stuff," he says, sidling up to me. "But come on. Forget it. Come at me. Come get me. Throw that out."

It is like a brother tugging the other to wrestle.

"Have fun with it. Yell."

"Arrrrwwww!" he yells, grinning. "Come on. I want you to yell."

Part of me wants to yell back. But the mundane part of me is still wary of this entire concept. I may be past my nervousness about being seen in public in garb but committing emotion beyond just determination is still a step too far for me. Losing myself in the moment just isn't happening. I am like the student in the movie "Dead Poets Society" who cannot let out a "wild yawp" to the world, the unabashed, un-apologetic roar of power Walt Whitman wrote about.

I can feel my face flush. I back up a bit. I am not ready to yawp just yet.

"Naw," I say. "I've got to breathe under here."

But as we start to mix it up I charge harder. I throw more shots. I swing a little wild. I stop worrying about what I am doing and just try to find a way through his arms and sword and shield. Once I slip a sword through to his shoulder or helm and I take a lot more, including a stinging bite on my rear end I know will turn Technicolor by morning. Talon laughs even as I hit him and keeps egging me on. I flail away.

At last we stop. I am sucking wind, drenched with sweat.

"That was good," Talon says. "Was it fun?"

I nod. "Yeah…that…was…good."

"He's smiling," Flynn says from the side.

He caught me.

In spite of myself, I am.

Act II, scene 2
The Squire's Choice

The note from one of the Kingdom's top fighters goes out by the modern courier of e-mail as the Chivalry and populace of the Middle Kingdom start the activities of the major Kingdom event of Baron Wars.

He has had it.

The death of his child, financial woes, accusations of domestic violence and a string of other problems have worn him down. He came to Baron Wars and set up his tent, but he stomped off the site shortly after and went home. In a burst of rage and frustration, he e-mails the rest of the Kingdom his plan.

"To my mother, sorry Mom. This is one kid who just could not wait for you to die first," he wrote on the public message board just before 2 a.m., before concluding, "I gotta go. Please, those of you who truly believe in prayer, pray for me."

He takes his gun and kills himself.

At Baron Wars, the old-timers and Kingdom leaders are buzzing. Could they have handled this situation better? Had they done the wrong thing? Should they have done something…anything…differently? The populace of the Middle Kingdom and of the Known World launches into debates over whether they should mourn the loss or whether their Society is better off without anyone with that much baggage.

At the very same event as Duke Andrew of Seldom Rest decides to carry out his final and fatal task, Valharic starts on a path of his own. At the moment Andrew types his final message, Valharic is leaning on Brannos for advice in a campsite discussion that keeps them both up past 3 a.m.

"I told him everything I was feeling," Valharic recounts later. "He helped me regain my focus."

Brannos cannot solve Valharic's marital and legal troubles, but urges him to stop his obsession with becoming a Knight or King. Within this hobby, each of his small setbacks were taking on too much significance and making him too frustrated and angry. He had hit the same wall many candidates for SCA peerages hit.

"It's watching your peers around you get Knighted knowing you can perform better than them," Brannos says, touching on many of the issues Diana Listmaker brought up. "At that point you tend to get angry because it's not you. Either you get so angry you turn away from the SCA or look at yourself and see why you're doing the things you're doing.

"The belt, the chain, even the coronet are just awards, they're just tokens. It's the path, the end of the path of being the best at what you do."

By morning, Valharic resolves to make a change.

"If I had not experienced everything, and I had not been in such a state of soul-searching and reflection, I don't think I'd have been able to listen to him," he says. But after losing a wife and two children, a crown or a white belt of Knighthood does not seem so overriding. The belt will never replace his wedding band. One piece of leather cannot take the place of that one piece of metal that changed his life. He can just fight.

"I quit focusing on being a Knight," he tells me later. "I wanted to be the best fighter in the SCA. Crown and being Knighted were just steps along the way. I stopped focusing on my short-term goals and on my long-term ones instead."

"You look at yourself…"

Baron Wars, held every May, is a mid-level event for the SCA, but a major one for the Middle Kingdom. Normally, the Kingdom holds it in a historic park outside Toledo with a picket fort built in the 1800s that allows for some unique battle scenarios. But three losses mar this year's version.

The first is the site. With the park service refurbishing the fort, the state has closed it for the year. Organizers had to look elsewhere and found a Scout camp, which works fine, but lacks the draw of the normal site. Other than an event about a month from now called "The Encampment at the Castle," it is normally the only event with anything resembling a fortress. "Encampment" uses the grounds of the old Mansfield Reformatory in Mansfield, Ohio, the prison used to film the movie *The Shawshank Redemption,* as its "castle" backdrop but has no fighting in the prison or on its walls.

The second is a tragedy linked to the event—the death of a former King in an auto accident on his way home from here in 1999. Thorbjorn Osis stood as a near-mythic figure in the Middle Kingdom and its neighbor to the north, the Kingdom of Ealdormere. Several years ago, while Ealdormere was still just a part of its parent Middle Kingdom, Osis, mundanely a former rower, had swept in from the north and seized the Midrealm Crown. He was almost larger than life. People who enjoyed the SCA party scene loved his enthusiasm and irreverence, best exemplified by his original name: Osis of the Livery, picked so that when he was inevitably Knighted, his name would become Sir Osis of the Livery. A few people told me the same, though unconfirmed story, of him ratcheting up his power on a "Rhinohiding" opponent who kept calling shots light until, after several progressively harder smacks, Osis bowled him over with a blow. He could offend someone one moment, then have a case of beer delivered to their tent in apology. Osis became one of the first kings of Ealdormere when it became a full Kingdom. But Osis, MKA Craig Cox, 32, of Richmond Hill, Ont., was killed mid-reign when he lost control of his truck while driving home through Ontario after Baron Wars. The truck flipped over and he was ejected and killed, along with a passenger. Followers planned a tournament in his honor at this year's event.

Andrew offered the latest stunner. He too had been one of the Kingdom's larger-than-life characters in its earlier days, training squires into Knights, using his home as stopovers for event travelers and driving people himself to many events. But Kingdom leaders knew about his personality flaws. He had been accused of several instances of wife-beating and he never recovered from the accidental shooting death of a four-year-old son. Then, late in life, injuries from a car accident left him in nearly constant pain.

In the Middle Kingdom's early days he had been a living legend, winning two Crowns in the early 1970s and a third in the early 1980s. But he became a quandary, particularly after his last win when his Queen abdicated because of a beating. A Knight who beats his wife violates the image of chivalry that Knights want to portray. Some thought he should lose his Knight's belt. Had he done some of these things before he became a Knight, he might not have made it. Once someone is Knighted, few have the courage and conviction to take the white belt away.

Many praise this Society for welcoming troubled people and overlooking their flaws. Diana Listmaker maintains that this group has saved many people who would otherwise have been lost and adrift. But being forgiving also has a flip side. By rarely drawing a line and refusing to tolerate immoral behavior, this culture of moral relativism can enable people to continue destructive behavior. The most infamous of SCAdians, East Kingdom Duke Aonghais dubh Mac Tarbh, had his white belt removed by the Chivalry only to have a King in another kingdom restore it. Then, even after he was convicted in 1994 of taking part in a murder-for-hire plot in Florida, the Society did not banish him. That step will not occur until late 2003, just months before he dies in prison.

Disciplining members for bad behavior is just one of many areas where this Society treads an unusual line between being just a hobby and expectations that it should be a moral authority. The Society opened up this Pandora's Box by trying to take concepts like honor and chivalry seriously. Just by putting high-minded ideals on the table, this Society sets an expectation of high standards for both its membership and for itself, even when neither may be better suited to meet them than groups like the National Duck Stamp Collectors Society or the National Taxidermists Association.

But it forever has to find a balance between enforcing those virtues and the danger of overstepping its bounds. Several Kings and Queens report that members have called on them to intervene in private disputes with their spouses. But when the Board of Directors "banishes" a Duke in the Kingdom of An Tir (Oregon, Washington and British Columbia) later this year, much of the populace there will howl that the Society's system did not provide proper due process. Someone's status and rank within this group is not something to be trifled with and many members resent the directors exerting any control over anything.

But the often-anguished debates and the losses, other than that of the fort, do not mar today's event for most. I haul my armor out for pickup fights after the main fighting events of the day—melees. Brannos, despite being up half the night counseling Valharic, takes charge as the highest-ranking Peer on the battlefield. He divides the fighters into sides and sets battle scenarios. With no royals on hand, everyone looks to his judgment. All afternoon, sides square off in practice battles. Since Darkyard dwarfs many other houses and even baronies, the typical battle is Darkyard against all-comers. Talon fights with the household all day, then laughs and jokes with the others as they walk the site in the evening.

When Valharic enters the Osis Memorial Tournament, nobody can beat him. Except Brannos. The two meet in the final and Brannos wins. But Valharic has started winning a larger battle.

His Gordian Knot has begun to loosen.

"Everyone around you hitches their wagons..."

In the weeks that follow, Valharic starts attending SFU projects sessions. He offers tips on armor, advice on how to throw and block shots and gives me a hands-on lesson in how to put a good grip on a sword. In seconds, he creates ridges on the handle by spinning a long strip of duct tape into a mini-rope to wind around the handle. The last week of May, though, he needs our help.

Crown Tournament is coming up this weekend. After skipping the last one, he is ready to try that test again. Finn and Tamara will give him a lift all the way to the site, about 14 hours away in South Dakota.

Midrealm Crown Tournaments usually do not have casual entrants. Unlike the West, where all competent fighters are urged to enter, Midrealm entrants are only elite fighters, or those looking to bump their reputation to the next step. Anyone with an Award of Arms can enter, but few do unless they are great fighters or want to make a point—either political or of devotion to a consort.

Valharic last fought Crown for the latter reason. This time, he will fight with his wife as his official consort, but he has no intention of making her Queen. He would rather show people honor, a quality he believes she lacked.

"I was not there to win," he tells me after he returns. "I was there to live down the other tournament, to show I could fight with courtesy and chivalry."

This time, the distance from the center of the Kingdom will limit the field. A lengthy drive and two nights of hotel charges rule out frivolous entrants. A few strong competitors have entered, including two previous winners. Palymar, already a Duke, will make the trek from Michigan, as will Valharic's household brother, Ragnvaldr. Ragnvaldr is a wild card. The scuttlebutt is that a wrist injury has limited his practicing and restricted his motion.

Valharic needs to look good. His helm is rusted and stained. The cloth cover on his shield is ripped. His lamellar body armor is missing a few rivets. And he is in a rush.

The group takes an unusual pride in Valharic's fighting exploits. He is like a kid brother making good. Everyone admires his superior talent and knows they cannot match his fighting skill. But the group feels protective of him. Everyone here shortens his persona name to the informal "Val" or still calls him "Tommy," not the more-adult "Tom," even though he is 27 and not the pre-teen they met him as.

At the same time, the group wants a taste of the top, to somehow feel a share of ownership in his exploits. Valharic may only be a squire and he has never won Crown, but Crown is not just any tournament. It is as big as it gets. We in the group are like low-level minor league baseball players with a teammate who just got the call up to

The Show. Whatever little thing we can do to help, any rivet we hammer, any sword we tape is going to be on stage in the Big Leagues.

William of Fairhaven, a Knight from Dayton, Ohio, who has finished in the finals of Crown before, says the dynamic is like that of "The Great White Hope."

"When you start to show you can win," he says, "everyone around you hitches their wagons. You're the horse that can go the distance."

Over the next few hours, we fix Valharic's lamellar. Flynn helps clean Valharic's helm with oiling and sanding. Talon removes the cloth from Valharic's center grip shield after taking off the tubing on the edge. A new layer of black fabric is slapped on, glued and then held on doubly well by the tubing going back around the edge. Talon and Valharic later collaborate on a design, just as in their art school days, by painting a Medusa head on the cloth. Painting on the cloth, instead of on the metal, allows a fighter to change designs several times in the life of the shield. It also means there will not be any chipping of paint and a sloppy looking shield. You can simply add new cloth and re-do it. Valharic does not have an official coat of arms. The Medusa head is Valharic's nod to the guardians of Hell.

We will all be checking the Kingdom e-mail lists late in the weekend for news.

Other fighters, though, have their own plans. Sir William of Fairhaven, MKA Pat Savelli, 35, is tired of having other people hitch their wagons, only for him to lose.

Mundanely a network designer for Xerox, he joined the SCA in 1982 after watching a demo with two SCA members in Crusader great helms slugging it out. Fighting was the draw that has pulled him along ever since. After a few hitches—having to rehab his shoulder and a bout with appendicitis—he turned serious about the sport in 1989. He became a squire and fought in his first Crown that year. Five years later, he was Knighted and was the chief marshal of the Kingdom in 1996 and 1997. He was even a marshal at Valharic's disputed Crown final with Edmund.

William has fought in so many Crowns that he has lost track of the number. Although he finished second in one Crown to Valharic's household brother Tarquin, William has begun to feel a little pressure, as the head of a household of 17 people, to come through.

He and his wife Mary, known in the SCA as Isolde de la Ramee', a laurel in Anglo-Saxon language, decided recently that they both wanted the throne. He has made an all-out commitment to winning. He started training. He plans to attend every crown tourney until he wins.

And he has a plan.

In his workshop, he builds a special weapon for an extra edge if he can reach the finals.

It goes into his bags for the drive to South Dakota.

Act II, scene 3
The Dance Goob's Tale

The Kingdom of Calontir never shies away from a good fight. The entire Kingdom covering Kansas, Missouri, Iowa, Nebraska and northern Arkansas is built around an army structure where the road to glory is to either man a key spot in the Kingdom's much-vaunted "shield wall" or knock yourself out bringing it water, beef jerky and soup to fortify the fighters.

But Tsire Tuzevo, MKA Sarah Vaughan, 25, of Des Moines, Iowa, couldn't care less about war. At the Kingdom's largest event, the Lilies War, she skips the steamy June battlefields, never picks up a shield or sword and avoids the constant re-telling of war stories.

She tells me she would rather "brawl" instead.

Huh?

As she talks, a beaming smile that would put the Cheshire Cat to shame bursts across her face. Fighters are carrying weapons off to the battlefield after a rainstorm, but Tsire does not even own armor. She is hanging out in a tent with a handful of musicians. I can't believe she would ever engage in fisticuffs.

I look at her, puzzled, but she hands me a bottle of ale she commissioned to be brewed especially for tonight. She cackles at the name printed on the label: Bar Room Bransle.

"That's a dance," she says, pointing at "Bransle." "It's just pronounced 'brawl.'"

Tsire and the musicians have gathered in this giant tent on the campground hosting the 15th Lilies War to practice for the main medieval dance event of this War: The Lilies Ball. Just a few years out of Iowa State University, Tsire has become one of the Kingdom of Calontir's major dance boosters. She sometimes hosts dance practices and dinners at her house, runs regional dance practices four times a year for the Kingdom and today is in charge of the Lilies Ball.

She has taken the charge and run with it.

In addition to the ale, she will offer dancers buttons saying, "Survivor. Lilies Ball XV." And she has prepared a program for the ball that plays off the names of the sides in this war: Lions vs. Wolves. The program reads "Lions and Wolves and Dancers…Oh My!"

Almost every local shire or barony across this Society has a dance practice or at least a few moments of its regular meeting devoted to dancing. But they rarely have live music. Instead of an orchestra playing period music, they often have to settle for CDs on boom boxes, just as Cleftlands had to back at its January event.

But at larger events, people who make playing medieval music their main pursuit gather to provide a band for the ball. And in a few cases, the balls have bundles of energy like Tsire running them.

"I'm a dance goob," Tsire says with a shrug, borrowing a Kingdom slang word often used for new enthusiastic fighters. "I dance and dance and dance. The last award I got, the Queen said, 'You dance and when you're not dancing you talk about dance and you teach about dance.'"

As the musicians start fumbling through one of the songs for the ball, her face erupts in a spontaneous smiley burst of glee.

"It just makes me so happy."

Vaughn has always loved music. She danced only a little as a child, but took voice lessons and played competitive piano while in high school. She also plays the guitar, the organ, the harpsichord and "kind of" plays the concertina, penny whistle, recorder and ocarina.

"I play anything I can get my hands on," she says. "Badly, but I can."

She joined the SCA four years ago while studying social work at Iowa State. At first, the draw was a chance to show off the firebreathing skills she picked up in college. But both she and her husband soon became very involved. Vaughn started a beginning dance, vocal and instrumental practice at her house, luring people in by offering dinner. She also did a lot of orientation for newbies and pulled them in as well. Soon she had nearly a dozen people at the practices even though the entire Ames, Iowa, group only has about 20 members.

When she moved to Des Moines she started a dance group and became an apprentice to Master Brendan MacRonan, one of Calontir's performing arts Laurels. By luck, his job as a technical writer for an insurance company is right across the street from the homeless shelter where Vaughn works. Together they are making period instruments. In her year as his apprentice, she has made one instrument, a lap harp she calls "a little clunky thing." But they are planning a portative organ, essentially a "baby organ" similar in size to an accordion. When finished it will have a keyboard that rests on her lap, pipes up the center and bellows in the back. They are also considering making a tabletop organ that would require a second person to do the pumping.

"He has never made one and I've never made one but we're going to do it together."

"Riding the -ish"

But her favorite part of this Society is dancing—re-creating the court dances of the Middle Ages and mixing in modern dances set to period music. Already enthusiastic about medieval dance, she is absolutely giddy about it today.

Just a week ago she attended a four-day Known World Dance Symposium in Boston that pulled in dancers and medieval-style musicians from across the country. There, she took classes from morning to night, sucking up instruction in Italian dance instead of the more English-style dances prominent in Calontir, and partying with the other dancers at night. The parties literally had them dancing in the streets near Boston University, no doubt confusing the BU students who have never before seen

Gelosia (a 15th century Italian three-couple dance) or Prexonera (a 16th century couples dance).

"I got to be with a group of people who are into and love doing what I do. I was all jazzed up. It's really uplifting."

Best of all, she was able to just dance and not spend half the time instructing newcomers on dances that pre-date mosh pits by 400 or more years.

"There wasn't the 'duh' factor," she says. "We would just go."

Practitioners of medieval court dance have more documentation to work with than the Middle Eastern dancers. Several dances, like Italian dances from the 14th, 15th and 16th centuries, have been recorded in writing and have a wealth of documentation, she says. The steps of others, like early Scottish and Irish ones, are lost because those cultures had mostly an oral system of relaying information, instead of using writing.

"It's kind of a shame because there's a lot of cultures I would like to know the dance of," Tsire laments.

At times, SCA dancers do what Vaughn calls "riding the -ish," performing dances that are "period-ish" but from the 1600s and not strictly in the SCA period. Others are simply folk dances.

"They're clearly folk dances," she admits. "We're trying to phase them out but they're really popular. The SCA kind of does its own culture on top of the real culture."

Groups often dance to "Scotland the Brave," a song most people recognize from Old Spice commercials, but the predominant dance to that tune is not period. One of the worst offenders is Korobushka, a Russian folk dance that the SCA dancers used in the days before the community had done enough research to find enough true period dances. The dance is "wildly fun" and "peppy," Vaughn says, and it caught on.

"It's wonderful fun but it's *so* not documentable."

And dances themselves evolve over time—even within SCA timespans. Two years ago, she says, an SCA dancer created a dance called "Quen Quer Que" to a 13th century cantiga. The circle dance had dancers facing each other head-on. But some dancers have added a body turn.

"In just two years it has added a swooshy style that wasn't intended by the creator."

"Guide, not toss…"

The band, now composed of several recorders, a harp and a dulcimer, is now playing a familiar song. I pause to figure it out and Vaughn jumps in.

"It's a Christmas song—'Ding Dong Merrily on High."

This one is for a dance known both as "Official Bransle" or "Toss the Wench." The English and French circle dance alternates Lords and Ladies in a circle that rotates rapidly. After a few revolutions, the Lords turn, put their hands on the hips of a Lady at one side and "toss" them across to their other side so there is a new Lady next to him.

"We have to teach tossing safely," Tsire laments. "The Lords don't always 'toss' the ladies. That's a misnomer. They move in front of him. They jump and he helps. We have to reinforce 'guide' not 'toss' because toss hurts. Smaller ladies tend to have problems with this because SCA guys like to prove they're strong and they go flying off."

Women who don't want to be tossed can simply yell, "I'll pass."

"But there's a number of ladies who like being tossed quite a large distance," she adds.

Finding men to fill out the dances is a major problem. I had seen recently-Knighted Sir Alaric try to fill that void at the Cleftlands event several months back. About 80 percent of the dancers, Tsire estimates, are women. In a Kingdom like Calontir, dancing is not particularly valued. She sees the Kingdom as dominated by its Old Guard Saxon culture. As Tsire puts it, the "Paleo-Norman" culture often consists of the same handful of middle-aged men sitting around campfires singing the same 20 songs event after event.

"It's very period combat-oriented—Og hit with stick," she says. "And dance is not manly. But I will challenge any fighter on the field to galliard as long as I can."

She gives a quick demonstration. The 16th century Italian dance uses six-beat music and is very much like a jig, with four leg kicks and a two-beat jump at the end as a drum accents the fifth beat. Her flurry of leg kicks kills any preconceptions I had about medieval dance. It is not just restrained, stately marching around a hall and simply touching upraised palms with your partner as you pass. Between the tossing and the galliard, parts of it clearly take some energy.

Vaughn makes one last pitch for men to join. It is the same argument I heard in favor of men doing belly dance.

"Dances are untapped chick resources," she says. "The men that figured this out dance because they realized the 80 to 90 percent women ratio. If they're not an absolute warthog they can so score."

Act II, scene 4
Manning a Shield

"**W**e don't lose."

The sentence comes out not as a brag or boast. It is an order.

Urien Vitalis eyes the row of five Darkyard and Darkyard wanna-be shieldmen in front of him. Only one of us in the group has any real experience on a shield wall. The other four, including me, all look back with a deer-in-the-headlights look. You want us to do what?

"Hit them. Hit them hard. Take them off their feet. I want to see shoes pointing in the air."

About 50 feet away stands a line of a half-dozen Cleftlands fighters, mostly newbies like me, who are themselves trying to grasp the intensity of what Urien is asking.

"We are Darkyard. We are Legio Draconis. We are an army and we do not lose. When we order the charge, you absolutely must drive them back. You must take their ground. You have to hit them as fast and hard as you can."

As I peer out at him through the grille of my helm and over the top of my borrowed warboard, I start to realize how seriously this household takes manning a shield in its line. I knew that before, but only in an abstract way. Today, in July, about a month before the Pennsic War, I find out for real.

"What do you need me to do?"

The Barony of the Cleftlands and Darkyard have not always been friendly. Many Darkyarders left the barony several years ago in frustration and aligned with Darkyard instead. Flynn had even urged me not to attend Cleftlands fighter practices because its approach differs from Darkyard's. In his view, Darkyard had it right and Cleftlands had it wrong. But that relationship has improved dramatically the last few years. Today's joint Darkyard-Cleftlands melee practice in the giant field of Cleftlands' Knight Sir William Ransom's house will mend fences further. Both sides hope to teach each other a few things about winning wars. Though I fought a couple of melees right after authorizing a few weeks ago, I have a lot of confusion to sort out. Today is my big chance.

Darkyard will help me find my way. The illustrious household has added a fourth win to its growing list of Crown Tournament victories. Valharic did not win Crown in South Dakota, but by all accounts put in a fair and honorable showing. Rather than being cutthroat, it was more important to demonstrate chivalry than to win. Twice, he offered a Knight a "point of honor" and offered to give up the same limb he had just taken from his opponent. The star was his former housemate, Ragnvaldr, who won his second Crown. His wrist injury was not as bad as rumor made it out to be. He will take the throne in September.

My own fighting test, my authorization, was an anti-climax. At Cleftlands' major spring-summer event, a regional "War Maneuvers," I suited up for the test. I had worried it would drag on endlessly under the blazing sun. Jen Detmar/Fionnhuala from the SFU group had a nightmare authorization test. Instead of using a small "heater" shield like I borrow today, she had to use her giant warboard. Because marshals wanted to make sure she could hit hard enough, her bout lasted 45 minutes.

By my authorization, I had come a long way since my first fight practice. To start with, it no longer freaks me out when someone tries to club me with a stick. I no longer flinch at a blow to the head and my shield is less trouble to hold up now than before. I have also been introduced to the bruises of this sport. After repeatedly leaving my left hip exposed to attack one fight practice, I awoke the next day with a grapefruit-sized bruise on my hip. And I am learning a practical lesson about armor. If it doesn't fit right, it can cause pain. The metal elbow protectors I have borrowed are leaving black, blue, yellow and red bruises on my arms. "Armor bites" are just part of the game.

With Flynn cutting his fighting to a minimum while he readies the house for his first child, Talon has taken charge of group fight practices. Valharic comes regularly and spends a good portion of his time teaching. I have struggled with the "wrap" shot, one of the SCA practices that ARMA detests. For a "wrap," you thrust your sword beyond or around your opponent and then snap it hard back toward you. The blade strikes your foe in the back of his helm, leg, back or—in a Brannos trademark—the buttocks. Trying that shot on my telephone pole made my arm throb, but Valharic teaches me a stretch that solves the problem instantly.

When I arrive at the event for my authorization, Valharic spots me and guides me to a collection of tents where a few Dukes (former two-time Kings) and the Kingdom's head marshal are having coffee and breakfast. We can do my test right now. And I will fight no easy foe. I will fight Valharic.

Fighting someone that good could be brutal. But I get off easy. Not only do I get to fight in the shade of trees, but my opponent is so good he is beyond being embarrassed to be hit by a newbie. The worst opponent for newcomers might be an average fighter frustrated that he is not better. Then he can make you a living pell, just to boost his sagging ego. Valharic takes the opposite approach. Though sensitive about not being Knighted, he recognizes there is no way I can make him look bad. In fact, he can help show the watching Dukes and Knights he is worthy by giving me a moderate challenge and staying in control. He does both.

The fight is as much a lesson for me in how better fighters can fight at many levels than it is a tough test for me. Just like in baseball, where pitchers throw at different speeds for batting practice, for warm-ups and in 9th inning jams, Valharic can ratchet his fighting back several levels. When I did things (more or less) right, I could hit him. When I made mistakes, he would strike me only with modest blows. Talon razzes me later that I was "gypped" by not fighting someone who would fight back hard.

At a later fight practice I paired up against Valharic again. As I approached to fight, he crouched and leaned back behind his shield. I had no target. I had no idea how to find an opening. I stared, searching, my eyes scanning him for a spot. When none came to mind, I tried swinging to one side and immediately shifting to hit the other.

My sword thumped against his shield. Even as I shifted for the second blow, I felt three quick slaps to my thigh, side and back. I had left myself open in several places with one move. If he wanted to show off, he could have crushed me up with each of those blows. Instead, not a single one left a bruise. But he had still made a point. I was leaving too many easy openings.

There were far more levels of fighting and skills to reach the Crown Tournament level than I imagined. As much as some of the armor looks terrible, as much as some people look awkward, as much as a rattan sword is far from accurate, there really is a set of skills to this sport that are not mastered in a day. This game may not be equivalent to masters-caliber chess in its complexity, but it's not checkers either.

I'm still at the Tic-Tac-Toe stage. If my one-on-one fights hadn't taught me that, my first taste of a melee made it clear.

A couple hours after authorizing, Talon handed me a Darkyard war board and I took the field. If I had trained in Detroit, every Darkyard fight practice would have put me through melee practice. But since I trained in a small group, the most I had tried was three on three.

I died quickly my first time out, taking a spear to the face. The second time I lasted longer. Even staying defensive, I made a kill when an enemy shieldman paid too much attention to the man on my right. One quick slap to the head and he went down. Maybe I wouldn't be hopeless after all.

"What do you need me to do?" I asked a commander as I stepped into a line for the third skirmish.

"Dress left and we're doing a penetration charge."

Since I was borrowing Hobbs' open-faced helm, my dumbfounded expression showed clear through the grille. He gave me the quick explanation: "Dress left" means to keep with the person to my left. If that person goes down, move close to the next one down the line. If the line splits into two units for tactical reasons, just stay with the left.

A penetration charge meant our line would hit the other line and try to punch a hole through the other side. A pulse charge would try to knock the other side back a few feet to disrupt them, but the entire Legion would stop instead of driving through.

"OK"

We charged. I wobbled trying to run while carrying a shield. Oh crap. Big 'ol Edmund with Sir Alaric were right in front of me. I ducked behind my shield, trying to stay low. With a giant thump I bounced off a wall of shields and stumbled backwards. I have no idea who I ran into because I had lowered my head behind the shield. Maybe I ought to look at what I'm doing.

In the next few battles, I learned more lessons: Stick with your group, react fast in a broken field and a tap on your shoulder and a yell to turn around does not mean a friend wants your attention. The spear to my face when I looked back gave me a clear message. SCA rules do not let you hit others from behind. Turning only opens you up, I told myself, put up your guard if you turn.

Today, as Urien puts us through charge after charge after charge after…I lose count…I am realizing that battles are where SCA fighting becomes more football than fencing. Darkyard's web site even has articles about training for the shield wall by using blocking sleds. Fighters often push and prop up their own fighting brothers to make the shield wall stronger. On a few of our charges, the row of fighters behind us leans into the shieldmen in front. Spearmen will even turn their spears horizontal for the charge and press it lengthwise against the back of two shield carriers to act as a brace. Fighting with such giant shields resembles a wall of riot police taking on looters. I later learn some branches of the Royal Canadian Mounted Police practice anti-crown tactics against SCA fighters.

Darkyard is not alone in using its shield wall aggressively. The Kingdom of Calontir lives off its shield wall.

The Calontir Shield Wall may be the Society for Creative Anachronism's most famous battle formation, deserving of the capital S and W. For 17 years it has muscled its way across battlefields and formed nearly impenetrable blockades on bridges and in castle doors. The Shield Wall redefined battle tactics for the entire SCA and made the fighters of Calontir the closest thing to a real, cohesive army the Known World is likely ever to see. And the Wall, and the teamwork it forces among the fighters, has created a sense of unity in the Kingdom unmatched by others. It has become as much a symbol of Calontir as the stylized "Calon" cross and golden hawk that make up the Kingdom's arms.

The Tale of the Shield Wall

Pavel Iosefovich was getting frustrated.

Each time he fought in battles against the Kingdom of Ansteorra, the Texans would fight with "big barn door shields" and with cohesion. After a smaller unit wiped out his larger one at his first Pennsic War, Pavel, MKA Paul Byers, 43, of Fayetteville, Ark., decided he had to try something different.

Pavel is such a legendary figure in Calontir that he is not just Pavel, but The Pavel. He is six feet tall and 280 pounds—"I'm a square block of muscle and fat," he says— but his reputation surpasses even that. He is one of those people you either love or you hate. You can't tell whether he should be hauled into court (for yet another award) or hauled into a real court to be committed to the loony bin. At times, he demonstrates chivalry in ways that surpass others on the field. At other times, he's just a loud-mouthed—and foul-mouthed—good ol' boy. And it's a wild card what he'll do next, whether he'll do tons of work to advance the Middle Ages pursuits or be the ringleader in a scheme to flaunt them.

His latest escapade was as a ringleader of the "Elvis Unit" that fought in a battle at Calontir's Lilies War a few weeks before I attended this melee practice. Donning shiny silver capes and parading velvet Elvis paintings to the battlefield as icons, they all picked names after Elvis songs. Pavel was Brother Hunka' Hunka' Burning Love. Calontir's King Valens, however, was allowed to just be The King.

But back in the early 1980s, Pavel made a landmark serious effort. One of the local baronies had a few giant rectangular shields called "scutums" by the Romans. Pavel experimented with the scutums, even trying a few out on a Pennsic bridge battle. They worked. He and the group held the bridge through the fight by setting up spearmen behind a solid wall of shields.

He returned home to Arkansas and wrote a paper for the February 1984, Kingdom newsletter urging the Kingdom to adopt the tactic and standardize both training and shield size. Soon fighters were ordering the 3-foot by four-foot T-6 aluminum shields and agreeing to ditch their old freelancing ways to carry a shield in the wall. Although aluminum, they are not flimsy. The metal is designed to stop aircraft ammo, has to be bent with a press and is almost impossible to dent with rattan. The Calontir scutum remains the same size and the same hefty 18 pounds. Now costing about $150, each is painted in the Kingdom's purple and gold, with just a corner for personal coats of arms. That tiny concession to individuals symbolizes Calontir's rule of Kingdom coming before self in battle.

"The first two years no one could beat it," he remembers. "They'd just charge at it and burn out."

The few households in Calontir, Pavel admits, were pretty much browbeaten into submission. And in a smaller area than the giant Midrealm, cohesion was still possible. Pavel estimates that the Shield Wall had its heyday about Pennsic 14, mainly because others had yet to adopt similar tactics. He believes the evolution of the Shield Wall makes it better today than it was in the past, but it less effective because it often faces others who have adopted the same tactics.

Today Calontir trots out its army and Shield Wall at major wars across the country to keep trying to make it better. The Wall is divided into a series of eight-man fronts with the most experienced fighters—the chivalry and a rank named after Saxon "huscarls"—holding shields in the front. Polearms and spears and archers stand right behind, with great swords, florentine fighters and new fighters behind them. Archers stand so close that they touch the shieldman in front of them. When bracing, shields overlap the shield to their left by four inches. And shieldmen often kneel behind the shields and brace them with their bodies.

"As a rule you'll stop the charge," Pavel says. "You won't get run over."

Although the scutum bearers carry swords, axes or maces, they rarely swing unless an opponent moves right in front of them.

"Your job is to hold them up so a guy with a 6-foot club can whomp them one," Pavel explains.

Other times, the wall will cave in just enough to let an enemy or two advance. Suddenly he is in a "kill pocket"—a smaller version of what Duke Baldar had tried to create back at the Gulf Wars field battle—where he can be hit from 270-degrees. The army has separate formations for field battles and for bridge battles. The Shield Wall has advanced on bridges with its front spearmen crawling forward on their knees as they push their shields. They have even lifted up the shields to drag enemy dead underneath and out of the way so their advance would not be blocked.

And each January, shortly before the big war in Arizona called Estrella, the Kingdom takes over the University of Nebraska's indoor football practice facility for war maneuvers in which newbies learn and veterans brush up on their skills.

In Calontir, Pavel says, the second fighter's motto after "No heroes" is "Cherish the goob." This is partly a reaction to early practices when newbies were considered pawns for the glory of Knights. Pavel remembers with disgust when he was new and a Knight used him as a living shield to block a spear thrust so the Knight could get a kill. Calontir's practice of giving new and lesser fighters manageable jobs and rewarding it partly explains the relatively high percentage of the Kingdom that fights and the fact that Calontir's army is 23 percent women, a total he believes is the highest in the Known World.

"We don't put our newbie goobs on the scutum," Pavel says. "It is an honor to be on the wall, especially in the first charge."

That is an honor that Pavel, as the father of the Shield Wall, still retains.

Life as a "speed bump"

Darkyard, though it values unit cohesion as much as Calontir, takes a different approach. All newcomers start on the wall, where as Jen had put it, they are "speed bumps" in the big charges, before graduating to carrying spears and polearms and doing the real killing. Both ways make sense. Newcomers start by authorizing with sword and shield. Only later do they authorize in using other weapons.

Today, Urien starts us with simple drills. He first sets fighters in two parallel lines and has them hold their shields out in between the lines to block the path. He then orders us to blast through with our shields, one by one, then rejoin the barrier in back.

"RRRRR," I growl as I run through, not quite yelling the war cry Urien wants. I may be comfortable enough with this culture to growl through clenched teeth, but not enough to open wide and yell.

Cat, back in medieval action after finishing her semester of an acting program, has no reservations. Suited up for this practice, she lets out the dramatic scream Urien wants.

"YAAAAAAAAH," she yells as she bounces off the shields like a pinball. She did not drill through cleanly, but she didn't let a shield send her flying like it was a flipper.

"All right!" yells Urien.

"That was a good yell," adds a shieldman in back.

Urien, who is not fighting today because his wrist is injured, then sets us in columns to charge against a wall set by the Cleftlands group. The two fighters I met back in January, Bernard and Bastian, are in the wall, along with Alaric's squire Stephan. Several times, Urien has us plow into the shields, trying to lower our shoulders and push them aside. Then, Urien has us swap roles. He has us brace to repel their charges or try to overpower them when both charging sides meet in the middle. While Urien tells us to be an irresistible force in our charges, a coach on the other side tells Cleftlands to be an immovable object. Most times, the collision is a stalemate.

When we pick up swords and fight line on line, I learn another key lesson. The man in front of you is not the only one who might hit you. Any of the other fighters in the opposing line may lash out with a surprise diagonal shot, catch you unawares and take you down. As I pay too much attention to the man in front of me, Stephan catches my helm with a snap from a diagonal.

Off to the side, Brannos has shifted into teaching mode again. He has two lines of spearmen practicing their footwork, the ways they grip the spear and how they thrust out to take a shot. Flynn, who is test-driving his new Roman name of Agrippa, joins the line with Talon and Ulfr. When Brannos shows them a way to maintain their defense and still strike, he has each line practice it on the other dozens of times.

The day finishes with two highlights. Cat, who fought Dagorhir for years, authorizes for SCA fighting in a bout against Lyonnete, the same woman whose authorization I watched in January. Cat borrowed old armor from Jocelyn le Jongleur, armor that Jocelyn's newer aluminum suit makes obsolete. This suit made of molded white plastic makes Cat look like a Star Wars stormtrooper. It was made to be worn under garb. Cat, though, will disguise the plastic by wallpaperng its entire surface with leather.

Brannos offers the other. One of the local Tuchux, the group of barbarians based on the *Nomads of Gor* novel, drops by to fight. Known as Tamoc, he has routinely fought well in SCA battles. Built like a weightlifter in his shirtless armor that consists of little more than a kidney belt, he and Brannos pound away at each other furiously. Their swords crack into each other with loud bangs. Each time that Brannos catches Tamoc with a blow, the two discuss it. One leaves a giant welt on Tamoc's side, but he keeps on.

"Did you see his sword?" Urien gasps at another fighter. "It bent when it hit him!"

As the day winds down and people grab food from a cookout Sir William provides, fighters gather in the driveway around Brannos to discuss the day's fighting. Fighting events with Brannos always turn out this way. Everybody learns something, either on the fighting field or in bull sessions afterward. He always has insights to share.

As Brannos leans back against the hood of a truck with the sun going down, a bottle of beer in one hand, a crowd forms a ring with him at the head. For two hours they exchange war stories under bug-attracting garage lights, but Brannos is clearly at the head of this "table."

Even the other Knights hang on his every word.

Act II, scene 5
The Pennsic War

Tommy: *Hey, look at that!*
Geoff: *What do you know? It looks like a village.*
Tommy: *Well it is.*
Geoff: *I thought you said there were no towns on the map around here.*
Tommy: *Well I did. Do you want to see the map?*
Geoff: *No, no. I believe you.*
Tommy: *Come on. Let's go down. There must be people down there. There must be food. That's what we're interested in…Funny it isn't on the map.*
—Brigadoon, Act I, scene I

I peek out my car window as I speed down Interstate 79 toward Pittsburgh, my eyes scanning the open and grassy fields to my right for the spot.

The giant open field of Coopers Lake Campground, cleared close to the highway, makes a tentscape spectacle for the drivers speeding by. The sight of this tent city of nomads is also a virtual welcome mat for those heading there. For several hundred yards, up hill and down, the normally grassy field is carpeted with tents. In between the rows of peaks and domes, between the rolling waves of canvas and nylon, swarms of scraggly and disheveled SCAdians in sleeping garb shake off the night's sleep. For the two weeks of the Pennsic War, Coopers Lake Campground in Slippery Rock, Penn., ceases to be a campground. It is no longer the place where a few residents live year-round in mobile homes. The vibes from the biker campout also held here every year do not exist. To most of the more than 12,000 camping here this week in August 2001, all of Coopers Lake could share the name of a small campsite within it for the authenticity-minded crowd: Enchanted Ground.

I pull off the highway and clatter down the dirt campground entrance road. Later today, a line of cars will back up down this road as the rush to War starts in earnest, but I am early enough to glide by unimpeded to park near the giant Troll tent. For the next week I will not leave the site. I will wear nothing but garb. I will camp in a tent, take very few showers and finally try my hand at this War's giant battles. That will complete the goal I set back in January. I will also try to meet the people that add flavor to an event that most typifies the Society's ongoing battle between period and party. Most of the SFU projects group is here at Pennsic this week. But Flynn, who has decided to change his name to Agrippa, stays home with Erin, who is too close to her due date to handle the August heat and hassle.

As a Troll booth volunteer hands me the stamped aluminum medallion that grants me admission, he asks, "Have you been to Pennsic before?"

"A couple times."

"Welcome home," he says, tossing me a knowing glance.

For most here, his greeting hits the mark. Pennsic is not just an SCA event. It is a happening, a defining event in their year. At a campfire on the closing day of Pennsic last year, one of the singers turned wistful as he asked everyone to savor the moment. We work all year, he told the gathering, and suffer the stifling mood of Mundania all for the chance to come back here. It is only at Pennsic, he said, that we really live. Not everyone agreed, but nobody objected either.

Watching him then, before I saw how much passion some members pour into this hobby, I had scoffed. I still consider his sentiment overblown, but now I better understand how this Society can have such importance. There are few things people can do in the "mundane" world with any degree of passion without others calling them nuts. Most people make their lives fit into one of the mundane world's culturally-acceptable boxes and never reach for the things they dream about. Pennsic, and the entire Society to a lesser extent, gives some people a chance to at least try for it.

The six months I spent on the obituary staff of my newspaper had hammered home how few people really reach for something, anything at all. Day after day, week after week, I wrote almost formula paragraphs about people who lived formula lives: Old men who "loved" working in their gardens and watching the Cleveland Browns on Sundays or old women proud to be lifelong residents of the same neighborhood and who "loved" to bake cookies. Families rarely could tell me why their relatives "loved" these activities or if they really did. Did watching the Browns or baking cookies really satisfy them? Did they wake up each morning itching to weed their gardens? The people that stood out were those driven by something, whether it be the woman who started a dress shop to cater to the high society of another era or the man who kept bees and gave the honey to the local ice cream stand. I sensed a spark in each of their life stories. Maybe caring about something deeply and throwing yourself into it is essential for lifting a life out of the day-to-day drone.

Pennsic is a setting for people to chase dreams of great deeds, pageantry, dance and even learning. The Middle Ages pursuits of nearly every person here will climax in success or failure in these two weeks. Exploits will be magnified in people's heads, all to be endlessly recounted mid-winter over coffee tables or at parties, with plastic tumblers of beer in hand. Events here are memorialized by the number of the War. Pennsic 14 was when they met their wife. Pennsic 16 was just before the wedding. Their son was only a few months old at Pennsic 19. If every Super Bowl is big enough to be numbered with Roman numerals, the Cooper family does Pennsic one better. They let the grass on the hill overlooking the battlefield grow tall and thick. Just before Pennsic, they mow the numerals into the thicket like a crop circle.

This year the numerals in the grass read XXX, a sign of the SCA times and the multiple forces at work at this event. That the SCA's signature event thrives at the age of 30 is a milestone. That the rowdy crowd overstuffing the site has dubbed it the "Porno Pennsic" or "Pornsic" is a sign that the forces of party vs. history are still at war.

Modern issues have also cropped up—some Internet search engines blocked the XXX and made it hard to find some web sites about this War.

For many, the War itself, the battle between the Middle and the East, is all that matters. For others, it is merely a backdrop and they will leave never knowing who won. Pennsic puts all of the sides of the SCA in a giant blender, then overflows it with the fringe and outsider groups that want to be part of the good time. Amtgard, the Kingdom of Acre, Dagorhir and Markland add dozens to the crowd. Many of the 12,000 make Pennsic their only medieval event of the year and come to party or soak up the atmosphere of a medieval-themed campout. A few stretch the bounds of medieval by hauling in gas-powered electric generators to power the refrigerators and VCRs they set up in their tents. Most just use the rows of food merchants set up in a mall-style food court for their meals.

Many believe Pennsic has ceased to be a true SCA event. It is a sanctuary for adults to drop off the mundane grid for two weeks. Teens and young adults can escape their parents. It is a place where a few dozen people can be found swimming au naturel in the site's "Classic Swimming Hole" or where suspiciously sweet-smelling smoke can waft from camps. It is also a stopover on the counterculture trail that next leads to pagan festivals in upstate New York. To borrow from Frederick of Holland, Pennsic is "related to" the SCA but not really even a re-creation of a typical SCA event.

Duke Finn, Valharic's mentor and the man in charge of running this year's event, believes it resembles the SCA less and less each year.

"It's become like Burning Man," he said.

It also has the most classes, the most merchants, the biggest medieval dances, the most performances of Middle Ages arts in the Known World and the largest competitive medieval battles in the world.

As I clear Troll, Valharic zips by on one of the golf carts reserved for event staff. Everyone else needs to unpack their cars quickly and get them out to the parking lot. Finn has needed help all summer planning for Pennsic, and Valharic has volunteered weekend after weekend. He has also spent hours helping build Pennsic's new fort. Valharic's work on this War has been like a Boy Scout's service project to become an Eagle Scout. A giant mundane trouble has also been resolved. Neither his wife nor her "friend" showed up in court to testify in his domestic violence case. He was cleared just before War. His marriage will be annulled a year later because his wife's divorce from a previous marriage had never been completed.

Today, though, Valharic is looking for Dame Alys Katharine, the boyhood friend's mother who used to drive him to events. At Pennsic, she is in charge of running a class schedule that dwarfs any kingdom university.

From across the country, experts and budding experts in medieval practices step forward at Pennsic to try to teach their craft. Attendees can spend an entire day measuring, cutting, then sewing a pair of 13th century shoes from scratch. They can turn string into rope, peruse embroidered Celtic designs, learn the details of ancient Celtic clothing or the Coptic tunic and then pick up a bodhran for a lesson in the Irish drum. In addition to the dancing and drumming at the Middle Eastern tent, European dance is taught in classes like "15th century Italian Dance for Dummies" or more specific ones like "Altezza d'Amore," advertised as "a fairly advanced dance from Caroso's 'Nobilita di Dame.'" Every hour, attendees can pick from about 20 classes in art, cooking, sewing, music and theater. Each one is free, aside from occasional copy or supply costs.

For five of the last six years, Alys, MKA Elise Fleming, 62, of North Olmsted, Ohio, has organized the hundreds of classes at Pennsic. When she started at Pennsic XXIV, the event offered a little more than 300 classes. Today, it has about 1,000. A single day's classes at the Pennsic University dwarfs the offerings at Kingdom universities.

"It has gotten to the point that this is all I'm doing," Alys says. Despite a crew of local assistants helping her manage the crush, her other major medieval interest and the one that earned her Laurel—creating virtual sculptures from a sugar paste—has fallen by the wayside.

She does not mind.

"We do funny things to have something that's ours, that's uniquely ours," she said. "This is something I could do."

The Teacher's Tale

As a child, Elise Fleming loved Middle Ages stories. She kept the interest as she grew up. On the wall of her house is a painting of a medieval court filled with lords and ladies, knights and a king that she rescued from a trash heap during remodeling of her school.

But she never really pursued the Middle Ages as a hobby until after her divorce in 1982. Until then, she had mostly been concerned with being a Spanish teacher in a local public school system and raising her children. She poured all her extra energy into teaching childbirth classes and using her organizational skills to help put together a childbirth guide still in use today.

But with her divorce, the SCA helped fill the new void in her life. As she started attending meetings regularly, her youngest son Matthew asked if she could drive a friend along. The friend was the young Tom Noble, now the Crown-hopeful Valharic. After feeling snubbed by Cleftlands, she became one of the main forces in creating a guide for new members called *Forward Into the Past*. Even without encouragement from the barony, she started to excel at the arts.

She began simply, trying to just be a good member. She baked and decorated cakes to bring to Baronial events and meetings. She even made and decorated one for the Middle Kingdom anniversary in 1989. She stayed overnight before that event at Kingdom founder Cariadoc of the Bow's house, then living in Chicago, and expected him to appreciate her work. He didn't.

"Have you ever tried to do anything period?" he asked instead. From authenticity-minded Cariadoc, that question was not just a question. It was a withering value judgment.

So Fleming started researching, learning about the old practices of using the pastes that could be made from natural gums to create decorations for the table. In one cookbook, she discovered a recipe for "sugar paste," with which someone could make whole plates and goblets from sugar. She learned that sugar plates from the Elizabethan era still survive, even though at dinners, they would usually sit on top of normal wooden plates, then be broken down and eaten.

She read of a gum tragacant that would make the sugar hold up better, then learned that modern gum paste was made of the same material.

She was off on her own path. With the paste, she made roses, boxes, bowls and plates with the Kingdom coat of arms on them and a goblet copied from one in the Cleveland Museum of Art. She then began teaching classes, which eventually led to her Laurel. It was something she could do where her efforts mattered.

Today she takes on the task of organizing classes at the War. Each spring, she is bombarded through March, April and May with e-mails. She then worries about properly formatting a schedule on her computer, sorting out land use patterns and making sure she has ordered all the proper equipment. Fleming must manage the schedule requests of teachers who dare not miss a certain battle, a certain ceremony or even other classes. Then because demand for some classes is so high, she has to arrange volunteers to man a sign-up tent that opens early in the morning the day before each class.

Though running this university has won her the respect of this Society, she has never had a chance at the top rank it offers: the Crown. Running the university and earning her Laurel and Pelican were things she could control. To be Queen, though, someone would have to step up and fight for her. Having Kings and Queens "by right of arms" blocks many capable people from those positions and often puts incompetent people in them. Alys is now in her 60s with gray hair. Her matronly build from three childbirths is not going to make any hot-blooded hot stick smitten. A few years earlier, she had joked on the Kingdom newsgroup, half as an invitation, that fighters looking for a consort ought to choose older women who are financially secure and have no other men they are attached to. As expected, nobody took the hint and asked her.

So she has long written it off. Running the Pennsic University is as large a role as she will ever have.

"Have Thee Not a Cow, Man"

I head to my camp past the unusual gates that households and the groups that camp together every year set up at their regular campsites. Some have painted wooden representations of their household arms a few feet across or post shields, suits of armor or skulls impaled on pikes at their gates to warn intruders off. For privacy, most camps box their borders with posts and fences they haul back and forth and re-install year after year. Roman Darkyard rents storage space for the two pillars it uses to make its gate. It adds the extra flourish of a mosaic of the household arms set into the entranceway ground. Darkyard's coat of arms fly on a flagpole higher than any other camp's in the sun-roasted field known as the "Serengeti." A few camps paint castle stonework on plywood with very mixed results. But the most common barrier is the "sheet wall"— sheets hung tightly along fence rails or between posts—often painted with heraldry or very non-period drawings and tongue-in-cheek cartoons. "Bard" Simpson in an Elizabethan ruffle calls out from one sheet wall, "Have Thee Not a Cow, Man."

Cat and I start setting up our tent, still a modern nylon one. We have not graduated to the period, or closer to period, pavilions of canvas with wooden poles. Cars are parked along the roadway past our campsite and people still wearing shorts and T-shirts drag coolers to their tents. Not only are garb standards here looser than normal in terms of authenticity, they often are ignored as people move in or out. Each year, they take a step toward failing altogether. At first, wearing a T-shirt in your tent was OK. Then that extended to wearing T-shirts in your own camp. Now, on moving days, a few people will walk across the event to the camp store in mundanes. I am still finding my way in this Society, but by now I respect it enough to drive here wearing garb pants and to throw on a tunic at the rest stop a few miles away, gawking glances from other "resting" motorists be damned.

I am still in the uncomfortable Phantom Zone between Mundania and the Known World when a singer by the name of Owain Phyfe wanders into the camp.

He offers the group of us still setting up tents the pick of many songs in several languages. We select Ukrainian. Phyfe, who also performs on the renaissance fair circuit and has several CDs, sings a tale of a gypsy to enthusiastic applause.

As he heads down the road, to play for the neighboring camp, I exhale. With that breath, my mind releases Mundane concerns.

The SCA mood is starting to take over. I will not come out of this trip for a week.

"If you can't score…"

"It is ever common that men are merriest when they are from home."
　　　　　　　　　　　　　　　　　　—Act I, Scene ii, *Henry V*

The bodies are packed into the courtyard between tents in the dark of night— "o'dark-thirty" in Pennsic time. Some 500 sweaty and garbed people in various stages of intoxication jam shoulder-to-shoulder and dodge tent stakes and poles.

A well-known Pennsic party spot along the lake known as Vlad's Pleasure Pavilion has set up a stage in its camp courtyard and ringed it with propane torches. The crowd overflows into the road as groups jostle and jockey their way forward for a better look at the merchandise—people.

Vlad hops on the stage from behind.

"Welcome to Vlad's slave auction," he bellows.

This "slave auction" has been a Pennsic tradition for several years with volunteers stepping forward to offer their services for bid. The money fuels the torches and beer taps that night and for parties in the camp the rest of the War.

The is a typical only-at-Pennsic SCA tradition: It has passing resemblance to history, turns into a camping version of a costumed fraternity party and becomes wildly popular for a crowd wanting to cut loose out of the mundane world. A cluster of campsites along the lake and in the "Bog" formed by a river running into it are filled with people who come to Pennsic more to relax and party than pursue medieval recreation. The geography of the campground almost creates two different worlds at War: The respectable Society establishment lives up on higher ground and looks down on the back-alley Bog revelry below. Until, that is, individuals want a party before returning to the safety up top. At their mundane homes, people can be embarrassed by acting up in front of neighbors or co-workers. Driving home after a night of revelry can pose a problem. But Walking Under the Influence is no crime here. It is a way of life.

Pennsic nightlife includes serious period-style activities like Kingdom courts, dancing in an open barn in the camp and the near-nightly Middle Eastern dancing at the cluster of tents making up Orluk's Oasis. Party crowds can pick from Hawaiian Luau cookouts, mini Mardi Gras parties and a string of other parties, including Men Without Pants, with gate-keeper guards making sure male attendees follow rules by checking under their kilts.

While sex is not directly for sale at this auction, it is clearly the thrust, so to speak, of the proceedings. Selling prices, other than for a few performing groups, have nothing to do with talent, but with looks and a would-be slave's willingness to shake it on stage. Tonight's auction will feature a parade of cleavage and pecs and chances for guys who can't buy a date back home to do so at this medieval-themed spring break.

Tonight, Vlad turns the stage over to a singer named Dankwert Maccabee Bathory just called Danx, who puts his mundane background in community theater to work. As if he were stepping forward in the spotlight in a musical, Danx launches into a song he tells the crowd was inspired by his first Pennsic.

The song would have image-conscious SCA members cringing. It would curdle the blood of those who want the SCA to be a true historical society, not a giant costumed fraternity party. But the crowd here whoops with approval as Danx belts out a rollicking, tongue-in-cheek tale of his quest for sex at Pennsic 25.

Punctuating verses with a chorus of, "If you can't get laid at the Pennsic War, you might as well go on home," he rattles of a list of the "virtues" of the ladies at several Bog camps. The song recounts sleeping with one woman, then heading straight out into the night to "knock uterus" again. The crowd follows every crude verse. When he roars, "If you can't score with a two-bit…" the crowd chimes in with "whore" right on cue.

When he steps off the stage to applause at the end, he quips, "I get a standing ovation. This is great."

Danx wrote "The Pennsic Song" himself after his first visit to the War at Pennsic 25. He no longer has the written lyrics, but he knows it cold from singing it about 50 times a year.

Asked how much of it is true, he laughs a deep laugh and says, "I don't want to answer that question."

But his view of Pennsic has changed since he wrote the song, much as the things he seeks from the event have. When he leaves Pennsic a week from now, his perception of the SCA and the role it has in his life will change even further. With a steady girlfriend and advances in his job as a disc jockey and master of ceremonies for functions, his real life will start snapping into place. The SCA will become more of a hobby and less of a lifeline.

Five years ago, though, it was what he needed. He was in the same dark place Kief av Kierstad, the Ansteorran Knight, had been in. In his case, he tells me, the trouble was gangs.

When he was 13, Adam Steinfelder of Long Island, had no friends and was an outsider.

"You know when you play tag someone is always 'it.' I wish I was 'it' because then I would have been a part of the game."

So he joined a gang.

"I was a mess," he admits, "but I found the group that would accept me. I know the shit I was doing was bad. I didn't want to do some of it. Shit, I didn't want to go to jail."

Someone pulled him aside and took him to SCA events. He saw the same structure, the same acceptance, the same camaraderie the gang gave him. He latched onto Andreas Eisfalke's very militaristic household, Bloodguard. While he struggled to meet the group's standards and dropped out, it showed him that a household, a unit that has a common goal, looks out for each other and protects each other, offers the same things his gang did.

The bowing and kneeling before people in the SCA threw him at first. But enough people followed through on their discussions of honor that the Society seemed like a better world. He tells me he once lost his wallet filled with $200 in cash. It turned up at lost and found, missing just one twenty. In its place was a note from the person who borrowed the $20 to travel home, apologizing for taking it and insisting on paying it back.

"I saw there were things I could do that were the right things. I could be OK. I could find acceptance even if I had to go back 600 to 700 years to get it."

The two auctioneers for the evening take the stage. One, known as Erik the Bard, has attended Pennsic since he was a teenager. Now 33, he is a Pennsic celebrity.

A master of self-promotion, salesmanship and think-on-the-fly banter, he has attracted attention at Pennsic with three big roles—auctioneer, as frontman for a semi-pro circus-style troupe called the Sloane Gypsies and by playing Satan in the Pentwyvern Goes To Hell party in the neighboring Pentwyvern camp.

The Tale of Satan

"I'm a tremendous, egomaniacal, attention whore," says Erik, MKA Steve Pack, 33, of Elyria, Ohio.

Pack, who works as a web designer for a branch of electronics supplier Pioneer-Standard, started his evolution into Satan at age 16. Hs first step was coming up with a makeshift costume and posing as a member of the SCA and Dagorhir to take advantage of their free admission to a local renaissance fair.

Then, to work his way into a group of performers called the Sloane Gypsies even though he had no skills, he taught himself fire-eating. He had no instruction and no books. He relied on intuition and his knowledge that the moisture in his wet mouth would prevent a burn—for a short period of time. He just had to avoid singeing his lips and had to find out how long the moisture in his mouth would last.

"You sort of play chicken with yourself to see how long you can keep the fire in your mouth before you start hurting yourself," he tells me. "I cooked my lips a few times, a few blisters."

He managed to learn. He was in. And he was soon off on a showbiz career among the SCA set. For the Sloane Gypsies' first two or three years at Pennsic he said, "we performed our asses off" for almost no pay.

"It was fun, oddly enough," he remembers.

The group eventually included members who could juggle and do magic tricks and even one who could lie on a bed of nails while Pack smashed cinder blocks on his chest with a sledgehammer. They started performing several weekends a summer at renaissance fairs. But the pay was low. The half dozen of them picked up other jobs. Even though Pack continues attending fairs, he now sells leather mugs and a brand of corsets to fair crowds.

"It pays better, sadly. It's like doing a Vegas show. When you do a booth, you get to perfect it. You can hammer the same line 500 times until you get it funny."

Running the Slave Auction and playing Satan for the party are his chances to perform before crowds. Helping run events in Vlad's camp also has other personal significance. He proposed to his wife, Rossana Fichera at a party here a few years back. In a full suit of armor.

His eyes light up as he recounts the tale. Though he does not fight, he borrowed a full suit of Milanese style plate armor. He surprised her with the armor and his proposal on stage.

"I know I am but a humble gypsy," he recalls telling her on the stage. "But I will strive to be your knight in shining armor,' which causes 1,000 people to go AAAWWWW."

He had met Rosanna, a former actress and now part-time palm reader, at Pennsic in 1987. He married her in 1999 in a ceremony in the same spot in Pentwyvern's camp that serves as Hell each year.

"I met her at Pennsic, got engaged there and got married there, so anniversaries are an easy thing."

At Pennsic, she is not just Steve Pack's wife, but "Babs," the wife of Satan. One night each Pennsic—around which most of Pentwyvern bases its War—Pack slathers red makeup on his body, pops on a pair of horns and a satin vest and takes the stage for a fire-breathing schtick as Satan.

The party draws such giant crowds that a line stretches a few hundred feet outside Pentwyvern's gates. Pentwyvern actually sets up a team of security volunteers and posts ID checkers at its gate to keep underage drinkers away from "Swamp Gas," the mixture of Everclear and Mountain Dew served each year from a punchbowl illuminated with glow sticks.

The camp has even built a propane gas torch that lights up in the letters "HELL." Pack gives the sweaty audience a monologue as Satan. He then gives way to such party games as bobbing for miniature bottles of booze, ring toss onto dildos and Drench-a-Wench, a wet tunic show courtesy of a dunking booth. Partiers can sign their souls away to Satan, pose for photos in his lap or submit to stockades where leather-clad "whip chicks" can administer a little light punishment.

"They're carnival games in every sense of the word," Pack says. The party pokes fun at the Satan myths, he said, though he understands how some outsiders who view the SCA and its pagan members as a Satan worship cult might get the wrong impression. The party, he says, was originally supposed to be five years of Hell and five years of Heaven.

"We couldn't come up with any good Heaven games," he jokes.

"The myth of Hell Nite is far beyond reality," he adds. "We never did become this evil. We just decided to see how far we could go. We want people to say, 'Oh my gosh. I can't believe they did that.'"

Up for bid in the "Slave Auction" is a performing group that takes a very different approach from the other "slaves." The Clan Tynker, an institution of the Kingdom of the Outlands, is in many ways like Erik the Bard's Sloane Gypsies were several years ago. They took Pennsic by storm last year with their act of juggling, fire breathing and dancing. But though they will perform at events like Hell Nite, starting something of that ilk is not likely in their future. The family is proud of being Christian.

The Tale of the Clan Tynker

Clan Tynker is the Kingdom of the Outlands answer to a circus family.

Unlike the weekend bards of the SCA, the five-member troupe from Santa Fe earns its living doing juggling and magic shows around New Mexico. They'll perform at birthday parties, company functions, restaurants and renaissance fairs. The group also takes the short play it wrote called "The Traveler's Tale" to schools around Santa Fe. They have performed at the Albuquerque Summer Fest street festival, the Debonshire

Renaissance Fair in Arizona and many SCA events. "They're the treasure of the Kingdom," one Outlands resident tells me.

Elijah, MKA Elijah Whippo, is the oldest and leader at the age of 24. Thin, with sandy and curly hair he has a wry smile and a deferential demeanor. He is a part-time artist who fights as well as performs. His set of Bayeux Tapestry armor takes the art of duplicating period sources to a unique level. Rather than guess whether those circles on all those fighters on the Tapestry are gambeson quilts or chain mail, he decided that all the Tapestry really showed was circles. So he just painted some on his jumpsuit.

"We have to go as literal as possible," he says, hiding a grin.

He has covered the grille of his helm with a white mask, on which he has doodled a line-drawing face and nasal guard. The circle eyes and straight-line mouth are straight off the Tapestry.

"I did it just to be funny. I wanted to see who would recognize it. Most people just said, 'What are you doing in a clown suit?'"

He and his sisters are also often spotted on the fencing fields in Grim Reaper armor, black robes and hoods with white skulls painted on their facemasks.

He is followed by Sarah, 23, known as Serendipity, who is the group's belly dancer. When not performing, she joins other SCA dancers around campfires. Maria, 21, known as Marygold, Rebekah, 20, and 16-year-old Sam round out the crew.

All of the Siblings grew up together in the SCA as their father sold knives and their mother sold Indian tapestries and scarves at events. Their father had done basic three-ball juggling for fun and taught Elijah the basics when he was 10. Elijah then taught his sisters, who took to it right away. Soon the whole Whippo family was juggling merrily away. SCA events were the perfect place to try performing. Elijah says events let them work out which tricks worked and which didn't in impromptu performances at campfires or for friends.

Elijah's skills picked up a new dimension when he started working at a magic shop called Fool's Paradise. There he learned new tricks to perform. When customers started asking for a magician or clown to perform at parties, Elijah grabbed the chance. He later filled out the act with his siblings. Today, all of the Tynkers can fire-breathe, a skill a circus performer taught them.

"Mom was a little scared," Elijah concedes.

"I went up in a fireball once," Rebekah adds. "It totally toasted my ears."

Sarah mostly dances, often with long wire "fire fingers"—mini torches extending several inches from her fingertips, which she quenches in her mouth. Other times she'll play the concertina while the others juggle.

Elijah does several magic tricks, usually close-range, small-scale tricks with cards and coins. He can juggle up to six balls at a time. The others juggle up to five or use pins or flaming sticks. Elijah can do "contact juggling," a slightly unnerving trick of rolling the ball up and down both the front and back of his hands or along his arms so that the ball appears to be floating. Stilt walking is a regular part of the act and Mary and Rebekah do a tumbling and trapeze routine from a portable pole. Brother Sam sometimes wears a bear suit and plays drums for the show or does a stand-up routine as a Pirate.

Their Pennsic journey started two years ago when Elijah went to Pennsic and did some busking on merchants row and at a few parties.

"I ran home and I was like, 'Oh my gosh, this is great. We all have to go."

So they packed into a car, drove cross-country, and launched into an insane performance schedule: about 10 half-hour shows a day wandering around the site, then three or four longer ones at night for camps and private parties. On either side of that, they'd fight in battles and hit the late-night parties.

"We didn't sleep," Rebekah says.

"We'd wake up, put on our armor and go fight," Elijah adds. "In the afternoon, we'd perform, then perform again at night. At midnight we'd go to parties until 5 a.m. or so, sleep a couple of hours and do it again."

All of their efforts left them with just $200 profit, but it covered their expenses and a speeding ticket in Oklahoma. They enjoyed the atmosphere and Pennsic's much-loved chocolate milk so much they plan to return several times.

Charging $300 an hour for a full five-Tynker show or $200 an hour for three members, they are having no trouble making a living. Their expenses are low. None are married or have children and they live in the family's solar and wind-powered adobe house. Cut into a Santa Fe hillside, the house has been built in stages by all of them.

"Our act is growing by itself, with the help of God," Elijah says. "It's getting bigger and bigger. But we have no big goals. It's not like one day we want to go to Vegas. If it's like this the rest of our lives, we're fine."

"A good old-fashioned War…"

Early the next afternoon, a giant cluster of Coptic-clad Darkyard fighters lines up outside their camp by contubernium, the Roman-styled units the Legion is broken into. Each has a separate flag with the contubernium's animal symbol: a bear, an elephant and Flynn and Talon's latest addition, a Krakken, the legendary giant squids that could pull ships to watery graves. The army rolls out along the road, bellowing the Darkyard song—"…for Forgan, and for…Darkyard!"—as it marches through the food court and across the road that divides Coopers Lake Campground. Cars on the road stop and let the army pass unbroken like a funeral procession. One of Talon's favorite household moments comes true: Darkyard being mistaken for an entire Kingdom.

"What Kingdom is that?" asks a woman out shopping.

"That's Darkyard," replies her friend. "And the whole Legion. That is so cool."

It cuts through the center of the site, past the Cooper store and to the Midrealm Royal camp.

Bardolph and Brigh are camping in the SCA version of the White House, a big grouping of jumbo pavilions with a giant courtyard surrounded by wooden walls.

Instead of a Rose Garden, Midrealm Royal has a heap of armor in its yard. Instead of Secret Service agents swarming the boundaries, two guys with big spears make up the guard. Retainers sit at the door, mini turrets covered with heraldry to each side, to check visitors against a list. Midrealm Royal serves as the private camp for the King and Queen, their retinue and heirs. It is also the meeting point and virtual function hall for specific events. Today, the crowds gather outside the gates.

Roak, the fighter and Middle Eastern dancer I met back at the February hafla, is now King of Ealdormere. He huddles with a group of his subjects gathered for the procession that is about to start. A group from the West Kingdom joins the crowd, followed by a token group from the Kingdom of the Outlands officially led by Queen Elinor. Unofficially, though, the Tynkers lead the spirited Kingdom. Rebekah and Marygold tower over everyone on stilts while Serendipity wears a mask. The Kingdom of Calontir adds its own flavor, singing as always, but accompanied by a bagpipe playing "Amazing Grace."

As the song ends, one person hollers, "OK! Let's go kill something!"

The mass starts its procession, hundreds strong, on the road in a sea of bright-colored garb and heraldry. The bagpipes continue and drums hammer a marching beat, in the spirit of high school bands at mundane parades, by ripping off military-style or Middle Eastern rhythms. The giant line stretches out into the battlefield and up the slight slope of hill to the gates of the Pennsic War's brand new castle.

Today's Pennsic opening ceremonies are the castle's coming out party. With Gulf Wars blazing the way, forts are becoming more common across the SCA. Pennsic needs to keep up with the medieval times. Finn had devoted $25,000 in Pennsic profits into building this 360-foot-long, six-foot-tall fortress with crennelations—the sawtooth of alternating short spots and high spots—in the wall for vaulting it and firing arrows through.

"This is the wave of the future," says Sir Miles Blackheath, one of the builders. "Pennsic is the granddaddy event. It seems right and proper that it should have a castle."

Of course, modern zoning codes do not have any easy way to deal with castles. So this one, with no roofs or floors other than the incline of dirt leading to its turrets, is technically just an oversized snow fence.

"Legally it's a fence," Miles explained. "It's a big bodacious fence, but that ended up saving us a lot of trouble."

The wood of the walls is still fresh, the heraldry painted on it still gleaming. The Middle Kingdom's royals, Bardolph and Brigh, have already have taken their spots on the stage set up in front of it, joined in a line with the royals of almost every Kingdom. The crowd fills the slope to the fort, packing both sides of a pathway that is left open. Trumpets blare and the chief herald of the host Kingdom of Aethelmearc addresses the crowd.

"Welcome to the 30th Pennsic War!" he yells.

The crowd roars.

"This year is the culmination of three decades of customs and traditions. Twenty-nine years ago the forces of the Middle and the East gathered for the first time in friendly competition."

The legend of Pennsic is that Cariadoc of the Bow "declared war on himself" when he moved from the Middle Kingdom to the East while still King of the Midrealm, then became King there. The truth is a complicated story of him playing a part in a string of challenges and half-hearted challenges between the Kingdoms. He has never written the true story down to set the record straight.

"I like the idea of oral tradition," he tells me. "That was the way it was and still is. The world is full of things people believe really happened but never did."

The herald at the war today continues that the first Pennsic drew 100 gentles. As the crowd laughs, another herald tells the crowd that by Pennsic X, there were 400 fighters and the War had its first bridge battle. By Pennsic XX, 8,000 people showed up and the old woods battle site had to be eliminated. Last year, Pennsic XXIX had 10,751 attendants. And now, this year's Pennsic is already the largest event ever in the Society.

Bardolph and the King of the East, Hanse, step forward. Both armies are ready for battle but nobody has officially declared war. At least until Bardolph offers a challenge.

"We come to crush your people," he says.

"I am Hanse, King of the East and I have many allies," responds Hanse. "We will do horrible things to you."

The two threaten each other and act as if they might start throwing punches. Hanse's Queen, Olivia, stops her King.

"I think we need to come up with another way to deal with this."

Bardolph has stepped back a few steps. He steps forward again and the schtick begins.

"Perhaps…" he pauses a second. "Thumb wrestling?"

He whips out his hand from behind his back. His thumb, covered by a prosthetic, is now a formidable foe at least a foot long. Hanse responds with, "Rock, Paper, Scissors?" and whips out an oversized set of fake scissors. Bardolph shoots back with "Lawn Darts?" and holds aloft a jumbo faux dart.

"Perhaps," adds Hanse, "A good old-fashioned war."

The crowd roars, then joins in with a chant of "Lawn Darts! Lawn Darts!" The Kings, however, settle on the normal war.

They seal that declaration by both grabbing the same arrow and snapping it in two, wishbone style.

"Dogs and wenches, Lord and Ladies…"

Within a few hours, fighters swarm the edges of the giant battlefield below the fort, strapping on armor or escaping the sun under the canvas pavilions that households and Kingdoms have set up. Non-fighting women dart back and forth, carrying milk jugs of fresh water to the fighters. The real battles of this War, the War Point battles that decide the winner of the war, will not start until tomorrow. Today, several smaller tournaments dominate the field as fighters get in extra fighting. Two tournaments offer a dramatic contrast in styles. A group of SCA fighters, striving for more authentic fighting standards, hold a Pas d' Armes, a more real re-creation of a medieval tournament. Everyone carefully picks and sews later-period clothing to match their reasonably-accurate later-period armor. Rather than "killing" each other in battle, they fight to "counted blows." The first to land a certain number of solid blows on the opponent wins. The atmosphere is of overstated civility. Every fighter bows to his opponent and to his consort before every bout. But just a few hundred feet up the battlefield, a tournament held by the fantasy-inspired Tuchux highlights their less-stately, but in many ways more realistic, fighting style. The Tuchux allow punches and kicks all over the body, along with sword blows, while their culture skips courtly formality.

"Dogs and wenches, Lords and Ladies, let's give them a howl!" calls a ringside bellower as the finals of this tournament is about to start.

"Aah-Rooo!" howls the milling crowd.

The battle pits SCA fighter Sascha of Darkmoon, MKA Kyle Gresham of Ft. Wayne, Indiana, against one of the 'Chux. The two launch into a battle of spear jabs. In the deciding fight, Sascha swipes aside a thrust well enough to knock the spear from the Tuchuk's hand.

As the Tuchuk bends over to pick up his weapon cautiously, he is an easy target to be not only stabbed, but knocked to the ground. The fight is Sascha's if he takes it. The SCA would stop the fight to let the fighter retrieve the sword. It's the honorable thing to do.

But the crowd of Tuchux, partisan up until that moment, starts yelling at Sascha as he holds back to let his opponent pick up his spear.

"Kill him!"

"Don't do it—just kill him!"

When the fight resumes, Sascha takes a giant clout from his opponent's spear. He loses because he followed the SCA honor code, not a Tuchuk no-holds-barred one.

"Nice guys lose," mutter some of the Tuchux.

"He could have had it."

"I would have clobbered him."

"I would have made him urinate himself."

Sascha, who has fought in this tournament four years running, tells me as he grabs a drink of water that he understands the differences, but he was only returning a courtesy another Tuchuk had given him before.

"Kicking, punching and grappling. That's the easiest way to even it up between you and someone else," he concedes.

On another part of the battlefield, more than 100 women fighters gather for their own tournament. Duchess Elina of Beckenham, MKA Tobi Beck, from the West Kingdom has organized this tournament, as she does at most major events, to try to coax more women into joining the ranks of fighters.

With her book, *The Armored Rose*, and frequent lectures at events across the Known World, the masses are building. So is the confidence of many women to give this sport a try.

Each of the competitors today will receive a certificate, reading, "Be it known unto all gentles that the bearer of this scroll hath competed with valor this day upon the field of the Tournament of the Armored Rose, Pennsic…While the Rose is beautiful, her thorns are sharp."

The Tale of the Armored Rose

The Somali suicide squads were coming over the walls.

Holed up with her troops in the U.S. embassy in Mogadishu, Lt. Tobi Beck of the U.S. Army Military Police, had a big problem.

She and her 30-man platoon were only supposed to be doing a simple escort job this day in February, 1993. But nothing was simple about peacekeeping in Somalia. They were under surprise attack and the lieutenant knew that if she didn't do something fast some of her platoon would go home in body bags.

There in Mogadishu, 9,500 miles from home, and with lives in the balance, Beck relaxed and thought back to her training.

"What would I do?" she thought, "…in an SCA bridge battle?"

Tobi Beck, born Tobi Cooley, is the product of very mundane parents and perhaps the greatest sibling rivalry duel in SCA history. Two years younger than her brother Alex, who went on to become Duke Baldar, Tobi skipped two grades in school and often ended up in the same classes with him.

Because of their strong physical resemblance, they would sometimes pass themselves off as twins. She insists with a grin that she found the SCA when she was 14, four months before her brother. She blitzed through the ranks of the Arts and Sciences to become a Laurel at 21, the youngest, she believes, in Kingdom of Trimaris history.

Her Laurel was in domestic sciences—spinning weaving, dyeing and candlemaking. She topped off her handiwork with the ultimate garb project for authenticity mavens—a "sheep to shirt" cotehardie. She collected wool from the hapless medical experiment sheep at her father's medical laboratory, spun it, wove it, dyed it (with natural dyes of course) and sewed the cotehardie by hand. She wove the trim for the dress herself and hand-embroidered it.

After all that, she gave it to a friend who wore it to events.

"If I had kept it I never would have worn it," she said. "Oh my God, all the number of hours I put into that. I would have wrapped it in tissue paper."

Meanwhile, she also took to fighting and became decent at it. Fighting, conflict and strategy were not a big issue for her. She had served in the Army's Strategic Force Unit, after all. She was scheduled to start a six-month training program shortly after one Pennsic when her life took a major turn. At the War, she met the man who would become her husband, Stephen of Beckenham, MKA Steve Beck. Stephen tracked her from battlefield to camp during that war before they hooked up as a couple. Their partnership has now lasted 10 years and they have lived in San Jose the last seven.

Elina says people sometimes take SCA wars too seriously.

"This is a game. I recognize it for what it is. But there are places in Somalia where this game saved my life. I would literally look at things and say, this needs to happen, based on what I learned in the SCA."

The SCA, she said, is a perfect training ground for commanders. It allows you to try out different battle scenarios and tactics with real people and real opponents, all without any real-life casualties. Then you get to try it all over again.

Military officials, she said, realize that SCA experience, particularly as a commander, benefits the military. The Army even gave her a pass from a training program when she cast her request for leave as a desire to defend a martial arts title she had won the year before.

Her commanding officer pulled out her file and flipped through it as he weighed her request.

"He goes, 'You want to go to Pennsic, don't you?" she remembers. "I was busted."

"He looks at the file again and says, 'Lieutenant, are you leading a unit at Pennsic?"

"Yes."

"How many are in your unit?"

"Thirty-five to 50."

"Well," he said. "You'll be getting more out of your week there than here."

Her SCA and military life crossed paths on one other notable occasion. On patrol rounds on her base, she stopped at the morgue to see the coroner hard at work trying to identify body parts from an airplane crash.

The coroner showed her a hand.

"She pointed at it and says, 'So is this a guy or a girl?"

Elina looked at it. It was medium-sized. The fingers were manicured but there was no nail polish. She had no idea, so she guessed.

"Girl?"

"No. Guy," the coroner replied and pulled out a set of electrodes and attached them to the severed hand. She zapped it with electricity and the hand closed. The coroner was now almost positive it was a man. The explanation: males typically make a fist with their thumbs in a different position than the one women use.

Immediately she made a connection with her SCA fighting. Some movements that men made naturally seemed difficult for her. Male trainers, including her husband, could easily do things that left her feeling awkward. Then she thought of how her drill sergeants had taught men and women different ways to fight with pugil sticks or how to shoot M-16s. She had asked her instructors why, but they didn't know. All they knew was that the different ways worked better.

"I did not get the complete how and why," she remembers. "But I knew it had to be something. I went on a quest to find out why."

The result is Beck's book, *The Armored Rose*, and a movement within the SCA to attract and teach more women fighters.

The SCA has had only one woman "King" or royal by right of her own arms. Duchess Sir Rowann Beatrice van Kampfer won the Crown in the Kingdom of Ansteorra in 1991 when she beat her husband in the finals. There are also several female Knights, a couple per Kingdom. But Beck wants to see more participants unafraid to strap on armor and swing stick. The more that fight, the more the attitudes of men fighting them change.

Her style uses a different sword grip from what most men use. She has her students position their feet the opposite way from men. Bardolph and Darkyard had taught me to have my shield foot forward and sword foot back. Elina encourages women to place their sword foot out in front because she believes it helps the mechanics of their blows.

"Women should not be treated differently," she says. "They should be trained differently."

Many fighters dismiss her theory as fighting "funny-footed" or "goofy-footed." Some see no advantages from it. But she has few critics of the pep talk that her book, and series of lectures at events around the country, give women.

The turnout today tells her she is making progress. She still has work to go toward her other goal: becoming a Knight herself.

Merchants Row

As I head from the battlefield toward merchants' tents, Brannos hovers at the edge of the field beneath a wide-open pavilion, watching fighters from the legion compete in the melees. He is not due on the field for a while. Sir Andreas, the Ice Falcon armorer, ex-King of the East and friend of Valharic, rehashes fights with him.

A young fighter walking by spots Brannos and his black and white Coptic tunic, recognizes him as Darkyard and shoots him a question.

"Do you know where Sir Valharic is?"

Brannos hesitates a second. One of the signs some Knights look for with candidates for Knighthood is that others treat them like Knights, even when they are not. This fighter has assumed Valharic to be a Knight.

"Val's not a Knight," Brannos replies with a smile. "He will be one day, but not now."

I soon reach the giant merchants' area, or actually just half of it. So many vendors flock to Pennsic, they are split onto different sides of the main entrance road. This market is several times the size of Gulf Wars'. Ice Falcon joins the crowd of armories selling the entire range of quality and authenticity. The Bored Housewife joins the garb merchants. Also in the mix are dumbeks, scores of books, pieces of leather for handiwork and ready-made laces, pouches and boots. Mixed in the rows of tents are knives, daggers and swords, Russian and Middle Eastern artwork, then spices and pigments for illumination and calligraphy. One night each War, Pennsic has "Midnight Madness," which brings the largest shopping crowds out late at night for a buying spree. Usually cool enough for people to wear cloaks or better garb than the heat and humidity allows, Midnight Madness is a time for parading past the shops to show off garb, to soak up the atmosphere when the flickering propane torches do not reveal modern flaws and to carry off a sack of materials for a year's worth of projects.

"We've had famous people buy our socks," a merchant named Roland Kein tells a browser at his sales pavilion. "Sockrates, Sockajawea, Socksquatch.

"I'm a known socksual offender, what can I say? You'll get a little socksual harassment if you stand here long enough."

Kein, who sells handmade baskets, furniture and the best assortment of felt hats found anywhere in the Known World, banters with his customers probably more than any of the merchants on the SCA circuit. Thirty to 40 weekends a year, Kein, 47, is on the road across the country, traveling as far as California and to Gulf Wars, along with events for re-enactors of other periods. Each year he'll drive about 30,000 miles. His white van, parked behind his tent, has 520,000 miles on it.

"People know me as the socks guy, the basket guy, the hat guy."

"If you make someone laugh," he explains, "it does one of two things—people will buy from people they like and two, people will remember you and be happy that they met you."

His hats, at $15 each, are huge sellers. His "hat blanks" are simple round wide-brimmed hats of wool felt that can be folded and pinned to create countless styles. By folding up the rim and pinning it to the dome, then stuffing feathers into the crease, it becomes a cavalier-style hat. Fold and pin the rim of a black hat blank to the dome in three places to form three even sides and you have the start of a pirate hat. With some trimming and pulling, the back can be folded up and the front tapered to a point, almost Robin Hood style.

In another tent amid the rows of merchants, a seller slides foot-wide discs of rolled ribbon onto dowels for display racks. These are not your typical shiny gift-wrap ribbons. The rolls have intricate and bright patterns in medieval styles. One tan roll, four inches wide, is stitched with a scaled-down, synthetic version of the Bayeux Tapestry. It doesn't tell the whole story, just repeats endlessly a small portion of the conquest tale.

It is one of the dozens of popular items that Calontir Trim sells.

"It's one of those things that goes for flavor, not for real authenticity," says the Byzantine owner, Andrixos Seljukroctonis. Though he is talking about the Bayeux Tapestry roll, he could be talking about his entire trim business or the entire SCA. All are about seeking a middle ground.

Calontir Trim is one of the largest and best-known merchants of the medieval-styled trims decorating the hems of thousands of tunics and dresses across the Known World. For a few dollars, anyone can buy a yard of Celtic knotwork, old Norse designs or Elizabethan accents to add a splash to their garb. The trim is flashy, it helps build the medieval mood of royals and nobles and makes it simple to accent garb. It also sits at the front of the simplicity vs. authenticity battle. Of course, here at Pennsic, Calontir Trim stands close to the forefront in its authenticity.

Leading up to this war, I have spent several weekend afternoons churning out several more tunics, both overtunics and undertunics, and a few makeshift cloaks for the rare cold night. I have concluded that Pennsic is responsible for lowering the quality of garb in the Society. People need to mass-produce items, rather than craft a few, to get by here. To move faster down the garb authenticity path, I had bought two books by Herbert Norris: *Ancient European Costume and Fashion* and *Medieval Costume and Fashion*. The books' drawings and descriptions of different styles, while not perfect, added to the overview that the Time Traveling Through T-Tunics class gave me. I still use a Simplicity pattern that is flawed in the eyes of serious garb makers. But I have stopped using grommets—metal rings for laces—on the neck. Though the metal can add to the medieval-ish mood, several garb-making web sites rail at them. In period, laces went through holes reinforced by stitches or by more cloth. Some period clothes have metal rings sewn with a few loops of thread to the outside of the clothing. Laces would then go through the rings. But even with my imperfect tunics and the pseudo jackboots I bought at Gulf Wars, I'm several steps ahead of most of the Pennsic crowd.

Every Pennsic, some people show up at Troll having heard about the party but needing to have the entire garb concept, and the idea that pizza cannot be delivered to their tent, explained to them. A crowd of hippie wanna-bes spends the week in the natural fiber shirts they dug out from beneath the Jefferson Airplane records in mom's attic or that they bought from NORML members at a Phish concert. Several others toss aside modesty along with their pants and shirts, and wear nothing but loincloths and boots. Likewise, a herd of women consider a pair of baggy pants and a halter top or sports bra a totally acceptable "attempt," even when herd is accurate in more ways than one. A few others, by choice rather than ignorance, make their own point by making accurately patterned garb from camouflage-print fabric or fluorescent nylon. But it qualifies as an "attempt" at medieval clothing.

Then, a portion of the crowd takes Hollywood as an unimpeachable source. Or Tolkien. Or any fantasy novel or television show. So out come the fantastical swords, chain mail bikinis and the *Xena: Warrior Princess* lookalikes. Not to mention the Tuchux, whose "wenches" wear skins and leather cowboy hats while many of the men strap spike-infested leather across their bare chests like Mad Max extras or candidates for the heavy metal band GWAR.

"If you ask what the average level of authenticity is at Pennsic, it's dreadful," Cariadoc tells me. "If you look at the best, it's wonderful."

Though I know the trims for sale at Calontir Trim are not truly period, I want to improve the look of my garb without spending hours and hours embroidering or weaving. Seeing the others here at Pennsic, I realize that even using that timesaver will still keep me huge steps ahead of the majority of this Society.

The Tale of Trim

"This isn't for the absolute, top-end most authentic piece you've ever going to do," Calontir Trim owner Andrixos, often just called Drix, tells me. MKA Steve Boyd, 39, Andrixos' summer breaks from teaching high school Latin are perfect for traveling to sell trim. "Were we heavily into real strong re-enactment, rather than somewhat looser re-creation, this wouldn't fly. People who are incredibly serious about every last detail aren't going to buy trim from me."

Using ribbon to decorate clothing was not common in the SCA's period—least of all in the early days. And many of the trims in Andrixos' stock display patterns that could be created in period only through hours of embroidery. He regularly has customers inspect the bright decorations and pass on a purchase, telling him they could create it themselves with a needle and some embroidery floss. He asks them to consider the time that would take.

"How much is your time worth?" he asks. "The thing I could make the most selling to people is their own free time. Sometimes I put it in terms of that. I'm selling convenience."

He had few choices when he started selling trim in 1988. He would pick and choose from scores of patterns to find the few that fit medieval style. The trim market has changed since then. Boyd now travels constantly to events and to trim factories in search of new patterns. He makes regular shopping excursions to the garment districts of New York and Los Angeles. He can spend $1,000 at a moment's notice to add to his stock of 1,600 large rolls of trim. While 400 sit in his "garage/warehouse" at home, he will pack about 1,200 rolls onto four-foot dowels that he squeezes into his mini-van.

Since the SCA and renaissance fair crowd buys trim by the mile, merchants have begun commissioning patterns. Promise a factory you'll buy about 1,000 yards and they will go to work. About a dozen variations of bright Celtic knots on black ribbon exist because a competitor, Pillaged Village, convinced a factory to supply them. Boyd will soon start commissioning a factory to make trims featuring the arms of SCA Kingdoms and large households.

He already has a monopoly on one existing trim—the several color variations of a pattern he calls "Welsh Knot." The tight, repeating knotwork patterns of that $5/yard trim are in thread on a background of cream-colored cloth. It is almost three inches wide and avoids the ribbon aspect of other trims.

He stumbled upon it when a met a British re-enactor in Wales who knew a factory that made it. It was not made for clothes, but for upholstery and drapery, and Boyd used the connection to build a stock of it. A few years ago, the factory owner stopped making it and decided to clean out its supply. Boyd bought him out.

"I have part of a storage unit full of it," Boyd said. "There is no more anywhere else. My understanding is that the loom cards for that particular trim were destroyed, so I am the only person who has that trim in the world."

Calontir Trim as a business, he says, earns him less than $20,000 a year. But the business enables him to go to SCA events, where he is a regular participant as both a fighter and a singer. He will soon receive his Laurel for the performing arts.

"You know," he observes, "drug dealers start selling because they need to feed their own habit. I'm pretty much the same."

Outside of events, Boyd makes many sales through his web site. At one point, he started noticing a shift in the call-in customers. Instead of the five yards SCA people would buy for a tunic, he was receiving orders for a single yard of many different styles.

Many of the trims on SCA clothing, he soon learned, can also end up as collars of dogs in major shows. He now sells about $8,000 a year in medievally-designed trims to the dog show world, another separate and intense subculture of this modern world, so owners can make their dog stand out to the judges.

"They say, 'I don't want to go to a renaissance festival but Smoochums here needs a new collar and that looks pretty good.'"

Battle Plans

As evening falls, commanders of the Midrealm and all its allies gather in a giant tent that serves as a conference room at Midrealm Royal camp. It can easily fit a few hundred people but there are only about 30 here now—commanders and trainees of the commanders—for a key planning session.

They have already met once to plan the first battle, the Woods Battle. Year after year, the Midrealm loses that opening battle of the War and plays from behind the rest of Pennsic. Allies usually compete to have a chance to command battles, but nobody volunteered for this one.

When Omarad the general offered it, Valharic jumped in.

It was another chance for Valharic to prove himself. Simply by volunteering for the job he had taken a step.

Talon was also taking a step forward. Last year a wrist injury prevented him from fighting, so he became an assistant, the aide de camp, of Omarad. He has the task again this War. Tonight he scribbles notes as Duchess Elina, the *Armored Rose* author from the allied West Kingdom, marks her plan for a "Mountain Pass Battle" on a greaseboard propped on an easel.

"I'm giving up the center because it's going to be the hardest to hold," she tells the crowd, watching from folding chairs.

The battle, not much different from Bridge battles, has three separate areas of land the sides will fight to control. Whatever side controls the banner in a 250-foot-wide section of field marked by hay bales, wins the point. Then, two 25-foot passages, one on each side, are each worth a point. The side controlling two of those areas at the end of the battle wins.

Elina plans to concede the middle section and win the banners on the two sides. The key is to make the East treat the center like a contested banner. By stationing a modest number of troops there to fight hard, the East will hopefully concentrate more of its own forces there than it needs. The East may take the banner and struggle to defend it for all 90 minutes of this resurrection battle. But in the end, Elina tells the commanders, the Middle will have extra reserves for the side passages.

"Let them waste all their troops in the center," she says. "Make a good hard move to the center. Make them think you want it. I want to taunt them on that one."

Since Elina estimates it will take 200 troops to sell that feint to the East, Omarad assigns the Midrealm regions containing both Darkyard and Cleftlands to the center. Though his troops are all but doomed to lose, the Cleftlands' Sir Alaric, who will command most of the sacrificial lambs, is eager for the task. Getting killed for a cause is not quite as final in this Society as it is in mundane wars.

But Alaric is not willing to concede the banner, so long as his assigned number of troops can win it without draining troops from the sides.

"We'll take the banner for you," he tells Elina.

"Drive on," she says.

"Do you want us to push for it?" he asks.

"If they are not defending it with all of their heart, yes."

On the sides, Elina wants fast troops to dash at the starting gun for the banners planted mid-pass and set up defense. On one side, Clan Prechain, one of partners in the Bastarmark camp at Gulf Wars, will go for the banner.

"Are they fast?" Elina asks.

"They're sprinters," someone shoots back.

"They're Celtic savages."

Elina spreads archery support for this battle, one of the few at Pennsic that allow it, across the field. Aside from simply whittling away troop numbers, she has one main job for them:Take out East leaders.

"If a target opens its mouth, shoot it."

Planning for the three Field Battles—two forces in an open field—becomes more muddled. Sir Gunther Von Brandenburg had mapped out plans for two out of the three but other commanders have concerns about a few aspects of them, so the plans are recast. Adding to the confusion is how to use archers in the one field battle allowing them or whether to even use them at all.

Brannos, ever-present at battle meetings as the Kingdom's former general and as commander of Darkyard, finds archers helpful in static battles where the sides compete over a piece of land, like the Mountain Pass Battle. Targets are more stationary—unless you are gaining lots of ground or losing it—and archers can pick people off. On the move in a field battle, archers can never set themselves.

"I won't have archers. I'll tell everyone to pick up a sword and board for this battle," he says. "Archers would get off two shots and then they'll be running away."

"With 800-man armies, will archers be effective enough to set up a scenario around them?" Omarad wondered. Combat archery is still so new to Pennsic that the commanders are not sure how best to use it.

"There's never been a mass battle on this scale with combat archers, short of…well, Hastings."

The Squire's Command

"We're going to win the woods," Valharic predicts the night before the battle.

That belief was a stretch. The Midrealm had not won a woods battle in years. Each year out, the East would take two of the three banners early and hold on for victory. Valharic believes he has found a solution to the problem. After his designated "runners" bolt through the woods in minimal armor to find the flags, he would simply cluster his forces around one, and hide the other among trees by simply not putting many troops near it. The masses of troops in other spots would draw the attention away but the couple of guards would go almost unnoticed.

The battle sets each side up on opposite sides of a patch of woods and a hill, with a couple of lines of evergreens cutting through the parcel. Valharic and the commanders even have maps of the parcel with items like "Spruce line" marked out.

Valharic's runners, wearing barely the SCA legal minimum in armor, take the front line at the start. They bump the other troops to the back, giving them a clear path for their sprint up the hill and into the woods. Other fighters clear the path of branches Fighting units huddle for last-minute pep talks. A group of non-combatant scouts in minimal armor meet to divide responsibilities and are each handed photocopied maps of the woods and told where units will be.

At the cannon's blast, the runners bolt. A second group, designated as immediate help for the runners also hustles into the woods. Valharic takes off down the path. Behind him, the bulk of fighters, heavy troops with big war shields and full armor march in and head for their assigned spots.

As Valharic settles about 100 yards into the woods, a front-line runner comes trotting out of the woods. Scouts follow a few moments later with news. The plan has doubly paid off. The Midrealm has snatched two banners. Now it just has to hold on for the rest of the 90 minutes. I have followed Valharic to watch the battle command and help keep time with a stopwatch. I can dive into battle to help out if needed.

The Midrealm and Eastern lines fight each other just a couple hundred feet ahead, the shouting, grunting and thump of spears on armor easily reaching Valharic. Fighters have divided into two giant masses, one to Valharic's left and one a few hundred feet to his right blocked from vision by the line of spruces. A stream of fighters who have been killed trudge out of the giant human fighting amoeba and march back down the path toward the starting line and resurrection area. There, water and Omarad await them. Omarad hustles them back up the hill. Fighting veterans know it and Gulf Wars had proven it to me: Making sure fighters resurrect to keep lines properly manned is crucial.

Resurrecting Darkyard fighters march up the hill then wait for other members of the Legion join them so they can charge back in as a unit. Scouts keep running up to Valharic and blurting messages. He then sends them right back out to specific areas to make sure troop levels have not dropped dangerously low. As time ticks away, Valharic sends scouts sprinting to Omarad to deploy 15 resurrecting troops here, 20 there.

With about a half hour left, the Midrealm suffers a key loss. Forces dwindled at one banner—a visible one—and the East makes a huge push while Midrealm troops resurrect. As soon as Eastern troops reach the banner, they snatch it and run off behind the lines to hide it in another spot.

The Midrealm has to find the banner. Fast. Or it will lose.

In a clearing, Brannos gathers a pack of more than 20 Darkyard returnees. They will gather as many household members as they can into one big unit to go hunt for the banner. Darkyard fights as a unit. It will not be split apart into multiple spots.

As Brannos gathers for a final, frantic charge, Valharic scampers through a spruce line and down a side path to where allies also search for the banner. The flag is gone. Nobody can find it.

The closing cannon shot fires. The battle is over. The Midrealm has lost.

I later learn that if troops had gone one way instead of the other on their last push, an almost random decision, they would have taken the banner back. At least Valharic's strategy worked. The captured banner he left almost unguarded stayed in Midrealm possession the entire battle.

Out of the Woods

The Midrealmers trudge down the hill. Many have no idea who won since trees and brush prevent them from seeing action not right in front of them. Talon, Ulfr, and Logan guzzle water at the bottom, their hair matted down by sweat. Of all the Pennsic battles, this one is likely the most tiring. Fighters swap stories—of how they died, of knocking some Easterners over in a charge, of tumbling past trees and brush in a collision.

"You fought like dogs today," Omarad tells his troops as a court forms at the bottom of the hill. Everyone had hustled in and out of the resurrection point and climbed the hill. Bardolph steps forward and calls Valharic before him. As Valharic kneels at his feet, Bardolph tells the troops that early in the week when the Kingdom had been looking for a commander for the woods, there was nobody. Only Valharic had stepped forward.

"For the first time in history," Bardolph shouts, in celebrating a small victory, "we captured two banners in six minutes."

"Hoobah!" the troops shout back in a cheer.

"Such deeds," Bardolph continues, "should be rewarded."

Sagging from the heat and their bruises just moments before, the Darkyard and Cleftlands fighters perk up. Could Valharic's reward be…?

Talon clenches his hands into fists that fidget and bob expectantly at his waist as he spits out the words, "Do it!" under his breath. Talon breaks his clenched jaw into a smile as Bardolph calls Sir Finn before him. Brannos and two other Darkyard Knights follow close behind. I cannot see Valharic's face but Talon now has a smile big enough for both of them.

"I'd like to beg a boon," Brannos says.

Brannos hardly completes his request before all of Valharic's friends turn giddy. Talon punches the air with a short celebratory jab. Valharic is going to become a Knight.

Bardolph puts Valharic on vigil and schedules his "elevation" to Knighthood at the gateway of the fort after the bridge battles a couple days from now. Brannos then announces that for Valharic's vigil, he will be at the castle the night before. Under Darkyard tradition, he will accept any challenge from anyone. All night until sunrise, if need be.

Valharic is mobbed with hugs, from the household's Knights he was squired to, from other house brothers and from other Knights and squires. Even Edmund. The Duke steps forward, shakes Valharic's hand and offers a bear hug.

But even with the welcome and congratulations from Edmund, there is still one hug lacking.

The Traveler's Test

The compact disc spins and my first-ever call to battle starts to ring out across Darkyard's camp the next morning:

The opening music of *Conan the Barbarian*.

I may be behind Darkyard's Roman columns among fighters wearing Coptic tunics preparing for a battle. But I pull on a tunic over my hockey shoulder pads to the soundtrack to a bad fantasy movie. I have no idea where this moment falls on the authenticity scale.

Violins bellow chords, kettle drums rumble and cymbals crash as the whole fighting household straps on armor, fastening buckles and tying knots for each other around the tables of the courtyard. Shoulder pads, gambesons and hockey arm pads go on beneath Coptics. Others pull lamellar coats or loricae segmentata on above the Coptics emblazoned with the Darkyard logo.

As the *Conan* music continues, I rummage through an old Army tent in the campsite for the rest of my armor. About 20 people have heaped their armor in piles inside. They are all like me, fighting with the Legion but not camping here, and grateful for a place to keep armor both close to the battlefield and out of the elements. It is morning, about an hour before the 10 a.m. field battles. Today's Field Battle is the same scenario I first saw when I pulled into Pennsic four years ago: the same battle that reminded me of *Braveheart* with two armies charging each other. In an hour I will be amid that mass of armor, bodies and hacking sticks.

I'm going to die.

Quickly, I strap on my leg armor as the bustle continues around me. Cat also puts on her armor. She will also try the battles here for the first time.

She is also going to die.

Once strapped in, I wander into the camp's courtyard where fighters tighten armor straps for each other. A woman named Berkana has set up shop in the courtyard with a paintbrush in hand. One by one fighters kneel in front of her so she can paint her answer to good luck charms—Viking runes—on their cheeks. I grab a tin cup from one of the tables and fill it with cold water. Darkard has covered the giant plastic water cooler with a handmade cozy of white cloth with Darkyard arms on it.

Everyone starts to line up by their contubernium. I join the line for Contubernium 1, a unit entirely of hangers-on from Cleveland. I step in behind Kollin, the unit commander. All I have to do, I keep telling myself, is follow his lead, his orders. I am not going to be fighting 700 Easterners, just the ones that Kollin steers us to. He will have to worry about the strategy and where Brannos steers him. Even though I have heard the overall battle schemes at the commanders meeting, I block them from my mind. Right here, right now, I am just a tiny piece of the Midrealm war machine.

The Legion starts marching to song, to the rumble of boots on the road and to the bellow of the Darkyard Song, "…hack and slash and slay the Eastern Army."

I sure hope so.

I march in silence. I do not really know the words well enough to keep up. Even when the others hit the end that I know—the shouts of "For Forgan! And for Darkyard!"—I stay quiet. I may have sewn a black and white tabard to wear over my tunic to match my unit. I may be carrying a Darkyard war board. But I am not fully a part of the team. I have yet to earn my spot. I am like a baseball rookie, recently called up from the farm team. I might have the same uniform but not the right to lead cheers.

When we hit the field, the Easterners already mass on the other side. Hundreds strong, they cluster around banners, growing in size by the minute.

The Legion lines up close to the edge of the field. I would not have to worry about my left. Since I am positioned a few rows of fighters from the front, I will not bear the brunt of any charges.

The more worries I can cross off my list, the better off I will be. I am stepping into totally new territory. The line starts moving and I just hold my shield up in front of me. Moving briskly, we have to cross about 100 feet. Simply moving with the group in heavy leg armor is a minor challenge.

The engagement does not go as planned.

Seconds into battle, an Eastern unit plows forward to our right. They do not actively attack us but are in position to sweep through our flank. When they end up less than 10 feet from us, we are in a no-mans land—threatened but non-engaged.

I have no instinct to guide me.

When a few Easterners make threatening moves, I let myself be drawn into a fight, instead of continuing straight ahead. Through the helm, things seem unreal. The frame of vision the helm allows makes the battle look like I am watching it on a television or movie screen. The sight of armor, bellowing foes, weapons slicing the air, shields splashed with heraldry and flags twisting in the air seems unreal. I have an odd moment of disconnect, as if the helm-vision and armor really set me apart from all this.

If I had practiced in more melees, I would have moved past this stage.

My closing foe clearly has.

With a slash of a polearm to my helm, I go down.

As my unit moves onward into a churning wall of swords, spears, polearms and shields, I lie behind dead, hoping I can do better next time.

The resurrection Mountain Pass Battle that afternoon gives me a chance to get my feet under me. Since it is a resurrection battle, I can fight, fail, and return for another try. The shock of the mass of troops on the field had 90 minutes to wear off.

I have made progress but I have learned how much more I need to learn.

Darkyard!

The East already has the middle pass by the time I reach the front line in that afternoon's Mountain Pass Battle. Midrealm fighters that got close to the banner at the start had been driven back and away—just as planned. As others fall in front of me, then head back to resurrect, I move up the ranks a step at a time, just as I would in line at an amusement park. The sides have settled into skirmish lines, jabbing spears back and forth, with small charges thrown in. I know the battle will be as exhilarating as a roller coaster when my turn comes. But remembering the enemy will try and smash me in the face, I edge forward with caution.

A spear takes down the shieldman in front of me and the call comes out, "Shield!" before he even rises to resurrect. I step forward. I am suddenly in the front lines.

The eyes of the Eastern spearmen dart from side to side, scanning my line for spots to strike. I do not need to attack them, just hold my spot as long as I can to provide cover for our own spearmen behind me. More-practiced shieldmen can actively foul blows aimed for their own spearmen with sword swats and their own shields. I just bunker behind my shield, holding my sword in front of my face to block jabs. An enemy spearman thrusts his spear at me several times, trying to ram it into my face. I manage to raise my shield quick enough for the tip to thump off it. Then, with a simple tactic of moving the head like a J-shape before he thrusts, he hits home on my face grille.

Clang.

My head jerks back, but only a few inches. My killer has courtesy. The idea is not to ram spears right through an opponent's head, just give it enough of a solid nudge to be clear. I lower my shield, raise my sword in salute, give a quick nod and bow of acknowledgement and head toward the back of the ranks.

Several more times I head back out, sometimes going down fast, other times lasting a while. Amid a few small charges, I even land a few blows in the press. I swat the top of an Easterner's head and he drops. My first kill.

As the time ticks away, the Midrealm forces in the middle are still fresh. We have never made a concerted push for the banner. To try to capture one of the side banners, the East has moved some of its troops away from the center. It is weak here. The

Cleftlands troops who have practiced slamming into each other in column charges all summer want real action.

"Why don't we just column charge all these people and take the banner anyway?" Stephan asks Alaric, his Knight and commander. Alaric checks with Elina to make sure his troops are not needed as backup for the side passes. He is not needed. He orders a charge.

Between resurrections, I can see only glimpses of the assault. Cleftlands fighters and the rest of Alaric's troops pound into the Eastern wall like a drill bit. They knock the Easterners clear off the banner and plow on past to create a little space. As I return to the resurrection point after being killed, I see Brannos, his eyes afire with energy, setting up a column of Legion troops for its own supporting charge. He moves like a lion tamer, with such confidence in his steps even the savage beast knows who is in charge. I should be resurrecting to get back on the field, but I cannot help but watch. The whole unit is so completely with him, so ready to follow his orders, that the fighters bounce on their heels in anticipation. The column sets off like a missile, boring right through the Eastern resistance, sending bodies flying and toppling in its wake.

I can only stare, mesmerized by the beauty of it, just as I would at the structure, balance and perfection of a museum masterpiece.

"Go! Get 'em!" I scream before I even realize what I'm doing. I am watching a home run clout soaring high on its way over the wall, a running back smashing through a tackle into the open field, a power forward launching himself over and through helpless defenders to slam the ball home.

The column punches deeper and deeper into the East ranks, leaving a trail of dead bodies behind.

I'd better help out.

I rush to resurrect and sprint toward the banner. The Midrealm fighters have it and are surrounding it with layer after layer of fighters, just like a tightly packed onion, to hold it in case the East makes a last-second push.

I run to the line of troops holding the East back across the rest of the Pass and go right to the front. These guys are NOT going to get through to that pack. Bunkering behind my war board, I deflect a few blows with my shield, my sword and my adrenaline. I even hold off an attempt to hook the top of my shield and pull it away.

The battle ends.

We have won the banner.

I have survived—and held—for several minutes of hurried attacks.

I have done none of the hard work. I have neither mounted nor repelled a serious attack. But I have helped, just as the other 200 people in this Pass have done, no matter how many casualties they inflicted or how many times they resurrected to keep up the pressure. The inexperienced, incompetent fighter that knew how to do little more than take up space had made a contribution simply by doing that.

And my side has won the whole battle.

Though we had lost one of the side passes and the battle plan had not fully worked, capturing this center banner meant the Midrealm had two. Elina marches past the troops holding the banner aloft and waving it to the troops.

"This is your banner!" she shouts. "This is what you did!"

As other Legion fighters bubble with stories of the battle, they launch into a boisterous chorus of "Darkyard!" raising their swords to the air in celebration.

For the first time, I join it. I have done something to help today. Somewhere in that battle, "I" and "they" somehow became "we."

"Darkyard!"

"For Forgan"

All of Darkyard forms a semicircle near the top of a hill on this campsite known as "Runestone Hill" in the twilight of that night, facing a few of the house's leaders standing beside a young tree. Everyone wears their dress garb—clean white Coptics or shiny metal loricas or helmets topped with a wolf pelt. As the sun was starting to wane, they had made the march from camp in formation, just as they did for opening ceremonies and for each battle. They again accompanied their march with shouts of "For Forgan! and For Darkyard!" which drowned out the Eastern court along the walkway.

Of all the moments of War, this night is truly "For Forgan."

The household planted the tree here after Forgan died as a memorial to him. Each year at War, Darkyard parades to the tree for remembrance and to make an offering of Forgan's favorite beverage, a can of Pepsi.

"Once again this is a wonderful year for all of us," Brannos says as he leads the ceremony. "We have great memories. Another of Forgan's children is going to be elevated. This is not a time, necessarily, to be sad. This is a time to celebrate because all of the people here remember him.

"We field great units. We field great kings and princes, barons and baronesses. All of these things have come about because of his influence. We have a great tree that grows bigger every time we come here. And we have a great household that grows bigger every time we come here."

Ragnvaldr, who will soon put Darkyard back on the throne, tells how he used to watch Forgan, his next-door neighbor, run battle scenarios with army men on his table. Today, he says, his connection to Forgan's household still feels strong.

"In the woods," he said, "I was very comfortable to be behind the black and white tabard."

Others offer stories, some on the verge of tears. Guys who would plow over any Easterner, who roar as they smack opponents in the heads with sticks, are silent except for the occasional sniffle. Finally Valharic steps forward. When he became a squire he had dreamed of returning his red squire's belt to Forgan at his Knighting when he would replace it with a white one. Forgan will not be here to take the belt back.

Silently, Valharic puts his hand on the tree. He drops to one knee as he lowers his head for a moment. When he lifts his head, he is crying. As his tears add to the Pepsi watering, he takes off his squires belt and returns it to Forgan the only way he can.

He ties it around the tree and leaves it there.

"The last blow..."

The crowd gathers at the gates to the castle after the Midrealm and East split bridge battles the next morning Valharic's "elevation" to Knighthood. Flynn/Agrippa and Erin have rushed to Pennsic from Cleveland for this milestone in Valharic's life. Bardolph and Brigh call a court and Brannos steps forward.

"Last evening Valharic did his vigil behind the walls of the gate," Brannos tells Bardolph. The challenges offered to him as his final test had included fighting, but a few oddball ones of balance, math, drawing and even a powdered donut fight.

"He accepted every challenge," Brannos continues. "He fought men three on one. He fought single sword. And he bellydanced."

"I believe the man a hero and once again we beg the boon for Valharic."

Bardolph nods out, "Summon the members of our most noble Order of the Chivalry."

Dozens of Knights drop to their knees in a circle before Bardolph.

"Noble Sirs, is it your judgment that Valharic is worthy to be numbered among you in prowess, loyalty and courtesy?"

When they all shout back, "Yes!" a herald hollers, "Their Majesties call forth Valharic."

In a white tunic with red clavi that Countess Rebekah has spent the last two days stitching here at war, Valharic kneels before Bardolph. His time has come.

Under Midrealm tradition, everyone elevated to a Peerage must have the support of at least one member of each of the peerages—the Royal peers, the Laurels, other Knights and the Pelicans. Valharic had been around long enough to have personal connections with each of his witnesses.

Tamara, wife of Finn and the former Queen that Valharic had served as champion for, attests that it "was my great, great honor to have this man accept the position of my champion during my reign."

Valharic, she said, went through several personal troubles during those six months but still held up his position. Only once did he find someone who would "gainsay" his Queen, and Valharic stepped in to quash him.

"I can think of no higher courtesy than that which he passed on to me."

Finn, a Laurel, praises Valharic's artistic talents both on paper and with his newly learned skills with glass.

As his Pelican witness, Dame Alys tells how she has known Valharic since he was still "the kid" at Pentwyvern of Dagorhir. He had gone to school with Alys' son and she has watched him with interest in the SCA all along.

"I have been absolutely delighted to see a teenager grow to be a young man and an even nicer adult. Every Pennsic, I have seen him grow more and more and he is the kind of person every mother would be proud of."

Ragnvaldr, once his roommate and who was squired to the same Knight on the same day at this very event, tells the crowd that Valharic's fighting prowess was clearly of a Knightly caliber.

"If you're not familiar with his prowess it's probably because you didn't see his off-hand shot crack you upside the head."

"Do we have a chain?" Bardolph asks. Each Knight wears a chain around his neck. But at their Knightings, none have the chains, spurs or belt they will actually use permanently. So each of the items presented at Knightings have been used before and have their own lineage.

Valharic is given a chain used in Forgan's knighting and spurs used in even Edmund's. Berkana, the Darkyard face painter who had helped him in his early years in the Society much like Alys had, fastens the white belt around his waist. Sir Calador, the same man whose own Knighting had sparked Valharic's outburst a year earlier, puts the chain around Valharic's neck.

Bardolph pulls the sword of state, Oathbinder, from its sheath and taps Valharic on the right shoulder, then the left, then the temple. Thus dubbed, Valharic swears:

"To ever be a good Knight and true,
Reverent and generous
Shield of the weak
Obedient to my liege-lord
Foremost in battle
Courteous at all times
Champion of the right and good
Thus swear I, Valharic Caligula Aurelius."

Valharic has one last thing to endure, before he is officially a Knight: his "buffet." At every Knighting, the newly dubbed take a traditional blow to the head or chest from the King to welcome him to the Chivalry.

"Let this be the last blow you accept unanswered," Bardolph says as he fires a solid open-faced punch to the kneeling Valharic's face.

With that, Bardolph wraps Valharic in a hug. Valharic beams from ear to ear. The other Knights leap to their feet and tackle him with hugs that border on buffets themselves. Just as football players can pump each other up by banging their helmets into each other, the Midrealm Chivalry punctuate their embraces with chest bumps or slapping Valharic's back as they hug. Even Edmund smothers him in a hug and smacks him. Valharic, who has just promised to let no blows go unanswered, fires back with a forceful shove to Edmund's chest. Instead of harboring hard feelings as competitors, they are now brothers in the order. They hug again.

The line of Knights soon dwindles, but a crowd of squires, who had been his brother only an hour ago, come up, followed by other fighters and his friends, including Alys and then Finn and Tamara, who had helped him make the last step. He smiles and laughs. The anger, bitterness and feeling of rejection from a year ago has disappeared. He has been recognized for his skills and efforts. He was no longer "The Kid." He is Sir Valharic. And he is no longer a wanna-be. He is a legitimate member of the Kingdom's highest fighting level.

Almost the highest.

He still has one last ring to grab, the one he so nearly caught at Crown Tournament 15 months ago.

War Pay

"Make your mark," Brannos snaps.

It is later that night and I have stood in line in the Darkyard camp with the rest of Contubernium One for my own final step of this war. Having served in this Roman army, I am entitled to pay. One by one we report to the table Brannos has set up in a tent. One by one, we sign our names to a ledger.

"This is for your food," Brannos says coldly, handing me a clove of garlic. Spices were valuable in Roman times.

"This is to buy a new pair of sandals," he says, handing me a coin. Soldiers' shoes, he continues, can easily wear down from marching and fighting.

The 10 Lira Italian coin is worth all of a few cents in currency once I walk out of this tent. But it holds far more value in acceptance, camaraderie and appreciation to each of the 80 combatants in line here.

"Dismissed," Brannos barks. "Next!"

When Talon's turn comes, Brannos awards him a double share—one for fighting, one for assisting Omarad all war. But Talon's biggest reward came earlier. Darkyard had welcomed him as a member, along with Bobbie, the SFU project group regular who had traveled to Gulf Wars this spring. Talon now wears a Darkyard tabard with the house arms of the moonlit tree on it.

Hobbs/Ulfr, who I have seen only in passing at this frantic War, has enjoyed his fighting. The improvement from a first Pennsic to the second is giant for most and has been for him. Even better, he and Amanda are now engaged. He had considered proposing on the battlefield, dropping to one knee in full armor in front of a mass of fighters, but chickened out. He did it back in camp.

When Valharic reaches home in North Olmsted a few days later, he pops his new elevation tunic into the washer. It was sweaty and covered with a little dirt from his efforts on the field. When it comes out, the grime is gone but the clavi have been transformed.

The red dye on the strips of fabric has washed away. As Valharic's focus now shifts to Crown Tournament just a couple months away, his Coptic's clavi have turned from red to gold.

Preparing for Crown

Miles away, William of Fairhaven is at his own home. He never left.

While Valharic and other Knights try to win this war for the Middle Kingdom, William stayed home to prepare for the October Crown Tournament.

William burned out on Pennsic a few years ago. He had attended 14 times, was Knighted at Pennsic, served as the Kingdom's head marshal at one War and was the top squire when his Knight was the Midrealm's War King. William had also captained several Kingdom champions' teams that fought against Eastern champions. It has become a grind to plan his vacations around Pennsic every year. He is not interested in fighting melee. Tournaments are all that matter. If he can win in October and be King next Pennsic, so be it. But he will not go to Pennsic again without being on the throne.

Two or three times a week he hits the weights for 90 minutes. Every day he spends a half hour on the treadmill. And he will attend one weeknight fight practice a week, in addition to an event most weekends. If he keeps up the pace, he will be a killer come Crown.

He also prepares at another level. He watches fight films. He started taping tournaments at his first Crown in 1989. He has filmed other Crowns and tournaments, and now has a tape library of about 100 events.

"If I want to learn how someone's fighting and I can't figure it out, I'll tape them," he tells me.

While the rest of the Kingdom wields weapons on the battlefield, William grips his remote control to scout potential opponents.

One after the other.

P.S. Oh yeah, I almost forgot. The East wins the War.

Act II, scene 6
The Knight's Tale: The Die is Cast

One late September Wednesday night, while members of the Society across the country are still sorting out how many participants they lost in the Sept. 11 attacks, the Viking known as Niall of Bork who runs most Cleftlands meetings finishes his weekly announcement of upcoming events in the Middle Kingdom. The Crown Tournament, he tells the group, will be on October 20 in Battle Creek, Mich.

"Anybody here fighting?" he asks.

People cast their gaze at the Knights of the barony. Only Valharic speaks up, ducking his head through the door, his hair soaked with sweat from the fighter practice next door.

"I'll be fighting," he says. His voice is deferential, not boasting. "…For Alys Katharine."

The announcement is met with indifferent silence. Though she runs the Pennsic University, Alys Katharine is a generation removed from much of the barony and Valharic is hardly a member here in Cleftlands. Sure, he lives in Cleveland and he started here, but his household is in Detroit and Cleftlands has mostly missed his coming of age. A few, remembering him from his immature days, do not even suppress their scoffing grunts. But some veterans smile at his choice of Alys. Even if they hardly know Valharic, Alys has the respect of many in this Society. Someone is finally giving her a chance.

"Never voted Queen of anything…"

Alys had been intrigued when Valharic caught her at Troll when she arrived at Pennsic a month earlier. She saw him at War every year and they would chat and catch up on things. But what was so urgent?

She finished her check-in business and tracked him down as he rode around the campground on a golf cart helping Finn run the War.

"I can't wait," she blurted. "What do you want?"

"He said, 'How would you like to be Queen of the Midrealm?'"

Her eyes widen as she recounts the moment, "I said, 'Woooo!'"

She had no idea Valharic had considered her. She had written off the notion of becoming Queen years ago. She was divorced. Her son was not a fighter. If Valharic won, serving as royals would transform how they regarded each other. She would be his partner on the throne, not just Mrs. Fleming, his friend's mom.

She accepted after thinking it over a few days. She then went to the Pennsic market to buy him a gift. She came back with a surviving Roman die made out of lead and held onto it for the day of Crown Tournament with a message in mind.

On her way home, a childhood memory rushed back. When she was eight she had gone to a church fair where she saw a fortune-teller.

The fortune-teller made several predictions, including that she would have three children. That one proved to be correct. She would also become a Queen. The idea stuck in the head of the Middle Ages-minded youngster through middle school until her socially rough high school years when she admits, "I was never voted Queen of anything." It did not resurface through the years as a mother, the years of being worried about childbirth classes or inner-city kids' Spanish grammar. And definitely not during her divorce and the solitude that followed.

Thanks to Valharic, the 55-year-old memory came back. And the door had opened for it to come true.

Most of the Cleftlands crowd shrugs off Valharic's announcement and goes back to planning the next event, fumbling through CDs for dancing or playing their weekly games of Mah Jong. Valharic, however, has his mind zeroed in on the tournament. It is another chance to reach for the brass ring, and this one is lining up nicely. The winner will be a War King, monarch at the Pennsic War that he loves so much. Most of the former Kings, the royal peers, have shied away from this tournament. This tournament also has some PR value for Valharic's reputation. By picking Alys Katharine he can quiet with one stroke the disapproving whispers about him fighting for his Tuchuk girlfriend. He can count on the support of the project group at Flynn/Agrippa's, which had just been renamed the more Roman "Portus Aurelius" in honor of both Forgan and its spot near a Great Lake.

Agrippa had offered more than a year ago, before the Crown Tournament that ended with Valharic's loss to Edmund, that he would serve on Valharic's staff if he ever wins Crown. He has made that commitment again, even though Flynn and Erin are celebrating the birth of their daughter. Madison O'Toole was born just days after the Sept. 11 attacks.

If Valharic just fights with honor at Crown as he had in the spring, and does not win, he will further bury grudges some still hold from the Edmund fight. Becoming a Knight took away much of that stress. He has trained for this fight more than ever. Even better, his mundane life has become more normal. He is a cook at a seafood restaurant and he and a friend, who has accompanied him to tournaments all summer, rent a house.

"Everything in my SCA career was going so well," he tells me later. "I was on a high from being Knighted. I'd been relieved of all the stress of dealing with all the things I'd been dealing with and just got to focus on what I cared about."

In the few weeks before Crown, he also cleans up his act—literally. He sheds his flimsy leather lamellar and trades up to a shiny coat of aluminum lamellar. With the help of Talon, he makes a leather back for it and fashions shoulders of leather dyed red and black. They secure the plates to the shoulders with cast metal discs emblazoned with Medusa heads. To his shield, he adds the image of a three-headed dog. Both the dog, Cerberus, and Medusa, were guardians of Hell. He intends to bring it to his opponents.

"I hoped it would be a little bit of an intimidation factor," he said of his new armor. The field is loaded with unbelts. The armor, his previous Crown experience and his new white belt might just cow some opponents enough to give him an edge. He packs the lamellar in his trunk and heads for Michigan on Friday, with Alys to follow.

"The Ultimate Cookie..."

Crown is the toughest test of a fighter's abilities.

The Society for Creative Anachronism has no national ranking system, no national championship. Though Pennsic includes a "Best of the Known World" tournament, many of the best skip it. Many of the veterans test themselves against each other in pickup fights out of the spotlight. They can take away satisfaction from beating someone, and both leave knowing who won. But those are informal. They have no stakes. The most basic measure from Kingdom to Kingdom is the number of Crowns won.

"It's the ultimate cookie," said former King Bardolph.

"If you didn't have a heavyweight championship, how would you say who the best is?" said Duke Baldar, the six-time winner from Trimaris.

Baldar's six Crown wins had been matched and would soon be doubled by the winner of the most Crowns ever, Jade of Starfall from the West. Jade would soon win his twelfth Crown in 15 years to stay undefeated in his string.

"The idea of losing Crown does not scare me," said Jade, MKA corporate consultant Jade Dauser. "In some ways it will be a relief because people will stop talking about me like I'm invincible. I'm not. I love the sense and thrill, the pomp and circumstance of fighting in Crown."

Of course, not all Crowns are created equal. Some discount wins from the West Kingdom, more by quantity than quality. Although it is the oldest Kingdom, the West has three reigns a year, instead of two everywhere else. That gives fighters an extra chance each year to win. Then, some Kingdoms are smaller than others or take tournament fighting less seriously. It is no different from college sports conferences. An Atlantic Coast Conference basketball title has a higher pedigree than the Patriot League. With no objective standard, the Crown of a Kingdom stands on its own and carries as much weight as its populace wants to give it.

The Society regularly debates whether this is the best selection process for leaders. For starters, someone like Alys is automatically barred from ever taking the throne unless someone fights for her, and wins. The system ignores any non-fighting skills or service. It also does not offer a test of a candidate's leadership abilities. An outstanding one-on-one fighter can become King even if others actively dislike him. This fall, the Kingdom of An Tir in the Pacific Northwest will break with tradition and hold a melee Crown, with the finalists each leading a small army against each other. That system has mixed results and the Society as a whole will ban any future Crown experiments.

The traditional system, however, does test candidates in more ways than just fighting skills. It is a pressure cooker. Crown will change your life for the next year. If you win, several friends become your staff. You will all travel almost ceaselessly as you serve as Prince, then King. One lightning-quick reaction in a fight, one opening spotted or missed, one blow thrown or not thrown at the right or wrong timing can determine the schedules and duties of several people. For several rounds, it can be on par with any other competitive tournament. But with each round, the real-life stakes ratchet up a notch.

Crown Tournaments test combatants in strategy and with many weapons. The hosting King determines what weapons can be used and who picks them for each bout. Fighters that are best with the sword may have to fight a crucial bout with a polearm, spear or mace. Sir William of Fairhaven built his secret weapon for such a spot. Kingdoms also differ on the number of fights per round. In the Middle Kingdom, it takes just one killing blow to knock you out of the brackets except in the finals, which are two out of three. Once defeated, contestants drop into a "losers' bracket." The winner of the losers' bracket can rejoin the main tournament. But other Kingdoms, including Atlantia, do every bout two out of three. And luck, ego, and confidence in your consort play a role.

Atlantia's King, Havordh, admits that luck played a major part in his Crown win. The Kingdom's best polearm fighter, Sir Vladimir Ivanovich Alexsandrov, probably should have won that day. But he had broken his polearm and was using a borrowed one by the time Havordh met him in the fourth round. Havordh barely beat him. At one point Vlad caught him three times in a row. But once was with the shaft of the weapon, once with the flat of the blade and only one, in Atlantia's two-out-of-three bouts, was good. If Vlad's polearm had not broken, Havordh said, the outcome might have been different.

That loss put Vlad into the losers' bracket so when he returned to the normal bracket in the semifinals he had to beat his opponent, Sir Gelmere, twice. The two bouts, with the long heavy polearms, lasted 15 minutes.

"The two of them exhausted each other," Havordh said. "He was so exhausted by the time we fought he wasn't in the fight as much as I was."

So Havordh won.

The recently departed Bardolph had lost a Crown final to Ragnvaldr (for Ragnvaldr's first Crown win, not the one that put him on the throne now) even though the winning blow never hit him. Ragnvaldr had taken Bardolph's arm and in a flurry soon after, Bardolph did not keep his "wounded" arm behind his back, as the rules require. A blow from Ragnvaldr hit Bardolph's basket hilt on his "wounded" hand. It had strayed too far in front and become an illegal obstruction. Bardolph went down.

Baldar's first Crown also ended in a strange way. He never used swords with thrusting tips since he normally slashes with the tip of his sword and never looks to thrust. In the deciding bout, Baldar remembers, his opponent took his leg, dropping Baldar to his knees. The opponent pounded away from above as Baldar cowered like a turtle beneath his shield.

"He was whaling on me," Baldar said. Like the polearm fighter in Atlantia, a broken weapon had forced Baldar to use a different one. The borrowed sword had a thrusting tip. As Baldar simply flailed away to stop blows, the tip caught his opponent's face-mask. His opponent stopped.

"He leaned forward and said, 'Did that hit me?' I hit him again and he said, 'Well, that did.'"

Of course, getting over the hump of a first Crown win can be the most difficult part. Several winners said the nerves hit them when they realized they might actually win. And from then on, battles became as much between egos as swords.

"The first time you're in the finals you're looking down a tunnel and a train's coming down the tracks," said Duke Finn. "You know there's going to be a train wreck, but you can just watch it."

For him, fighting became a passion "when it went from being a physical thing to a chess game with a stick."

Bardolph agreed and said his mental approach played a critical role in his win. People had urged him, he said, to treat Crown Tournament like his work as a state trooper, like a life-or-death situation when he's wearing the badge. That approach would make him his most ruthless. But it offended his reverence of fighting as an honor sport.

"I was always appalled," Bardolph said. "If I thought I would fight to the death I would win Crown, but I wouldn't take a single blow."

But then someone suggested scaling back the life-or-death mindset just one level, to a situation where he would be justified in using deadly force and the opponent was going to jail. He tried it. He just remained a state trooper in his mind, with garb as his uniform and a sword as his sidearm for the day.

He won.

"In my mind there was nothing my opponent could do to change the outcome."

Even when legged, he was not bothered. He said he knew marshals were there, but once the call of "Lay on" came, he only saw his opponent. Time, he said, slows down as your awareness and ability to process information skyrockets. His bouts all seem much longer as they happen than they look on videotape.

"I've talked to others who have been there," Bardolph said. "Their focus and concentration level is such that the entire planet could fall away. I'm guessing unless you reach that level of concentration you'll never win a Crown.

"Fighting at that level is a blast. I'm afraid it might be addictive. There's something about fighting at a really high level that is just an ultimate rush, whether you win or lose."

Finn took the mental part further for his first Crown win, starting his battle months in advance. He had psyched people out so badly, he said, a Kingdom officer congratulated him on winning—the day before the fights. Finn made sure he beat all of the top competitors in fights before Crown. He did it by fighting them when he was at his best and they at their worst—at events their home baronies hosted, when Knights had to help run the event. I remember Sir Alaric at the Cleftlands event back in January setting up, explaining armor to outsiders, serving feast and on and on.

"Those days, they're performing at their worst. I come in fresh as a daisy and beat you up in front of your friends. My goal is to make it as easy as possible for you to accept that blow in that split second you have," he said. Beating them each already made all of his opponents accept the idea they might lose to him—even if their previous meeting had been a mismatch.

When Finn won his first crown, he had the luxury of winning his semifinal bout before his opponent, Jafar, had his semifinal. Finn had time to prepare even as Jafar was simply advancing.

For the actual fight, Jafar, then an unbelt, stood on the field armored. Finn came out mostly unarmored and put on a show highlighting that he was a Knight. He had his squires bring out his helm, his sword and his shield and arm him on the field while Jafar watched by himself. Finn won easily.

This time, Finn is not fighting and is playing the role of coach for Valharic. He has spent months leading up to this Crown Tournament coaching Valharic on his mental approach. Valharic had fought a final before, so he no longer had that obstacle. But another of Finn's pupils here today has also been to a final before, the same Knight who set his plan for an extra edge in this tournament months ago.

William of Fairhaven.

The Die is Cast

Valharic wakes up the morning of Crown with a clear mind. All the distractions are gone. He is ready.

"I knew I was going to win," he tells me later. "Sometimes I get nervous, but I was absolutely calm. I could visualize the victory."

When he arrives at Harper Creek High School in Battle Creek just before 9 a.m. to sign up for the tournament, the school's gym already has been converted. A gallery is reserved for spectators. With the bleachers still folded up, there is room for people to set up seats and "day camps" like the ones that had packed the Twelfth Night hall. The Dragon thrones sit at half court for newly crowned King Ragnvaldr and Queen Arabella. The basketball court is only for fighting.

Valharic spots Alys as he straps on his armor. She walks over and tells him about the fortune teller's prediction that she would be a queen. While the fortune teller never could have imagined this scenario, the possibility is no longer nebulous. Today, she has a tangible chance. That is up to Valharic.

Then she hands him the Roman die.

"The die is cast," she says.

Julius Caesar made that same proclamation on his way to becoming emperor, as he led his troops over the River Rubicon and back into Italy from Gaul in 469. The event has become a metaphor for points of no return and pivotal moments in history and in life. Caesar was at that moment defying the Roman Senate and making civil war unavoidable. Today, as the Crown Tournament of the Middle Kingdom is about to start, everything has been set. Valharic has trained for the fights. He has set himself mentally. All he has to do was carry it out.

"I meant it either way, win or lose," Alys explains later. "The die is cast."

Valharic holds the die and focuses on that thought as he finishes armoring.

The opening rounds look easy to Valharic. He even tells Alys she does not have to watch his early fights. But three people in the tournament look to be challenges. Valharic has faced them all several times. Paruig Mac Morcat, a Knight from Columbus, Ohio, has given him tough bouts, but Valharic is confident he can beat him. There is also Sir Alasdair MacFhearguis, a Viscount from Minneapolis, in the heart of Northshield. Alasdair has a chance to become the first from that region in years to become King. He and Valharic are an even match, often locking into long battles in tournament after tournament. Then there is William of Fairhaven.

Normally about 5'10" and 225 pounds, William has shaved off 10 pounds with his training. Finn is his coach. And his secret weapon waits in his bag for just the right moment.

Valharic launches into his fights. In the past, he often had no plan of attack and would throw several shots to set up a kill shot. Fights took longer than he wanted, and he would wear out. Here, he has decided to limit his shots. Virtually everything he throws is designed to be a killer. And they are. Jeffrey Mandragora goes down in the first round. Kieran McCloud in the second. Straum, a fighter on the Knighthood watch list, falls victim to Valharic in the third. And in the quarterfinals, the Knight with the most distinctive persona in the Midrealm, the Aztec Sir Ix goes down. When they finish the bout, Ix gives Valharic yet another omen. The person who knocked him out of Crown the last five times, Ix tells him, went on to win. Meanwhile, William of Fairhaven plows through the other side of the bracket, never losing, and often winning decisively.

In the semifinals, Alasdair, one of the fighters Valharic has concerns about, is up. About the same size as Valharic, Alasdair is just as mobile and both normally use a center grip shield. "The only difference is I'm a little bit stronger and he's a little bit faster," Valharic said. At the last Crown Tournament in South Dakota, the two had fought a war. Today, since Alasdair emerges from the losers' bracket, he will have to beat Valharic twice.

Instead of the long battle Valharic anticipates, it ends in a flash. A thrust from Valharic catches Alasdair's face in just seconds.

"He was moving towards me to throw and I kind of caught him flat-footed. He cocked his arm. That's it."

Valharic has made the finals. All that stands in his way is William of Fairhaven.

"This is it..."

Both William and Valharic look to Finn for advice on how to handle the match, but Finn declines to pick between them. He cannot help one of his friends beat the other. They are on their own.

All of the Midrealm Knights come in close, as they traditionally do, forming a ring around the fighting area. All of the Ladies of the Rose—the former Queens—form around Alys and William's wife Isolde, both for the traditional moral support and to break things up if the emotions from the duels spark a consort fight.

The finals are best two of three. Each fighter can pick the weapon for one of the first two rounds. Once they use a particular weapon in the finals, it cannot be used in another bout. Valharic has first pick. His specialty is sword and shield. He could use that form now. But he expects King Ragnvaldr will call it for the third fight, if needed. Guessing he will get that style anyway, he goes for his second-best option, the longer two-handed swords often called bastard swords.

As the fight starts, Valharic pushes the pace with three quick blows at William's head and shoulders

"I was envisioning hacking him in half from his head through the center of his body," Valharic remembers later.

William blocks all three. Valharic's strategy of throwing almost nothing but killing blows has not worked. The two end up in a sword press—each pushing against their swords as they lock with each other. As they break out of the press, each swings and hits home. The blows nearly kill them both. William's sword smashes Valharic's shoulder, a killing blow since it was with a two-handed great weapon like a bastard sword. Valharic, aiming for William's hip—also a killer with these swords—misses. The blade hits William's thigh, just a little too low to count as a kill. Those few inches mean Valharic is "dead" and William has only been legged. The first bout is William's.

"Oh my god!" Alys worries on the sidelines. "That was HIS choice of weapon but he LOST."

Alys goes to Valharic and asks if he is OK. He is. Alys is more nervous than him.

"It's all right," Alys tells herself, bracing to lose what may be her only chance at the throne ever. "It was nice that he asked me. I'll do my Academy Awards smile and look like a pleased loser."

William announces his weapon choice. It is time to hatch his plan.

"This is it. It's a good place to be." William remembers later. "But I knew nothing's a lock. There's nothing that's a guarantee."

William knows most everyone practices with standard-sized weapons. Everyone fighting at Crown knows how to fight with a spear or polearm or axe. But he knew that nobody would practice with extra-short spears. He had cut two spears down from the six feet that most Knights use to just four feet—a drastic difference, but still legal. The cut makes the spears even smaller than the bastard swords, turning them into sword-sized weapons that can poke and thrust, but have no blade for hacking. And since he has planned for this, he has practiced with them. Fighters can adjust to such changes in weapons. But at a Crown Tournament, there is no time to practice and recalibrate your sense of range. In the very first exchange of blows with the weapon, the opponent will be just a little off, but William will not. He counts on that advantage.

Both competitors must fight with the same style weapon and because nobody else would have a spear of that size, William brought a matching set. He hands the extra to Valharic. Valharic must adjust, or he dies.

The two charge. In a flurry of jabs from William, Valharic drops to one knee. The barrage continues with jabs at Valharic's head. Valharic covers his face like a boxer, pulling the head of his own spear in front of him as a guard and turning his face away. That move gives William a clear shot at Valharic's forehead and top of his head, but spear thrusts to the head do not count unless they are to the face. William's thrusts hit the helmet but do not count. William launches more and jabs at Valharic's face. One blow, he thinks, might have struck home, but he is not certain and Valharic does not fall.

William abruptly stops his attack and steps back.

"I don't recall hitting you in the leg," William says. Valharic tells William that he had not been hit in the leg and had only slipped on the slick floor. The marshals talk.

Alys cannot hear as Valharic, William and the marshals wave their hands and talk. She cringes. Has Valharic lost? Is "Rhinohiding" an issue? She sighs with relief when they reset to fight again.

Valharic regroups. Only inches separated him from losing.

"I got head fixated," William admits later. "I kept thrusting him in the side of the head."

"If he had shifted to my body," Valharic concedes, "It probably would have been over."

They re-set to fight again. William charges. Valharic starts to step back. In one move, he shifts the spear from two hands to just his left and snaps off a lightning thrust. The blow lands cleanly.

They are tied.

"I retreated just enough that he thought I was fading," Valharic says. "I used it like a fencing foil. At full extension I hit him in the face."

William's trump card has not paid off. He broke his game plan, very much like Baldar's first Crown finals opponent, by backing off and not slugging away until Valharic dropped.

"There was no reason for me to stop the fight," he says later. "The momentum was lost. My fault. My bad."

And the blow that might have landed? "I give it no consideration," William says.

In the breather between bouts, Valharic has a quick message for nervous Alys.

"The die is cast," he tells her. She laughs.

As King, Ragnvaldr picks sword and shield—Valharic's strongest form—for the deciding bout.

"I won," Valharic says to himself. "There's no way this man can beat me sword and shield."

And Valharic has a plan now. William is now in his territory. All day he watched William "bowl over his opponents and fight like a bulldog" by hitting them with leg wraps, towering over them and pounding them after they dropped to their knees. Valharic refuses to let William think he can bully him.

He charges and hits William with a plowing version of his signature shot. Valharic launches to his shield side. He jams his shield against William's before throwing a back-hand slap at William's head. William hits the ground from the collision, not from the sword swipe that whistles through the air right over his helm. Valharic had caught William off balance and sent the message. William hops up, sputtering that Valharic accidentally stepped on his toe, tripping him.

Valharic could re-start the fight with William on his knees and Valharic standing over him. Instead, he lets William start on his feet.

Valharic thinks the last skirmish has set William up for a winning blow. He knows William has a videotape library of other fighters, and guesses William knows the jump with the backhand head shot is Valharic's bread and butter. Valharic also has just used it in the shield collision.

"I knew that he'd be watching for it."

He is right. William is watching for it, but not because of the tapes. As it turns out, very few of Valharic's bouts are in William's library. The move, William says, is common for left-handed fighters like Valharic.

When the deciding bout re-starts, Valharic steps forward, jumps and starts that same shot again. William shifts his arm to block it. If Valharic continues that shot, William's shield will be there.

But mid-shot, Valharic turns over the wrist of his sword hand. The hack becomes a thrust right at William's face.

William freezes for a split second. The sword knifes through the spot William's shield had been covering and hits home.

William topples to the ground. Valharic is the winner. There will be no debates with marshals over this. There will be no hard feelings.

Sir Randolph, the chief marshal, comes up to Valharic and drops to one knee at his feet.

"Congratulations, My Prince."

Little Tommy Noble is going to be King.

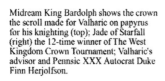

Midream King Bardolph shows the crown
the scroll made for Valharic on papyrus
for his knighting (top); Jade of Starfall
(right) the 12-time winner of The West
Kingdom Crown Tournament; Valharic's
advisor and Pennsic XXX Autocrat Duke
Finn Herjolfson.

Brannos (top) holds a laurel wreath over Valharic's head as they walk to the stage for coronation with Talon standing guard to the left and Flynn, now Agrippa, standing guard to the right; Members of the Kingdom populace (above) swear fealty to their new king and queen; Alys Katheryn and Valharic (right) leave the hall after they are crowned.

Valharic's lifelong goal of becoming King is realized as
Duke Ragnvaldr places the Middle Kingdom crown on his head.

Britannia
Britannia founder Dan Shadrake (above) directs fighters before a battle.

Fighter Steve Wade (above) loves beating shields to a pulp like the one below.

Shadrake challenges fighters in a show battle at Hawkstone Park, believed to be the burial place of King Arthur.

Regia Anglorum
Shoemaker Anna Deissler (top left) explains her work at the Chippenham Viking festival; Kevin Crowley (top right) sells woven trim his wife made: Fighters (left and below) prepare for their Vikings versus Saxons battle.

The Ermine Street Guard
(clockwise from top left) The battle formation known
as Testudo or "tortoise"; a campsite featuring a real
leather tent; lining up at Portcheseter Castle; food
items on display; officers show off their gear: Mike
Garlick with his cornu.

King Valharic implores his troops at the Pennsic War (top and above right); Dankwert Maccabee (above) leads the Middle Kingdom army in a rousing post-battle song; Brannos (kneeling) refuses to give up in his duel with Eastern Duke Lucan even after the other Midrealm Knights have already lost to the East.

Sean/Flynn/Agrippa and his daughter Madison, 11 months, in a break from attending to King Valharic. (top left) Craig/Hobbs/Ulfr drums for Middle Eastern dancers. (top right) Rob/Talon/Titus prepares to fight in the Unbelted Champions battle at Pennsic. (right) The "Something For Us"/Portus Aurelius projects group in their improved lamellar armor. (below)

Act III, scene 1
The Prince's Tale: Becoming a King

April, 2002 Common Era
Anno Societatis XXXVII

> *"...For 'tis your thoughts that now must deck our kings..."*
> —Prologue, *Henry V*

The thrones sit open right in front of him.

Though the Cleveland National Bohemian Hall is packed with 700 people, most of whom revere the Middle Kingdom thrones and hold at least a slight desire to have the right to sit in them, Valharic's path to them is free and clear. The populace of the Middle Kingdom bows their heads to him and nothing blocks the walkway between seats. There are no more opponents, whether they be other fighters, bad impressions or character questions.

The only thing left in his way is Ragnvaldr.

But Ragnvaldr is not there to rain blows on him or take the crown. He is there to give it away.

Valharic has passed the fighting tests. He has passed the tests of honor and service. He has no need to rush or anxiously snatch it and set off the strong feelings that his attempt at Crown two years earlier had spawned. The die has been cast.

He heads with purpose toward Ragnvaldr and the thrones, which stand before a giant Dragon flag. Kynar in his full dress armor and wolf glaring out from above, and Kollin in lorica segmentata and a crested helm, lead the procession that sends a message to the populace. You're not just getting a new King today. Hail your Caesar.

Brannos, who had been named a Pelican for all the service he has done with his teaching of fighters, walks right behind him every step of the way. Above Valharic's head, he holds a crown of leaves in a Roman show of support. Romans who were believed to have the favor of the gods would have such crowns held aloft for them, often by slaves. Brannos as the carrier of that halo only amplifies the symbolism—the Kingdom's virtual god of Knighthood respects this new King enough to play servant to him.

Valharic stands silent and grim as Ragnvaldr runs through a list of his attributes.

"I show no virtue that befits the dragon thrones," Valharic shoots back. "Show me I am not the man you speak of."

The head marshal, Sir Randolph Lee, steps forward. Valharic, he says, would show true courage as King. Valharic again takes issue. His courage, he says, would not match the Dragon thrones.

Sir William, who had been so close to having Valharic's spot today, steps forward and attests Valharic would do well as a new King. Valharic again denies it.

Suddenly a grubby beggar with stringy hair springs to the front.

"He has refused the throne!" the vagrant yells, thrusting his finger in a jab toward Valharic nearly as quick as the deciding face thrust at Crown.

Almost as fast, he is dragged back by Talon who is posted spear-in-hand as a guard at the front of the stage with Agrippa and Ulfr on the other side.

"Three times you have refused the throne," Ragnvaldr queries Valharic. "Will you also refuse your sovereign?"

"That," Valharic replies, "I cannot do."

Moments later, his household watching, Finn and Tamara bearing witness and a contingent of his old foam-fighting foes, all bigger of belly and grayer of head, reveling in seeing one of their own making good, his boast comes true. When Ragnvaldr sets the crown on Valharic's head, he is no longer a braggart kid.

He is King.

"She was so deserving…"

The last week had been a blur. So had his entire six months as Prince.

The breakneck pace had begun the instant Sir Randolph congratulated him at Crown. The ring of Knights swarmed him with congratulations. It was the second time in three months the Chivalry he had struggled to be part of for so long had congratulated him. The first time it had been to welcome him as an equal. After Crown, it was in honor of him becoming their prince.

"Oh my God, he won," was the thought flashing through Alys' head in the instant Valharic landed the winning blow and changed the course of their lives for the next year. "It wasn't until the moment William fell that you know he actually won. It's real. From then on, the rest of the day was not in our hands."

It took Valharic 20 minutes to free himself from the barrage of hugs and back claps to catch up with Alys. Ragnvaldr broke up her stunned and excited chattering and whisked them off to try on several crowns for fit and for Valharic to collect the Kingdom's sword for the Prince. He was then whisked off to a Chivalry meeting, then hurried to the celebration feast.

Quickly, he changed into dress tunic. Valharic was short one key item for the celebratory feast—a place setting. Of course, he had a set of his own, but he had no intention of staying if he had lost. He might have been confident, but not enough to pack a set of feast gear.

"The food was awesome," he says when a loaner set saved the day. "Food never tasted better."

When court opened after feast, Ragnvaldr and Arabella called for Valharic. The man who had been his roommate years before now crowned him Prince. Valharic then crowned a beaming Alys.

"She was so deserving," Valharic says. "I was just excited I got to be the one to do it."

"It's your job…"

At Pennsic there is often a class called "Oh Bleep! We won crown. Now what do we do?" The title is only half tongue-in-cheek. Prepared couples can keep the pressures and problems in perspective and have their best experiences in the SCA. If not, they can be miserable. For six months, every public word you utter, every tunic or dress you wear, every smile or scowl is scrutinized. Every minor faux pas will become part of your legacy. No matter which Kingdom you rule, the pressures and pains of being King and Queen are so great that some people who might win Crown Tournament do not enter because they do not want the responsibility that comes with winning.

For starters, many new royals need new garb. Most people have a few pieces of very nice garb and a huge pile of lesser "everyday" garb. Royals don't get to have an off day. They can't very well go around wearing their well-worn T-tunic with a crown. They need exceptional garb—garb befitting a royal—every day of every event. Make that two sets, day garb and feast garb. Most Queens change for feast and court. Kings often have to change from fighting garb to feast garb, something they are used to, but now the fighting garb has to be better. They may need to brush up on their persona, too, and make sure their garb, armor and persona all match. They are an example.

Then they have to spend their days in meetings making decisions on Kingdom officials and awards. They need to be comfortable with public speaking since they'll be running court. And they'll need to be fresh and full of vigor when the event site opens at 10 a.m. on Saturday, even if they pulled into the hotel at 2 a.m. after a six-hour drive the night before. Dozens of people will approach them at events to hit them up for favors. Every one of them will remember exactly what they say and what the royals say back, even if the King and Queen are dashing from meeting to meeting.

The Royals become public property. Their travel plans, food and drink preferences and intimate details of their clothing sizes are posted on web sites, right down to their waist and bust sizes. Local sewing guilds use the measurements to fashion expensive and ornate clothing for Their Majesties, but Royals can kiss modesty goodbye.

At Atlantia's university in February, Havordh and Mary-Ellen were still Prince and Princess. From their Crown Tournament in the fall through February, they had one weekend without an event—Christmas. From the first week of January through March 10, they had no weekends off. They took a break on the 10th only because they had to pack for Gulf Wars.

"All of your friends want you to come to their events," Havordh said. "Instead of this being just the thing you do on weekends, you get 20 e-mails a day, you spend time talking about who gets awards, where events are going to be and who we have to talk to to get X, Y and Z done."

"It becomes less your hobby and more of a job. It's your job to make sure everyone else is enjoying themselves as much as possible."

When Valharic returned to Cleveland with the dismantled Prince's throne and other pieces of regalia, it all went into Agrippa's basement. The SFU meetings, once a sidelight even within the household, will become nerve central not just of Darkyard but an entire Kingdom.

For the next six months the throne leaned against the solid, brick wall of the Armory between events.

So did its new owner.

Valharic depended on the SFU projects group to make his time on the throne work. Agrippa, Talon and Ulfr all became part of the staff that accompanied him to events to play the servants and bodyguards that enhanced the role. As such, they all needed matching uniforms and armor. Valharic took his role as War King seriously and wanted to keep pushing the image as a warrior King. His staff needed to support that.

Through a large group order, they purchased hundreds of already-punched aluminum lamellar scales. Talon helped construct red and black backplates and shoulder flaps from leather. Helms were polished with a coat of oil and a power sander.

In the final week before coronation, the group flurried to finish their look. Talon tinkered with his lamellar while Agrippa dug through old Army duffel bags of gear for extra pairs of knee-length Roman leggings for other staffers. Ulfr had to scrounge a pair of caligae, the Roman-style leather sandals.

At the last Tuesday night meeting before coronation, the women of the group, Erin, Wanda and Bobbie, brought down their final work. A reign needs more than just armor. They had made Agrippa, Ulfr and Talon each a red Coptic tunic with yellow/gold clavi as their uniforms. Although Valharic already wore some of the pieces they had made for him as Prince, their best work would be unveiled Saturday. For Valharic's first court, Erin was finishing a long tunic with two intricate roundels—red circles—each embroidered with a coiling green dragon. Wanda/Juana had another showpiece in the works. On the giant red cloak Valharic would use for the reign, she was still satin-stitching the figure of a giant, vicious Midrealm dragon ripping apart a prone tiger, the symbol of the enemy East.

On Friday night, friends from several states packed into the homes of Agrippa, Talon and Valharic's parents. Agrippa and Valharic scampered down to the Cleveland National Bohemian Hall to help unfold tables, set chairs and string up the rope boundaries for fighting. Decisions had to be made to make sure things would go well.

One big decision, a bitter and highly-politicized fight over who should be the Baron in Cleftlands, was being made by Ragnvaldr and Arabella. Before stepping down, Ragnvaldr polled the entire barony over whether people supported Laurelen Darksbane (the Elvish Knight), and his wife, Baroness Ithriliel. Though more than half of the barony supported Laurelen, only a third supported Ithriliel. Valharic and Alys had been assured that the whole issue would be settled by coronation, but Valharic had to urge Ragnvaldr to not leave it until that morning. Pushed by Ragnvaldr, Laurelen resigned.

"I Swear It To the People"

On Saturday morning, as 700 gentles drive past the real world Finn Tavern (with a battlement-topped logo no less) and down the mundanely named Mead Road to witness the changeover, that issue is only a topic of whispers. Today is about the new King and Queen. The populace packs the seats. Since coronation is a showy event, many of the gentles wear their best garb. The Kingdom cleans up pretty good when it wants to. The gathering has the atmosphere of a wedding, even though the "I swears" are a little off. I half expect ushers to ask the incoming crowd, "King side or Queen side."

Darkyard's Legion is as single-minded today as it is on the field. A household flag joins the row of banners on the second floor railing, accompanied by Forgan's arms. The arms of Valharic's mentor will look down on this moment, even if Forgan cannot be here. A flood of black and white Coptics rims the hall with contubernium flags popping above them like candles on a cake. Countess Rebekah's apprentices are still at work sewng Valharic's night court garb, stitching on jewels as fast as a snap to the helm. Valharic pulls on his day garb, a long purple tunic with gold cuffs. Talon, Ulfr and Agrippa put on their new tunics, the tight leggings, Roman sandals and their show armor of lamellar. They all cluster in a back room as Ragnvaldr finishes his final court.

Ragnvaldr and Arabella plow through a laundry list of awards and recognitions: for banners of all of the Kingdom's award badges, for painting a King's shield for Ragnvaldr, and for serving as their staff. They even sneak in an award of arms for Buster Ragnvaldrsson, which is accepted by someone else. Of course it is. By Buster's handler. Buster is the husky who has accompanied them to events for the last year. He is out in the car.

Once Valharic is crowned, he has no hesitation in swearing the oath of King. Ragnvaldr reads off the requirements.

> "A King is not an all-powerful sovereign. A King is a man given the duty to govern.
> A King must bear the heaviest burdens and strike the mightiest blows
> Ever the foremost in battle and last in the most desperate retreat.
> A King has no right to the common joys of living, no freedom to indulge in
> personal interests, tastes and biases.
> He is a sacrifice to the common people, a man who lives to serve by ruling,
> protecting the Kingdom by disciplining all private inclinations and sentiments,
> submitting himself to absolute objectivity and justice.
> And in the time of famine or leanness, he must wear the finest raiment and
> laugh the heartiest at the lightest board of any man in all the Kingdom.
> He must place his people's needs above all else.
> To be King is to respect all manner of things that many people hold dear,
> even though the King may not.

Valharic's voice, solid and resolute, grows to near shouts when he swears to follow each one "until death takes me or until the world ends."

"I swear it to the people," he barks.

He cracks his first grin as he faces Ragnvaldr, just before Ragnvaldr tells the crowd, "Midrealm, behold your King." When Valharic turns to face his populace, he is serious again. Only the bellow of "Darkyard!" from the clapping crowd breaks his stare. He cuts the clapping short. He orders his staff to the front with a bark. They march into place. He has already set the tone. Orders will be delivered—and followed—with a snap.

They ought to be. This is a military reign.

"The crowns get the flotation cushions..."

Even with all the crying, the emotion and pageantry, this coronation is pretty dull as SCA coronations go.

After all, there are no inquisitions, no pig guts, no hurricanes and no murders.

Each of the SCA's 17 Kingdoms has its own approach to coronations. The Midrealm, one of the oldest, generally has fairly serious ones. So does Calontir, once a part of the Midrealm. And the West, the oldest of all, is known for following the same exact script almost every time.

"The West is very hidebound when it comes to tradition," said Duchess Elina of Beckenham. "They are in love with the wording. They are in love with the ceremony. They will not change it."

At the moment the new King is crowned in the West, the banner with the arms of the new King is rolled up and taken off display.

"I am no longer Elina of Beckenham when I am crowned," she explained. "It's Elina Regina. It may as well be Elina West."

The banner of the outgoing King is unfurled. He has his identity back.

Some Kingdoms have multiple sets of crowns but the West has just one. Pieces of the original crown made by Diana Listmaker for the First Tournament were stripped off and cast into the crowns made by Henrik of Havn 25 years ago. The populace of the Kingdom donated silver dollars to be melted down for the crowns.

The Kingdom considers its crowns so important, the West's guide to incoming royalty issues stern warnings for mistreating them, even ordering new royalty to have a retainer hold the crowns for them—level to the ground, mind you—outside while they use the bathroom.

"If the plane you're on goes down over water," the guide says, only half tongue-in-cheek, "the crowns get the flotation cushions."

The Midrealm had a set of crowns treated so poorly that damage to them is left as a warning against how badly things can go wrong with a reign.

Albert Von Dreckenveldt was the unfortunate prince of the Midrealm under the infamous Michael of Boarshaven who he called "truly psychotic." After Michael did things like chop one of Albert's garden hoses into tiny sections and surprise people with mood swings, he'd steal sparkplugs out of Albert's lawnmower. Soon, Michael's Queen and his heirs refused to sit on stage with him. The Queen quit and the heirs followed.

"So he got mad and resigned," Albert said. The Kingdom had to file suit in court in Champaign, Ill., to retrieve the crowns while Albert, the stand-in King, had to use cheap copper sheet replacement crowns. When the crowns were returned, Michael had ruined them.

"They had these semi-precious stones on them," Albert said. "Michael took a screwdriver to them and pried them out. I don't know why. I don't know what he thought he'd get for them."

The Kingdom had to have the crowns rebuilt, but intentionally left one jewel missing. The hole would serve as a reminder and caution about what can go wrong.

As for the ceremonies themselves, other Kingdoms like to mix in a few surprises and wrinkles.

In the Kingdom of Ansteorra, the winner does not get a free pass. The Lions of Ansteorra, the select group of the Kingdom, gets to put the new King to test at coronation. The Lions are the keeper of the sword of state. They take the sword from the outgoing King and decide whether the new one is worthy to receive it. In front of the populace, the Lions question the new King about chivalry, the crown and responsibility to determine his worth.

"He's won the crown by right-of-arms but he's not won the right to hold that sword," Sir Kief av Kierstad explained. "It is never scripted. Sometimes the questions that come out of our mouths are interesting. Sometimes it's only a minute or two. Once it lasted 15 minutes with the older members grilling him."

"I've never known anyone to fail in the answers, though sometimes we grumble about the answers. I don't know what the hell we'd do if someone couldn't answer."

Then there is the schtick, where the blurry lines between real and theater bleed even more toward acting. The Prince and Princess are the children, the heirs, of the departing royals who then become counts, countessess, dukes or duchesses. But in the real world, former kings are not Dukes—they're dead. A few SCA monarchs follow suit deciding to depart both the throne, and their mortal Current Middle Ages life, in style.

Roak of Ealdormere was once crowned Prince after the outgoing couple decided to "poison" themselves and spent the rest of the event walking around as ghosts. In Trimaris, the string of coronation tragedies has stretched on so long that people joke about the "Dead Kings of Trimaris."

"We go for a more theatrical type thing," Baldar said.

Baldar once turned up at his step-down with a fake stump on one arm and a pump that made it ooze blood. His persona is Viking and Viking tradition, he said, does not allow a King that is not whole of body. So his Queen slit his throat.

At his last coronation, Baldar planned an elaborate play involving a coup. He had someone come in with a small army of supporters insisting the usurper had been elected King. A bishop persona crowned the imposter, who started setting up a court.

"People were getting more and more agitated," Baldar said.

The event was outdoors at a lakeside. Suddenly a horn blast comes across the lake. Baldar and his house had borrowed a Viking ship and the crew rowed at full speed across the lake, Baldar standing at the head.

"Our boat rolls up and beaches itself. All these Viking warriors come out of the boat, we had maybe 30 to 35, and they all had live steel."

The usurpers charge to the water. A Saxon monk runs toward the shore holding a cross and ordering the heathens from the land. A Viking chops him with an axe, breaking the cross and sending blood everywhere. The Vikings swing their steel at the traitors. One is caught flush in the chest and entrails and blood pours out. The Vikings are victorious in the end and the ground is littered with dead, blood and guts.

This had been planned carefully. The axe was realistic-looking foam. The disemboweled traitor had hidden a metal chest plate under his tunic along with plastic bags of pig guts. The knife cut the tunic and gut bags but never touched him. In all, 23 packets of fake blood spurted from mock wounds.

The Midrealm today, however, escorts its interrupting beggar away with no bloodshed.

"Behold your Queen"

In the back of the room, Alys' entourage has lined up side by side with arches overhanging the gap between rows. Roses cover the arches in a nod to the Order of The Rose, which will soon be called up for Arabella as she steps down. Alys comes down the aisle, led by her staff. A red veil covers her white hair and her white and purple dress is covered by a purple cloak and shiny trim along the borders.

She plows through her oath. When Valharic's urging to swear her oaths "to the citizens" comes out as an order, not even slightly a request, Alys does not flinch.

"I swear it to the citizens," she replies, with even more force than her promise to the King just before. She may owe this position to Valharic. But she owes the importance of it to her populace.

"Midrealm!" Valharic orders. "Behold your Queen."

His first real order to his populace is met with resounding applause.

His task is no longer to become King. For the next six months, he has to *be* King.

Act III, Scene 2
Wimples On: Imagine You Are Back in Time

"If you're writing about us, your job is to inform people, right?" asks the Viking after a patrol of Saxons cuts down his band of fighters on the battlefield.

He had grunted at the mention of the SCA, disdain infusing his voice. He had heard all about the dubious garb. He had heard about plastic on the battlefield.

"It's worse than that," he says, half to me, half to a kinsman hovering nearby. "People wear armor made out of carpet."

I start to tell him carpet armor barely exists anymore but he keeps rolling.

"You have a responsibility to tell people the difference between the SCA and re-enactors," he says. It is almost a value judgment and challenge—more of a challenge than his band of Vikings had mustered in their skirmish against the Saxons today, here in Chippenham, England.

The SCA, says Thorold, an officer of Regia Anglorum, Britain's premier Dark Ages re-enactment group, borders on fantasy. Little separates it from Live Action Role Playing (LARP) groups or foam popsicle fighters with inauthentic weapons and clothing. *Real* re-enactors use real weapons, accurate (or no) armor and the look of their camp and clothing should be, and is, a huge leap up from the average SCA event.

"If you are not authentic, then you are, by definition, fantasy," he says.

With that one sentence he sums up neatly why many serious re-enactors and Middle Ages experts look down on the SCA.

Standing between two handmade, wood-framed cloth tents, his position rests on solid ground. He has trimmed his wool tunic with tablet weaving, not ribbon trim. Every tent fits Regia's late Dark Ages period—all wooden A-frames with plain canvas, no nylon. Everyone has authentic clothes, right down to footwear. Virtually every fighter hits the field in turnshoes even for battle, with no combat boots or cross-trainers to be found. Members have hand-sewn much of their clothing, all wool or linen, with a few pieces of raw silk thrown in. And they have all left watches and cell phones under skins in their tents.

As a Saxon woman walks by, Thorold's eyes zero in on a sheet of paper in her hand with the day's itinerary photocopied on one side.

"You shouldn't have that out here," he scolds. "It's not wimples off yet, is it?"

With that phrase—"wimples off"—he hammers the second of his wedges between the SCA and the British re-enactment community. And he hits it harder than any of the re-enactors have ever been hit by a weapon. The call of "wimples on," is the order to shift into period and the authenticity rules kick in. At "wimples off," everyone stands down and the rules go out the window. The lines that are blurred in the SCA with all the Coke cans at the feast table and plastic on the field are clear here. They may as well call out "Lights, camera, action!" to start them and "Cut!" to stop the show. And since Regia, like most of the UK's re-enactment groups, considers itself on stage for the audience, those commands might ring more true.

I made the flight across the Atlantic the first weekend of May, 2002, a long bank holiday weekend in the U.K., to see the re-enactors at work (literally, since the groups are paid). My plane reversed the route of some of the early Viking passages to North America by arcing over Newfoundland and Greenland as it headed for Gatwick Airport. I am yet again using 21st century technology to reach my destination. But the time shift far exceeds the five hours of time zone jet lag. I have traveled to the Old World from the New World to delve deeper than the SCA or even its roots. I am headed to the places that inspired the *idea* of the SCA. Here in Britain, castles and battlefields stand for more than just names in books. People can find them around the corner or at the next exit off the Motorway. As I study the map in Gatwick Airport's arrivals lounge, my eye catches a name of a town about 10 miles north of the M25. Hertford. I smile. Duke Edmund's persona home. It is still a place where people live. It reminds me that here, the Middle Ages is not someone else's history, like the SCA world is for us American pretenders. It is the history of the Brits' backyard, of their families.

It also reinforces the main idea I left home with. Groups here have two advantages Americans do not: real historic sites for events and real artifacts to study and copy, all at reachable museums.

Can they pull the Middle Ages off any better with these tools, I wonder?

The results, I learn, are mixed. While they may be after many of the same things as the SCA, the approaches differ as dramatically as driving on the left side of the road instead of the right.

Britannia: "Crowds love to see the wood chips fly..."

"Sorry we're a little disorganized," Dan Shadrake says, grinning as he tightens a rope on a pavilion in a valley in Hawkstone Park, possibly the resting place of the real King Arthur. "Had a little too much red wine last night."

Shadrake's group, Britannia, recreates as closely as it can the times of the actual Arthur. His book, *Barbarian Warriors: Saxons, Vikings, Normans*, had conveyed a seriousness and attention to detail. Today, the rowdy, rough-and-tumble class clown side of him steps forward..

"We're just a bunch of ex-football hooligans," he says. "This was the only way we could get violent with each other without being arrested."

He flashes the same grin again that nearly spreads from ear to ear of his largely bald but white-fuzzed head. He is joking about the violence—but not completely—and the group mirrors his split personality. Britannia is made up, as members openly say, of "weirdos" who like to expend huge quantities of spirit on the fighting field, then recharge with the same amount of spirits at the pub afterward. Other times, they hit the books as hard as their swords hit shields and try to glean as many truths as they can about a terribly undocumented era.

As Shadrake heads off to help with a tent, fighters shuffle through gear and debate what weapons to use.

"Do we have an extra axe this weekend?" one asks.

"Yeah, I think we have one more."

"Good. I want to use an axe today."

They toss each other knowing glances and crack devilish smiles. Someone's going to get it. But the next question for the would-be axe-wielder is not, "Who are you after?" It just has the same tone.

"Whose shield?"

Someone, it seems, has brought a fresh new shield to today's battle. The virgin sword-blocker has none of the gouges, scrapes or chips that a seasoned shield should have. And the wanna-be axe-wielder is only too happy to do the honors of breaking it in. If axe hacks on the newly painted wooden shield wow the audience, all the better.

"The crowds love to see wood chips fly," explains another fighter, Steve Wade. The 29-year-old computer worker fits the pattern of Middle Age enthusiasts hitting the keyboard to fund their habits of hitting people with swords.

"Anyone that has a shield last more than a season is a nancy-boy, really," he says.

"I tell them we were in *Gladiator*…"

My first contact with Britannia came through Shadrake's book. Brannos had lent it to Ulfr from his library at Brannos' Keep. The Brassey's History of Uniforms series has several books, all detailing the uniforms, equipment and basic military practices from several eras, including the American and British Civil Wars, the Napoleonic Wars and the Mexican-American War. Shadrake, now a designer and artist for the British magazine History Today, and his wife Susanna, who has written several historical documentaries, turned out their *Barbarian Warriors* book with countless diagrams of weapons and armor, instructions for lacing lamellar and making mail and at least 150 color and black-and-white photos of artifacts or re-enactors in action. His book and another Brassey's volume on Living History can open a few SCA eyes on just how far Brit re-enactors are willing to go for authenticity.

Britannia's web site boasts "Battle Re-enactment and Living History 400-600 AD" and trumps a very promotional plug—"As featured in Ridley Scott's Epic *Gladiator*." The Portus Aurelius crew would sometimes watch the opening of *Gladiator* to revel in the energy of battle and so Ulfr could decipher the shout of "Ihr Seid Verfluchte Hunde!" from the Germanian barbarian behemoth. I would scan the troops for anyone I had seen in Shadrake's book. No luck. It did not help that Britannia's standard garb is post-Roman and *Gladiator* had Romans from a few hundred years earlier fighting Germania. The film crew gave Britannia different outfits so spotting them by their typical look is impossible. Shadrake didn't care.

"If the money's right I'll wear a blue teapot on my head and stand there starkers," he says.

Shadrake has another explanation for why I cannot spot them.

"I personally am about 200th from the left in the opening battle scene."

Some in his group can pick their fleeting glimpses out of the pack. Wade gets a vague nod from Russell Crowe as Maximus stalks the battle line before the fight. Britannia's big moment, Shadrake says, comes when a row of archers dip their arrow tips into a line of flame to fire. Lots of combat extras—from other groups, Shadrake pointed out—said they could follow directions and raise their bows in unison to fire. But they made mistakes and wasted shots. The frustrated directors could give Britannia's guys, Shadrake boasts, just one take to somehow get it right. They nailed it with a cascade of arrows.

Many shifted sides a day later, changing costumes to add to the Germanian masses in camera shots of the battlefield in Bourne Wood, near Farmham, Hampshire. There, they fought alongside Chick Allan, who played the monster Germanian leader. Allan, 39, is not part of Britannia. But as head of the Edinburgh, Scotland-based Clanranald Trust and a leader of the Scottish Federation of Medieval Martial Arts, he is a part of the re-enactment community. In between TV and film gigs, both on screen and as a fight trainer, he will attend a few major re-enactments and play the bagpipes with his band Saor Patrol. And deliver some clouts to Britannia troops whenever they meet.

"He's actually hit me around the head with a large latex mallet," says Wade, as if that clout carried the same meaning as a dubbing.

"I enjoy fighting against Britannia," Allan later says of his foes, as he sits at his computer, miles away from sword range in Edinburgh. Thanks to modern technology my queries did not have to be sent via a cannon-fodder messenger and answered with the Snicker-Snack of a vorpal blade. "They are not whimpish and can give a good fight as much as take one—except when I dig them with my huge Warhammer—ha-ha."

Allan was hired for *Gladiator* after working with the fight director on the BBC production of *Ivanhoe*. Britannia also fought in that film. Shadrake's crew landed parts opposite another celebrity with a Middle Ages bent, Rowan Atkinson, and played Robin Hood's merry men in the Black Adder millennium celebration film, *Back and Forth*.

"Some of my friends think it's cool. Some of them think I'm a real dweeb," Wade says of his link to the group. "People think it's a really crap hobby until I tell them we were in *Gladiator*. Then they say, 'Can you get me in?' I just say no."

Though Wade can identify with the image problem the SCA can face, even he is a little taken aback by some of the SCA's practices. Britannia never spends the whole weekend in Middle Ages mode and members do not adopt period names or personas.

"During shows we may use names, simply for the benefit of the audience," he says. "Re-enactment is a silly hobby. We're silly blokes in silly costumes and it's a bit Dungeons and Dragons. Some people take it far too seriously."

This weekend is the group's first major outing of the year. As the summer goes on, the group will hit several parks and festivals to do demos of equipment and fighting and charge the museums, historical sites or festivals for the show. Shadrake estimates the group earns 3,000 to 4,000 Pounds ($4,500 to $6,000 at the exchange rate of the moment) to pour into their gas tanks, equipment expenses and their beer mugs. Britannia has 36 pints of beer on hand for tonight.

"An army marches on its stomach," Shadrake says.

The likely biggest event this summer will include repeat performances at a recently excavated amphitheater in London where archaeologists found the remains of a gladiatrix, a female gladiator. Britannia and the site drew sellout crowds of 2,000 people for its last set of shows and the crowd noise even added insights for the historians. Since the crowds could be heard throughout the entire square mile of original old London, Londinium, they learned how noise may have carried around arenas back then.

"An enthusiastic amateur can sometimes shed so much more light than an academic and professional," Shadrake says.

He set off down that road by taking his fledgling group off on 26-mile march 11 years ago, all in armor and loaded with gear, to see how far and fast fully equipped Roman soldiers could march. That laden marathon between Chelmsford and Colchester, England, took the group 10 hours.

Besides the forced march, Shadrake plays the taskmaster when it comes to authenticity. Unlike the SCA, where standards are up to the individual, UK re-enactment groups have a narrow focus and a narrow mission. And the heads of the group have no fear of rising to the role of authenticity Fuhrer to keep everything up to par, even to academics. Shadrake studied old Coptic tunics at the British Museum and London's Victoria and Albert Museum before he put the entire group in Coptics, just as post-Roman Darkyard does. Of course, Britannia uses all wool and Darkyard, needing to survive August midday heat in Pennsylvania, does not. Modern equipment goes out of sight for shows. All the weapons match artifacts from the period as do the armor styles—lamellar and shirts of small metal scales. His small carroballista is made of true period materials—no bedposts topped with bows. Even the tents have wooden stakes, chopped out of chunks of wood. And the shields are edged with sinew, not heater hose, though he has no problem with using dog chews—soaked until soft and stitched together.

"The group here under Dan is pretty authentic," says Derek Clow, who at 67 is one of the group's elder members. "As for Romano-British history, he's brilliant."

"The audience is half the battle..."

"King Arthur..." Clow says into a microphone as spectators gather for Britannia's show.. "...What a load of rubbish."

His voice carries easily to the few dozen families with children in tow standing at the double rows of yellow hazard tape strung along the edge of the field. About a dozen fighters already command the field in matching tan Coptics with green clavi. They are on patrol for any bands of Saxons infringing on their territory. But as Steve Wade warned me, "the audience is half the battle." To keep the crowd happy, each half hour show is a virtual play, with a beginning, middle and end.

Today, the park visitors who paused their hikes through the park to watch, will be treated to their best look—"as best as we know today"—of life in the era of the true Arthur, not the myth but a warrior. Best accounts suggest he was a chieftain, a fierce fighter who helped fill the post-Roman leadership void until the Saxons eventually did his kingdom in. Shadrake pulls on his helmet, unsheaths his sword and picks up a shield. He is now in charge of the Roman unit on patrol.

When the band of Saxons emerges from a path from the woods, the unit snaps to attention.

"You're on Roman land!" Shadrake bellows. When the Saxons hold their ground, he charges and the two lines collide mid-field. Shields smack into each other and a din rises of swords chopping wooden shields and of yelps, grunts and screams. Roars accompany roundhouse sword swings and as blows lands, the recipients sometimes hit the ground with screams that would draw a chorus of "Hold!" at an SCA battle. But it is all an act.

Every blow is pulled and turned from hack to slash just before it hits someone, making it into a gentle brush. Almost anyone can get their shield up in time to block the exaggerated blows, which only means the attacker has a chance to chop wood. If a blow will clearly hit shield instead of flesh, that amounts to a green light to slug away.

As both lines of fighters collide, sword blows grow even more obvious and telegraphed but still work fine as wood chippers. One by one the Romans fall to the turf in deaths that would make Dagorhir enthusiasts happy. The Saxon trespassers take the day.

"What you just saw did actually happen," Clow booms over the loudspeaker. "Not on this scale but a much larger scale, which is why you all speak English instead of Latin."

The show ends with all of the fighters setting themselves in a line facing the audience. With a shout and a roar, they charge at the crowd, swords drawn as if to run a picnicking mom through the belly. But they pull up at the yellow tape as kids ooh and aah. Their point, giving a taste of what it is like to face such a charge, has been made.

"That went pretty much as I expected," Shadrake says, as he pulls off his armor. "Except they won."

The spectators crowd around the fighters for a chance to hold swords and shields and touch armor. A few grade-school kids smash a shield with a sword and grimace as the blade vibrates, like a batter in baseball jammed with a pitch.

"There's a lot of comedy and ad-libbing," Shadrake admits. "You can't be too serious about it. You know you're doing well when people don't leave to buy ice cream."

The crowd disperses and Britannia's work for the day is done. The 36 pints of beer are waiting, all cool for sweaty fighters. But despite all his assurances that he does not take this too seriously, Wade, Shadrake and a few others go back into the field with swords. An hour and a half later, they are still fighting, sword on sword, practicing parrying blows with the weapon, lunging and hacking wildly, and adding to their sweat.

They might not be as officially competitive as the SCA. But they are as hard to pull off the field as Brannos.

Regia Anglorum: "It's just ecstasy for me..."

The band of Viking invaders moves cautiously across the field, their leather shoes churning the grass. Their round shields hang near their waists but are ready to snap up in an instant should anyone take them on. The Saxon troops (Weren't they the invaders just yesterday?) start across the field toward them and their leader steps to the front and issues a challenge: Leave our land or die in battle. As the Viking leader pauses to take it in, a sound breaks the silence.

"Oh, that you could know...," comes a voice over a loudspeaker. "...the thrill of being on the edge of death and come away unscathed. Imagine you are back in time, that you are there so many years ago."

And the audience, standing three deep at the double rows of safety tape strung at the boundaries of the battlefield, waits urgently for the charge.

The setting is Chippenham, Wiltshire, site of several skirmishes between Saxons and Vikings in the 9th century. But what time it is today depends on whether you're on the field or outside the safety tape listening to the melodramatic play by play. In the 21st century, this is the Chippenham Viking Festival, an annual event along the quaint banks of a river. The local history museum has set up a tent of exhibits in the bankside park but the entertainment of the day is Regia Anglorum. The *paid* entertainment.

The city has hired Regia to set up camp at riverside, do historical arts demos and perform two battle shows, one in the afternoon and one at night. The group has several hundred members across the U.K. but in scattered chapters. About 50 people have made it to the group's first big event of the spring. The fees all fund the group's replica Viking ships, a permanent period two-acre site in Kent and expenses for hardship cases. Otherwise, each member pays their own way, just like with most re-enactment groups.

"We take the view that the members do it for nothing but the society does it for money!" explained the group's national organizer Kim Siddorn. "This is how we can afford to buy five ship replicas and be well on the way to building a permanent site in Kent, none of which comes cheap.

"The real purpose of the site will be to sit in our long hall, behind our ramparts, and amuse ourselves. We want to sit in a structure that is so close to the period we recreate."

The show starts as soon as someone walks through the gate to Regia's camp. By the time I pull in from Shrewsbury, Siddorn has already called wimples on and the authenticity standards become very clear. Safety tape draws a solid line between the period re-enactor zone and the modern visitors. Inside the tape, no one wears modern fabrics or non-period garb. There are no rattan swords or aluminum shields. The weapons are real, if blunted, spears and swords and all-wooden shields. Only the authenticity stars of an SCA Kingdom could live up to this standard. Everyone has hand-sewn leather shoes of period patterns. No trainers. No New World moccasins. No East German Army surplus boots. The base level of knowledge and appearance easily surpasses that of the SCA. And since Regia focuses on one period, like a large household, the look stays consistent.

Regia Anglorum, which means "Kingdoms of the English," normally covers the years 950 to 1066, the last days of the Saxon empire before William turned from wanna-be to accomplished conqueror. Sometimes they will drop back to 743, the start of Viking raids on Britain, or as far forward as 1350 and can play a variety of roles: Saxons, Vikings, Celts and Normans.

Kevin Crowley of Bracknell, whose "authentic name" is Ketil Thorkeldon, hovers between tents, a block of wood heaped with tablet weaving sitting at his feet. He makes a virtual prototype of a Regia member though he has been around a while and has a long wispy beard with a few gray hairs to match his age. Bracknell has been in Regia since 1988.

Crowley estimates that half of the people who join Regia quit within a year because of the high standards.

"We have split marriages up," he says.

The A-frame tents and Regia Anglorum's garb paint the base authentic picture. Wool stands as the fabric of choice for the knee-length overtunics, though members use linen for undertunics and some overtunics. Regia rules, Crowley says, allow wool blends but only if wool makes up a minimum of 60 percent of the fibers. The colors have to be ones plausible in period. Members can buy wool already dyed, even by modern methods, but the resulting color must be accurate.

"If we can't dye it that color using natural dyes, you can't have it," Crowley says.

Then Regia imposes garb restrictions based on the rank of the person someone portrays. Unlike the SCA, there is no assumption everyone is a noble, and darker colors indicate status. Lower-rank people need to wear clothes with light coloring.

After that comes the sewing. Regia encourages members to sew their clothes by hand, but allows sewing machines for seams, particularly ones that will take stress. But people hand sew all hems or at least "oversew" them by adding a visible layer of accurate stitching over the machine stitches. Several of the members on the field have done so, oversewing the tiny and close machine stitches with longer ones about a half centimeter long.

"Unless you look really closely, you can't tell," says Crowley, whose wife machine-sewed his seams in between churning out yards of tablet weaving as trim for cuffs and bottom hems. In addition to making braid for her husband, she gives it away, sells it or trades it for items made by other Regia members.

Anna Deissler, sitting on a stool nearby struggling with the leather for a pair of turnshoes, trades her shoes for the trim. She has made several shoes for members and has been done research that would make any SCA shoemaker jealous.

Thanks to Regia's reputation for trying to make museum-quality items, the curators of the Jorvik Viking Center let her handle full shoes on display, then inspect pieces in back.

"When you get all the little fragments you can see the seams and you can see underneath," she explains. "That taught me more than the whole boots."

At the moment, her challenge is making a pair of turnshoes, actually high boots with toggles for straps. The toes do not want to come out. But that struggle is part of the fun.

"I just love kit-making," says Deissler. She joined Regia two years ago for the costume making, weaving and dyeing, even though it interferes with the career her PhD in molecular genetics could earn her. "I'm getting better and better at making museum-quality reproductions. My family thinks I'm bonkers, but I think they're bonkers too."

Even some Regia members look at her as odd, for reasons that would make her welcome in the SCA. Deissler dives into Regia's mission with a rare zeal, but she also regrets Regia's lack of a campfire culture. There will be no group parties with a shared 36 pints of beer tonight. Regia is not big enough to have several cultures under its "Big Tent" like the SCA. To satisfy one desire, Deissler indulges her love of songs and filk with other medieval enthusiasts. Then with Regia she spends hours perfecting accurate kits, even down to her undertunics. Even just using linen will not satisfy her. So she scours newspapers for estate sales and asks for the antique linen, which the sellers often all but give away because the fabric may not pass modern muster and can be shaded funny.

"It feels so real. It's hand-woven and hand-dyed and the dye is uneven," she says "It's just ecstasy for me."

But even with all of that work, Anna decided to take another step and hit the battlefield.

"I came for the kit-making side, but I got a bit cold and bored," she says. "When you're running up and down in battle you get warm."

"Nothing harder than a handclap..."

Anna wears an outfit that surpasses even the better SCA court garb. She sunk 200 hours of embroidery into the wool tunic to put complicated Byzantine—"imported" as she puts it—designs on the cuff and bottom hem. The embroidery would have taken longer, she says, if she had not used coarse fabric. The thread was all hand-dyed with madder for the red, woad for the blue and weld for the yellow. She bought rust-colored cloth for the sleeves from a handweaver in Donegal, Ireland.

She pulls on a pliable leather tabard as armor and straps on her antler handle dagger at her waist. With no true helm, she simply pulls a leather skull-cap over her head, hair tucked underneath. She has no qualms about taking the field in such a valuable kit.

"I just make sure I fall on my shield, not on a cow pat," she says.

The sexist attitudes of some in the SCA aside, Regia has the same historical objections to women fighters as the SCA once did. It's not accurate. So when she takes the field, Deissler shifts the spelling of Anna to an authentic one that makes it a male name and she fights as a male.

But in a big shift from the SCA, she has no problem with people pulling blows and going easy on her or refusing to hit her because she's a girl. None of the fighters here hit anyone hard.

All blows, explains Crowley standing nearby, are "nothing harder than a handclap."

I ask him to hit my bare arm like a "telling blow" in Regia combat. The brush is so light I would never consider it a good SCA blow. Even bare-armed, it is so soft I would not even owe an SCA opponent the courtesy of yelling "Light!" in explanation for not taking it. The "blow" is barely a graze.

Britannia and Regia offer convincing evidence that any portrayal of the Middle Ages depends on how you set priorities. Regia sets authenticity as its number one goal, trumped only by safety in some situations. Mood, cost, difficulty and such notions as "The Dream" fall very far behind. Regia uses real, though blunted, weapons with no duct tape or foam-swelled thrusting tips to be found. And Regia eliminates the troubles the SCA has with armoring early-period personas, by using soft blows and putting almost no one in armor. Most remain unarmored "squishies," in Regia jargon. Fighters do not need a face grille on their helms and many have no helm at all. Using little armor fits Regia's period: Chain mail and helms would have been out of the price range of all but the upper class in true Saxon times.

But limited armor means limited targets. With no face grilles, head shots are not allowed. Hitting the back is also out. Fighters cannot hit below the knees, just like in the SCA, or lower on the arms than the elbow. Blows must be below the neckline because nobody wears a gorget. And because Regia and its clients set some of its shows too early in history, oftentimes nobody can even wear a coif.

For the few people that make authentic armor, Regia has an illogical system of handling blows, in which armor protects body parts it doesn't even cover. Since fighters are never allowed to hit an opponent's head, a helm would have no legal target to protect. So Regia has decided, in a leap of logic, that wearing a helm allows a fighter to ignore blows to the arm. Because Regia does not want to shrug off blows to the body, chain mail shirts are deemed to stop leg blows instead.

Regia makes the same tradeoffs with archery. It will not consider using golf tube arrow shafts or heads like Baldar Blunts. Regia uses plain wooden shafts with 35-pound bows and small dense rubber tips almost invisible to the audience. Forget shooting a charging opponent in the face, like I saw over and over at Gulf Wars. Shooting higher than the chest is banned and archers are urged to shoot for legs. Archers cannot "kill" people, just drop them to their knees. And archers are allowed to fire at opponents only at prescribed points in battles, not in the chaos of melees.

"We don't like the idea of distracting fighters," says Thorold, the Cambridge-based chimney sweep who serves as Regia's Missiles Officer. "It's a potentially dangerous distraction."

Even with all those restrictions, Regia fighters insist the battles are fully competitive. To a point, they are right. Everybody tries to land blows on their opponent within Regia's restrictions. It does take some extra skill to get a blow past defenses and then pull it back. In every confrontation the loser "dies," the winner keeps fighting and Regia does not dictate which side will win a battle. If a set outcome is needed, Regia will stack the chosen side with extra fighters. The fighters who want to survive a battle and walk off victorious even avoid the better fighters on the other side.

But Regia has the same core problem that any re-creation of medieval fighting has, whether it uses the forms of the SCA or ARMA or Regia: It can't be done accurately without injury. Most participants in any group have blind spots for the compromises their style makes. They take it as a given that their group's chosen compromises for safety—whether those come in appearance, the allowed targets, the armor rules or in the limits on how hard to hit—are the best balance available. Regia has a right to look down on the accuracy of the materials the SCA uses. But its members fail to understand the advantages that the SCA style offers. Regia fighters blanch when I tell them Valharic won a fully competitive Crown with a face thrust. When I ask why they do not jab their opponents in the face with spears, they invoke safety as justification for the restriction. The idea of requiring armor that would allow them to hit more targets is out of the question for them. That would compromise their accuracy. True, I respond, but would a real Saxon spearman avoid a chance to ram his spear right through his opponent's face? Is banning that kind of blow really accurate? They don't have a good answer, because there isn't one. No group has found the perfect answer to replicating killing without actually killing.

Regia's North American head understands both forms of fighting and sees value in the cultures of both groups. George Johnson, 52, holds the Saxon rank of Eorl in Regia and is a Duke in the SCA. He has been King of the Midrealm three times under the name Talymar gan Llwynn and a Knight since 1979. Mundanely a schoolteacher in rural Ohio, he is currently seeking his doctorate in education while he tries to build Regia beyond a handful of participants on this side of the Atlantic.

"I wouldn't pick one over the other," he says. "Both of them have attributes I enjoy, and both have things the other doesn't."

He says he is not an "authenticity nut," but is sometimes bothered when local SCA groups put on demonstrations at schools or for civic groups with gear and costuming filled with inaccuracies.

"You take a typical SCA fighter and stand him in front of students. Can he say everything he's wearing is right? Ninety-nine percent of them can't. At least for one outfit, I want to say everything I have is right—the right clothes, the right colors, the right shield. I do it down to the socks."

But Regia fighters, he says, do not quite understand where the competition in their fighting falls short. Though the members of Regia and ARMA see great holes in SCA fighting and armor, he says SCA fighters easily surpass them with competition.

"The SCA has realistic combat," he says. "It's full speed, full contact. It's very realistic. The SCA is just the opposite from Regia. To maintain the authenticity of the fight, we are more inauthentic in the armor."

The SCA's other allowances also have a little appeal, he says, particularly after fighting a 90-minute battle up hill and down, in the woods and in August heat.

"When I'm tired and stinky and I want a beer, I don't have to worry about someone seeing my cooler."

"Shadows in the landscape..."

"Wimples off" comes late afternoon and the Regia bunch stands down for a break and dinner. A few cook items at their site but they do not bother with period food. A feast did not make the itinerary. Others walk along the river, over a footbridge to the local fish and chips takeout. The lone merchant sells Saxon and Viking belt fittings and jewelry from a large tent. He is doing a booming business in flimsy toy swords for children. The crowd starts building as evening falls. Regia has one more show tonight followed by a ship burning on the river. Families have started pouring down the hill toward the encampment. As modern Celtic music comes from the loudspeakers (Not 9th century music?) a few of the Regia fighters gather on the field and practice. They do not practice real fighting, but a set of moves, blows and grappling to get the finale choreographed just right.

The two camps of Vikings and Saxons gather at opposite ends of the field as music continues to swell from the speakers, first classical music a few centuries off. Then, for all the claims of authenticity, Carmina Burana joins the mix—a 20th century backdrop to a 9th century skirmish. And it shifts just before battle to the soundtrack of *Gladiator*. It is all for the audience, but is no more authentic than *Conan* in Darkyard's camp. The audience here is both the reason for the high points and the excuse for low points. The narration that comes over the loudspeaker moments later pulls in the crowd but is melodramatic.

"We are storytellers," comes the voice. "We are all shadows, shadows in the landscape..."

It smacks of *This is Spinal Tap* and the introduction to a song about a historical site less than an hour from here:

In ancient times, hundreds of years before the dawn of history, lived a strange race of people—the druids. No one knows who they were, or what they were doing, but their legacy remains, hewn into the living rock—of Stonehenge.

The night's battle pits 12 fighters against 13, not Regia's best turnout, which can top 100 combatants at some events. The battle does not re-create any specific fight and represents a typical minor skirmish between Saxons and Vikings. It follows the typical "re-enactorism" plot. One side—the Vikings—is trespassing on the other, this time the

Saxon kingdom of Wessex. When the sides spot each other, the Saxon leader orders the Vikings out.

"Retreat! There is no shame in leaving!"

"Death to Wessex!"

"Death to the Vikings!"

The two sides charge and sword hacks fly. They tone down the blows compared to Britannia. New shields are too costly to replace. If they want one to break in a show they build a cheap "destruct-o-shield" just for that. The sides retreat and come at each other again in a step-by-step march. After three charges and retreats, nobody has fallen. No dead. No wounded. After three charges.

Perhaps seeing many photos of Regia before I came has dulled the spectacle that the armor and weapons can present. Perhaps watching Britannia yesterday has me inspecting Regia's fight with more pickiness and attention to detail. But limiting casualties to make a battle last longer for spectators does not convince me of the authenticity of the fighting.

After a few more charges, the dead finally start mounting. Injured fighters hit the ground and writhe for show only to have their throats slit as they lie there. The Wessex leader and the Viking leader, Einar, take each other on. The choreography kicks in, with giant blows blocked and one tumbling the other to the ground by the arm. The battle ends when the Viking that Einar argued with betrays him, runs up and spears him from behind.

The warriors roll the hefty Einar onto a shield and carry him aloft toward a Viking ship docked at the bank of the river. Hundreds of spectators converge near the ship. The fifth flaming arrow fired at the boat sets it ablaze. The crowd cheers and the boat burns. As I watch families trudge up the hill to their cars, children cackling with glee as they chop the air with their new toy swords, I soften my skeptical eye at the fight. It had hit home with the audience. Perhaps Regia has the right balance in how it handles its battles. And, perhaps, the real battle of the day is not Saxons vs. Vikings. It is Regia's knowledge winning a skirmish against a fading and sometimes-forgotten history.

I leave Chippenham with one more visit to make. I head south to one of the first Roman settlements in Britain.

Ermine Street Guard: "They lived here..."

Mike Garlick sounds for a moment like a cranky old man.

His white hair gives him away as a senior citizen. His complaint only adds to the image. The 67-year-old resident of Whitcomb, Gloucester, is a retired maintenance engineer for the chemical industry. Garlick is angry at changes in his town, at old and familiar things yielding to the bulldozer to make way for the new.

"It's sacrilege," he gripes about a road unearthed for a new one. "It annoys me every time I drive it."

The road in question dates back a little earlier than the fond memories of his childhood or teenage escapades—almost 2,000 years earlier.

Ermine Street was an original Roman road and an entire village formed around it. So did one of the best kit-oriented groups in the re-enactment world: The Ermine Street Guard. Just as archaeologists unearthed seven Roman buildings beneath the road before the new construction, Ermine Street Guard has spent the last 30 years unearthing ways to make near perfect reproductions of Roman equipment.

"We don't cut any corners," Garlick says. He, like many of the Guard's members, has been with the group the entire 30 years and takes satisfaction in paying attention to details.

"You know that you're doing it right. As right as you can."

If the wolf skin tied by the paws around his neck and over the metal bands of his lorica segmentata did not make enough of a statement, the horn he rests on his shoulder stands as evidence of that commitment. Called a cornu, it looks somewhat like a cross between a hula hoop and an oversized French Horn. Garlick made it himself. He started by measuring an original cornu at a museum in Naples and finished by reproducing a real mouthpiece he studied at a museum in Edinburgh.

"It's exactly the same as the original. I turned it up on my own lathe. I know the sound that comes out of this is exactly what the Romans heard.

Today the Ermine Street Guard is the entertainment, or the teachers, depending on your point of view, at Portchester Castle along England's southern coast. Advertised out front as the Imperial Roman Army, the Guard will show off the equipment and formations of the Roman Legions. But the Guard, unlike other re-enactment groups, will not fight. They have put too much care into their gear to turn it into "destruct-o-shields." Skipping fighting allows them to put all of their energy into crafting superb gear, all to match the last half of the first century shortly after the 43 A.D. invasion of Britain, instead of learning the right moves to sell fake blows to an audience.

It is just one way the Guard differs from other re-enactors. Whereas Britannia boasts of its involvement in *Gladiator*, Guard members have helped some documentaries but are glad they are not associated with anything so Hollywood.

"It's junk!" snarls Garlick. "It's pure and utter junk. I've only watched it once—and under duress."

What was so wrong? a visitor asks.

"The beginning, the middle and the end," a passing Guardsman adds.

Romans, Garlick says, would never have fought the opening battle scene that so many others almost drool over. Romans did not fight in the woods unless they had to. Garlick says Romans fought in units—blocks of men that stab from behind the curved shields. In the woods, the Romans broke their ranks far too much and the individual fighting would not have happened unless things had gone so badly for the Romans they could not regroup. The Guard will show the formations today, he promises, though it will not stage any battles.

The setting will help cover for the lack of action. Portchester Castle was once the site of a Roman fort in its pre-castle days and in the early days of the Roman presence in Britain. The castle bears little resemblance to what it looked like in Roman times. Most of what remains was built about 1,000 years after the Romans left the island, about twice the chronological anachronism as Tudors driving cars. But it fits the "medieval" mindset. While the physical setting may be a bit off, it has a giant plus over any SCA event.

"You know that Roman troops exercised in this very yard," Garlick says. "They lived here."

Ermine Street Guard has set up a camp at one end of the courtyard that devotes just one tent to modern needs. Tourists who stop to see their show walk away with Guard postcards and pencils or have an armored soldier hammer them out a coin between two metal casts. Two hand-stitched tents dominate the rest of the camp. They go a step beyond groups that use tents made from canvas instead of nylon: Each of the Guard's tents is hand-sewn from 70 goatskins. "We have some real masochists in the Guard," one infantry man mutters as he points out the handstitching holding each of the skins together. Vegetables and fish in pottery bowls spread on a table while a cook stirs a bacon and vegetable stew bubbling in an iron pot over a fire.

Armor and weapons make up the bulk of the display, most of it on show as members wear it around the site. The Guard, like the real Romans, take a long-range approach with their gear. Romans owned the armor their men wore on campaigns until they served 25 years. At that point, the soldier could retire and sell it back to his unit for use by a newcomer. "He wore his pension on his back," one Guardman put it. All of the Guard's gear belongs to the Guard. Members pay just 20 pounds a year to be in the Guard and are often issued a full loaner kit that they must return. The Guard pays for the materials needed for new projects out of its performance fees. Individuals use the things they make, but all items belong to the Guard. Garlick estimates individual kits would cost 2,000 to 4,000 pounds new—$3,000 to $6,000—but even relative newcomers are outfitted like veterans for events out of the Guard's inventory.

The Guard takes one shortcut with its shields. It uses plywood as the base instead of the real Roman method of using hoof glue to hold together a lattice of hand-cut thin wood strips. But the Guard follows a Roman painting process—painting the wood first, then putting a covering of linen over it while the paint is still wet. Armorers then paint the unit's designs over the linen.

Most Guardsmen wear the Lorica Segmentata, the heavy armor that hides the body behind overlapping bands of steel. The bands wrap around the body, with the edges tucked under the next one like segments of a collapsible telescope. These were only used, Garlick says, in the colder and wetter reaches of the Empire. Hollywood makes the common mistake, he says, of putting this armor on Romans in other settings, even the Middle East, because it is easy to make. If the armor is "Roman," that's good enough for most directors. Guard members make theirs by bending the metal carefully around large water pipes to prevent creasing it.

With their Loricas, as with their helmets, members can tell you the exact academic classification of their equipment. Martin John White, known in the Guard as Marcus Javelinus Candidus, wears a Lorica known as Corbridge Type A, partially based on finds from the town of Corbridge near Hadrian's Wall. An armorer's box, excavated from the old Roman garrisons there in the 1960s, produced several key pieces of evidence. Corbridge Type B, for example, uses hooks in some places instead of straps.

White also wears items based on finds in Vindolanda, another site along Hadrian's Wall. He has a pouch based on finds there. Instead of a notepad, he carries wax tablets—thin sheets of wood that have been scraped and hollowed to form a wide reservoir for wax—to etch notes with a stylus. His sword, a point of pride for the Guard, is a gladius that is a near exact copy of one on display in the British Museum that was found in the Thames River. Romans had two main swords—a spatha they could swing from horseback and a gladius, which was mostly a stabbing short sword. White carved a mold for the gladius' scabbard using the British Museum piece as a model, then cast it using pewter—his one concession in accuracy since the original is bronze.

"I've got to go to work tomorrow…"

The 30 soldiers, all chanting and marching in unison, head into the open field within the castle walls. Spectators, including children tugging at parents' arms, stand two-deep along the ever-present safety tape. Garlick marches in the lead with his cornu, in a line next to the commander, a banner carrier called a "signifer," and the "imagnifer," a man carrying a bust of the emperor Vespasian. Hammered out of silver, the imago perches atop a staff. All wear animal skins around their necks in Roman style. Garlick's horn blasts quick command tones. In battle, commanders could broadcast orders across a field via the cornu player. But a small PA system works better for giving lessons to an uninitiated public.

One of the commanders tells the audience a bit about the Guard before explaining rules of the Roman Army. Soldiers, he tells the crowd, had to serve 25 years and be devoted to nothing but the army.

"If they were married when they joined," he says, flashing a grin to the crowd only a fraction the size of Shadrake's, "they were instantly divorced…We'll take volunteers later."

The soldiers turn their backs to the audience to show the neck guards of their helmets. The ridges on the helmets' brow, the commander says, gave protection from sword chops. As for the strips of leather and metal that dangle like tassels from the belt over the groin, he says, "They provide at least psychological protection."

Soldiers would carry a pilum, a spear, as they marched into battle and throw it at the enemy as they closed. If the pilum hit an enemy, that was great, but if it hit a shield it would lodge in the wood and make the shield heavier and more awkward and give the Romans an advantage. The closest Guardsmen come to fighting today is demonstrating training using wooden swords and lead-weighted wicker shields. The Guard brings out a few horseback soldiers to demonstrate cavalry by chopping cabbages off the top of stands with their spathas and attacking a couple of foot soldiers with wicker shields.

As a group, they demonstrate several formations. The basic one has a line of men marching in tight together, each secure behind his shield, with just his gladius extended out to stab. They also demonstrate a wedge formation known as the cunaeum and one called the testudo—tortoise—that Roman used to move troops amid a hail of arrows or rocks. In the testudo, the front line holds the shield as normal, while the soldiers at the edges face their shields out and the ones in the middle of the ranks hold the shields over their heads to provide a canopy.

The biggest "oohs" and "aahhs" come from the siege equipment the Guard has set up inside the castle. In a row for the audience to inspect are an onager, a ballista and a catapulta, a mini ballista about the size of SCA "ballistas." Each fires mock oversized arrows or wooden balls the few hundred feet across the courtyard, where they smack into shields used up as targets.

"Each of these machines," the commander tells the crowd, "can shoot an awful lot further than they will, but we are restricted to keeping them within the castle walls."

The audience leaves happy—just as happy as those for Britannia and Regia Anglorum. The equipment and materials are exceptional but something falls short— no real fighting. Regia, which covers all aspects of pre-1066 life, could duck fighting with better justification than a group that builds itself around an army. Guard members shrug it off.

"We're re-enactors," Martin White says. "We know the Romans walked in gear 20 miles, but we don't have to do it. We can't go at this full tilt. I've got to go to work tomorrow."

Act III, scene 3
The Illuminator's Tale

The skins of dozens of slaughtered and eviscerated sheep and goats are strewn around Gabrielle's workshop, some in entire hides, others chopped in pieces. She has ground others into jelly for her ancient craft. Chunks of belly blanket her table.

Her poisonous potions and powders pack her shelves, along with more than 150 volumes detailing the magic of this arcane art. She has filled a chest at the end of her table with distillations of earth, ground powders of Malachite and Azurite, the coating from clusters of wasp eggs and scrapings from copper that has been exposed to vinegar.

Scalpel in hand, Gabrielle slashes open the neck of a freshly plucked plant. She squeezes its life juice into her latest brew, all for its special powers.

A vision she had years ago set her on this alchemist's path, her life's calling.

It is time to put all these concoctions to work.

Gabrielle, MKA Diane Calvert, is no witch. And her shop is no laboratory for turning common items to gold—at least not in a chemical sense. Her creations are actually re-creations of medieval-style illuminated pages. From her storefront studio, she crafts both "scrolls" for the Society's European Kingdom of Drachenwald and illuminated greeting card designs and commemorative decorations for private collectors and businesses.

Born in Texas and trained in New York City, Gabrielle/Calvert now splits her time between a second shop and studio in Paris and this shop in the French village of Noyers sur-Serein, a town the French government advertises as one of the 100 most scenic villages in France.

On her work days she leaves her 15th century half-timbered house just a short distance from her main studio and shop, then changes into her 14th century French garb to put on a better show for walk-in customers as she works on her latest commission.

Her arrangement, which would qualify as a dream for hundreds of scribes in the Society, was not intended to be permanent when she started it 10 years ago. It was going to be just a "sabbatical" from her real job as a textile consultant for the Macy's department store chain.

"Guess what?" she asks, grinning. "I never went back."

"It illuminates the room…"

More than a year before I meet Gabrielle at the SCA's European Kingdom of Drachenwald's largest event, Doublewars, Edmund had told me how he had changed over time from simply basking in the atmosphere of SCA events to taking responsibility for making them come alive for others.

But Edmund is a fighter. He at least was able to fight for himself at first.

If your main pursuit is drawing and painting illuminations—re-creating the work done for centuries by monks mostly on the pages of Bibles—you start off doing work for others. Just as monasteries had scriptoriums filled with monks inking page after page, all in selfless work for the glory of their Lord, nearly every local Society group has a scribe's guild whose job is to turn out scroll after scroll—actually flat pieces—for their King to give as awards, all to other people.

Scribes might do work for themselves or friends on their own, but the work that counts in this Society is all for the Kingdom.

"It is a common problem with artists," quips Cleftland's scribal guru, Aiden Elfeadur, who earned his Laurel in illumination. "We don't do art for ourselves."

At every Cleftlands event I managed to attend, at least a half-dozen scribes would spend the afternoon holed up in a room off to the side painting the designs—the illumination that brightens up a page—and carefully scripting a matching style of calligraphy to the period and style of the art.

Alys Katharine, now Queen of the Midrealm, is making a point of praising the local scribes and others for their work at almost every event.

"The scribes of Cleftlands are absolutely amazing," she says in one court. "If you have not seen the scrolls produced by these people, you should."

Shortly before Alys and Valharic were crowned, I had ducked into a talk at a February event called the St. Valentine's Day Massacre in Kalamazoo, Mich., to learn a little about the history of writing and artwork in a class taught by Dr. Tom Amos, the rare books librarian from Western Michigan University. Though not well known in most circles, Western Michigan hosts a respected medieval scholars' conference every year.

Other than the shorter messages carved into stone, Amos tells the class, most writing had to be done on papyrus sheets until about the year 350. Those sheets were made by harvesting the reed, slicing it thin and mashing the slivers criss-cross into a sheet, before letting it dry out. Some people, particularly Romans, also made wax tablets. Those pieces of wood covered with a layer of wax that could be gouged to mark words served as the Etch-a-Sketch of the time, Amos said.

By 350, parchment, the flattened and dried skin of sheep and goats, had become far more widespread. And rabbit skin too—"for very short manuscripts," he laughs. Around then, "codex" manuscripts—made by folding sheets of parchment over a few times, cutting them, and sewing them together into books—started being produced.

Paper was not common until 1240, although the first European paper was likely used in Spain as early as 1135.

Most of the Society's scribes make scrolls from paper, which they will paint with a glorified watercolor known as gouache. Both the paper and paint are much simpler, cheaper and easier to come by than the parchment or period pigments. The scribes will then rummage through reprints of pages from old prayer books, music and Bibles for designs to copy. Their results usually come close to work done in period. But just as with anything else in this hobby, it comes down to the same question: How medieval do you want to be?

"Authenticity is something to be strived for, not insisted upon,' says Aiden, MKA Steve Otlowski, a front office worker for Cleveland's St. John Cathedral. He, like most of the Cleftlands Scribes, who he hosts for scribal workshops at his duplex not far from Cleftlands meetings, uses paper and gouache for most scrolls and saves parchment for higher-level awards. The old ways and materials, though, are still valuable.

"Learning the actual period techniques teaches you things," said Aiden. His stashes of period pigments, he says, add an entirely different texture to the "medieval graphic arts" than the "ultra-smooth" paint from tubes. And his favorite scribal decoration, gold, looks different when done with gold paint, than with "shell gold"—shavings mixed with something to adhere it to the paper—and even more different from his specialty, gilding with real gold leaf. He is now an expert in gilding, the craft of putting a binding agent on a page and pressing gold leaf onto it to create highlights in just the right shapes and places.

Aiden bought his first book—a set of pages—of gold leaf when he was just 15. Talking about his first encounters with gold, his eyes gleam almost as much as the Books of Hours and the antiphonal pages—choir note pages—he beheld in the Cleveland Museum of Art as a teenager.

"The larger a piece of gilding is, the harder it is to get smooth," he says. "These were just pristine. When you use real gold in a book, it doesn't just sparkle. It shines. It illuminates the room."

While he may use paper for basic scrolls, he will regularly use real gold.

"You just can't imitate it."

Gabrielle, though, refuses to cut any corners. She believes strongly that imitating any part of this art, not just the gold, is impossible. She will study book after book of medieval illuminations to learn exact styles and forms. She re-creates them using the exact same materials and exact same processes as the monks and the illustrators that followed them. Each of her creations is on parchment of lambskin or goatskin. And she makes each of her paints herself, even grinding up gems on her own for specific and authentic colors.

"If you make an "illumination' from non-period products," she tells me, "you may have created an absolutely beautiful painting, but it is not medieval illumination."

"I don't do anything that is not period..."

Diane Calvert's Middle Ages dreams started, quite literally she says, with a sort of dream when she was 14.

"I had a vision," Gabrielle/Calvert recalls. "It was not a dream. It was as awake-type vision. All of a sudden I knew who I was in the 14th century. I knew my family. I knew who I was."

She started scouring libraries in search of records about the family. She failed in that task, but the research had an unexpected benefit: she learned about the Middle Ages along the way. That interest received a kick-start when she moved to New York to be with her second husband. There she earned an Associate masters degree in medieval studies from Columbia University.

She also started studying at the School of Sacred Arts in the same city, learning textile design to become a consultant for Macy's, and studying illumination and calligraphy with local medieval enthusiasts.

Her job at Macy's sent her on so many trips to Paris to check out fashions, she even had her own apartment in that city. But her husband, a human resources director at Citicorp, grew tired of corporate life. He spent a chunk of his corporate pay to buy the apartment and the two moved to Paris. Both her illumination skills and her dive into medieval life took off from there. The village where they bought a home soon after and where she has set up shop just adds to her inspiration.

"Any part of this village I could turn into illumination," she says.

Her gallery and studio sit in an 18th century house, built after a 17th century fire destroyed all of its predecessor except its original 12th century foundation. In the shop, she keeps her cash box out of sight in a drawer and hides her credit card machine. But she works in the middle of the room to give customers a view from all angles.

"I don't do anything that is not period in the gallery," she said.

Her home is half-timbered, with its big, dark wooden beams exposed throughout. But she and her husband are still working on restoring it. In the 17th century, a time that qualifies as incredibly old on its own, the owners updated the house to their supposedly modern standards. Since, Gabrielle says, "it was considered de classe" to show the timbers which made it look like a "poor man's house," the owners plastered over it all. Calvert is now ripping out all the stucco and meeting 15th century standards to restore 200 years of age.

It is an exaggerated lesson in how people view styles—in homes, in cars and in clothes. Items perceived as modern when they are made lose value because they are used and second-hand. They later go out of style, then look tacky and wrong before somehow gaining the cachet of vintage. Eventually they become valuable antiques that people covet. A year later when I am house hunting I think about her house every time I see something that is out of style. Will that formica counter top be a museum item some day? Will people a few hundred years from now try to re-create the post-World War II bungalows that sprouted across the United States? Will someone someday have dreams of living in a shag-carpeted ranch house?

As she restores her house, she has to pay careful attention to every detail to satisfy both herself and local historical officials. In the SCA, though, the only standards come from herself. She blanches at the shortcuts other scribes use.

"You will never catch me with a tube of gouache in my hand," she vows.

She never uses paper either.

She always uses parchment, buying entire goatskins or sheepskins, from suppliers and cutting it into pieces for separate projects. One sheepskin usually makes a half dozen 8"x11" pieces. The prime spots are the belly and sides, but the short leg sections can be soaked and boiled—just like making soup—into a jello that can be used as glue.

"Parchment is the illuminator's best friend," she said. "It is totally forgiving. And it is period."

Unlike paper, which absorbs inks, the parchment does not. The pigments are mixed with binding agents to make the paint stick to the surface. Forget about fixing mistakes with an eraser. With parchment, you can add a little water and blot it off. If permanent ink has dried, just scrape it off.

Western Michigan's Amos had made the same point, noting that most pictures of period scribes show then with both hands full—one holding a quill pen, the other holding a knife eraser. The ability to scrape paint off of parchment has also been a boon for historians trying to recover old records. New cultures or the winners of the latest war would often recycle entire books by scraping the text away and reusing the parchment pages. Today experts can raise the old text with a chemical process.

"Some parts of classical culture have been found only by being discovered under something else written in the early Middle Ages," Amos said.

New scribes may be satisfied making a scroll that looks simply "medieval," but Gabrielle says 12th century French illuminations look different from 12th century Italian, and both would be different from 14th century illuminations. Each culture had unique styles of portraying backgrounds, faces, fighters, arms and positions of people, both in the style of drawing and roles the figures serve in the piece. Figures in period illuminations will be stylized, but their expressions will be made clear in standard ways—much as in today's cartoons—and she tries to match those fine points.

Then she has to pick colors. Color coordinating with a modern sense may satisfy some, and may look just fine on someone's wall, but she wants to use only pigments available to that time and place. Just as detail-oriented fabric dyers do not want to use out-of-period dyes or mordants, Gabrielle matches pigments to time.

Most of her pigments come from semi-precious stones, earth and plants. Right out the back door of her gallery she will pick Greater Celandine, a weed her neighbors try to eradicate, and often just dip her brush into the stem for yellow—pale in the spring, more golden in the fall. Dried parts of Indigo, Woad, Rose Madder and Saffron also make good colors. She will crush Azurite for a blue with a green tinge, Malachite for another bluish green, Cinnabar for rust color or Chrysocolla for turquoise color.

"When you add water to the ground powder, it's like magic seeing the color just explode."

Ground egg shells make good whites—white shells make white, brown ones a little bit ivory—that are transparent enough to be used to highlight already painted areas. Verdigrine, a deep bluish green, comes from the rust flakes from exposing copper to vinegar fumes. Adding to her pigments are the bags of reddish and yellowish earth she dug from a chateau construction site near Noyers.

"Every batch of earth, every stone you get, is slightly different in color."

Despite her expertise, she has virtually no rank in the SCA, largely because she has not been in the club long enough. Unlike up-and-coming artists—or bards, or fighters, or seamstresses or cooks—she says she has just one goal, independent of awards. It would make Brannos proud and would be one Valharic can understand.

"I just want to be the best illuminator I can be."

Act III, Scene 4
The King's Tale: The Day Is His

"For never two such Kingdoms did contend,
Without much fall of blood…"

—Act I, scene II, *Henry V*

Valharic stalks the battlefield as survivors and "dead" clear the field after a crucial battle here at Pennsic XXXI. He searches for his commanders as marshals tally the results.

For the last 90 minutes under the August sun, Valharic's Midrealm Army has clashed with the East over a wall of hay bales that stretches a few hundred feet across the grass. Both sides have struggled that entire time to control five key spots—each marked by a hay bale bagged in a sack—that would determine the winner of this, the "Hadrian's Wall Battle." As Valharic hunts for his officers, he knows his forces have seized at least two. One more will give his Kingdom the battle and even the score of this Pennsic War that he must win.

He just has to. He has staked his entire reign on it.

But his fighters and the enemy East Kingdom have clawed and scrapped for the other bales every minute of this battle. Any late surges by the East would take the battle from him. From the sidelines, I watch him pace and fidget, his anxious eyes searching for news. If I could help his cause, I would. But I am stuck on the sidelines due to health problems, and all I can do is root. I was skeptical about this world when I started my journey and I may have had doubts about Valharic, but his unabashed desire to win is infectious. Some Kings take a far more reserved and dignified approach to battles—as much as any man in a dress prancing around in a field can be dignified. Most kings are older than Valharic and almost set themselves a step above the fray, much like a college sports coach who stays calm to steady his emotional team. But it's not just King Valharic that wants this win. The Tom Noble part of him wants it too. He may be King of the Middle Kingdom and he may be commander of an army several hundred strong but Tom Noble is still an unmarried, unemployed 28-year-old struggling to wrestle his mundane life into submission. If I could lend my sword to either of the wars he is fighting, I would. But both are up to him.

As he searches the field for any sign of the results, he knows not if the day is his.

As the Midrealm points pile up, the worry dissolves from Valharic's eyes. The Midrealm wins one, then two, then three. Even outnumbered in forces, the Midrealm has won the battle. The Pennsic War is tied. The Midrealm also takes the fourth bale and when the final bit of news comes in, Valharic thrusts his fist into the air and leaps atop a hay bale as fighters crowd around.

"Bale Five was Red! Bale Five was Red!" he shouts, still pumping his fists. "That was another for the Midrealm."

He jumps down and spikes a water bottle in celebration. The Midrealm has returned a decisive drubbing from the day before. He hurries back to he Kingdom's trailer. Decorated with a castle façade, it is jokingly known as the QE2. Valharic climbs up to its dais where the thrones and Alys wait. Troops crowd around in growing numbers.

"Hail Caesar!" they roar, then follow with the name the army has given itself, Latin for "invincible dragon."

"Draco Invictus!"

The Roman color of his reign has caught on. Both he and the troops are having fun with their new chants and cheers. Even the scroll-making scribes picked up on the theme, jokingly exclaiming, "Draco Inscriptus!"

Valharic's unit commanders march up one by one to sling their prizes, the red and blue pillowcases that covered the contested bales, onto the stage like hunters with their catch.

"I can't express what you've done for me today," Valharic shouts, practically in tears. "This is the stuff of legend. There are men who will hold themselves cheap because they were not here today. They were back in their camp with an ice pack on their heads."

The crowd roars with laughter.

"We will march to New York!"

"Roma Victa!"

Some in the crowd have chills, a tingle running up their armored spines at Valharic's unrehearsed words. The young King hits a nerve with his passion and words that remind them of Henry V's St. Crispin's Day speech of "We few, we happy few."

"Man, oh, man, did it ever give me serious goosebumps!" gushes Saradwen Ariandalen, a woman who has carried water to fighters at the Pennsic war for years and has heard more than her share of battlefield speeches. "One of my Squire brothers was next to me and he turned to me and said, "Serious goosebumps, man, that's what it's all about!" He was grinning ear to ear, as I was, also wiping away a tear."

Even Jocelyn le Jongleur, who has listened to Kings in other Kingdoms, tells me she has never heard a more charismatic speech in the Society.

"On the battlefield he has the charisma of a King—a good one," she says. "The magical moment he created on the battlefield will not be forgotten. It will be cherished. People might ask, 'Why the hell are they doing this silly thing?' That moment stands in majestic answer."

But while the Current Middle Ages gives people a stage to try to bring their medieval fantasies to life, it does not guarantee an outcome. If it were all a story, Valharic's speeches would make an Agincourt-style victory a foregone conclusion. Sometimes, though, the irresistible force of one dream runs up against the immovable object of someone else's. The more than 700 fighters in the East Kingdom army also want this war for their own storylines.

They are not about to give it up just for Valharic. He will have to win it.

"We had arrived…"

Valharic's push to pull his war effort together started even before his coronation. In January, three months before taking the throne, he and Edmund took a trip together to Atlantia to build alliances. The immediate target was hard-hitting Atlantia and Duke Cuan McDaig, who had commanded woods battle wins for the East and who Valharic saw as key. Atlantia agreed to side with the Midrealm. Cuan would command the woods. But Valharic also won over Edmund and vice versa. The two had their first long talk since their disputed Crown on that trip, and returned supporting each other. Valharic, who had resented Edmund for so long, called the Duke up in court to recognize him for an exceptional portrayal of his Saxon persona. Edmund could now join Valharic in post-battle banter, sharing drinks and cigars, without suspicion. At Pennsic, he would lead small units of troops into battle for his young King with energy. And most importantly, Valharic let go all hard feelings from the disputed Crown. After William of Fairhaven lent me a videotape of Valharic's fight with Edmund out of his tape library, Valharic watched his younger self on tape with me and admitted the fight was close. Watching himself in the semi-finals against another Knight, he watched a blow hit him.

"Uh-oh," he blurted out before pausing to rewind and watch again. "I think I'm dead…I don't like to see that."

And he is now glad he did not win against Edmund.

"Ultimately, the best man won the day—the best to do the job," he told me. "I believe very much in fate and it was not my day. I believe I would have been a very poor King if I had won."

Now that he is King, he has Darkyard behind him, with Brannos and Ragnvaldr to give him advice. But just as before his coronation, the Portus Aurelius group is Valharic's primary support staff. Although Countess Tamara served as chamberlain down in Cincinnati and made many of Valharic's events, his Cleveland friends took on much of the day-to-day business. Valharic's marital breakup had cleaned out his limited savings and, unemployed after the restaurant where he worked closed, he has been unable to foot the bill for his reign. So Alys covered some of it and Flynn/Agrippa bankrolled the rest of it temporarily until the Kingdom travel fund could reimburse him. And he became Valharic's driver. The van Agrippa bought after his daughter was born would carry the Kingdom regalia, Valharic, Talon and Ulfr on the royal progress.

It was not without its tensions.

Alys had her own staff, and it was sometimes a challenge to coordinate plans between two royals living a couple of towns apart and their respective staffs. Royals who are romantic couples will travel to events together. In many cases, Alys and Valharic attended different events completely separately. Alys' eyesight at night was not perfect. So Calum, the same fighter who often trains others at Cleftlands, drove her to events in his position on her staff as Queen's Champion. Other staff coordinated favors for her to hand out and turned the piles of items in her house into gift baskets for other royals. Calum took on the extra duty of accompanying her on a full week trip across Northshield, hitting events on bookend weekends and local meetings the nights between.

They made an interesting pair on the thrones. While she was the oldest SCA Queen ever, Valharic looked even younger than he is and some looked at him as a "frat boy" King. As he sat at court, a few in the populace—often middle-aged women—would invariably remark on how young he looked. "What a cute little King," one woman told her neighbor at an event. His staff saw it countless times, as if significantly older women felt a combination of mothering instinct and attraction to his appearance on the throne in regalia. Sitting on the throne also helped his dating prospects with a younger crowd.

"There were a couple of groupies after him," chuckles Alys. More than a few people, she said, had called him "the hottie King."

And they played their roles—he as a warrior King, she as supporter of arts—to the hilt. For basic awards, Valharic would keep a normal tone of voice. For fighting ones, the 'warrior King" would bark orders in the same tone as a military commander. Alys, remembering how she had been ignored, went out of her way to welcome newcomers.

At other moments, Valharic was struck by the emotional impact some awards had on recipients. He handed one woman a scroll that was the first her own daughter had ever made. The surprise made her cry. Another woman at another event received a small, but real, sapphire as part of her award. Her jaw dropped and stayed there even as she went to her seat.

He was able to make his first Knight in a ceremony that affected even him.

"You kind of relive your own Knighting," he said after the dubbing. "When he said his oath I don't think there was a single Knight who wasn't thinking on his."

Valharic and Alys had to deal with a few fires in their home barony. After Laurelen's resignation, the barony launched into nasty debates over details in Kingdom and Society law, both written and unwritten. Though Laurelen had a few pointed comments to make, he stuck by the resignation he had offered. Whether he was treated poorly or brought the trouble on himself, his insistence that his resignation stand, without appeal, prevented fights that would have damaged the barony and tainted the reign of Valharic and Alys. They still took heat for it.

"The crap that went on!" she exclaimed to me. "There were people that I have known a long time that sent some rude and discourteous e-mails to me."

Others in Cleftlands, though, supported the reign. In addition to the scribes, others in the barony built Valharic a Roman-styled chariot to carry him into Pennsic court sessions.

The time and energy devoted to the reign also posed a challenge. Valharic struggled to find a good job after the restaurant where he worked closed. With no job and no family, he focused on his reign. Every weekend, he was anxious to head to events as early as possible. But his entourage had to finish the workweek and worry about other mundane issues. Valharic's Crown win had come just weeks after Flynn had become a father. Talon and Wanda/Juana Ileana were seeking a house, then moving into it. Ulfr and Amanda did the same.

The relationship between Valharic and the rest of Portus Aurelius settled into an odd symbiosis. It had started before coronation. The women in the group churned out new Coptics for his staff, then Valharic's coronation tunic and the dragon cloak. Valharic awarded both Erin and Wanda Willows, a mid-level arts award for their hours of work. William of Fairhaven had observed that others "hitch their wagon" to Crown contenders for the vicarious chance at the spotlight. Once someone wins, though, their friends simultaneously pull the wagon and are pulled by it. Valharic received garb he never could have made or afforded, and Erin and Wanda had a stage for their handi-work to receive the attention and note it deserved. Agrippa noted one day that such symbiosis fits SCA period—serfs provided labor and crops to their lord, who in turn provided protection. It just plays out today with a little different spin.

For Agrippa/Flynn the reign also brought serious sacrifices and rewards.. Many parents center their lives on a new child, particularly their first, and other pursuits lose attention. But Agrippa lost weekend after weekend of his newborn daughter's first year. In return, his SCA commitments grew beyond what they had ever been and it gave him a platform to show his talents for organizing and tending to details as well as his efforts in service.

It was at War, where he ran staff meetings to coordinate the schedules for Valharic and Alys, that he realized how much his perceptions of the SCA had changed in the months since Valharic won Crown.

"We had arrived," Agrippa said. "Our group, our generation had gotten there. I was walking around Midrealm Royal and thinking I was in a position I never expected I'd be in the SCA. I was the guy wearing moccasins and glasses at Pennsic 16. Now at Pennsic 31 I am running Midrealm Royal."

The rest of the staff also jumped into prominence. Ulfr, though a relative new-comer, soon became friendly with Kingdom and Society powers. Talon, who shifted his name to the more-Roman Titus Oceanus, attracted enough attention to make the Kingdom's team of unbelted—non-Knighted—champions. The team fights the cham-pions of the East every year in a battle that counts as much toward winning the war as other larger battles. In return, Ulfr/Hobbs and Titus/Talon had to spend hours follow-ing Valharic at events and standing guard behind him at court after court after court. When locals eagerly volunteered to fill in for them and stand on stage behind Valharic, they sometimes took breaks in the parking lot or fields behind the stage. Or they dis-creetly passed notes with inside jokes on stage as Valharic and Alys handed out awards.

The sense of humor also cut both ways. Even outside of events, and even in Agrippa/Flynn's basement armory, Valharic would sometimes order the others around, grinning all the time, as their King. "Your Majesty," Agrippa would reply with a smirk, "We're not in public anymore. You're in *my* castle." Valharic and the others would tease Agrippa about his penchant for launching into very opinionated speeches—"He's on his soapbox again," Portus Aurelius members, even Erin, would say. So as Pennsic started and the staff all borrowed portable radios to communicate Royal plans across the site, they stuck him with the handle of Soapbox. Talon was Snoop Lupus Lupus. Ulfr was Forkbeard.

When Valharic finishes his reign a few months from now, he will make Agrippa a "court baron"—a largely ceremonial position of honor that differs from "landed" barons, who actually run baronies—as a reward for his help. Even at Pennsic, Agrippa frets that Valharic will do that for him and not for Erin.

"Tommy's reign was very good because it got me on the radar," he said, but the toll fell to his wife. "She was the one who made all the sacrifice. I got to travel. I got to go to the events. She was the one keeping my house together, keeping my child together, making the garb for Val for the next week."

Over the years, in fanciful dreams as he slept, he would imagine placing a crown on his wife's head. He will not be able to do that, he tells me at war, even if he is named a Court Baron, and Erin will have earned her coronet—a baron's crown—with her own work. But it could be a nice moment if they receive them as a team, with each of their efforts helping make it possible for the other.

"I know I'm not going to become a Knight," he says. "I'm damn positive I'm never going to win a Crown Tournament. I will never be able to give her a crown. But I worked as hard as I could for a year so she could get a coronet."

When Valharic bestows the honor upon them both in the fall, just over a month after this Pennsic War, he makes that dream come as close to true as Agrippa can ever expect. Valharic also focuses goals in the Society for both Ulfr and Titus/Talon by naming them both squires. As they end their vows, Valharic will put a knife against their throats, saying, "Your life is in my hands." Then, grasping their hands around the same knife, he will put it to his own throat. "My life is in yours."

Even as the others saw Valharic as their connection to the elite SCA world, in a few pensive moments he saw that their real-world successes were rapidly leaving his behind.

One night the group jokes about a trip to the neighboring Kingdom of Ealdormere and some of the attention Valharic would receive as a royal. "They've got some nice women up there who will rub your back," Valharic quipped.

"I wouldn't mind being part of that," deadpanned Ulfr, but Talon reminded him he would need a white belt or crown to attract that kind of attention.

"What if you hang near a white belt or crown?" Ulfr asked, in mock hopefulness.

"You get a good view of the back rubbing," Valharic shot back.

"So I just live vicariously through you?"

Valharic paused.

"Yeah, and you all go back to Mundania to your houses and your women and your bank accounts and I live my mundane life vicariously through you."

The Traveler's Change

Since I had met one of my main goals at Pennsic XXX by fighting in the major battles, my own approach to the SCA has shifted. I had left that War bubbling with excitement about this hobby. Just nine months earlier, I had scoffed at some of the makeshift equipment, at the passion many display for this game and at many of the "attempts" at clothing. But somewhere along the way, I had started looking beyond those shortcomings and started seeing things in a more forgiving light. It is easier to criticize something you don't know and never try, I realized, than it is after you have struggled through the same, often difficult, tasks.

My trip abroad, though, opened my critical eye again.

The bad armor—not much different from what I wore myself—looks even worse to me now that I have seen people who get it right. The bad equipment looks far more jarring now that I have seen better camps. My mundane tent embarrasses me. My garb that I had spent hours sewing now looks wrong. It may match the quality of most everyone else in this Society, and is even better than some, but it's not real. It's not medieval. It's medieval-ish. The re-enactors all had "kits" that it would take a lot more work to equal. Even the Society's own European Kingdom of Drachenwald had far better garb. I felt self-conscious at their Double Wars event where I met and interviewed the illuminator Gabrielle. My trim was all just glorified ribbon, not the much more authentic weaves I saw there. My East German army boots now seem like an adolescent attempt to feel big and powerful by adopting the feel of Nazi jackboots. Even the pair of shoes I made at Pennsic bothers me. They are very close to a medieval style. But they do not match the time that my persona, such as it is, is supposedly set in.

Months ago, Flynn/Agrippa had joked about his own failed garb attempts that "you often hate what you once were." I'm doing him one better. I have started to hate what I still am.

When I returned home through London, I spent a few frantic days dashing around the city searching for clues. I had visited the British Museum twice before on earlier trips to London, but my passes through the medieval sections had been cursory. "Cool old stuff," I had thought as I breezed through displays of archaeological finds about 1,000 years old. "Neat armor." This time, though, I skipped the throngs around the Rosetta Stone and around the Egyptian caskets. I bee-lined for statues where I could see for myself the sandals sculpted on a Roman soldier: they had closed toes instead of being open. Cat and I stopped at a display of surviving shoes so she could sketch details and sort out a pattern. My eyes perked up at the displays of the Roman wax tablets found along Hadrian's Wall. None of these things had ever really mattered before in a tangible way. Now I could put them into context. I could imagine a world in which these items were useful. And I could envision making them. From there we ran just a few blocks away to an art store Gabrielle had recommended for its exquisite selection of parchment and pigments for illumination. We left with a sack full of items to show off to the Cleftlands scribes. Then we dashed to the Victoria and Albert

Museum. There, giant shelves have sliding racks to display fragments of cloth from many cultures and times. We ogled the remnants of the Coptic tunics—the style Darkyard wears—and were amazed at the intricate designs and motifs that were often woven straight into a tunic. When the tunics wore out, the clavi were cut off and sewn onto new clothes to save work.

Upon our return, I would have plowed hours into making a far more authentic fighting kit. Were it not for the health problems that ended my short-lived fighting career, I would have joined the Portus Aurelius group in making a set of lamellar armor to match Darkyard's period and Valharic's staff. Instead, I settled for making a few Coptic tunics to match his Roman reign. Though I took the simple route and satin-stitched simple strips of cloth onto tunics with my sewing machine as clavi, I knew just how it fell short and vowed to do better when I had more time. Ulfr and I talk about meeting after Pennsic to make good 9th century garb, starting with shoes. Cat and I will buy a small inkle loom at Pennsic to weave accurate trim ourselves and instead of shopping for more ribbon trim I will seek out natural-looking weaves already done and pay more for them. I will shop at a booth named "Raymond's Quiet Press," which both sells how-to pamphlets and reproductions of real period cloak clasps and belt buckles made from sketching artifacts then sculpting molds to match them.

I realize as Pennsic approaches and my apartment becomes a tornado-struck mess of cloth and thread and camping supplies that I am starting to move down the path many SCAdians follow. It is no longer enough just to get by. It becomes more important to be more specific about period and persona. I am no longer an outsider wondering whether this group is crazy.

I have become one of them.

"He took this war very personally…"

Over everything hangs Pennsic, particularly for Valharic. A War King, especially one who takes melee just as serious as tournament fighting, has Pennsic as the climax of the reign and the focus of much of his energy. Valharic made it even more so.

"Winning was his measure of success for his reign," Flynn/Agrippa tells me later. "He didn't come in with an agenda. He didn't change rules. He didn't try to rewrite the awards structure. He didn't have anything he wanted to do, except win Pennsic."

"If he could have given a liver to win that war, he would have," Valharic's friend Kollin, the fighter who commanded my unit at last Pennsic, also tells me. "He took this war very personally. He would do anything to win except compromise his honor."

Though he became such quick friends with the East King, Darius Orientalis, that they called each other by cell phone constantly to share news and plan months ahead of the War, he wanted to win. Landing Cuan was the first step.

Then Ealdormere, a Kingdom he had counted on for support, threw a curve. Its King, Sarnac Kir, was a friend and his wife Jolecia had made Valharic a tunic to wear at

Crown Tournament. Sarnac, who lived right over the U.S.-Canada border from Detroit, trained with Darkyard and Darkyard practices had groomed him for both his Knighthood and crown. But Sarnac sided with the East, he said, because an Ealdormere commander who had assisted Valharic in the woods the year before still stung from that loss and he wanted to beat Cuan. Sarnac continued attending Darkyard fight practices, though many of the fighters drew mental targets on him for practice and at War. Brannos and Calador still welcomed him but a few would not mind laying an ass wrap on him.

As the East set out on a mission to line up allies, Valharic's delay in courting others may have hurt. The Midrealm, if everyone came out, might have enough fighters to beat the East on its own. At one event, touching on the themes of Henry V's St. Crispin's Day speech, he told his troops he would love to see the Midrealm win the War with just its own troops.

His agreement with Darius to shift troops if either side was up by more than 100 made it far less urgent to gather masses. Once Ealdormere went to the East, Darius had told Valharic that would be enough. Valharic attended the Lilies War outside Kansas City in June hoping to make his case to Calontir. But Eastern Duke Ronald Wilmot, the East's warlord for the war, had already courted that Kingdom. They had committed.

The Middle was short allies.

Cuan would need to work some magic.

"You make me so proud..."

Here at Pennsic, though, the War effort is not working out the way Valharic had hoped. Last year, I was like most every fighter at War, enjoying just playing the game. I was happy just to survive and fight another day. But watching this Pennsic with an eye on how the Knights, Kings and commanders viewed it, I see how the game's honor sport system can falter. Other re-creation groups, like ARMA and Regia Anglorum, lose a giant part of this endeavor by not having fierce competition. But the emotion of competition and the drive to win also fuel resentments the other groups avoid.

Valharic's push to win has trouble right out of the starting blocks. The woods battle starts late and communication between marshals and the Middle Kingdom is confused. The starting cannon for battle goes off while the Middle and its allies still wait for the five-minute warning to line their troops up. The runners, instead of being perched at the barrier ready to go, have to jostle past other troops. The East takes control early and wins the battle Valharic counted on, both because of the confusion and a few tactical errors.

The interplay that follows between the Midrealm and Ealdormere the rest of the war oscillates between playful and hostile, between a fun game and something to be taken personally.

Valharic, with Flynn, Talon and Ulfr fighting alongside him, tries to keep things playful by trying to jokingly take Ealdormere's Queen hostage in the woods battle and ransom her. But she thwarts them by swatting her own head with her sword and falling dead. Marshals will not let Valharic carry her "body" out of the woods to continue the game.

But a few Midrealmers grow angry when Ealdormere, formerly just a part of the Midrealm, captures a Midrealm banner in the battle and parades it around the War, hangs it in the Ealdormere camp and displays it like a trophy at its court. Ealdormere even parades the banner past Midrealm Royal in a taunt. Then, Duchess Eanor of Amberhall, the woman that Sarnac had chosen as his champion—the one to fight to uphold his honor if he is challenged or insulted—gives it to the East.

"For Our Kingdom to capture and hold the Midrealm banner was, for us, an incredible moment," Sarnac said. "It was an inspiration to our Kingdom and our Army and for many was a symbol of our coming of age."

After the Midrealm returns the drubbing in the woods by sweeping all five banners in the Hadrian's Wall Battle and prompting Valharic's impassioned battlefield speeches, Valharic's own Champion decides he has to avenge the capture for the Kingdom and his King's honor. The soon-to-be-Knighted Vitus Atold Von Atzinger, MKA Sean Garrison, of Louisville, Ky., challenges the overmatched Eanor to a bout.

He clubs her quickly and efficiently, five blows to one. A few observers cringe at a man beating a woman, even on the fighting field. Even Sarnac cries foul. But most understand that King's champions have to be able to fend for themselves. It is mostly a ceremonial post, but sometimes—particularly if your King thumbs his nose at another and the target fights back—champions have to live up to the name. If she was not up to it, she had no business accepting that post.

Eanor, though, thanks Vitus for the bout. Whatever happens on the fields of War, she tells the crowd that gathered to watch their fight, the bout will be the highlight of her war. Both Valharic and Vitus are so wound up from the War that this bout draws the emotion out of both of them and puts it on display. Having an army fight for him in battle, then having his champion fight to settle something for his Kingdom, moves Valharic to tears.

"I love you like a brother," he tells Vitus.

"I will be yours forever my King," replies Vitus as they fall into a hug, tears pouring down their faces.

They pull apart and Valharic composes himself again. He pauses as his eyes scan the crowd.

"Go away," he orders. "I'm crying."

The Hadrian's Wall battle won decisively by the Midrealm is one of the few bright spots of the war, though the Kingdom's champion archers who had been improving steadily the last few Wars beat the East for a War Point for the first time in years. But the Midrealm loses the field battle. I watch from atop the QE2 as Darkyard and the Legion grind through an Eastern unit, then turn with a flood of other allies to try to sweep across the East. Initiative looks to be all the Midrealm's. But "dead" bodies have piled up. To avoid crushing them, the marshals call a hold to clear the dead. Momentum is lost and the East wins the battle. When the sides fight a series of three bridge battles, the Middle wipes the East out in the first, blowing fighters off the passages between hay bale lines standing for bridges, and plowing right on through to the other side and into the Eastern backfield. But on the final two battles, the East crushes the Midrealm when late-arriving units join the Eastern forces. According to Duchess Elina, the *Armored Rose* author who commanded that first bridge battle for Valharic, the Midrealm had a 25-man advantage on the first, then was down by 90 for the second and close to 200 for the third. Accusations start flying that the East had held people back to avoid the troop counts that are supposed to keep the sides within 100 fighters of each other. Easterners claim that some units arrived late because they made a mistake on the battle time.

A crestfallen Valharic praises his troops for trying.

"The battle of the day was hard fought," he tells the gathered troops. "I asked you for your hearts and you gave them to me. I never could have dreamed that anything could have made me as proud as your performance at this war."

He dropped to one knee in front of everyone, tears again welling in his eyes.

"I thank you on bended knee. You make me so proud."

"Much easier to blame the other guy…"

As that news filters across the War, Midrealm fighters grow angry at the East for cheating. The usual stories of Easterners not taking blows and of fighters "resurrecting" in non-resurrection battles make the rounds. Even Alys, who hardly ever attended battles before becoming Queen, fumes on the sidelines as she watches. She is angriest after watching Eastern units at one of the bridge battles hang by the sidelines with the already "dead" fighters, then charge in to fight.

"To want to win so badly you're willing to be dishonorable is not the SCA," she snaps. Months later she will still be bitter. "I'd darn well rather lose than win with deception."

By the final day, the Midrealm is way behind the East in War Points. But battles between selected champions for the two Kingdoms could still pull it out for the Midrealm.

As the East King Darius gives each of Eastern Knights on the "belted champions" team—a select group of Knights—special tabards in the Eastern blue and whispers a message to each, Valharic and Alys try to rally their champions. For Valharic to somehow win this War, his Knights will have to take this battle.

"Gentlemen, you know how much I admire you, each and every one of you," Alys tells the Midrealm Chivalry. "Fight honorably. I have heard some things about the other side that I am not happy about."

Her voice turns steely for a moment. "You do *not* do that to my children."

One by one, the Knights hand Alys their Knight's chains, symbolically putting their honor in their Queen's hands.

"They were very heavy," Alys said. "In more ways than one."

The Middle loses, yet again.

As his companions fall, Brannos tries to make a stand. Out of the mass of colliding shields and flailing weapons, Brannos emerges, locked into a one-on-one duel with Eastern Duke Lucan von Drachenklaue, one of the best fighters in the Known World. While the other Knights from both kingdoms continue fighting as units against each other, Brannos and Lucan square off one-on-one, their duel migrating off to a corner of the battlefield, apart from the mass. With a quick slash, Lucan strikes Brannos' leg. Brannos drops to his knees, now at a severe disadvantage.

He can see the battle rage, then dwindle to a few fighters. Then only Easterners remain standing. The East has taken this battle too. The Midrealm will lose this long, frustrating Pennsic War and Brannos' household brother's dream of winning is over. If Brannos gives up, nobody would notice.

But Brannos will not go down easily.

"Brannos believes," Valharic tells me, "that if he gives his opponent anything, he's taking something away from him."

He continues fighting Lucan as fighters pick themselves up off the ground after the battle. A crowd of Eastern fighters is still alive, ready to pound Brannos into the ground if he somehow beats Lucan. But Brannos continues fighting off attacks and waiting for a chance to strike.

Both sides gather round and form a ring to watch the duel between the best of the two Kingdoms. Brannos and Lucan stare each other down. They feint. They shift. They each throw blows that the other blocks. All eyes watch as the two duel, Brannos refusing to concede the fight.

After several minutes, Lucan slips a blow through to Brannos' chest and Brannos drops. Even that extra, determined effort is not enough to keep the East from winning.

"Hail Brannos!" cheer the Midrealm troops. Valharic give Brannos a hug, then hugs every one of the Knights as he returns their chains.

"Gentlemen, I have never cried before from watching a battle," Alys tells them. "I hold you family and you hold my heart."

Long after the battle is over, Valharic tells me that Brannos' refusal to quit typifies Brannos' attitude about fighting.

"If he'd given any less of a performance, whether it mattered or not, he'd be compromising everything he holds dear," Valharic says. "He's one of the people who when they fight for something, they actually fight for something."

Off to one side, Talon prepares to fight with the unbelt champions. He has rapidly improved as a fighter (once he no longer had incompetent fighters like me to train) and this battle gives him a chance to try to even the results of the War a little, both for himself and for his friend the King. Once his battle starts, the Midrealm seems to have an edge and plows through the East. But somehow the East never breaks. The East wins. Midrealmers start complaining again about Easterners not taking blows.

The complaints continue as individual battles by champions begin. Though Valharic and Eastern King Darius are friends and while many of the fighters left the War not caring who won, much of the Midrealm population is bitter. Kollin, who has commanded my contubernium last Pennsic, is so discouraged he almost dismisses this War as pointless.

"I put it this way to people," he says. "If you played chess with someone who kept cheating just to win, would you play anymore?"

Sarnac, the Ealdormere King who practices with Darkyard but sided with the East, calls the view from the Eastern side, though, "eye-opening."

"I was on the other side and heard Eastern fighters say the same thing…'That guy just wouldn't die'…'I don't know how hard I have to hit them before they take it', so its not just the Midrealm.

"I think that any time you put people in a situation where so much attention and emphasis is placed on one battle like these are, you are going to have people on both sides that just don't want to lose, no matter what. Also I believe that, in many cases, its much easier to blame the other guy for not taking your blow than admitting that you didn't do well, especially if you don't know him."

Not Turning His Back

Though Valharic's battlefield court speeches had recalled enough of Henry V to give troops the feeling they were fighting for a real cause, he did not assume Henry's role completely. His side did not win, though not through lack of caring. He also refused to follow one of Henry's leads. When the young Prince Hal matured into a King, he turned his back on the revelry of Falstaff and his tavern friends, telling them:

Presume not that I am the thing I was;
For God doth know, so shall the world perceive,
That I have turn'd away my former self;
So will I those that kept me company.

Valharic is not willing to make such a cut. This is a hobby. Real world Kings have real consequences—often deadly and very compromising ones—if he associates with such company. But the SCA is a club. It is for fun. Nobody dies for real. Nobody loses houses or crops or real land. No boundaries are at stake. And cutting loose is part of the appeal of the SCA for many.

So Valharic chooses to honor it. He offers his services as a cook at the infamous Slave Auction. He and his staff just set ground rules. By midnight, every night, his crown would come off and go back to Agrippa's tent at Royal. Valharic could stay out as late as he wanted and party. After midnight, he was just himself, not the King. And instead of casting aside his old friends at the party camps of the Pennsic Bog—the Society equivalent of Falstaff and the rest of the tavern crowd—and hanging them for imperfections, he holds a late-night court in one of the Bog camps and hands out awards to people he believes have been overlooked.

"They're not just a lot of fringe people wearing vampire teeth and elf ears," he said after taking a little criticism. "I wanted to give back to my roots. I had the opportunity not to overlook them."

Even in 2004, almost two years after this Pennsic, he still believes that recognizing a crowd that even members of this Society consider odd, was the only right thing to do. It just offered one of the benefits of the SCA to a more extreme crowd.

"There are a lot of people that are in the game and they're whole people," he says. "But with any escapism, they're looking for acceptance and something they're not getting in the mundane world. These camps give acceptance. They nurture probably a little more and are more understanding than other people in the SCA, on even a baronial level or a Kingdom level or a Society level.

"The SCA keeps a lot of people from falling through the cracks. But there are still cracks that people fall through. This group fills a lot of the cracks."

Many Society veterans, when discussing their evolution in the group, say when they start out they are just swept along in the "magic" that veterans create for them. Over time, they take on more and more responsibility for creating that magic for others. Many Kings and Queens, by the time they become royals, have already made that shift. But some, like Valharic, sit in a no-mans land in between. They may be in a position to inspire passion. They can spur people caught up in the magic to grand and dramatic deeds. They can give people moments that make their dreams of heroism seem real. But they also have their own struggles and storylines that can use a boost back. Valharic may have made the War for some with his battlefield speeches, but the effort of his troops, the cheers, the chants for King and Kingdom meant just as much to him. He was just a year removed from being an unbelted squire who wondered if he was good enough or would ever be accepted. The response from his troops and the populace told him he was. Though he did not win Pennsic, he had achieved enough on this stage to take that confidence and feeling onto the mundane stage.

"A man can fight," he had told his troops through a choking throat after the Kingdom's battle win. "He can fight for the honor of his Queen. He can put a crown upon her head. And he can call himself a King. But only through the might of an army can he be called a Caesar."

With tearing eyes, the man who had both bragged and longed to be King as a little boy, looked out at his undermanned but victorious army.

"Today, my army has made me a Caesar."

THE TRAVELER'S EPILOGUE

July, 2004 Common Era, Anno Societatis XXXVIII

Thus far, with rough and all-unable pen
Our bending author hath pursu'd the story
In little room confining mighty men
Mangling by starts the full course of their glory.

—Epilogue, *Henry V*

A few clarifications before I update the progress of many of the characters since we last saw them:

The vast majority of this book was researched with first-person observations or in one-on-one interviews in person or by phone. I attended dozens of classes at events that are not recounted here, but which I used to build background. In addition, after watching the British re-enactment groups, I visited multiple museums in Oslo and London and constantly compared the exhibits there to my impressions and to the historical details I learned in my travels across the Current Middle Ages. However, because the Middle Ages is such a broad period with many distinct cultures, I concede I am not an expert in every part of it. I may have made errors in my historical information, though most anything that is debatable is quoted as coming directly from a source.

The description of fighting in this book is exactly as I saw or experienced it happen, with a few exceptions. I had started this project expecting to write about the good and the bad of fighting and to include details of any injuries I might suffer. But though I cracked or broke ribs three times—two from shield collisions in charges and the third from an Eastern spear stab at a Pennsic bridge battle—I did not mention them in the main text. All three breaks, I later learned, were due to my having prematurely brittle bones because of a longstanding medical condition and are not an accurate reflection on this sport.

I personally attended all of the events described that took place in 2001 or 2002, with the exception of Valharic's Crown Tournament win. An auto accident on the way there prevented me from attending and the account here is reconstructed from videotape graciously provided by William of Fairhaven and from interviews with the participants. William of Fairhaven also provided me with a videotape of Valharic's Crown finals against Edmund that preceded my journey. Injuries from that accident also limited my activities and research during Valharic's time as prince and his time on the throne. Though I already owed the entire Portus Aurelius/SFU projects group thanks for putting up with constant questions as I researched this book, I owe them extra thanks for their understanding and help following the accident.

Many people I interviewed and many events I attended are not included in this book, including Aethelmearc War Practice (Pennsic Lite, as some call it), Grand Outlandish, the Lilies War, Great Western War and Drachenwald's Double Wars because of length and too many characters spoiling the already-crowded mix. Fencers, target archers and experts on the heraldry of coats of arms are also omitted mostly for space. I hope to present descriptions of those events and pursuits in some form later if there is an audience for them.

Since the end of Valharic's reign, the Portus Aurelius group that was so central to running the Middle Kingdom has all but stopped meeting. All of the members of the group are still friendly but Flynn/Agrippa needed a break, to both be a parent and start his own private law practice. Mike and Jen Detmar, the couple that attended regularly when I started, now only hover on the fringes on the SCA while they pursue other hobbies. Talon/Titus, now married to Wanda/Juana, still holds fight practices and Hobbes/Ulfr is still in search of the ultimate fighting kit, a journey made all the more difficult by his constant vacillation between the Viking era and the far more ornate later-period armor and garb. But the group's major goal—helping each other make garb and gear—became moot after the frenzy of supporting Valharic's reign. The improvement from the "Big Belt Club" I started with is dramatic. Everyone in the group had reached a plateau, if not their ultimate one, through his reign and has to start almost anew on future goals.

Most of the people in this book continue in this hobby, much as before.

Omarad stepped down as the Kingdom General but still fights almost constantly. Edmund continues attending events and setting an example for people in his area.

Bastian, Bernard and Lyonnete, who all authorized to fight at the first Cleftlands event I watched, continue to fight and are active in the barony. The deposed Baron Laurelen Darksbane still attends fighter practices regularly, still wears his "scary" helm and still instructs fighters as a good Knight should. Alaric and his squire Stephan are also both very active, Alaric serving as the Pennsic battlefield coordinator in 2004 and Stephan as the Cleftlands Seneschal.

The Middle Eastern segment of the SCA still thrives, despite the 9/11 terrorist attacks and the U.S. wars in Afghanistan and Iraq, and can still count on Baron Durr to hold haflas where Chengir will always be ready with a story.

Thomas Longshanks' translation of the Catalan cookbook continues and he has expanded the project to include a newly discovered version of the same cookbook. His mundane job is taking up more of his time than before and he estimates it could take years to finish. So he and his wife hold an annual feast to show off the recipes he has translated in the last year. The recipes are available for $12 by contacting him at a5foil@ix.netcom.com. Less than a year after I met him, he was named a laurel for his research in medieval food and cookery.

Gulf Wars continues drawing large crowds, including Baldar's House Asgard. Rules for combat archery are still debated and Baldar has started producing his own design of helm Anti-Penetration Devices for arrows to meet the new rules. Sir Erika was named a Pelican in 2003 for her service to the Kingdom of Trimaris, much like Brannos up in the Midrealm, for going beyond the call of Knighthood to teach.

Andreas Eisfalke was the King of the East Kingdom in February 2003 when his Marine unit was called to Iraq. He brought supplies to fighters across Iraq, including in the capital Baghdad, and missed the end of his reign before returning home in July. The SCA Board of Directors agreed to waive its requirement that Kings attend the coronation for their successor, so Andreas could take the title of Duke.

"No matter how angry you can get at somebody in the SCA, it can't compare to war," he told me a year after his return. "The war really kind of brought it home…we really are part of a big family. Despite the petty squabbles we have from time to time, you're all family members."

Alys Katharine is searching for her next project after the end of the reign, the end of her time running the Pennsic University and her retirement from teaching at the end of the 2003-04 school year.

"I don't have any cause right now," she said. "At some point, I'll have to re-invent who I am."

Darkyard, the household that welcomed my feeble attempts at fighting, continues churning out Kings. In the spring of 2004, 10 years after his last reign as King, Brannos swept almost untouched through another Crown Tournament. He will become King, with Rebekah his Queen, as this book is released. Erin, who had to be the head assistant to Flynn/Agrippa when he was the chief assistant to Valharic, will turn that situation around. She will serve as chief of staff for Brannos and Rebekah's reign. Talon/Titus had improved so much as a fighter he reached the quarterfinals of that Crown.

And Valharic has used his experience on the throne to help him succeed on brand new stages. He may have lost Pennsic and he may not have cast out old friends as the "real" Henry V did, but at Pennsic he followed Henry's path in one important way: he met and established a serious relationship with an educated royal from another Kingdom. At a Pennsic dinner party thrown by an allied Atlantian, he met Duchess Ariell the Golden and moved to Charlotte, N.C., to live with her soon after. MKA Courtney Hester, the bank officer for corporate real estate, has given his life, he says, far more stability than he had in the past. They became engaged just before Pennsic in 2004. He now works for a grocery store chain supervising portions of its catering and hot foods services.

"I think I got a lot of confidence from being King—with dealing with people and being more diplomatic—that has helped me in my mundane life," he tells me. "I went from working entry-level positions to now moving into corporate positions."

For Pennsic in 2004, he will have another major change. He has fit in so well in the Kingdom of Atlantia he was named its warlord—the equivalent of general—and will command Atlantians, not Midrealmers at Pennsic. And he will command them as allies of the East—not the Midrealm. The Atlantian King had offered that allegiance to the East Kingdom before picking Valharic, so Valharic will have to fight against his friends. He'll still camp with Darkyard, though, and will hopefully use his status on both sides of this War to mend a few fences and misperceptions.

That would be a difficult position, if he were not able to step back a little bit now. He can be a leader now, instead of someone needing acceptance. He sees more of a responsibility to the game.

"The next generation here in Atlantia is really moving up here...or starting to...or needs to," he says.

But his personal Middle Ages dream is still the same one he set after his long talk with Brannos at Baron Wars: To be the best fighter in the Known World.

"I'm still not there," he admits. "I'm not the best. But maybe someday..."

My own involvement with the SCA has dropped dramatically because of the demands of completing this book, lingering auto accident injuries and the need to catch up on mundane responsibilities. Those duties have made my pendulum of judgment of this Society swing again, this time retreating from the authenticity swing it had upon my return from Britain. I have not made new shoes. I still have mostly medieval-ish, not authentic, garb. My loom sits unused. Though I feel almost a moral obligation to do better, reality is interfering with that goal. For Pennsic in 2004, I have become more forgiving of shortcomings and am glad this Society is also forgiving. I am glad that others will not pass harsh judgment.

But the Current Middle Ages keep changing how I look at things in the modern world, even as I concentrate on mundane pursuits. I see people at the mall wearing shirts with vertical strips coming down from the shoulders, and instantly think, "Clavi!" I have to restrain myself from telling them their fashion is Roman-inspired. I cannot watch movies anymore without reflexively objecting to blatant inaccuracies. And when I bought a new home, I found that making armor had helped me overcome my white-collar college-boy phobia of cutting, chopping, removing or breaking something, even to repair it or rebuild it. After almost freezing at simply cutting a cowhide for my armor, I had no trouble at all scraping plaster off my new bathroom ceiling and stripping paint from walls.

My worries about what others, even perfect strangers I will never see again, think of this hobby have also disappeared. On the way to a recent event, I simply strolled into a fast-food shop in full garb—tunic, boots, pouch and hat—without any hint of self-consciousness. Instead of darting in and out quickly, Cat and I actually bantered with a very amused clerk and filled him in about the SCA as he handed us a super sized "trough" of Coke and our takeout "feast."

"Have fun at your battle," he said, grinning.

"We will, M'Lord," I shot back, drawing an even bigger smile from him. "We will."

0-595-32530-0

Printed in the United States
70066LV00004B/20